Childhood Cultures in Transformation

Childhood Cultures in Transformation

30 Years of the UN Convention on the Rights on the Child in Action towards Sustainability

Edited by

Elin Eriksen Ødegaard and Jorunn Spord Borgen

BRILL SENSE

LEIDEN | BOSTON

This is an open access title distributed under the terms of the CC BY 4.0 license, which permits any non-commercial use, distribution, and reproduction in any medium, provided the original author(s) and source are credited. Further information and the complete license text can be found at https://creativecommons.org/licenses/by/4.0/

The terms of the CC license apply only to the original material. The use of material from other sources (indicated by a reference) such as diagrams, illustrations, photos and text samples may require further permission from the respective copyright holder.

All chapters in this book have undergone peer review.

The Library of Congress Cataloging-in-Publication Data is available online at http://catalog.loc.gov

Typeface for the Latin, Greek, and Cyrillic scripts: "Brill". See and download: brill.com/brill-typeface.

ISBN 978-90-04-43365-6 (paperback)
ISBN 978-90-04-43368-7 (hardback)
ISBN 978-90-04-44566-6 (e-book)

Copyright 2021 by Elin Eriksen Ødegaard and Jorunn Spord Borgen. Published by Koninklijke Brill NV, Leiden, The Netherlands.
Koninklijke Brill NV incorporates the imprints Brill, Brill Hes & De Graaf, Brill Nijhoff, Brill Rodopi, Brill Sense, Hotei Publishing, mentis Verlag, Verlag Ferdinand Schöningh and Wilhelm Fink Verlag.
Koninklijke Brill NV reserves the right to protect the publication against unauthorized use and to authorize dissemination by means of offprints, legitimate photocopies, microform editions, reprints, translations, and secondary information sources, such as abstracting and indexing services including databases. Requests for commercial re-use, use of parts of the publication, and/or translations must be addressed to Koninklijke Brill NV.

This book is printed on acid-free paper and produced in a sustainable manner.

Contents

Foreword   VII
   Gunn Helene Engelsrud
Preface   IX
Acknowledgements   XII
List of Figures and Tables   XIII
Notes on Contributors   XV

1 Introducing Childhood Cultures in Transformation   1
   Elin Eriksen Ødegaard and Jorunn Spord Borgen

2 In the Best Interests of the Child: From the Century of the Child to the Century of Sustainability   13
   Liv Torunn Grindheim, Jorunn Spord Borgen and Elin Eriksen Ødegaard

3 On Equal Terms? On Implementing Infants' Cultural Rights   37
   Pauline von Bonsdorff

4 Children with Severe, Multiple Disabilities: Interplaying Beings, Communicative Becomings   54
   Kristin Vindhol Evensen

5 Spaces for Transitions in Intergenerational Childhood Experiences   74
   Czarecah Tuppil Oropilla

6 Managing Risk and Balancing Minds: Transforming the Next Generation through 'Frustration Education'   121
   Ida Marie Lyså

7 Children's Food Choices during Kindergarten Meals   138
   Hege Wergedahl, Eldbjørg Fossgard, Eli Kristin Aadland and Asle Holthe

8 Children, Food and Digital Media: Questions, Challenges and Methodologies   162
   Karen Klitgaard Povlsen, Stinne Gunder Strøm Krogager, Jonatan Leer and Susanne Højlund Pedersen

9   'Children at Risk' in Public Health Policy: What Is at Risk?   178
    Jorunn Spord Borgen, Gro Rugseth and Wenche S. Bjorbækmo

10 'Childish' beyond Age: Reconceptualising the Aesthetics of
    Resistance   197
    Susanne C. Ylönen

11 Approaching Agency in Intra-Activities   214
    Liv Torunn Grindheim

12 Studying Families' and Teachers' Multilingual Practices and Ideologies
    in Kindergartens: A Nexus Analytic Approach   229
    Anja Maria Pesch

13 Studies of Child Perspectives in Methodology and Practice with
    'Osallisuus' as a Finnish Approach to Children's *Reciprocal* Cultural
    Participation   246
    Liisa Karlsson

14 Global Paradoxes and Provocations in Education: Exploring Sustainable
    Futures for Children and Youth   274
    Jorunn Spord Borgen and Elin Eriksen Ødegaard

    Index   297

Foreword

While you read this book thousands of children around the world are suffering. More than 30 years after the 1989 United Nations Convention on the Rights of the Child (UNCRC) established a global standard for children's rights, the gap between the ideals espoused in the convention and the hardships still faced by children around the world is tragic and shocking. Despite the formal establishment of a "children's bill of rights", political calculation and economic concerns still take precedence over the wellbeing of millions of children: children who live in the Moria refugee camp, indigenous children in the Brazilian rainforest, orphans who have lost their parents in the COVID-19 pandemic. Not to mention the countless children who are struggling to contend with the dark corners of the digital world and social media, the ones who are trapped in violent relationships, dealing with poverty, deprived of cultural stimulation or crippled by existential anxiety about the destruction of the natural world and their diminishing chance to enjoy a viable future on our planet. Moreover, global politics are unstable, and leaders threaten or engage in war without thinking of the consequences for children and young people's lives. Nevertheless, children are not without hope. Inspiring young people such as Greta Thunberg and Malala Yousafzai cry out for justice and sustainability, and their voices are heard around the world. They influence and inspire thousands of other young people to speak up for their right to education, peace, and preservation of the wilderness and natural world.

This is where we are today. But how can the perspective of the Nordic researchers who contributed to this book shine a light on to how we understand children and childhood cultures? How do the researchers amplify the voices of the most vulnerable children, and contribute with knowledge, ensuring that they are not drowned out in the clamor of globalisation and change?

All chapters provide up-to-date knowledge and discussions of various methodologies and philosophies in childhood studies and beyond, and they discuss findings and relate to ongoing debates over current knowledge in the field. By doing so, the book highlights the complexity of cultural studies of childhood in an inter-disciplinary manner and argues for an awareness pedagogy and transformative research agenda. Even though the studies presented in this book are derived from a Nordic researcher network, the authors believe that childhood is simultaneously local and global, and therefore that research on the lives of Nordic children can offer useful insights for people who work with children around the world. The work of these researchers provides rich empirical descriptions and new knowledge to help readers understand the conditions of the children in their studies – how they live their lives in the twenty-first century, how childhoods vary and how culture matters in their specific contexts.

Ask yourself: How can the book you now hold in your hand help you rethink what you know about children? Children's voices are the most fresh, vital, and authentic voices of our time; we can learn much from them – if we take the time to listen. When we become aware of the paradoxes, inconsistencies, tensions, and contradictions that exist in children's lives and their possible impact on a sustainable future, we are called to action.

"To make the world a better place for all children" may seem like a dream, but a path to that better world can be built. With its contributions of knowledge and insight, this book can help show the way – for the benefit of the children of today, and those who are yet to come.

Gunn Helene Engelsrud
September 2020

Preface

When the BIN-Norden Child Culture Research Network invited to a conference in Oslo, Norway, called *Fears and Pleasures in Nordic Childhoods* in 2016, we raised provocative questions to the Nordic network of 300 researchers. The response was engaging and rich. Through a series of panels and a range of papers and course for master's students at the conference, supported by the Nordic Council of Ministers (Nordplus – Higher Education fonds), we stated that childhoods can no longer be seen as a world within a world, but as different experienced childhood(s). Our previous uniform understanding of Nordic childhood was challenged as the conditions for cultural participation by children and adolescents are negotiated and co-constructed in new ways through interaction between the local, regional, and global and interferences through migration, refuges, travels, media, digitalisation, world economics, etc. The editors of this book were at that time leaders of the network and invited researchers to contribute to this book. Soon an interdisciplinary group of researchers, working in the Nordic region, agreed on taking the challenge to renew existing understandings of childhoods and education though developing their papers, and also researchers in the outskirt of the network were invited to give a comprehensive contribution.

The BIN-Norden research network was established in the 1970s and for the last 25–50 years, researchers in the fields of child culture, educational science, sociology and media have focused on studying and viewing children and young people in their own rights in order to grasp their perspectives and then both critique and analyze the child culture industry, child culture professions and the instrumentalisation of childhood and education. The book is a result of a three-year project entitled *New Nordic childhoods – Paradoxes and transformation*, supported by Nordplus. In the final stage of the book the authors provided additional support. Through the BIN-network the researchers have been engaged in questions concerning children's views on questions like:
– What life experiences do you have?
– What future world do you want to live in?
– What do you want to change?

They have also been occupied with the voices of child experts as teachers, childcare workers, teachers in arts, health and nutrition experts. Their questions have been: 'How do children and young people express their creativity and meaning-making?', 'How do we conduct research with children?', 'How can we develop good education with children and young people?' 'What are the critical factors to achieve sustainable futures?' and 'What do the cultural sector and the educational sector offer children, what are their practices and how can practices be changed?'

Papers and panels have given us perspectives from children, young people, professionals, and experts, e.g. the need for nature and the environment to be protected and for world leaders not to start more wars. Digitalisation and media play a huge role in children's and young people's lives. We know too little about the diversity of children's voices and meaning making, e.g. the infants and toddlers, the importance of agency, language, and culture. We know too little about how macro and micro cultures impact on children's lives. There are paradoxes in the policies directed towards children, families and education.

The 1989 United Nations Convention on the Rights of the Child (UNCRC) established a milestone for the 20th century. Many of these ideas still stand, but time calls for new reflections, empirical descriptions, and knowledge as provided in this book. This book investigates and uncover paradoxes and ambivalences that are actualised when seeking to make the right choices in the best interests of the child. Our main argument for this book is that the history of the UNCRC's adoption and the continuous debate over children's rights and the best interests of a child must never be regarded as set in stone, and now it is timely to put the UNCRC in action towards sustainability.

Our hope is that this book will encourage and provoke debates and inspire new research, practice, and policy development. The many chapters of the book hold a multitude of perspectives all related to the UNCRC.

Special attention is directed to the conceptualisation of children and childhood cultures, the missing voices of infants and fragile children, as well as transformations during times of globalisation and change. All chapters contribute to understanding and discussing aspects of societal demands and cultural conditions for modern-day children age 0–18, accompanied by pointers to their future.

We open the transformative landscape on childhoods, both within educational institutions, such as kindergartens and primary schools and outside of them like family and cultural arenas like media, health and cultural arts institutions. The chapters of this book provide analytical arguments and empirical examples of paradoxes, inconsistencies, tensions and contradictions that exist in children's lives and point to possible impacts for a sustainable future. Even if the studies presented in this book are derived from a Nordic researcher network, these authors agree upon the new concept of childhood as both local and global simultaneously, and provides rich empirical descriptions and new knowledge to help readers understand the conditions of the children and how they live their lives in the twenty-first century, how childhoods vary and how culture matters in their specific contexts. All chapters provide up-to-date knowledge and discussions on methodologies and philosophies in childhood studies and beyond and discuss findings and relate to articles in the UNCRC. In doing so, the book highlights the complexity of cultural studies of childhood in an inter-disciplinary manner and argues for an awareness pedagogy and transformative research agenda.

Acknowledgements

We acknowledge the institutions that have supported the Nordic cooperation and the publishing costs. The process of writing and publishing this book has been supported by Nordplus Higher Education fonds (Nordic Council of Ministers), Research Council Norway (projectcode 275575), University of Jyväskylä, Helsinki University, Aarhus University, Norwegian school of Sport Sciences, UiT – The Arctic University of Norway, Norwegian University of Science and Technology and KINDknow research Centre, Western Norway University of Applied Sciences. Last but not least, we want to thank all the children, youths, teachers, child experts from a range of fields and librarians who have participated and supported the studies disseminated in this book.

Figures and Tables

Figures

5.1 PRISMA-inspired work flow (based on Moher et al., 2009).   82
5.2 Year of publication and methodologies.   106
5.3 Methods used.   107
7.1 Effect of availability and accessibility on food-item intake. The data is shown as mean ± standard deviation of the percentage of children who chose the food items.   148
7.2 Distribution of vegetable intake when offered at Kindergarten A (A) and Kindergarten B (B).   151
8.1 SAP Design Led Innovation (DLI) process.   172
8.2 The process of Design Squiggle by Damien Newman (thedesignsquiggle.com), licensed under a Creative Commons Attribution – No Derivative Works 3.0 United States License (https://creativecommons.org/licenses/by-nd/3.0/us/).   172
12.1 Traditional bilingualism: Two autonomous linguistic systems (Garcia & Li Wei, 2014, p. 14).   233
12.2 Interdependence (Garcia & Li Wei, 2014, p. 14).   233
12.3 Translanguaging (Garcia & Li Wei, 2014, p. 14).   233
13.1 Child studies, childhood studies, studies of child perspectives, the child-centered view, and social participation in different contexts.   249

Tables

4.1 Communication as technique.   63
4.2 Communication as contextual impressions.   65
4.3 Communication as causally linked to diagnoses.   67
5.1 Experimental questions.   75
5.2 Results matrix.   85
5.3 Journal field of study.   108
7.1 Informants and number of participating children at the two kindergartens.   141
7.2 Types of food item registered at lunch during four observations at each kindergarten.   146
7.3 Number of food items eaten and availability of various food items for each individual child at lunchtime at the two kindergartens.   147
7.4 Combination of toppings and spreads on the slices of bread for different age groups at the two kindergartens.   149

7.5   Combination of toppings and spreads on the slices of bread at the two kindergartens.   149
7.6   Dietary intake of various sandwich fillings from the lunch at two kindergartens.   150
7.7   Intake of nutrients during lunch at two kindergartens.   152
9.1   Words related to public health policy in two Public Health White papers (Documents A and B).   184
13.1 Differences between the currently predominant child research approach and the studies of child perspectives.   253

Notes on Contributors

Eli Kristin Aadland
(PhD) is an associate professor at Western Norway University of Applied Sciences. She is educated as a teacher in food and health and has a PhD in health effects of lean seafood. Her field of interest is in food and health and outdoor activity in teacher education, and she has published several papers in the field.

Wenche Schrøder Bjorbækmo
(PhD) is professor of physiotherapy for children and adolescent at the Faculty of Health Sciences at Oslo Metropolitan University. Bjorbækmo has been leader of two work packages in the research program FYSIOPRIM (Physiotherapy in primary care). Respectively the work package: Individually adapted physiotherapy; "effect" and experience, and: Clinical tool for registration and use of patient data in clinical practice, an implementation study of an eTool (Tablet with apps) in clinical practice. Her main research interest is on how children experience to move and being active in daily life; how children, their families and clinicians experience the physiotherapy encounter, and currently how systematic ways of using video in the education of master students specialising in physiotherapy for children and adolescents might mediate the integration of theory and practice in physiotherapy in primary care.

Jorunn Spord Borgen
is professor (dr.art.) at University of South-Eastern Norway. She is also a visiting professor at the Western Norway University of Applied Sciences. The expertise is studies in arts and cultural education and physical education in kindergarten, primary and secondary education and in higher education, the relationship between policies, professional development and practices in kindergarten and school. Professor Borgen has built research capacity through research leadership in Oslo Metropolitan University, The Nordic Institute for Studies in Innovation, Research and Education (NIFU), as special advisor for Research Council Norway (RCN), through PhD-programs and member of boards. Among international expert roles is from 2015 an expert for the OECD Education 2030. She is currently member of the leader team of the research project *pARTiciPED* granted by Research Council Norway (RCN). She served as a board member on the BIN-Norden Child Culture Research Network and later rose to the head of the board from 2013–2018. Professor Borgen has produced more than 150 publications and presented papers as a keynote speaker at several national and international conferences.

Gunn Helene Engelsrud
(PhD) is professor at the Western Norway University of Applied Sciences, Faculty of Teacher Education, Art and, Sport. She has presented and published national and international papers on children's movement and bodily experiences. Her expertise is in qualitative research, phenomenology, embodiment, teaching and learning in higher education. Among her latest publications related to children and childhood are contributions to the journal *Physiotherapy Theory and Practice* (2018) and the book *Physical Activity and Sport in the First Ten Years of Life* (edited by R. Bailey et al., Routledge, forthcoming).

Kristin Vindhol Evensen
has a PhD in sport sciences, an MEd in special needs education, a minor degree in adapted physical activity, and a BEd as a kindergarten teacher. She is an associate professor at Department of Teacher Education and Outdoor Life Studies at Norwegian School of Sport Sciences and has practiced her profession as a pedagogue in heterogeneous areas of Oslo, where families from wide ranges of socio-economic backgrounds meet in public institutions (e.g., kindergartens and primary schools). Professor Evensen's work has been conducted in mixed groups wherein children with and without various disabilities share space and time as well as in special groups for children with intellectual disabilities and autism spectrum disorders in ordinary schools. Throughout her work, Evensen has been particularly interested in subjective movements as a pedagogical resource that can bridge the apparent gap between subjective expressivity and symbolic language.

Eldbjørg Fossgard
(PhD) is an ethnologist and professor emerita at the Western Norway University of Applied Sciences. She has a teacher education and a PhD in ethnology. Her research focus is on food culture and especially on social and cultural aspects of food and meals in schools and kindergartens.

Liv Torunn Grindheim
(PhD) is professor of early childhood education at the Western Norway University of Applied Sciences. Currently, she is the leader of the work package "Conditioning Children as Explorers" at the KINDKNOW Centre, which is hosted at the Western Norway University of Applied Sciences. Professor Grindheim has been involved in several research projects. She has presented and published national and international papers on children's everyday lives in early childhood education, Children's rights, children as citizens, play, and sustainability.

Her main research interests are children's exploration, children as citizens, sustainable education in early childhood, and early childhood teacher education. Grindheim is board member of BIN-Norden.

Asle Holthe
(PhD) is currently the Dean of the Faculty of Teacher Education, Arts and Sports and associate professor at Western Norway University of Applied Sciences. He is educated as a teacher, including food and health, and has a PhD in health promoting work. His research interest is in subject didactics and in food and meals in kindergartens and schools.

Liisa Karlsson
(PhD) is a professor at the University of Eastern Finland (School of Applied Educational Science and Teacher Education) and an adjunct professor at the University of Helsinki (Faculty of Educational Sciences) in Finland. Her research interests include child perspective studies, childhood studies (of children aged 0–17 years), subjective well-being, participation, agency, reciprocity, empowerment, reflexive listening, child culture, interculturality, humour, practical theory, learning, inquiry, participatory pedagogy, study enjoyment and engagement, participatory operational culture, collaboration, interaction, and qualitative methodologies (e.g., narrative ethnography, narrativity, storycrafting methods, multimethodology). Professor Karlsson is the project director for the research project "Children tell of their well-being – who listens? Listening to children's voices and receiving their stories" (TelLis, grant no. 1134911) and the principal of the research and development project "KOTO – Integration through arts and skills – research-based asylum seekers' integration project using workshops, and development of voluntary work with methods from arts and skills". She serves as a board member of both the BIN-Norden Child Culture Research Network and the Finnish Society for Childhood Studies.

Stinne Gunder Strøm Krogager
(PhD) is associate professor at the Department of Communication and Psychology, Aalborg University. In 2013, she completed her doctoral thesis on children and young people's use of media and food at Media Studies, Aarhus University, Denmark. Ever since she has among other issues published on children and young people's media use and relationship to food in, e.g. *Nordicom Review* and *NORA – Nordic Journal of Feminist and Gender Research*. Also, she is editor-in-chief of the Nordic journal, *MedieKultur: Journal of Media and Communication Research*.

Jonatan Leer

(PhD) is head of food and tourism research at University College Absalon, Roskilde (Denmark). He has published widely on food culture in journals like *Food and Foodways, Food Culture and Society, Anthropology of Food, European Journal of Cultural Studies*. His PhD was on food and masculinity. He has authored three books in Danish and edited the books *Food and Media* (Routledge, 2016) and *Research Method in Digital Food Studies* (Routledge, 2021) and contributed to numerous anthologies including *Alternative Food Politics* (Routledge, 2018), *Food and Popular Culture* (Bloomsbury, 2017) and *Food and Instagram* (Bloomsbury, 2021). Jonatan is visiting lecturer at the University of Gastronomic Sciences in Pollenzo, Italy, and member of the Danish gastronomic academy.

Ida Marie Lyså

(PhD) is employed as a postdoctoral fellow at the Norwegian Centre for Child Research, Department of Education and Lifelong Learning at the Norwegian University of Science and Technology (NTNU), where she is engaged in a project that explores present and future imaginations among youths in Ghana. She holds an MA in Anthropology from the University of Bergen and a PhD in Interdisciplinary Child Research from NTNU. Her doctoral research focuses on disciplinarian practices in urban Chinese kindergartens that are approached as relational, everyday practices. This study was based on eleven months of ethnographic fieldwork in two kindergarten in Shanghai (2011–2012). The study aimed to explore how disciplinarian practices were visible in relationships between teachers and children in kindergartens, how children experienced, related to, and partook in such practices, and how everyday disciplinarian practices were connected to contemporary views of and future concerns for the situation of children in the urban Chinese context. Lyså's research interests include qualitative child research, methodology and ethics, and cultural diversity in childhood experiences.

Elin Eriksen Ødegaard

(PhD) is professor and director of the Kindergarten Knowledge Centre for Systemic Research on Diversity and Sustainable Futures (KINDKNOW) at the Western Norway University of Applied Sciences, where she has built research capacity in early childhood education towards sustainability. She is also a visiting professor at the Arctic University of Norway (UiT). Professor Ødegaard often employs narrative and visual methodology in her research. She has received research grants from Research Council Norway (RCN), was supported by the Nordic Council of Ministries. Professor Ødegaard was President of OMEP Norway (World Organisation for Early Childhood) (2009–2013) and led as secretary for the BIN-Norden Child Culture Research Network (2013–2018). She is currently World OMEP Treasurer and Vice-President of Association for Visual Pedagogy. From 1998–2020, she has published more than 150 articles and chapters, and has been invited as a keynote speaker both nationally and internationally. She has co-edited or co-authored 8 books, e.g. *The first 1000 Days – Becoming* (Springer, 2019), *Children's Exploration and Cultural Formation* (Springer, 2020) and *Studies of Exploration in Education: Cultures of Play and Learning in Transition* (Bloomsbury, forthcoming).

Czarecah Tuppil Oropilla
is currently a PhD research fellow at the Western Norway University of Applied Sciences, Norway, where she is also involved in the KINDKNOW Centre. She holds a BS in Family Life and Child Development from the University of the Philippines and was awarded an Erasmus Mundus scholarship for an International Masters in Early Childhood Education and Care, a joint programme of Oslo and Akershus University College (now Oslo Metropolitan University), the University of Gothenburg, the Dublin Institute of Technology (now Technical University Dublin), and the University of Malta. Oropilla has taught undergraduate and preschool classes at the University of the Philippines and has managed operations of an international roleplay facility for children and their families in Manila.

Susanne Højlund Pedersen
(PhD) is associate professor at Aarhus University, School of Culture and Society, Department of Anthropology. Her research areas are anthropology (Homeliness, Place and space), Ethnography, Identity, Participant observation (Institutional Ethnography), Pedagogical anthropology (childhood anthropology), and Theories of learning (Educational anthropology). She is member of the research group Education, Teaching and Philosophy, and Man and Cultures. Among her latest publications is a contribution to the journal *Communication Research and Practice* (2020).

Anja Maria Pesch
graduated from UiT with a PhD in Early Childhood Education and Care in 2018. Her dissertation explores views on multilingualism among ECEC teachers and parents of multilingual children, their relation to the teachers' and parents' linguistic practices, and the choices they make for the children's language development. The work also discusses the influence these views may have on the collaboration between ECEC and parents of multilingual children. Professor Pesch teaches early childhood teacher education at UiT and serves as a member of an interdisciplinary national network in research on early childhood

multilingualism and second language development, the interdisciplinary research group "Language and Identity Encounters in the Arctic (LAIDA)" (UiT), and the Research Group in Early Childhood Education and Care (UiT). Her main research interests are early childhood multilingualism, ECEC institutional work with multilingual children and their parents, and semiotic landscapes (Schoolscapes).

Karen Klitgaard Povlsen
(Lic. Phil.) is associate professor emeritus, School of Culture and Communication, Media Studies, Aarhus University, Denmark. Dr. Povlsen has been involved in many research projects on media, children and adolescents, 2018–2022: ReNew: Image of the North (NOR-H+S), member of the committee in charge at AU; 2013–2019: Taste for Life, funded by Nordea Foundation; 2008–2012: Cool Snacks, work package leader of Children and Media (National Research Fund); 2006–2010: MultiTrust, work package leader; Trust in media (Funded by Agriculture and Organics). Her main research interest is popular media fictions and audience studies. She completed her PhD (Licentiate) with a dissertation on fashion and food in women's magazines at Aalborg University and has published five books, ten anthologies and more than 150 articles and book chapters.

Gro Rugseth
(PhD) is associate professor at the Norwegian School of Sport Sciences. She has presented and published nationally and internationally on obesity and lifestyle change, on physical education, disability and inclusion, on white paper analysis of current discourse in public health politics and on qualitative research methods in health science. She has been part of the European project DEDIPAC – Determinants of Diet and Physical Activity; Knowledge Hub to integrate and develop infrastructure for research across Europe, and of the research group Society, Health and Power (SHEP) at University of Oslo. Among her recent publications are articles published in *Health Care for Women International* (2020) and *Phenomenology & Practice* (2018).

Pauline von Bonsdorff
(PhD) is a Professor of art education at the University of Jyväskylä. Professor von Bonsdorff has authored roughly ninety scholarly publications on topics including the aesthetics of childhood and children's agency, imagination, the theory and philosophy of art (namely architecture), art education, arts in school, environmental aesthetics, and phenomenological aesthetics. She is currently writing a book on aesthetics in childhood by drawing on current empirical infant research, childhood studies, philosophical aesthetics, and phenomenology. Professor von Bonsdorff has extensive experience in research supervision

and assessment and serves as a reviewer of many international journals and publishers. She led the research project "Spaces for Children: Aesthetic Practices, Children's Life-world and Agency" and was a member of the steering group of "Artification and its Impact on Art". She has held numerous scholarly positions of trust, including a chair of the Finnish Society for Childhood Studies, the Finnish Society for Aesthetics, and the Finnish Society for Research in Art Education, was a member of both the Research Council for Culture and the Society of the Academy of Finland and member of the BIN-Norden board.

Hege Wergedahl

(PhD) is professor of health promotion and prevention at the Western Norway University of Applied Sciences. She holds a PhD in biochemistry from the University of Bergen, Norway and focuses on the mechanism of the fat-lowering effects of the intake of edible oils and proteins. Since 2008, Professor Wergedahl has worked at the Western Norway University of Applied Sciences, and her research focus shifted from biochemistry and nutritional components to the health-promoting aspects of food and meals for children. Her competences and research interests include food and meals in kindergartens and primary schools, the nutritional content of foods and healthy meals, guidelines for food and meals in kindergartens and primary schools, and dietary interventions in kindergartens and primary schools. Professor Wergedahl is considerably experienced in leading research projects, and she also teaches topics within food/meals and methodology for the BS and MS in Early Childhood as well as the MS in Physical Activity and Diet in a School Environment programmes.

Susanne C. Ylönen

holds a PhD in Art Education and is currently a postdoctoral researcher at the Department of Music, Art, and Culture Studies at the University of Jyväskylä. Her doctoral dissertation *The Fighting Crab Monster* (2016, written in Finnish) explores the field of child cultural horror and delineates how different aesthetic choices – such as aesthetic sublimation (fear and awe-inspiring renditions), aestheticisation (beautifying approaches), and aesthetic sublation (disgust-inducing, possibly humorously degrading interpretations) – are used within discourses such as risk speech, cute talk, psychologisation, and peer cultural meaning making in order to achieve particular performative aims, from spreading horror to containing and ridiculing it. Professor Ylönen is currently working on the subject of aesthetic sublation as a form of pop-cultural meaning making by tracing convergences of, for example, disgust and cuteness in diverse case studies – from Hodor doorstops (TV-serie) to zombie picture books and violent clowns. This research is being funded by the Finnish Cultural Foundation.

CHAPTER 1

Introducing Childhood Cultures in Transformation

Elin Eriksen Ødegaard and Jorunn Spord Borgen

Abstract

In this introductory chapter we present how the book open the transformative landscape on childhood, both within educational institutions, such as kindergartens and primary schools and outside of them like family and cultural arenas like media, health and cultural arenas.

Keywords

cultural studies of childhoods – best interest of the child – right to participation and the right for protection – Nordic glance on transforming childhoods – sustainability

1   Introduction

Around the world, organisations, researchers and individuals in and outside of politics have been and still are, inspired by the United Nations Convention on the Rights of the Child (UNCRC) (United Nations, 1989) and more recently the adoption of the 2030 Agenda, which includes the Sustainable Development Goals (SDGS) (UN, 2015, 2017). These global policy documents commonly advocate for the best interests of children and hope to put an end to inequality and injustice, protect the most vulnerable and secure life on planet earth.

Both agendas clearly outline the world and future we want, but children, families and educators often experience uncertainty related to the paradox of the gap between vision and practice. In this book we provide rich descriptions, constructive critique and recommendations for transformative research and practices. The UNCRC was declared in 1989 and reflect ideas of children and childhoods and the world views at the time it was drafted (1979–1989). Many of these ideas and world views still stand, but time calls for new reflections, empirical descriptions and knowledge as provided in this book.

This book combines discussions, empirical research contributions and new methodological and philosophical perspectives on research within the theme of societal and cultural conditions for modern-day children between 0 and 18 years of age, accompanied by pointers to improve the future of these children. Special attention is directed to the conceptualisation of children and childhood cultures, the missing voices of the infant and the fragile child, as well as the paradoxes and transformations identified during times of globalisation and change. Paradoxically, children and young people can behave as adults when searching the internet for inspiration, knowledge and entertainment. While the experts who wrote the UNCRC wrote their drafts on typewriters, today both children and adults live in a new reality of technology and multiple worlds of learning possibilities that sometimes makes children more knowledgeable than adults (Veermann, 2014). Available information, opportunities for agency are not necessarily the problem in all occasions since given agency and voice does not take away the complexity for children and young people. Both children and adults face dilemmas and uncertainty when trying to figure out what is the best choice for them.

Childhood can be seen as a sheltered world unto itself, but the realities of a diverse society, an increasing awareness of the impact of climate change and health concerns due to pandemics have given rise to an entirely new range of childhood experiences. An often-forgotten dimension in child and youth studies is that childhood, the experience of being a child and education itself essentially form a temporal, geographical and generational phenomenon (Alanen, 2001; Massey, 2005; Uprichard, 2008; Kraftl, 2020). In an age of globalisation, the boundaries between cultures are blurred, and the relationship between them becomes important (Lee, 2020).

The past three decades in which the UNCRC has been operative have been a period with much discussion about the different constructions of children and childhood (Crowly, 2020; James & James, 2004). Understanding the child while also understanding society are two sides of a coin. The authors of this book share the perspective that 'being' and 'becoming' are not in fact conflicting discourses and, therefore, will consider them together. When the child is seen as both 'being and becoming' the agency that child has in the world can increase (Uprichard, 2008).

A key outcome of the new social studies of childhood is that children are seen as active social agents who participate in the creation of knowledge and daily experience of childhood (Uprichard, 2008, p. 9). From this perspective, which is also the perspective of the authors of this book, children are seen as future agents. These perspectives have had increasing international recognition (World Organization for Early Childhood Education, 2017; Samuelsson,

Li, & Hu, 2019). The general intellectual, ethical and cultural climate, what we call the zeitgeist of our time, will create conditions for what is considered right and wrong, while relational, material, geographical and bodily senses and impressions will shape conditions for what children can or cannot experience and learn (Hackett, 2016; Rautio & Stenvall, 2019). A few of these experiences will be very similar to the experiences children have had for generations, regardless of where they are born and live, while others are more or less time- and place-specific, such as whether children spend time in institutions in China or in Nordic Countries or whether they play (un)supervised outdoors or (un)supervised indoors with touchscreens, virtual reality games, etc.

During the 20th century, efforts to develop successful global policies for children have been concluded with the UNCRC and ratification by most countries, but there are still many bumps in the road as the authors of this book remind us. This book is an argument for why we have to reconsider the future, bringing in relational and contextual knowledge when considering the best interests of a child. The rich descriptions and contributions take us far beyond the discourse of school and educational success, as seen in so many projects dealing with children and youth in education. This book reorients the view of children and young people being merely objects of education. The collection of chapters open the transformative landscape on childhood, both within educational institutions, such as kindergartens and primary schools and outside of them like family and cultural arenas like media, health and cultural arenas.

2   The 30 Years of UNCRC

UNCRC (United Nations, 1989) holds two central children's rights that need to be balanced: the right to participation and the right for protection. The Convention stresses that every child has rights, whatever their ethnicity, gender, religion, language, abilities, etc., and on these grounds, the Convention must be seen as a whole as all the rights are linked and important. According to Lucy Smith,[1] the General Measurements of Implications (2003, no 5) underlines four principles as general for the whole Convention: article 1 about how the best interests of the child shall be a primary consideration in all actions concerning children, article 2 about non-discrimination, article 6 about children's right to life and the maximum extent of possible survival and development and article 12 about children's rights to express their views freely in 'all matters affecting the child'. These views are being given due weight. The latter is the most radical, along with articles 13 to 16 regarding freedom of expression, freedom to be of any or no religion, the right to meet with friends and to join groups and the right to privacy (Smith, 2008).

The authors of this book consider the right to relax and play (article 31) and the right to freedom of expression (article 13) of equal importance as the right to be safe from violence (article 19), the right to guidance from adults (article 5) and the right to education (article 28) – which must develop every child's personality, talents and abilities to the full (article 29).[2] However, for any child and adult, these rights have the potential to be paradoxical. In spite that UNCRC is being implemented in laws and regulations in most countries, crime, suppression and unjust decisions are present in many children's lives, also in the name of the child's best interest. What is 'the best interest of the child' is not a question with a straightforward answer. A parent and teacher will easily disagree with children in certain questions. Children's voices on these matters will simply collide when meeting cultural expectations. These are problems that will be illuminated and elaborated on in this book.

Because difficult and impossible decisions need to be made, without parental or child consent, societies, experts and professionals need ethical guidelines. What is considered the child's best interest is essentially a personal and individual norm that experts, professionals or parents use as a guide (according to their own values) when considering the suitability and appropriateness of approaches to making choices or decisions. Determining the child's best interest requires a value judgement – what is an interest, whose interest, what is the best interest in this situation, time and place? Although the child's interests should be the sole focus for concern, children's interest cannot be decided without taking into consideration, validating or scrutinise the information coming from those who make decisions on their behalf. The common assumption is that parents seek their child's best interest, informed and supported by experts and professionals (Dan, 2018). However, experts and professionals does not by mandate relate to their personal norms, but rather to their position as their child's best expert and advocate. Unfortunately, experts can give the wrong advice based on prejudice, lack of sensitiveness, professionals can have bad judgment and parents can harm their children in the name of their best interest. Furthermore, many countries and territories are not able to follow guidelines provided by the UNCRC and, for example, secure education for all. UNESCO (2019) reported that despite the considerable progress on access to education and participation over the past years, 262 million children and youth aged 6 to 17 were still out of school in 2017, and despite rapid technological changes presenting opportunities and challenges, the learning environment, capacities of teachers and quality of education have not kept pace. Refocused efforts are needed to improve learning outcomes for the full life cycle, especially for women, girls and marginalised people in vulnerable settings (UNESCO, 2019). Conflict of interest exists, and since the public has different values and norms, policies regarding child culture and education will also be areas of dispute and disagreement (Urban, 2018). *Agency* and *participation* have been key concepts over these last 30 years with the convention, and research has been occupied with the relation between social structure and the individual social actor (Vuorisalo, Raittila, & Rutanen, 2018) within sociological and interdisciplinary frameworks. The extent to which these studies have had an impact on policy, family and institutional lives and practice varies (Gradovski et al., 2019).

The history of the UNCRC's adoption and the continuous debate over children's rights and the best interests of a child must never be regarded as set in stone. Researchers suggest that children live in diverse conditions and that present concerns may move beyond the context of the UNCRC and pave the way for rethinking the entirety project of children's rights (Quennerstedt, Robinson, & I'Anson, 2018). This book intends to contribute towards such a dialogue. The chapters will present analytical arguments and empirical examples of paradoxes, inconsistencies, tensions and contradictions that exist in children's lives and point to possible impacts for the future.

3   A Nordic Glance on Transforming Childhoods

The original driving forces for a Nordic glance on childhoods were cultural and geographical. It is important to rethink what a Nordic glance entails, and this book will provide a multifocal glance that goes beyond geographical and cultural boundaries. In Nordic research, the question of 'Nordic added' value is often raised but is difficult to articulate (NordForsk, 2011). The creation of knowledge and the use of knowledge will always be intimately tied to networks. Knowledge production is therefore a social process. In small countries like Nordic ones, researchers act on an international level, concurrently, Nordic researchers act in Nordic networks, and childhood, child culture and educational research have a particularly strong standing, according to NordForsk[3] (NordForsk, 2011, 2018). The Nordic-added value from this book will be new scientific knowledge with examples of how the UNCRC is used in research, how it motivates and justifies research and how the UNCRC has become a self-evident mandate for a researcher to consider. The contributions are a result of a longstanding cooperation and exchange, some of which is funded by Nordic ministries and research councils in Nordic countries.

This book was initiated by researchers connected to the BIN-Norden Child Culture Research Network. This network was established in the 1970s and connects almost 300 researchers. For the last 25–50 years, researchers in the fields of child culture, educational science, sociology and media have focused on studying and viewing children and young people in their own rights in order to grasp their perspectives and then both critique and analyse the child culture industry, child culture professions and the instrumentalisation of childhood (Borgen & Ødegaard, 2015). The editors of this volume have organised three conferences in the Nordic countries in cooperation with the University of Copenhagen (in 2014), the Norwegian School of Sport Sciences, and the Western Norway University of Applied Sciences (in 2016), and the University of Jyväskylä and the Finnish Society of Childhood Studies (in 2018). Alongside these conferences, a three-year project entitled New Nordic childhoods – Paradoxes and transformation was supported by the Nordic Council of Ministers (Nordplus[4]). The dialogues in these conferences and network meetings have challenged the idea of one Nordic childhood and one dominant discourse (Borgen & Ødegaard, 2015). The papers for these conferences include examples of paradoxes within the Nordic welfare system and examples of newly changing Nordic childhoods. This book will analyse a selection of these papers and add several more to provide a collection of new discussions and ideas regarding local transformation in a global society. Paradoxes are a common feature in these works, some of which include taking parenthood seriously, having higher birth rates than more traditional family cultures, making legislations for parents to spend longer periods of time with their infants, having institutionalised childhood, encouraging children to be independent from an early age, and experiencing what some would call a modernisation of the family. The editors of the book worked as a leading team of the BIN-Norden Child Culture Research Network from 2012–2018.

Even if the studies presented in this book are derived from a Nordic network, some of them present international global-oriented perspectives. Even if the Nordic model and the Nordic welfare system are often internationally associated with 'happy childhoods', time for self-organised play and nature activities (Aasgaard, Bunge, & Roos, 2018), this book does not claim a Nordic identity; these authors agree upon the new concept of childhood as both local and global simultaneously.

4   Central Insights and New Knowledge from This Book

Several interesting topics are presented in the chapters of this book in an aim to identify the zeitgeist of our recent times. The book provides rich empirical descriptions and new knowledge to help readers understand the conditions of the children and how they live their lives in the twenty-first century, how childhoods vary and how culture matters in their specific contexts. All chapters provide up-to-date knowledge and discussions on methodologies and philosophies in childhood studies and beyond, and discuss findings and relate to articles in the UNCRC. In doing so, the book highlights the complexity of cultural studies of childhood in an inter-disciplinary manner.

Chapter 2, "From the Century of the Child to the Century of Sustainability", written by Liv Torunn Grindheim, Jorunn Spord Borgen and Elin Eriksen Ødegaard show how perceptions and mobilisation of the UNCRC has changed over time. The authors present significant transformations of understandings of childhood in the Nordic context over the past 120 years, pointing to the challenges that researchers face when doing research for problem-solving in achieving the rights of children, especially children's right to be heard, right to protection and right to play. They argue for transdisciplinary research designs to approach paradoxes and ambivalences they have identified.

Children's intellectual capacity and right to be heard in matters that concern them have been increasingly acknowledged and given more importance both in research on children and in childrearing. In Chapter 3, "On Equal Terms? On Implementing Infants' Cultural Rights", Pauline von Bonsdorff argues that a slight 'adultocentrism', that is, the modelling of children on adults, runs through the UNCRC, (with the examples of articles 13, 14 and 29), that diminishes its relevance and applicability, especially when it comes to infants.

In Chapter 4, "Children with Severe, Multiple Disabilities: Interplaying Beings, Communicative Becomings", Kristin Vindhol Evensen discusses how these children's transitions between interplay and communication, embodiment and expression, subjectivity and objectivity, expressivity and interpretation and being and becoming are understood and described in research and included in UNCRC articles 12 and 13. This analysis could help inform experts, professionals and families about how to best communicate and listen to children with severe disabilities. The chapter also contributes to the discussion on challenges studying the cognitive discourse of human rights in line with the arguments put forward in Chapter 3 by Pauline von Bonsdorff.

The UNCRC upholds the view that children are competent, strong, active, participatory, meaning-makers and fellow citizens who have the right to be involved in decisions that affect them and who have the freedom to express their thoughts and opinions. This sentiment is echoed in Chapter 5, "Spaces for Transitions in Intergenerational Childhood Experiences", written by Czarecah Oropilla. This chapter explores where and how space is given to listen to children, especially in inter-generational interactions, through a literature review on inter-generationality across institutions and contexts and through the use of multi-modal methodologies. Oropilla also points to how research and practice that take the opinions of both children and adults into consideration will further the UN's 2030 Sustainable Development Goals and Agenda.

In Chapter 6, "Managing Risk and Balancing Minds: Transforming the Next Generation through 'Frustration Education'", Ida Marie Lyså describes the phenomenon 'frustration education' in contemporary urban China. She presents the societal transformations that have taken place in China over the last decades and explains how these changes have been accompanied by changes to the perceived challenges of children in contemporary and future Chinese society. The chapter gives a rich and unique description of how the staff in kindergartens is trying to build future citizens by specific pedagogies. Here, the best interests of children are presented as being intertwined with the best interests of society as a whole.

Children's freedom to choose and food practices in everyday life is examined in Chapters 7 and 8. In Chapter 7, "Children's Food Choices during Kindergarten Meals", Hege Wergedahl, Eldbjørg Fossgard, Eli Kristin Aadland and Asle Holthe examine children's food choices during lunch and how these choices contribute to children's dietary intake. In Chapter 8, "Children, Food and Digital Media: Questions, Challenges and Methodologies", Karen Klitgaard Povlsen, Stinne Gunder Strøm Krogager, Jonatan Leer and Susanne Højlund Pedersen discuss the results of their study on children in sixth and seventh grade home economics classes involving the use of digital media in relation to their everyday routines and food practices. This chapter argue for that the digital media offer new possibilities of inviting children to express their views freely as the article 12 of the UNCRC proposes.

The cultural context of childhood is changing. Conditions on children's agency and cultural participation are being negotiated among adults and children and constructed in new ways. For example, Chapters 9 and 10 discuss risk and resistance as being negotiable. In Chapter 9, "'Children at Risk' in Public Health Policy: What Is at Risk?", Jorunn Spord Borgen, Gro Rugseth and Wenche Bjorbækmo examine how children's future health risks arise in the Nordic context and how such risks are outlined as problematic in two Norwegian health policy documents. The chapter provides insight into the conception of risk and its dependence on the various interpretations of the phrase "in the best interest of the child" (United Nations, 1989, art. 3). It also challenges the understanding of children's right to express their views freely in "all matters affecting the child" (art. 12).

What is considered suitable or desirable behaviour for children is under constant negotiation in day-to-day interactions between children and adults. In Chapter 10, "'Childish' beyond Age: Reconceptualising the Aesthetics of

Resistance", Susanne C. Ylönen explores the concept of 'aesthetic sublation', that is, a performative mode of meaning-making that seeks to degrade an object (Ylönen, 2016; Korsmeyer, 2011). She discusses this phenomenon as a form of resistance related to inter-generational negotiations. As such, the chapter relates to UNCRC article 31, which presents the child's right to engage in play and recreational activities as long as they are "appropriate to the age of the child".

Liv Torunn Grindheim analyses how actors can be traced in an intra-activity in Chapter 11: "Approaching Agency in Intra-Activities". With reference to childhood studies and the UNCRC, that legalise children's right to express their views, she claims that it is time to challenge the dichotomy between agency and structure. By considering material-discursive forms of agency, she demonstrates how actors can be traced in an activity involving Polydron (toy for construction). She claims that Polydron, children, teachers, families, the economy, play, learning, and the position of mathematics in education emerge as actors in one sense or another. Thus, the space for agency between actors and structures can be identified and widened.

Anja Maria Pesch, in Chapter 12: "Studying Families' and Teachers' Multilingual Practices and Ideologies in Kindergartens: A Nexus Analytic Approach", discusses which insights an applied nexus analytic approach may contribute with to the field of childhood studies. Based on ethnographic fieldwork in two kindergartens (one in Norway and one in Germany), she argues that the analysis shed light on the complexity of intersections of linguistic practices and the study of it. The practices and choices made by parents and teachers involve values of specific languages and codes and create conditions for the children's own linguistic practice. A question deriving from this complexity is then which forms of linguistic practice may be in the best interest of multilingual children.

In Chapter 13, "Studies of Child Perspectives in Methodology and Practice with 'Osallisuus' as a Finnish Approach to Children's Cultural Participation", Liisa Karlsson discusses the methodology and practices used in research on children's perspectives and participation as a cultural phenomenon, specifically in Finland. Conducting research on children can be justified in terms of children's rights and learning needs, as noted in this chapter with reference to article 12, UNCRC.

Chapter 14, by Jorunn Spord Borgen and Elin Eriksen Ødegaard explores the future of education as articulated by a group of children and a group of child experts selected by the authors, highlighting the similarities of their perspectives. The chapter suggests some qualities that a sustainable future would require in relation to the UNCRC articles 28 and 29. The chapter is especially tied to Chapter 2, which states that, when designing sustainability research, the best interest of the child should be considered. This requires a transformative research agenda. An informed discussion, as provided in this book, will be a necessary starting point in reimagining children's rights for the twenty-first century.

Notes

1 Lucy Smith (1943–2013) was a member of the U.N. Committee on the Rights of the Child, and as an expert she monitored and reported on the implementation of the United Nations Convention on the Rights of the Child. Smith was also Norway's first female (full) professor of law (1987) and served as rector of the University of Oslo (1993–1998).
2 These statements are paraphrases from the UNICEF website: https://www.unicef.org.uk/what-we-do/un-convention-child-rights/
3 NordForsk is an organisation under the Nordic Council of Ministers that provides funding for and facilitates Nordic cooperation on research and research infrastructure.
4 Nordplus, the Nordic Council of Ministers' program in the area of lifelong learning, financed a Nordic master's course on Nordic Childhoods in Transformation that were embedded in these three conferences and organised as sessions and research tasks for master students.

References

Aasgaard, R., Bunge, M. J., & Roos, M. (2018). *Nordic childhoods 1700–1960: From folk beliefs to Pippi Longstocking*. Routledge.

Alanen, L., & Mayall, B. (2001). *Conceptualising child-adult relationships*. Routledge. https://www.researchgate.net/publication/278406453_Alanen_L_B_Mayall_eds_2001_Conceptualizing_child-adult_relations_London_RoutledgeFalmer

Borgen, J. S., & Ødegaard, E. E. (2015). Barnekultur som forskningsfelt – et interdisiplinært vitenskapelig emne [Children's culture as a research field – An interdisciplinary scientific topic], *BARN, 33*(3–4), 5–17.

Crowly, A. (2020). *Global report 2019 Progress towards ending corporal punishment of children*. Retrieved April 19, 2020, from http://endcorporalpunishment.org/wp-content/uploads/global/Global-report-2019.pdf

Dan, B. (2018). The child's best interest: Ethical guide or ideology? *Developmental Medicine & Child Neurology, 60*(1), 4. doi:10.1111/dmcn.13608

General Comment No. 5. (2003). *General measures of implementation of the convention on the rights of the child* (Arts. 4, 42 and 44, para. 6). Retrieved April 24, 2020, from https://resourcecentre.savethechildren.net/node/9689/pdf/general_comment_no_5_crc.pdf

Gradovski, M., Ødegaard, E. E., Rutanen, N., Sumsion, J., Mika, C., & White, E. J. (2019). *The first 1000 days of early childhood: Becoming* (Vol. 2). Springer Singapore.

Hackett, A. (2016). Young children as wayfarers: Learning about place by moving through it. *Children & Society, 30*(3), 169–179.

James, A., & James, A. L. (2004). *Constructing childhood: Theory, policy, and social practice.* Palgrave Macmillan.

Kraftl, P. (2020). *After childhood: Re-thinking environment, materiality and media in children's lives.* Routledge.

Lee, Y. Y. (2020). Beyond the dichotomy: Engaging a deeper dialogue about our interdependent futures between the western and non-western horizon. *ECNU Review of Education, 3*(1), 160–163. https://doi.org/10.1177/2096531120905210

Massey, D. B. (2005). *For space*. Sage.

NordForsk. (2011). *Rethinking Nordic added value in research.* Nordic Council of Ministries. https://www.norden.org/en/publication/rethinking-nordic-added-value-research

NordForsk. (2018). *NordForsk strategy 2019–2022.* Nordic Council of Ministries. https://www.norden.org/en/publication/nordforsk-strategy-2019-2022

Quennerstedt, A., Robinson, C., & I'Anson, J. (2018). The UNCRC: The voice of global consensus on children's rights? *Nordic Journal of Human Rights, 36*(1), 38–54. doi:10.1080/18918131.2018.1453589

Rautio, P., & Stenvall, E. (2019). *Social, material and political constructs of arctic childhoods: An everyday life perspective.* Springer.

Samuelsson, I. P., Li, M., & Hu, A. (2019). Early childhood education for sustainability: A driver for quality. *ECNU Review of Education, 2*(4), 369–373. https://doi.org/10.1177/2096531119893478

Smith, L. (2008). FNs konvensjon om barnets rettigheter [UN's Convention on the Rights of the Child]. In N. Høstmælingen, E. S. Kjørholt, & K. Sandberg (Eds.), *Barnekonvensjonen. Barns rettigheter i Norge.* Universitetsforlaget.

UNCRC. (1989). *United Nations Convention on the Right of the Child.* Retrieved April 21, 2020, from https://downloads.unicef.org.uk/wp-content/uploads/2010/05/UNCRC_united_nations_convention_on_the_rights_of_the_child.pdf?_ga=2.259582415.454887985.1587459175-44770236.1585716747

United Nations. (2015). *Transforming our world: The 2030 agenda for sustainable development* (A/Res/44/25). UN General Assembly. https://www.ohchr.org/CH/ProfessionalInterest/Pages/CRC.aspx

United Nations Educational, Scientific and Cultural Organization (UNESCO). (2017). *Education for sustainable development goals: Learning objectives.* United Nations Educational, Scientific and Cultural Organization.

United Nations Educational, Scientific and Cultural Organization (UNESCO). (2019). *Special edition: Progress towards the sustainable development goals.* UN Secretary General.

Uprichard, E. (2008). Children as 'being and becomings': Children, childhood and temporality (Report). *Children & Society, 22*(4), 303.

Urban, M. (2018). (D)evaluation of early childhood education and care? A critique of the OECDs international early learning study. In L. P. Michel Matthes, C. Clouder, & B. Heys (Eds.), *Proving the quality of childhood in Europe* (Vol. 7, pp. 91–99). Alliance for Childhood European Network Foundation.

Veerman, P. (2014). The aging of the UN Convention on the Rights of the Child. In M. Freeman (Ed.), *The future of children's rights*. Brill | Nijhoff. https://doi.org/10.1163/9789004271777_004

Vuorisalo, M., Raittila, R., & Rutanen, N. (2018). Kindergarten space and autonomy in construction – Explorations during team ethnography in a Finnish kindergarten. *Journal of Pedagogy, 9*(1), 45–64. doi:10.2478/jped-2018-0003

World Organization for Early Childhood Education. (2017). *Higher investment for Early Childhood Care and Education (ECCE): Declaration of the 69th assembly and world conference of OMEP.* http://worldomep.org/index.php?hCode¼POLICY_03_04

CHAPTER 2

In the Best Interests of the Child: From the Century of the Child to the Century of Sustainability

Liv Torunn Grindheim, Jorunn Spord Borgen and Elin Eriksen Ødegaard

Abstract

The 1989 United Nations Convention on the Rights of the Child (UNCRC) established a milestone for the 20th century, which is often referred to as the 'century of the child'. Despite the UNCRC being accepted in most countries, suppression and injustices are still present in many children's lives. To gain more insight into how to come closer to achieving equitable conditions for generations living interconnected lives in their situated local, but globally entangled, nature and cultures, this study investigated how children's rights to protection, to be heard and to play and recreation are promoted, actualised and expended in the wake of the century of the child. We start by presenting significant voices and changes that occurred during the 20th and 21st centuries and point to paradoxes and ambivalences that researchers encounter when aiming to discover what is in the best interests of the child. Research that has enhanced our knowledge on children's protection, participation, play and recreation revealed that children's lives, historical voices and legal rights and changes in global and local societies, nature and research are entangled and offer both new and contradictive knowledge about children and childhood. The uncovered paradoxes and ambivalences call for transformative research designs that are problem-oriented and transdisciplinary, as we as experts, together with citizens and policymakers, seek to make the right choices in the best interests of the child.

Keywords

century of the child – sustainability – UN Convention on the Rights of the Child – transformative research designs

1 Introduction

The United Nations Convention on the Rights of the Child (UNCRC) states that the best interests of the child should be a primary consideration in all actions concerning children (United Nations, 1989, art. 3). The UNCRC has been accepted by most countries; however, crime, suppression and unjust decisions continue to exist in and impact the lives of many children: all in the name of the child's best interests. Even in the Nordic countries, which are recognised for their child-centred approach to children and families in matters of education, public services, child culture industries and art, children continue to be abused and neglected, and their voices continue to be too easily ignored, both in everyday life affairs as well as in more important life decisions, such as those that have a huge effect on their future.

Attitudes towards children are deeply culturally grounded. Positioning ourselves among researchers who study childhood, children and children's cultural formation and examine these attitudes, requires an awareness of the context within which we operate. We can start by pointing to Ellen Key's influential book *The Century of the Child* (2018) that was published in Sweden in 1900. This book influenced not only Swedish society but also the Nordic and European spirit of interest in children's agency and personhood. The establishment of the BIN-Norden Child Culture Research Network in 1970 and the 1989 UNCRC can both be traced back to Key's influence. The influence of *The Century of the Child*, reified as worries for the children of future generations, is also evident in the world's ecological awakening and the 1987 Brundtland Report (World Commission on Environment and Development [WCED], 1987) that pointed to sustainable development as 'development that meets the needs of the present without compromising the ability for future generations to meet their own needs' (p. 29).

Since the 1980s, studies on childhood, child culture and developmental psychology have begun to establish common themes that have inspired other fields, such as education, philosophy, health and law. For many years, these fields have been less universalised and more contextualised (Borgen & Ødegaard, 2015). Children are understood as individuals who contribute to their own and others' cultural formation through interpersonal interactions in local communities but also through participation in the global sphere via travel, migration, television, the Internet and social media. As such, we see an increasing interest in developing policies based on universal solutions, legislation and efforts (Biesta, 2015). Both approaches attempt to meet the uncertainties of our rapidly changing and internationally interconnected contemporary society, where we must also face the enormous challenges presented by unsustainable methods of distributing and managing natural, cultural and human resources. In some parts of our world, children still do not have access to childcare and education, and poverty among children exists in both developed and underdeveloped countries (Eriksen, 2018). Acknowledging these challenges, we are convinced that universal solutions based on research from 'yesterday' cannot adequately address contemporary and future challenges. Despite this, we also know that historical and cultural knowledge must be handed over to the next generation; not doing so would be a disservice to the next generation. Thus, we have a pressing need to understand and accurately depict the current conditions of children's lives, encompassing their play, learning, well-being and cultural formation. This chapter, therefore, is structured around the question: *How are children's rights to protection, participation and recreation promoted, actualised and expended in the wake of the century of the child?* By looking backwards to the century of the child to understand ways of viewing children and childhood, we aim not only to gain insight into how to re-establish what might have been left out of children's lives but also to determine how to come closer to realising equitable conditions for generations living interconnected lives in their situated local, but globally entangled, nature and culture.

We begin by presenting some significant voices and changes from the 20th century, especially those from the Nordic context in which we are embedded, and point to paradoxes and ambivalences researchers encounter when they seek to identify actions and ideas that are in the best interests of the child. We approach our examination through the lens of three central themes. The first considers departure from children's right to protection, the second from children's right to be heard and the third from children's right to play and recreation. We sum up by viewing the paradoxes and ambivalences identified as conditions for transformative research practices that promote sustainability and the involvement of a variety of stakeholders and disciplines.

2 The Century of the Child

Taking a historical route, the perceptions of both women and children have been significantly impacted by the fact that references to a 'human' have traditionally been perceived as references to a grown man. Many voices have suggested opposition to this main discourse on man and instead have emphasised the resources that children have and bring to society. These historical thoughts and actions are manifold, but a common thread is the radical thought of children as humans in their own rights. Ellen Key (1849–1926), a Swedish intellectual, is one of the first strong Scandinavian voices to advocate principles concerning the rights of children. In her famous book, which she titles with her designation of the 20th century, *The Century of the Child* (Key, 2018),[1] Key writes about the neglect of children and advocates making children the focal point for political reform and education, promoting child-centred approaches to teaching and learning. Her ideas were embraced and further developed in Germany and the United States and were disseminated back to the Nordic countries in anonymous intertextualities by Elsa Köhler[2] and Charlotte Bühler[3] (Hauglund, Key, & Thorbjørnsen, 2001).

Key was familiar with the philosophies of both Karl Marx and Friedrich Nietzsche and oriented herself politically toward social democracy. She fueled the process of the social inclusion of children and the full membership of boys and girls in the human structure (Hällström, Jansson, & Pironi, 2016). The child-centred focus in Key's writings and the close relation to Rousseau's beliefs are exemplified by what she opined about education:

> To suppress the real personality of the child, and to supplant it with another personality continues to be a pedagogical crime common to those who announce loudly that education should only develop the real individual nature of the child. (Key, 2018, p. 108)

She referred to the 'soul murders in school' (p. 203) and to kindergartens as 'canned education', meaning that kindergartens were like factories where children learned to model others rather than to express themselves. She argued that the Froebel dictum, 'Let us live for the children', must be changed into a more significant phrase, 'Let us allow the children to live' (p. 242). Accordingly, she was very critical of corporal punishment. She wrote that one should never beat a child, because beating seldom makes children realise what error they made; it only awakens feelings of revenge. Furthermore, bodily punishment appeals primarily to the 'beast in man', the beast that one otherwise strives so diligently to obliterate in the child (Ambjörnsson, 2014). Even though her visions were close to those of Rousseau (and argued against some of Fröbel's didactics on modelling patterns), philosophical ideas from the 17th and 18th centuries, what she proclaimed was radical and not set into the juridical system until much later.

We trace the heritage of the establishment of children's rights to Key. One such effort to establish children's rights was the Norwegian parliament's passage of the Castbergian Child Laws[4] in 1915, which granted children born outside of marriage the rights to inheritances and to bear their fathers' surnames. These laws also ensured financial support for unmarried mothers by expanding the maintenance obligation. Thus, these rights were strengthened through legal protection (Andersland, 2015).

The 1924 Geneva Declaration of the Rights of the Child (League of Nations, 1924), recommended by the League of Nations, is another early document that specifically addressed children's rights. Then in 1948, the UN General Assembly approved the Universal Declaration of Human Rights, a revised and expanded version of the Geneva Declaration that states that all humans should be protected, as outlined in article 1: 'All human beings are born free and equal in dignity and rights'. This document formed the basis of the 1959 Declaration of the Rights of the Child approved by the UN General Assembly (Smith, 2008), which represents a milestone in the establishment of legal rights for children. The 1959 Declaration, which specifically focused on the rights of children, was seen as necessary in spite of the passage of the UN's Universal Declaration of Human Rights that had been approved in 1948, establishing the rights of all human beings. Each of these laws legitimised voices like Key's that argued that children are vulnerable and should have their own rights.

The first effort to establish the 1989 UNCRC was initiated in Poland in 1978. The original plan was to finalise the draft by the end of 1979, which was the International Year of the Child. The first suggested work from Poland was close to a confirmation of the principles in the declaration from 1959, upon which most states had agreed. Since the period from 1959 to 1978 saw a change in the ways both human rights and children were understood, several nations wanted a more radical declaration (Smith, 2008). After ten years of work and negotiations, the nations agreed upon a convention that represented a radical view of children's capabilities and rights; in addition to giving primary consideration to the best interests of the child and children's protection, it also stated that children had radical rights, like the right to express their views freely in 'all matters affecting the child' and for those views to be given due weight (arts. 12–13); children's rights to play and to engage in cultural life (art. 31) were also established. On 20 November 1989, the UNCRC was finally established and was put into practice on 2 September 1990.

In the wake of the century of the child and despite the UNCRC being accepted in most countries, issues such as crime, suppression and unjust decisions are still affecting the lives of many children. Regarding children's right to protection, it is uncomfortable to realise that corporal punishment remains an issue in child rearing practices. In 2019, Japan became the last reported country to prohibit all corporal punishment of children (Crowly, 2020). We see a growing awareness of violence against children as a fundamental human rights issue. Many countries face multiple serious and challenging issues like war, corruption and poverty. Thus, children are often not prioritised, and their right to protection is not fulfilled.

Another important issue in the wake of the century of the child is ensuring that more countries prioritise children's rights in every respect in order to achieve sustainable futures. By giving children individual rights, we indicate awareness of children's unique experiences, capabilities and vulnerabilities as a group that needs protection. At the same time, by establishing these rights for children, we also forward an individualistic approach that can overlook notions of humans as interrelated and dependent across generations, structural power-relations, economies and cultural and natural contexts and artefacts. Taking these paradoxes and ambivalences on board, along with the ecological awareness prevalent in part of the 20th century and in the 21st century, we see a surge towards sustainability. A strong voice that contributed to drawing attention to the interdependence of economy, poverty and natural resources and to the huge impact that our management of these resources will have on future generations is the 1987 Brundtland Report (WCED, 1987). In the report, reducing poverty and distributing resources more evenly are central to addressing both present and future needs, together with acknowledging the importance of our ability to live rewarding lives, which are dependent on human relationships and cultural belonging. Therefore, in the best interests of the child, it seems necessary to move from the century of the child to the century of sustainability.

3 Paradoxes and Ambivalence When Approaching the Best Interests of the Child

What it means to be a child and what childhood entails are concepts repeatedly negotiated when dealing with issues impacting children's lives and in cultural, historical, natural and institutional discourses (Cunningham, 2005; Dahlberg, Moss, & Pence, 2013). Voices like Key's and the establishment and worldwide acceptance of the UNCRC have, on one hand, established children and childhood as important both here and now and for future sustainability. On the other hand, these voices and rights are rooted in the global North and are easily construed as opposite to the concept of childhood in the global South (Nieuwenhuys, 2013). This can be exemplified by the Nordic welfare model. The Nordic welfare model that was established after the second world war was founded on ideals with the aim of establishing social welfare, health care and social security for all citizens, including children, as a public responsibility (Satka & Eydal, 2004). The Nordic welfare states have an explicit goal of regulating spaces and relations for children in 'the best interest' of the child. The core ideal is equal opportunities for all children (Korsvold, 2012). At an institutional level, the Nordic countries often serve as role models for good social practices. However, forwarding the Nordic welfare state as a role model forms a paradox to our conviction that universal solutions cannot form the answer for contemporary and future problems.

From the 1990s to the present, both international and Nordic political and structural changes have greatly impacted the Nordic welfare states and children's lives in geographically and culturally similar, but politically different, neighbouring countries (Juncker & BIN-Norden, 2013; Korsvold, 2012). Nordic childhoods are multicultural, intermediated and digitalised. The emphasis on children's agency and their legal UNCRC rights have given them a position in society-at-large, and therefore, childhood can no longer be viewed as a special kind of life-world; rather, children are, at all levels, participants in society across sectors (Juncker & BIN-Norden, 2013). Children's participatory potential, along with their need for protection and recreation, have been and continue to be explained and researched.

For the last 25–50 years, researchers in the fields of child culture, educational science, sociology and media have focused on studying and viewing young people in their own rights in order to grasp their perspectives. This research both critiques and analyses the child culture industry, child culture professions and the instrumentalisation of childhood (Borgen & Ødegaard, 2015). To reject the idea of modern childhood as a Western discovery or invention, postcolonial perspectives, in their broadest sense, are concerned with challenging the unquestioned, routine 'us vs. them' approach (Nieuwenhuys, 2013, p. 5). Postcolonial perspectives offer an abolition of this contradiction and instead present a conceptualisation of childhood(s) as the unstable and contingent result of a contextual encounter (Nieuwenhuys, 2013, p. 5). Furthermore, research about materiality as an actor in children's cultural formation, often departing from theories presented by Deleuze and Guattari (1988), is brought to the table. Emerging research points to sustainability raising awareness of how children and humans are entangled through nature, culture, materiality and economy and how their contexts are governed (Grindheim, Bakken, Hauge, & Heggen, 2019). How to meet the paradoxes and ambiguities in these entanglements are core issues in research seeking to identify the best interests of the child.

In the following, we point to three themes that we see as emerging and characterised by paradoxes and ambivalence concerning children's protection, participation and recreation in the wake of the century of the child – all with the overall aim of being in the best interests of the child (United Nations, 1989, art. 2). The first theme takes departure from children's right to protection, which is an overall aim of the UNCRC. We find the concepts of protect or protection referenced in articles 2, 3, 15, 16, 17, 19, 20, 22, 25, 31 and 38. The second theme is children's right to be heard (United Nations, 1989, arts. 12–13) and the third is children's right to play and recreation (United Nations, 1989, art. 31).

3.1 The Right to Protection

Quite recently, the COVID-19 pandemic revitalised the ambivalence of children's right to health protection (United Nations, 1989, arts. 3, 24). Although the virus hits and harms worldwide, the ways countries regulated children's lives during this situation differed, although the various regulations are legitimate in reference to the best interests of children and to inter-generational solidarity. Building upon the same situation and arguments, some countries closed early childhood education institutions and schools, while other kept them open (Drageseth, Berg, & Odland, 2020). Paradoxes and ambivalence on how to protect children in their best interests challenge ways to distribute responsibilities among generations, structures, cultures and established knowledge.

Adults' expectations regarding children seem to be constantly removed from structures established in the best interests of the child and are, instead, projected onto the individual child (Spyrou, 2018). This forms a contract with the web of structural and relational factors and interrelated dynamics that regulates children's spaces for relative autonomy and agency. 'Agency' has been a key concept in the social studies of children and childhood since the 1980s, where studies have been occupied with the relation between social structure and the individual social actor (James, Jenks, & Prout, 1998; Qvortrup, 1999). Agency in the sociology of childhood is understood as individual capacities, competences and activities that persons use to navigate within their given context (Robson, Bell, & Klocher, 2007). In child and childhood (or child-related) research, this awareness of children's agency from the 1980s is often referred to as 'children as beings', rather than 'children as becomings' as future adults and citizens, which indicates that children's lives here and now are of interest and importance (Bae, 2009; James & James, 2004). In contemporary research, it is acknowledged that both children and adults are in a constant state of movement and must learn more throughout their lives than was previously necessary. In that sense, no human being possesses all the knowledge that is needed to live his or her life; all of us are engaged in the continuous act of becoming (Holloway, Holt, & Mills, 2019; Uprichard, 2008). In addition, the view of children as agents with competences also creates some ambivalence; in more modern times, close connections have been made between competences and responsibilities (Lee, 2001). This way of understanding responsibilities, which is taken for granted, is also challenged when children come forward as competent. Even if competent, children also need protection and are not to be responsible in the same ways as adults. Indeed, the views of the child are to be 'given due weight in accordance with the age and maturity of the child' (United Nations, 1989, art. 12.1). The issue of responsibility also forms an ambivalence towards children's involvement for sustainability; although children can exercise agency and contribute with fresh points of view, the responsibility for pollution is a heritage from the older generation and is first and foremost the responsibility of the adult generation. Article 24(c) states that children have the right to a healthy environment with no dangers and risks of environmental pollution. The ambivalence of children's involvement, responsibility and right to protection must be balanced and future oriented (cf. Brundtland Report, WCED, 1987).

How to balance the paradoxes and uncertainties when children are experts in the experiences of their own lives and are entitled to protection is a continuous challenge in research aimed at understanding the conditions in which children live. Children are enmeshed with other people, materials, cultures and nature, living within or on the edge of systems that govern their lives. Furthermore, these paradoxes and ambivalences challenge our thinking about what we can know, and about research methodology, and indicate that research about children's participation needs to be viewed in terms of time, context and relations (Mannion, 2009); this also applies to studying children's culture and cultural participation (Borgen, 2011). A singular emphasis on children's 'own' culture can leave the political, societal, institutional and social structures that form conditions for children's participation and protection in the shadows.

We have traced an overall ambiguity related to children's right to protection and distribution of responsibility. Even if children are accepted as being persons here and now (and not only as future adults) who have agency to influence both their own and their peers', teachers', parents' and cultural workers' lives in their given material, cultural, economic and natural contexts, they also have an overall right to protection from all forms of physical or mental violence, injury, abuse, neglect or negligent treatment, maltreatment or exploitation, including sexual abuse, while in the care of their parent(s), legal guardian(s) or any other person responsible for the care of the child (United Nations, 1989, art. 19). In addition, they have the right to the protection of their 'child culture' (United Nations, 1989, art. 31), protection from pollution (art. 24) and protection from the heavy burden of earlier generations' uneven distribution of resources. This calls for considering ethical concerns in childhood research far above national guidelines.

3.2   *The Right to Be Heard*

Research reveals that while children are given the right to be heard (United Nations, 1989, art. 12) through freedom of expression (United Nations, 1989, art. 13), freedom of expression is often conceptualised as participation, meaning ongoing processes of information-sharing and dialogue, which involves children experiencing their own contributions and participation, together with those of others, in their daily lives (Bae, 2018, p. 50). However, these rights are restricted compared to those held by adults (Qvortrup, 2009). Children's spaces for participation are often held apart from those held by adults, and consequently, children do not necessarily have control over their structural conditions. Thus, in childhood studies, identity is generally framed in the context of adult–child relationships (de Castro, 2004). This can lead to their being subtly controlled by their parents and other guardians (Hennum, 2010) through the practices of welfare professions and institutions (Cockburn, 2010; James, 2011), justified as being in the best interests of the child. However, research also depicts how children can make room and space for themselves in contexts that are not governed in the best interests of the child (Mannion, 2007), like children living in the streets in Bolivia who negotiate control over specific areas (James, 2011). Also, in Estonia, children had implicit influence due to changing political regimes that differed radically as it came to family and childcare politics (Vihalemm & Müürsepp, 2007). Children's participation and use of media is a topic of concern; however, these concerns also lead to children's cultural and societal participation becoming visible and debated in public (Gaini, 2006). The ways in which children raise their voices – by being a nuisance (on the streets) (James, 2011), by not being as physically active as adults want them to be (Borgen, Rugseth, & Bjorbækmo, 2021), by being aesthetically resistant (Ylönen, 2021) or by expressing anger (Grindheim, 2014) may also cause concerns. Although children's rights to participate are restricted, children are heard in a variety of ways and contexts that are not limited to spaces structured for democratic participation by adult generations. Thus, the entanglements between culture and generations can both empower and disempower children.

Children's right to be heard is also of relevance for research methods and ethics in child-related research. The historical perspectives and changes in child-related studies reflect how both vertical and horizontal processes interact in this research field. This can be exemplified by the way a report about children's humour (Bregenhøj & Johnson, 1988) was met in the 1980s. This report was recognised and debated in public newspapers regarding issues of children's burlesque language culture and researchers' ethical responsibility towards visibility of such language-specific humour. The debate revealed a contradictive view between the public and researchers related to children and children's culture. The debate revealed that in the public view, children's culture happened among children when they were on their own and could only be scientifically examined by looking 'through the keyhole into children's "rooms"' (Ekrem, Tingstad, & Johnsen, 2001, p. 158). Thus, children should be understood from the adult perspective, and no interest was left for children's perspectives or for children's participation in society-at-large. This view was contrary to childhood research designed to capture children's perspectives.

In the wake of the century of the child, researchers continued to discuss and explore children's perspectives. For instance, in her meta study of child culture research, Marianne Gullestad (1991) discussed the idea of capturing children's perspectives and how it is a challenge for researchers that requires imagination as well as insight into children's everyday routines. The discussion centred on the idea that children's perspectives are not perspectives on children but are perspectives from children's position in society and culture (Johansson, 2003). An awareness is emerging in contemporary research of the need to focus on children and childhood in spaces for transitions in intergenerational childhoods (Oropilla, 2021) and in the embodied interplay and communication between multiple disabilities and the sensitive significant other, techniques, contexts and objective medical knowledge (Evensen, 2021). There are also suggestions concerning an existential approach in the understanding of both the infant and the involved adult in more reflective ways, emphasising reciprocal models, and more than cognitive capacities and infant's ability to imitate (von Bonsdorff, 2021). Children are resources in iterative research design processes as users of software (Povlsen, Krogager, Leer, & Højlund, 2021). Research seems to come closer to emphasising entanglements between humans, non-humans, objects and different phenomena (Grindheim, 2021), and between cross- and transdisciplinary designs (Borgen & Ødegaard, 2015; Karlsson, 2021). This awareness is of specific relevance when aiming to capture children's perspectives in order to meet the intertwined challenges of children's position and participation when approaching sustainability (Grindheim et al., 2019).

3.3 Right to Play and Recreation

Research reveals that many childhood-related topics circulate around the twin poles of fear and pleasure (Borgen, Ødegaard, & BIN-Norden, 2016). A childhood suffused with an awareness of risks and dangers is a phenomenon in contemporary Nordic society. For example, in our rapidly changing society, globalisation, commercialisation and digitalisation are all factors that might cause both pleasure and danger. Children are, both implicitly and explicitly, exposed to cultural artefacts, certain kinds of physical spaces and places, certain types of human age communities and certain varieties of timeframes, all of which are embedded with more or less incongruous signs and shifting modes of how to act, relate and think, open for children to take up, conserve and transform (Ødegaard, 2011). These norms and paradoxes for children's participation in society provide grounds for new understandings of the transformation of childhood in a globalised era. This creates an uncertainty as to how children might exercise their rights to play and recreation (United Nations, 1989, art. 31), since what is considered 'good' for children is difficult to know: what are the fears and what are the pleasures, and for whom?

In many cases, these changes and the pleasures connected to children are also sources of fear and anxiety. The image of childhood as a refuge from the horrors of the world is challenged in the global, digitalised media by images of refugee children, alone or with their families, living hand to mouth in camps or en route to asylum, struggling to survive the nearly insurmountable challenges of endless war, cynical profiteering, hostile or fearful citizens of European countries and forces of nature that can take their lives in a moment. Several of the UNCRC rights of these children are not met, such as their rights of protection as refugees (United Nations, 1989, art. 22); they lack food, shelter and medical supplies (United Nations, 1989, art. 24), and they have been stripped of central aspects of childhood: the creation of child culture through play, fun, fantasy and youthful control of space and material (United Nations, 1989, art. 31). In the Nordic countries we are stuck on the idea that we are protecting 'our' children, limited to Nordic youth. This forms a paradox for those who have concerns about sustainability and who press for more even distribution of resources, who advocate for children's right to life, play and recreation globally and who fight politically for solidarity by forcing Scandinavian governments to give shelter to children from the Moria camp of refugees before they are all affected by COVID-19 (Save the Children Campaign, 2020).

Even when children are not subject to any threats, many adults feel that they must be protected by teaching them how to manage risks later in life (Lyså, 2021). Vulnerability and risk go hand in hand with protection and care and what is perceived as appropriate play and recreation. The presumed romantic innocence of children may be an attractive idea to adults; however, this romanticism can manifest itself as anxiety about the eventual, inevitable loss of innocence. Again, here, we trace paradoxes and ambivalence; on one hand, childhood can be seen as a temporary idyll, full of pleasures to be romanticised, forgotten or deemed 'childish' later in life. On the other hand, children themselves can be perceived by adults as sources of pleasure and hope for the future, for example, by performing at high levels and developing some sort of unique or extraordinary talent (Lyså, 2018). Ideas linking children and childhood with pleasure are supported by cultural imagery from high art to advertisements: a mother cradling her child is one of the most iconic images of domestic bliss.

The concepts of risk and risk prevention are brought into early childhood education by political documents and white papers, by several professional knowledge bases, by general cultural discourses, by parents and by children themselves. An example is the debate about risk and play. Competing discourses on children's play and recreation debate how to balance guarding children's safety with allowing children to play in physically and emotionally stimulating and challenging environments, which in Scandinavian research is often synonymous with being outdoors in nature (Sandseter, 2007; Sandseter & Sando, 2016). Indeed, Little, Wyver, and Gibson (2011) argued that regulatory factors and requirements for playground safety can be identified as having 'a detrimental impact' on the quality of play. Also, Gill (2007) pointed to the paradoxes and ambiguities that a societal misreading of risk can result in when children face a myriad of restrictions that are intended to support them. If children are restricted from activities that involve taking risks, they will not learn how to assess and respond to risk. From our point of view, we might, thereby, also restrict children from developing extended abilities to cope and to contribute to a higher degree of sustainability by having the courage and competencies needed to face the risk of challenging the status quo of unsustainability.

Emphasising fears and pleasures as they relate to recreation and play might form a contesting approach to children's lifeworld and what is in the best interests of the child. It involves more than facing the ambivalence of safeguarding and challenge; once more, we depict the overall tendency to look to explanations within the individual child. Gurholt and Sanderud (2016) outlined how 'risky play' might be closer to explorative play, where children seek challenges when natural environments invite them into forms of play that may involve risk of physical injury, than to an understanding that children innately seek physical danger and that risk is essential for children's growth (p. 318). We need ways to come closer to understanding children's perspectives, which can provide more insight into relational, situated and contextual play activities, play tools and moods of play practices that are sliding, shifting, displaying and exceeding areas of interest, as, for instance, outlined by Karoff (2013). Finding ways to perform research in order to understand and depict the conditions of children's lives and play and, thereby, support their rights to play and recreation is an ongoing challenge.

3.4 Summing up – Paradoxes and Ambivalence in Child-Related Research in the Nordic Context

From this (rather short and superficial) mapping of research in the wake of the century of the child – all aiming at what is in the best interests of the child – we point to several paradoxes and areas of ambivalence when investigating how children's protection, participation and recreation are promoted, actualised and expended. It is depicted that children's protection, participation and recreation are enclosed by paradoxes and ambiguity that supply the grounds for gaining new understandings of the transformation of childhood in a globalised era. This underlines that, in research involving children, it is crucial to reflect upon procedural, methodological and conceptual matters. In all areas where children are in focus, ethical considerations are also of vital importance; ethical dilemmas, aspects and deliberations comprise methodological issues. We find that these challenges are difficult to manage in a single research tradition. Therefore, these paradoxes and areas of ambivalence can be seen as conditions for transformative research practices that foster sustainability and the involvement of a variety of stakeholders and that take a more future-oriented and imaginative strand to research designs.

4 Facing Paradoxes and Ambivalence in Research through a Transformative Research Approach

The complexities, contradictions, paradoxes and uncertainties in childhood contexts call for a variety of perspectives to gain insight into how to facilitate sustainable living. In the BIN-Norden network that began in the 1970s, researchers from different disciplines, such as ethnography, sociology, art and history, as well as those who took an interdisciplinary approach, began to question the way in which children were understood. BIN-Norden has emerged as a robust and active children's culture research network, where the subject of research – children and young people and their culture – is shared across disciplines, classifications and sectors. During this period, the sociology of science has problematised the notions of dense disciplinary boundaries versus the knowledge migration of researchers between the disciplines (Sandström, Friberg, Hyenstrand, Larsson, & Wadskog, 2004). A disciplinary specialisation has become an overly narrow box for exploring many of the issues that are relevant in our time, something the BIN-Norden network exemplifies through child culture research.

A key event (Taylor, Flanagan, Cheney, & Seibold, 2001) that is explicitly recounted as spawning the terms 'interdisciplinarity' and 'transdisciplinarity' is the first international conference on interdisciplinary research and teaching in Organisation for Economic Co-operation and Development member countries (OECD) in 1970 (Apostel, Berger, Briggs, & Michaud, 1972; Klein, 2013). Cross-disciplinary science is, according to Sandström et al. (2004, pp. 15–16), an 'umbrella term' for multidisciplinary and interdisciplinary research. These different approaches can be taken by collaborating researchers who represent different disciplines or by researchers seeking to acquire a knowledge base from another field in addition to their own. A multi (multiple) disciplinary research design may involve different researchers with different competencies working side by side, often through separate work packages and an agreed division of labor. Each discipline helps to illuminate one aspect of the topic or problem being investigated, and no direct contact is established between the various knowledge bases, such as the disciplines, represented by the researchers. Nevertheless, the collaboration is characterised by the addition of new knowledge about the topic or problem. Multidisciplinarity is a condition for both interdisciplinarity and transdisciplinarity. In interdisciplinary scientific work, the approach is to integrate the knowledge that the researchers possess with the aim of elucidating a topic, problem or area of knowledge together. The different fields of knowledge agree on a common conceptual apparatus and actively exchange theory and method (Sandström et al., 2004, p. 16). This requires professional interaction and close communication between those working in collaboration. Whether the research can be characterised as multidisciplinary or interdisciplinary depends on what forms it takes and what consequences it will have (Nicolescu, 2014). According to Klein (2013), debates about the definition of interdisciplinarity are related to concepts such as interrogation, critique, transgression and transformation, as well as to the quest for reconfiguring, reformulating and resituating, and they can be linked to struggles for social change that began in the 1960s and 1970s (p. 196). The struggles for social changes emphasised are close to the struggles for children's rights in the 20th century.

The sociology of science deals with how concepts and working methods change over time and how new concepts become valid. 'Trans' means transgression, and transdisciplinary research may be the current term of choice when trying to tackle a complex problem where there is disagreement as to what the problem is. Transdisciplinarity contains possibilities for syntheses or compositions that appear as new content. For example, a research team may develop a research design and conduct research through a division of work that distributes roles and responsibilities between multiple members, where the team comprises researchers as well as members who are not researchers.

The integration in transdisciplinary research can, thus, consist of both horizontal and vertical elements: collaboration between researchers in different disciplines and people who know the problem area, for example, through their professional practices or from being affected by it in other ways. Augsburg (2014) referred to two 'main schools' of transdisciplinarity. In the first main school, represented by Nicolescu's ontological notion of reality as plastic and simultaneously outside and inside us, a subject/object interaction (2008, p. 12), 'We are part of this Reality that changes due to our thoughts, feelings and actions. This means that we are fully responsible for what Reality is' (Nicolescu,

2014, p. 25). In the second main school, the 'widely recognized current (frequently referred to as either the Swiss, Zurich, or German school) focuses on transdisciplinarity as a research approach to addressing complex societal problems such as those related to sustainability' (Augsburg, 2014, p. 235). Here, 'transdisciplinarity is conceptualized as problem-focused with an emphasis on joint problem solving at the science, technology, and society interface that goes beyond the confines of academia' (Augsburg, 2014, p. 235).

The paradoxes and ambivalences we trace in the wake of the century of the child appear to go beyond the confines of academia. Several considerations required examination, like political fights for children's rights. Childhood is political and cannot be identified and discussed from one perspective alone. Meetings between disciplinary perspectives, and between research-based knowledge and general understandings in society, contribute to changes in understandings and concepts about children's culture and childhood. Therefore, the transdisciplinary approach appears to be of high relevance for childhood research in the century of sustainability.

In accordance with the paradoxes and ambivalences we find in the wake of the century of the child, when taking departure from the UNCRC, we find Klein's (2015) conceptualisation of transdisciplinary research to be of specific relevance. Klein (2013) argued that 'calls for transdisciplinarity arrived at a moment of wider crisis in the discourse of human rights accountability' (p. 197). Klein (2015) offered perspectives on how problems in the world can be met and solved and argued that, since the future is unpredictable, we will also need several conceptualisations of transdisciplinarity.

> As an epistemological project, transdisciplinarity will be aligned more closely with the discourse of transcendence. As a method of knowledge production, it will be linked with utilitarian objectives [problem solving], although they range from manufacturing new products to new protocols for health care and environmental sustainability. As a form of critique, it will continue to interrogate the structure and logic of the university and its role in society. (Klein, 2015, p. 15)

Augsburg (2014) departed from Klein's (2015) hypothesis that transdisciplinary individuals can contribute to the evolution of transdisciplinarity's discourse, and the question of how one becomes a transdisciplinary individual and how to take a transdisciplinary approach in research. Becoming a transdisciplinary researcher requires being an intellectual risk taker and institutional transgressor, as well as transdisciplinary practices and virtues, creative inquiry and cultural relativism. Augsburg (2014) argued that the 'transdisciplinary attitude' has paved the way for considerations of transdisciplinary skills, characteristics and traits, along with individual transdisciplinary virtues and practices, and that these can be trained (p. 244). While heterogeneity can be viewed as transdisciplinarity's biggest threat to success, it is also its fundamental characteristic. Thus, transdisciplinarity presupposes an ethic of shared knowledge that differs from traditional academic norms and structures (p. 234).

From our point of view, this can be a way to gain new insight into a variety of understandings, including how to facilitate the best interests of the child in the century of sustainability. In line with Augsburg (2014), who stated that transdisciplinarity presupposes a moral philosophy of shared knowledge (p. 234), we see that the paradoxes and ambivalences that we trace also call for a methodological ethic, which must be expanded and trained to identify conditions that change, interfere and contradict. These arguments serve as motivation for more insight and research practices that can face the contemporary uncertainties by undertaking transdisciplinarian research methods and more imaginative strands to research.

5   Summary

Conducting research in the best interests of the children presents challenges. Investigating how children's protection, participation and recreation is promoted, actualised and expended in the wake of the century of the child reveals that children's lives, historical voices and legal rights, and changes in global and local societies, nature and research are entangled and offer both new and contradictive knowledge about children and childhood. From our outline, where the 1989 UNCRC is seen as a milestone for ensuring children's protection, position and well-being, we face some of the same challenges referenced in the arguments for establishing the UNCRC. Children are still being neglected in several parts of the world, and corporal punishment is still an issue. In addition, we see that by giving children individual rights, we not only increase awareness of both children's vulnerable position and their unique capabilities, but we also forward an individualistic approach that can leave notions of humans as dependent across generations, structural power-relations, economies, cultural and natural contexts, and materials in the shadows. Taking a closer look at how the rights to protection, participation, and play and recreation are promoted, actualised and expended in the wake of the century of the child seems to lead us to what Klein (2013) pointed to as the crisis of human rights accountability. It calls for avoiding universal solutions and colonialisation and for fostering sustainability in ways of organising our human, cultural and natural resources. Seeing the paradoxes and uncertainties as conditions for change and transformations in research as well as in practices, this chapter argues for future-oriented and sustainable transdisciplinary approaches to research designs and practices as we, as experts, together with citizens and policymakers, try to make the right choices in the best interests of the child.

Notes

1 Soon after it was published in 1900, the book was translated into 13 languages.
2 Elsa Köhler (1879–1940) was a Swedish psychologist and educationalist whose legacy was the creation of links between German Froebelian ideologies and Swedish pragmatism. She was an early advocate for the acknowledgment of children's self-activity and learning through play (Tallberg Broman, 1995).
3 Charlotte Bühler (1883–1974) was a pioneer child-oriented psychologist who is known for the contributions her research on early ages made to the understanding of human beings' tendency to strive for personal satisfaction in sex, love and ego recognition, their tendency for self-limiting adaptation for the purpose of fitting in, belonging and gaining security, and their tendencies toward self-expression and creative accomplishments and toward integration or order-upholding (Woodward, 2012).
4 The law was named after Johan Castberg, a member of the radical wing of the Liberal Party, who became a politician and head of the Labour Democrats. Throughout his political life, Castberg was a proponent of women's and children's rights and of bringing social differences into balance.

References

Ambjörnsson, R. (2014). Ellen Key and the concept of Bildung. *Confero: Essays on Education, Philosophy and Politics,* 2(1), 133–160. doi:10.3384/confero.2001-4562.140515

Andersland, G. K. (2015). *De Castbergske barnelover 1915–2015* [*The Castbergian child laws 1915–2015*]. Cappelen Damm.

Apostel, L., Berger, G., Briggs, A., & Michaud, G. (1972). *Interdisciplinarity: Problems of teaching and research in universities.* Organisation for Economic Co-operation and Development.

Augsburg, T. (2014). Becoming transdisciplinary: The emergence of the transdisciplinary individual. *World Futures,* 70(3–4), 233–247. doi:10.1080/02604027.2014.934639

Bae, B. (2009). Children's right to participation: Challenges in everyday interactions. *European Early Childhood Research Journal,* 17(3), 391–406.

Bae, B. (2018). *Politikk, lek og læring. Barnehageliv fra mange kanter* [*Politics, play and learning. Kindergarten life from many sides*]. Fagbokforlaget.

Biesta, G. J. (2015). *The beautiful risk of education.* Routledge.

Borgen, J. S. (2011). The cultural rucksack in Norway: Does the national model entail a programme for educational change? In J. Sefton-Green, P. Thomson, K. Jones, & L. Bresler (Eds.), *The Routledge international handbook of creative learning* (pp. 374–382). Routledge.

Borgen, J. S., & Ødegaard, E. E. (2015). Barnekultur som forskningsfelt – Et interdisiplinært vitenskapelig emne [Child culture as research field – an interdisciplinary scientific issue]. *Barn, 33*(3–4), 5–17.

Borgen, J. S., Ødegaard, E. E., & BIN-Norden Conference. (2016). *Fears and pleasures in Nordic childhoods*. Book of abstracts for the BIN conference 2016. http://bin-norden.org/wp-content/uploads/2016/10/Book-of-abstracts-BIN-Lysebu.pdf

Borgen, J. S., Rugseth, G., & Bjorbækmo, W. S. (2021). 'Children at risk' in public health policy: What is at risk? In E. E. Ødegaard & J. S. Borgen (Eds.), *Childhood cultures in transformation – Reorientation and new readings of children and childhood* (Chapter 9). Brill | Sense.

Bregenhøj, C., & Johnson, M. (1988). *Blodet droppar, blodet droppar: Skolbarns humor [Blood is dripping, blood is dripping: School-children's humour]*. Alba.

Christensen, P., & Mikkelsen, M. R. (2008). Jumping off and being careful: Children's strategies of risk management in everyday life. *Sociology of Health & Illness, 30*(1), 112–130. doi:10.1111/j.1467-9566.2007.01046.x

Cockburn, T. (2010). Children and deliberative democracy in England. In B. Percy-Smith & N. Thomas (Eds.), *A handbook of children and young people's participation* (pp. 306–317). Routledge.

Crowly, A. (2020). *Global report 2019 Progress towards ending corporal punishment of children* [PDF file]. http://endcorporalpunishment.org/wp-content/uploads/global/Global-report-2019.pdf

Cunningham, H. (2005). *Children and childhood in western society since 1500*. Pearson Education.

Dahlberg, G., Moss, P., & Pence, A. R. (2013). *Beyond quality in early childhood education and care: Postmodern perspectives* (3rd ed.). Routledge.

de Castro, L. R. (2004). Otherness in me, otherness in others: Children's and youth's constructions of self and others. *Childhood, 11*(4), 469–493.

Deleuze, G., & Guattari, F. (1988). *A thousand plateaus: Capitalism and schizophrenia II*. Althlone.

Dragseth, S. S., Berg, N. & Odland, A. M. (2020, 2. April). 25 barn fra hele verden – slik rammer koronaviruset livet vårt [25 Children all over the world – this way is the corona virus effecting our lives]. *Aftenposten*. Retrieved April 8, 2020, from https://www.aftenposten.no/verden/i/xPkPmB/25-barn-fra-hele-verden-slik-rammer-koronaviruset-livet-vaart

Ekrem, C., Tingstad, V., & Johnsen, H. (2001). BIN-Norden – en historisk och kulturell kontekstualisering [BIN-Norden – a historical and cultural contextualisation]. In U. Palmenfelt & T. K. Marker (Eds.), *Refleksivitet i barndoms- og børnekulturforskningen* [*Reflectivity in childhood and child culture research*]. *Tidsskrift for børne- og ungdomskultur, 43*, 149–170.

Eriksen, E. (2018). Democratic participation in early childhood education and care – Serving the best interests of the child. *Tidsskrift for Nordisk Barnehageforskning, 17*(10), 1–15.

Evensen, K. V. (2021). Children with severe, multiple disabilities: Interplaying beings, communicative becomings. In E. E. Ødegaard & J. S. Borgen (Eds.), *Childhood cultures in transformation – Reorientation and new readings of children and childhood* (Chapter 4). Brill | Sense.

Gaini, F. (2006). Internet chatting in the Faroe Islands. New forms of communication among young people. In *Fróðskaparrit 54* (*Annales Societatis Scientiarum Færoensis*) (pp. 62–70). Fróðskapur (Faroese University Press).

Gill, T. (2007). *No fear. Growing up in a risk averse society*. Calouste Gulbenkian Foundation. https://content.gulbenkian.pt/wp-content/uploads/sites/18/2007/01/01175447/No-fear-19-12-07.pdf

Grindheim, L. T. (2014). 'I am not angry in the kindergarten!' Interruptive anger as democratic participation in Norwegian kindergartens. *Contemporary Issues in Early Childhood, 15*(4), 308–318.

Grindheim, L. T. (2021). Approaching agency in intra-activities. In E. E. Ødegaard & J. S. Borgen (Eds.), *Childhood cultures in transformation – Reorientation and new readings of children and childhood* (Chapter 11). Brill | Sense.

Grindheim, L. T., Bakken, Y., Hauge, K. H., & Heggen, M. P. (2019). Early childhood education for sustainability through contradicting and overlapping dimensions. *ECNU Review of Education, 2*(4), 374–395.

Gurholt, K. P., & Sanderud, J. R. (2016). Curious play: Children's exploration of nature. *Journal of Adventure Education and Outdoor Learning, 16*(4), 318–329. doi:10.1080/14729679.2016.1162183

Hällström, C., Jansson, H., & Pironi, T. (2016). Ellen Key and the birth of a new children's culture. *Journal of Theories and Research in Education, 11*(2), 1–25. doi:10.6092/issn.1970-2221/6373

Hauglund, E., Key, E., & Thorbjørnsen, K. M. (2001). *Barnets århundre og Ellen Key: 8 nøkler til en låst tid* [*The century of the child and Ellen Key: 8 keys to a closed time*]. Akribe Norsk form.

Hennum, N. (2010). Mot en standardisering av voksenhet? Barn som redskap i statens i disiplinering av voksne [Towards standardisation of adulthood? Children as tool for state disciplinisation of adults]. *Sosiologi i Dag, 40*(1–2), 58–75.

Holloway, S. L., Holt, L., & Mills, S. (2019). Questions of agency: Capacity, subjectivity, spatiality and temporality. *Progress in Human Geography, 43*(3), 458–477.

James, A. (2011). To be(come) or not to be(come): Understanding children's citizenship. *The Annals of the American Academy of Political and Social Science, 633*(1), 167–179.

James, A., & James, A. L. (2004). *Constructing childhood: Theory, policy, and social practice*. Palgrave Macmillan.

James, A., Jenks, C., & Prout, A. (1998). *Theorizing childhood*. Polity Press.

Johansson, E. (2003). Att nærma sig barns perspectival [To come closer to children's perspectives]. *Pedagogisk Forsking i Sverige, 8*(1–2), 42–57.

Juncker, B., & BIN-Norden. (2013). *Børn & kultur I Norden. Nordiske forskningsperspektiver i dialog. Historien om et projekt* [Children & culture in the Nordic countries. Nordic research perspectives in dialog]. Scandinavian Book A/S.

Karlsson, L. (2021). Studies of child perspective in methodology and practice with 'Osallisuus' as a Finnish approach to children's reciprocal cultural participation. In E. E. Ødegaard & J. S. Borgen (Eds.), *Childhood cultures in transformation – Reorientation and new readings of children and childhood* (Chapter 13). Brill | Sense.

Karoff, H. S. (2013). Play practices and play moods. *International Journal of Play, 2*(2), 76–86. doi:10.1080/21594937.2013.805650

Key, E. (2018). *The century of the child* [eBook]. Project Gutenberg. https://www.gutenberg.org/wiki/Gutenberg:Permission_How-To#Citing_Project_Gutenberg

Klein, J. T. (2013). The transdisciplinary moment(um). *Integral Review, 9*(2), 189–199.

Klein, J. T. (2015). Reprint of "Discourses of transdisciplinarity: Looking back to the future." *Futures, 65*, 10–16.

Korsvold, T. (2012). Dilemmas over childcare in Norway, Sweden and West Germany after 1945. In A. T. Kjørholt & J. Qvortrup (Eds.), *The modern child and the flexible labour market: Early childhood education and care* (pp. 19–37). Palgrave MacMillan.

League of Nations. (1924). *The Geneva Declaration of the Rights of the Child* [PDF file]. http://cpd.org.rs/wp-content/uploads/2017/11/01_-Declaration_of_Geneva_1924.pdf

Lee, N. (2001). *Childhood and society: Growing up in an age of uncertainty*. Open University Press.

Little, H., Wyver, S., & Gibson, F. (2011). The influence of play context and adult attitudes on young children's physical risk-taking during outdoor play. *European Early Childhood Education Research Journal, 19*(1), 113–131.

Lyså, I. M. (2018). *Duties and privileges: An ethnographic study of discipline as relational practice in two urban Chinese kindergartens* (Doctoral dissertation). Norwegian University of Science and Technology.

Lyså, I. M. (2021). Managing risk and balancing minds: Transforming the next generation through 'frustration education'. In E. E. Ødegaard & J. S. Borgen (Eds.),

Childhood cultures in transformation – Reorientation and new readings of children and childhood (Chapter 6). Brill | Sense.

Mannion, G. (2007). Going spatial, going relational: Why "listening to children" and children's participation needs reframing. *Discourse: Studies in the Cultural Politics of Education, 28*(3), 405–420.

Mannion, G. (2009). After participation: The socio-spatial performance of Intergenerational becoming. In B. Percy-Smith & N. Thomas (Eds.), *A handbook of children and young people's participation* (pp. 352–364). Routledge.

Nicolescu, B. (2014). Multidisciplinarity, interdisciplinarity, indisciplinarity, and transdisciplinarity: Similarities and differences. *RCC Perspectives, 2*, 19–26. www.jstor.org/stable/26241230

Nieuwenhuys, O. (2013). Theorizing childhood(s): Why we need postcolonial perspectives. *Childhood, 20*(1), 3–8.

Ødegaard, E. E. (2011). Deltakende handlingsrom i barnehagen – dynamikk og vilkår [Room for participation in kindergarten]. In T. Korsvold (Ed.), *Inkludering, barn, barndom, barnehage* [*Inclusion, children, childhood, kindergarten*] (pp. 130–151). Fagbokforlaget.

Oropilla, C. T. (2021). Spaces for transitions in intergenerational childhood experiences. In E. E. Ødegaard & J. S. Borgen (Eds.), *Childhood cultures in transformation – Reorientation and new readings of children and childhood* (Chapter 5). Brill | Sense.

Povlsen, K. K., Krogager, S. G. S., Leer, J., & Pedersen, S. H. (2012o). Children, food and digital media: Questions, challenges and methodologies. In E. E. Ødegaard & J. S. Borgen (Eds.), *Childhood cultures in transformation – Reorientation and new readings of children and childhood* (Chapter 8). Brill | Sense.

Qvortrup, J. (1999). Childhood and societal macrostructures. In *Child and youth culture*. Working paper 9. (s. 3–22) [PDF-file]. Odense University. http://citeseerx.ist.psu.edu/viewdoc/download?doi=10.1.1.120.4643&rep=rep1&type=pdf

Qvortrup, J. (2009). Childhood as a structural form. In J. Qvortrup, W. Corsaro, & M. Honig (Eds.), *The Palgrave handbook of childhood studies* (pp. 21–33). Palgrave Macmillan.

Robson, E., Bell, S., & Klocker, N. (2007). Conceptualizing agency in the lives and actions of rural young children. In R. Panelli, S. Punch, & E. Robson (Eds.), *Global perspectives on rural childhood and youth. Young rural lives* (pp. 135–148). Routledge.

Sandseter, E. B. H. (2007). Categorising risky play – How can we identify risk-taking in children's play? *European Early Childhood Education Research Journal, 15*(2), 237–252.

Sandseter, E. B. H., & Sando, O. J. (2016). "We don't allow children to climb trees": How a focus on safety affects Norwegian children's play in early-childhood education and care settings. *American Journal of Play, 8*(2), 178–200.

Sandström, U., Friberg, M., Hyenstrand, P., Larsson, K., & Wadskog, D. (2004). *Tvärvetenskap – En analys* [Cross disciplinarian science – An analysis]. Vetenskapsrådet.

Satka, M., & Eydal, G. B. (2004). The history of Nordic welfare policies for children. In H. Brembeck, B. Johansson, & J. Kampmann (Eds.), *Beyond the competent child: Exploring contemporary childhoods in the Nordic welfare societies* (pp. 33–62). Roskilde University Press.

Save the Children Campaign. (2020). *Evakuer barnefamilier fra Moria nå!* [*Evacuate families with children from Moria, now!*]. https://evakuermoria.org/?utm_campaign=evakuer_barnefamilier_fra_moria&utm_source=facebook&utm_medium=social&utm_content=video_med_birgitte_om_evakuer_barna_fra_moria&fbclid=IwAR2txypQ3o5xSmnB2CNVnPu5hFlVsvdfvXbk0Wb5NUTRG7n_Tq-hsbUPdc0

Smith, L. (2008). FNs konvensjon om barnets rettigheter [UNs convention on the rights of the child]. In N. Høstmælingen, E. S. Kjørholt, & K. Sandberg (Eds.), *Barnekonvensjonen. Barns rettigheter i Norge* [*The convention on the rights of the child: Children's rights in Norway*] (pp. 15–27). Universitetsforlaget.

Spyrou, S. (2018). What kind of agency for children? In S. Spyrou (Ed.), *Disclosing childhoods. Research and knowledge production for a critical childhood studies* (pp. 117–156). Palgrave Macmillan.

Tallberg, I. B. (1995). *Perspektiv på förskolans historia* [*Perspective on preschool history*]. Studentliteratur.

Taylor, J. R., Flanagin, A. J., Cheney, G., & Seibold, D. R. (2001). Organizational communication research: Key moments, central concerns, and future challenges. *Annals of the International Communication Association, 24*(1), 99–137. https://doi.org/10.1080/23808985.2001.11678983

United Nations. (1989). *United Nations Convention on the Rights of the Child*. https://downloads.unicef.org.uk/wp-content/uploads/2010/05/UNCRC_united_nations_convention_on_the_rights_of_the_child.pdf?_ga=2.259582415.454887985.1587459175-44770236.1585716747

Uprichard, E. (2008). Children as beings and becomings: Children, childhood, and temporality. *Children and Society, 22*(4), 303–313.

Vihalemm, R., & Müürsepp, P. (2007). Philosophy of science in Estonia. *Journal for General Philosophy of Science, 38*(1), 167–191.

von Bonsdorff, P. (2021). On equal terms? On implementing infants' cultural rights. In E. E. Ødegaard & J. S. Borgen (Eds.), *Childhood cultures in transformation – Reorientation and new readings of children and childhood* (Chapter 3). Brill | Sense.

Woodward, W. R. (2012). Charlotte Buhler: Scientific entrepreneur in developmental, clinical, andhumanistic psychology. In W. Pickren, D. A. Dewsbury, & M. Wertheimer (Eds.), *Portraits of pioneers in developmental psychology* (pp. 67–87). Psychology Press.

World Commission on Environment and Development (WCED). (1987). *Our common future/The Brundtland Report.* Oxford University Press.

Ylönen, S. (2021). 'Childish' beyond age: Reconceptualising the aesthetics of resistance. In E. E. Ødegaard & J. S. Borgen (Eds.), *Childhood cultures in transformation – Reorientation and new readings of children and childhood* (Chapter 10). Brill | Sense.

CHAPTER 3

On Equal Terms? On Implementing Infants' Cultural Rights

Pauline von Bonsdorff

Abstract

How can we implement infants' cultural rights? Is there even reason to confer such rights to non-speaking children, or is it enough that we recognise slightly older children as culturally active individuals? Acknowledging children's intellectual capacities and their right to be heard in matters that concern them are important threads in research on children and ideals of childrearing during the last hundred years. This development is parallel with the one leading from the *Declaration of the Rights of the Child* in 1923 to the UN *Convention on the Rights of the Child* in 1989. The spirit of human rights that informs these documents cannot be underestimated. Yet reading the Convention carefully one observes that infants, literally "non-speakers", are challenging in the discourse of human rights, which emphasises speech and language. What is an infant, then? While non-speakers, infants are highly social and communicative, using their whole body in multimodal, active and responsive gestures. This is often overlooked in both research and practices, as I show in my chapter. Instead of noticing the similarities between infants and adults, infants still tend to be represented as different and "other", as compared to the adult. I suggests that we need a more holistic approach, which does justice to infants' playful, interactive and affectionate initiatives. We need to be sensitive not just to what is generalizable, but also to particular contexts, situations and cultures of interaction. This way it might be possible to better acknowledge and cater for infants' cultural rights.

Keywords

children's cultural rights – infant communication – infant aesthetics – play – imitation theory – copycat babies

∙∙∙

I held a baby who was just under two weeks old and looked at her. She seemed to look back, although due to her dark blue eyes I could not see exactly where she was focusing. I showed my tongue. After a short while, she showed hers. I put my tongue in one corner of the mouth. She responded with the same gesture, and we went on for a short while. A few days later, as I held her again in a similar situation, she initiated the game by showing her tongue. And I showed mine.[1]

1 Introduction

According to empirical research and theoretical and methodological arguments especially from childhood studies (James, Jenks, & Prout, 1998; Corsaro, 2018) we should consider children as agents. From the point of view of culture, this means they are persons capable of contributing to culture in their families and communities. The development of this view in the research community is parallel with the implementation of the United Nations Convention on the Rights of the Child from 1989 and is part of the same intellectual current.[2] Moreover, research about infants' cognitive and communicative capacities from the late 20th and early 21st centuries has brought about a recognition of the continuities in human development from infancy through to childhood and adulthood (Gopnik, 2009; Reddy, 2008; Stern, 2010). Due to this body of research, we can now acknowledge that infants are similar to older children and adults in many respects rather than just different, even categorically, from them.

In terms of cultural rights, infants however pose a challenge to the ethos and formulations of the Convention. This challenge is related to their condition as individuals who do not speak and to a slight bias, in the text of the Convention, towards the normative idea that human beings are autonomous and rational. The child, as it appears in the text, is primarily a speaking child, as implied by locutions such as "freedom of expression" (article 13:1) and "freedom of thought" (article 14:1).[3] There is no mention of communication and interaction as processes where we influence each other and create meaning together. Rather, children are either speaking subjects who voice their thoughts and express themselves, or subject to education (article 29).[4] This creates a lacuna with regard to implementing especially infants', but also older children's cultural rights. Yet especially in infancy, intersubjectivity and interdependence are paramount, and communication is highly reciprocal and embodied (Malloch & Trevarthen, 2009a).

The Convention might be symptomatic of an "adultocentric" (Kennedy, 2006, p. 67) view of human beings; one that suits the rational adult but is less fitting for children, let alone non-speaking infants. In this Chapter I discuss, in a partly constructive and partly critical mode, how we might think about and act with infants in ways that make more justice to them as cultural beings that are both similar to and different from older people. I start by outlining an "existential" approach that recognises the embodied, relational, and affective dimensions of infant agency and takes into account the situation and context of interactions. I then turn to cognitivism in child psychology, more precisely to the "imitation theory" of new-borns' responses to facial gestures. My conclusion is that the term imitation is problematic, because it overshadows infants' agency. Similar problems pertain to the popular media phenomenon of "copycat babies". In different ways, both science and popular media tend to "other" infants: to portray them as radically different from "us" in ways that suggest inferiority (Powell & Menendian, 2016).

As expressed in the Convention, the goals of education are the development of "the child's personality, talents and mental and physical ability to their fullest potential"; the development of respect for others, cultural values and the natural environment; and the preparation of the child for a "responsible life … in the spirit of understanding" (29). I argue that we can best support these qualities if we treat the infant on equal terms: encountering the infant in ways one would like to be encountered, with respect, curiosity and understanding. To end, I suggest that if we look at infants acts in terms of play, recognising multimodality and improvisation, we can better understand their cultural agency, for example in co-creating communicative events.

2   An Existential Approach

Research on infants from the 1970s onwards has radically changed the understanding of their cognitive and communicative abilities. Overall, the change has been from seeing young infants as mechanically responding creatures, driven by instincts and needs and not yet in control of their own movements, towards seeing infants as communicative persons who, while awake, are more or less constantly making sense of their surroundings and, although unfamiliar with cultural conventions, have already acquired some cultural learning. We know for instance that newborns can recognise auditory elements such as their mother tongue, their mother's voice, and music that they heard while in the womb (Stern, 2010; Moon, Lagercrantz, & Kuhl, 2012; Huotilainen, 2012).

In the existential approach, I include research that emphasises infant's intersubjectivity, embodiment, (pro-) active behaviour, creative imagination and multimodal communication. Rather than separate, these aspects support and build on each other. The researchers that I include in this approach (see below) are sensitive to the question of what it is like to be a baby, and recognise the subjective character of infant experience and its irreducibility to mechanistic or objectifying explanations. In other words, while e.g., neurophysiology enhances our understanding of infants' embodied mind and its capacities, such knowledge cannot replace the question of what it is like to be (in) that body and situation.[5]

Infants' dependence on adult caregivers is undisputable. Yet the recognition of how much this dependence is social in character, rather than simply related to the fulfilment of physical needs, is more recent. The distinction between "primary" and "secondary" intersubjectivity (Trevarthen, 2001) suggests that the fundamental form of sociability – of being with and acting with others – does not presuppose a developed sense of self, i.e., self-awareness or self-consciousness (cf. Delafield-Butt, 2018). Rather, as suggested by Margaret Donaldson (1978) and Daniel Stern (1985/2000, pp. 69–123), the infant who interacts with a parent is first a deictic and relational self who acts from its present situation without having internalised, and even less reflected upon, a self-image, not to speak of self-identity. Being with others, rather than being alone or separate from others, is the default mode of infant existence and part of infant subjectivity. While infants are awake, especially in interactive situations, and often while they sleep, another person often holds them. The younger the infant, the more connected – to use Suzanne Zeedyk's key concept – it is, unable to change location and thereby enlarge its world to any significant degree without the help of others (Zeedyk, 2012). This does not mean, however, that infants are unable to separate self and other, only that their present and accumulated experience, including self-other relationships, differs significantly from adults' experience.

Colwyn Trevarthen (2011) describes exchanges between infant and parent as a "sharing of experiences". The formulation underlines that the experience is a joint creation that would not exist if either party were missing. It also indicates that experience is in the world, in a space between people, rather than just a mental occurrence. In a similar vein, Vasudevi Reddy criticises the idea of a "gap" between minds. In her "second-person perspective", infant and parent understand each other precisely through engagement and participation (Reddy, 2008, pp. 7–42). Maurice Merleau-Ponty (1945/1992) likewise pointed to the relevance of co-creating and sharing situations for understanding others. In these models, the emphasis is on connections within a dynamic, fluctuating exchange – rather than on the attempt to reach or identify the "content" of another mind, conceived as a static object. We understand each other in and through acting together partly because we change and grow precisely in these interactions, which the participants create jointly (Mühlhoff, 2015).[6]

Analyses of infants' early interactions indicate that the child is more than just reactive. Overall, there seems to be no reason to suppose a stage in infant development where the baby is unable to contribute in unexpected ways to social interactions, in however minute a manner. The premature baby that vocalised in response to the father's talk while kangarooing on his chest is an early example of infants' willingness and ability to have a conversation or join into what another person is doing. A recording showed that the infant contributed in meaningful, vocal ways to the father's talk, with exact timing (Trevarthen, 2018, p. 22).

Without recording, the premature infant's contribution to the conversation might have gone unnoticed. The communicative agency of young infants can indeed be hard to detect because it is low-key, but also because the recognition of the communicative intention of multimodal gestures might go unnoticed. Infants communicate and process things with their whole body more than adults do, and expressive gestures involve tensions and postures of the torso and movements of feet and legs in addition to hands and arms (Trevarthen, 2011). Mostly the eyes have a key role in communication, yet visual impairment is no hindrance to personal contact. There are many ways to turn towards or away from another and to signal contact or withdrawal. Moreover, the borderline between intended and spontaneous is probably open and permeable rather than fixed beforehand. When the other person recognises a gesture and responds, the gesture is more likely to become part of a cultural repertoire.

Overall, infants' communicative agency is embodied, multimodally gestural, and highly dialogic. The last feature is visible in their capacity for timing in socially interacting with an adult, often in situations where the focus is on enjoying the exchange itself. In a landmark book, Stephen Malloch and Colwyn Trevarthen (2009a) introduced "communicative musicality" to characterise infants' innate communicative capacity. Several features however invite us to use the term aesthetic here (cf. von Bonsdorff, 2018). First, the exchanges are multimodal rather than musical in the narrower sense of referring only to auditory qualities. Moreover, they are sensuous, expressive, intrinsically meaningful, (with form inseparable from content),[7] and enjoyed for their own sake,[8] for the fun of it. Finally, the infant's agency is – like the parent's – creative and imaginative: it is forward-looking and creates variations on earlier acts rather than mere repetitions.

3 Imitation Theory: The Computational Baby

The cognitive approach differs in important respects from the existential, and is part of the legacy of Jean Piaget, whose primary focus was cognitive rather than social development.[9] Cognitivists, such as Paul Harris (2000) and Alison Gopnik (2009), typically study infants and children with a view to rational thinking, and admire their capacity for understanding logical relationships such as causality and counterfactuals. Infants' and children's thinking is, in other words, assessed against criteria of logic, and explained with reference to mental maps and models. Moreover, children are studied as individuals, whose subjectivity is basically located in the brain. When it comes to understanding other persons, the idea is either that the infant simulates the other person's behaviour and likely feelings (simulation theory) or constructs a theory of the other's mind ("theory-theory"; see Reddy, 2008, p. 20).[10] In other words, cognitivists presuppose that infants perform complicated operations of rational thinking and inference but lack any primary sense of intersubjectivity.

The particular cognitivist theory that I shall look upon in more detail is Andrew N. Meltzoff's explanation of responsive facial gestures in infants, a phenomenon usually referred to as imitation (Meltzoff, 2005). My aim is to indicate the limitations of the cognitive approach, as it sidesteps the potential social intentions of the infant and fails to account for its embodied and interactive situatedness (of by default being-with-another). Meltzoff's theory is cognitivist and mentalist, and even computational. On the one hand, it assumes that infants react to gestures due to innate mechanisms in the brain, while they on the other hand make rational comparisons ("if a, then p"). This is why the infant in imitation theory appears to be a computational baby.

Meltzoff observed that his new-born, only 42 minutes after birth, repeated the gesture of tongue protrusion that he had performed while looking his child in the eye (Meltzoff, 2005, p. 70). The fact that infants respond to an adult's facial gesture by repeating the same gesture, and may initiate the same gesture in subsequent situations with an adult, is now well recognised and widely researched by Meltzoff and others. Significantly, the phenomenon is discussed in terms of "imitation", and when initiated by the infant on a later occasion, "deferred imitation", which reportedly has happened after a delay of up to 24 hours (Meltzoff, 2005, p. 71).

According to Meltzoff, (2005, p. 56) imitation is innate, it precedes the understanding of other people, and these are causally related. He stipulates three conditions for imitation: "(1) the observer produces behavior similar to that of the model, (2) the perception of an act causes the observer's response, and (3) the equivalence between the acts of self and other plays a role in generating the response"; adding however that the "equivalence need not be registered on a conscious level" (Meltzoff, 2005, p. 55). He also specifies that imitation takes place with novel acts and after a certain temporal delay, thereby distinguishing it from mere entrainment.

What does this mean in a situation of interaction between infants and adults? The first condition is unproblematic. The second condition however implies the causal activation of a particular mechanism. The infant does not make a choice, but is compelled to respond, and the reaction is purportedly due to the "imitative brain". Accordingly, Meltzoff's analysis is in terms of physiological rather than intentional activity. Imitation is a "matching-to-target-process" which includes the activation of exteroceptive and proprioceptive feedback loops. Infants identify relevant body parts and then attempt to perform the gesture they have perceived. A supramodal framework couples the observation and execution of acts, and enables the infants to repeat an act without knowing how their own face looks. This connection is innate: "exteroception (perception of others) and proprioception (perception of self) speak the same language from birth" (Meltzoff, 2005, p. 72).

The third condition of imitation, "the equivalence between the acts of self and other", is key in respect to Meltzoff's "Like-Me" hypothesis. When infants realise that the adult is like them, they acquire "a tool for cracking the problem of other minds." (Meltzoff, 2005, p. 75). Through coupling their own mental states (emotions, beliefs, intentions, etc.) to acts, and then registering the equivalence between self and other, they become able to understand the other. If I cry when I am unhappy, others are unhappy when they cry. Meltzoff assumes that there is a "lingua franca of human acts" (Meltzoff, 2005, pp. 75–76).

As we have seen, Meltzoff's focus in analysing responsive acts is the act itself rather than its communicative or social intentions and functions, not to speak of context. His perspective is thoroughly third-person: there is no attempt to grasp intentions from a first-person perspective, nor to draw upon second-person engagement in the situation (after all, the seminal insight came through interaction with his own child). This perspective is in harmony with the idea that the intersubjective element follows from the act, rather than being an ingredient of it.

In emphasising the developmental function of imitation for understanding other persons, Meltzoff restricts imitation to infants and demarcates it from adult life, where, as he writes, "certain bodily movements have particular meanings. If a person looks up into the sky, bystanders follow his or her gaze. This is not imitation; the adults are trying to see what the person is looking at" (Meltzoff, 2005, p. 65). Nevertheless, with a view to adult culture, if I feel that another imitates me, my reaction is likely to be either amused, baffled, or offended, depending on the situation. Not so if others respond to what I do: I then get a sense of mutuality, regardless of whether I think they got what I meant or not. Meltzoff also describes the function of imitation in infancy as learning a culture. However, the theoretical framework suggests that culture in imitation theory is more about socialisation and repetition than about variation and creativity. Overall, imitation theory pulls the understanding of infant agency in a hierarchical direction, where the adult is a model for the infant. The infant reacts, rather than acts, by imitating an act performed by an adult. However, the fact that the infant does not always respond has perhaps gained too little attention. While an infant would hardly perform a particular facial gesture without the adult performing it first, the adult's gestures may be a reason, but not a cause, for the infant's gesture. The distinction is important since it points to choice and intention.

There is an additional problem, related to the contingency of the facial gestures. Meltzoff claims that infants connect a particular gesture with their own "felt meaning", and then project this meaning on others who perform the same gesture. Nevertheless, the facial gestures used in the experiments may lack particular meaning in the culture, or the meaning they have may be irrelevant. To show one's tongue is a naughty, derogatory gesture in some cultures, while in others it signals a greeting. If new-borns protrude their tongue, they may just test how the air feels. There is no intrinsic "felt meaning" attached to the act – and whatever it might feel like probably has no communicative relevance (which Meltzoff also does not suggest).

Meltzoff can also be criticised for intellectualising the infant in three respects: in his privileging of vision, in the view of the infant self, and in the hypothesis thesis. Referring to how actions "look like" to the infant, or what a "new-born sees", he fails to notice how vision is imbricated in the total, multi-sensuous perceptual and embodied situation (Meltzoff, 2005, p. 75).[11] To be born is to leave a mother's body, be received (mostly) by another adult, and then returned to intimate contact with mother for nursing and rest. When facial gestures are initiated, even if within one hour from birth, the newborn has already been addressed vocally, touched and held by adults. In these situations, people have probably looked the baby into the face, trying to catch attention and make contact. Adults as totalities with faces, gesturing and supportive bodies and vocalisations are familiar from the start of life. In these situations, interaction and communication in several sense modalities (sometimes tacit, sometimes more explicit) are paramount.

Through the multimodal and embodied immediate life-world, infants are connected to the world around, not separate. Infants live through and with other people. The multimodal and relational experience of the world makes the comparison between what is "seen" and "felt" dubious. Rather than reflection, implied by Meltzoff's phrasing, there is response from within a situation of primary connectedness. This connection is internal and runs like cords through the situation, rather than external, as when a cord binds two separate items. Furthermore, it is unlikely that infants experience their self or that of others in terms of mind-body –dualism. To separate "felt events" and "perceived events" presupposes a distinction of internal and external, but as argued above, the new-born self is neither articulate nor autonomous in a self-conscious way. More likely, in situations where facial gestures are initiated, new-borns recognise being addressed by another creature who, in a way that tickles their curiosity, is familiar and yet presents something new.

Finally, similar problems pertain to the idea that infants hold a hypothesis, however intuitive, about the similarity of self and other. This again presupposes an understanding or minimally a felt awareness of self and other as separate; but such an understanding probably does not yet exist. Although intelligent and exploring, new-borns hardly think in the scientific style. Rather than a hypothesis, there is a dawning felt sense, accompanied by experiential knowledge that grows in action. I shall elaborate on this in a later section, having first looked at some material from popular media.

4 Copycat Babies

Youtube searches for material on interactions with infants, using search terms such as "still-face experiment", "facial gestures babies" (or "infants"), "tongue protrusion" (with "babies" or "infants") or "facial gestures imitation infants" yield interesting results. I have made these searches at intervals from 2015 to 2019, and the material that comes up changes. Overall, however, there are three categories. First, some of the videos represent the popularisation of science for a larger audience, with interviews of renowned scientists.[12] A second group comprises videos made for therapeutic or educational purposes, e.g. to help parents interact with their babies, support them in becoming more communicative and developing socially, or be more sensitive to the infant's gestures and intentions. Thirdly, there are homemade videos of infants' gestures, sometimes with interactions between infants and parents. These are the most interesting here. For ethical reasons I do not provide a list of the videos as it would be an unnecessary act of poking at behaviour that, while appearing in a less favourable light, hopefully was produced (by the adult/parent) without bad intentions. In addition, as intentionally recorded, the videos do not necessarily give a sense of what the everyday interactions between these infants and their parents are like.

There is naturally a rich variety in the videos but they also share some features. Often they focus on the infant's face and hands; sometimes they show the whole body. The babies are filmed in situations of active gesturing and vocalising, and appear "cute", "funny" or even "adorable". This is emphasised by the adult laughter that often accompanies the scene.

In one video, a mother is interacting with her baby vocally. The mutual vocalisations are clearly the focus of the video, although the infant, at two months, also makes lively gestures especially with her hands and arms. The mother is bent over and focusing on her child. She vocalises, and waits for the baby to respond, but then gives back more or less the same vocalisation, as if imitating or copying her child. Lying on her back, the baby looks confused at times; she frowns and looks away although she cannot escape the situation. On closer inspection, there seems to be many moments of standstill or interruption: the situation does not develop and the vocalisations remain separate. The mother's behaviour is enthusiastically forthcoming rather than attentive, and the baby is not fully "in" the situation either. One gets the sense that the performance is for the camera rather than a genuine, spontaneous dialogue. The mother is stimulating the baby to vocalise rather than interacting with her.

Some videos focus on tongue protrusion. In one of these, a mother is encouraging her child vocally and by touching tongue and mouth with a cloth. The act seems completely unnatural, and devoid of any context or meaning. In videos of babies performing "funny tongue movements", it is often not clear whether they respond to someone or not. The main purpose seems to be performing for amusement, but without the performer's (the infant's) consent or intention to amuse others.

In many of the videos, the infant's gestures are imitative in the colloquial sense: one person does something, and another repeats it. There is no need to understand context because the focus is simply on the quality of an act, not on the agent's intentions. This is the way imitation is performed in circuses or in contexts where the aim is mockery: to show someone's way of acting, make the audience aware of it, and laugh. Part of the videos seem to be set up for the camera, which raises the suspicion that the baby is trained to do the trick – this at least could be the case with many videos of tongue protrusion. There is a certain uncanny similarity to pet videos. Nevertheless, if the aim is to show what the infant is able to do, then laughter introduces a paternalistic perspective. Usually, we do not laugh at people acting smartly, but some laugh at people who misunderstand, make other mistakes, or act stupidly. From this perspective, the videos represent a practice of "othering", i.e. of representing the group of infants and toddlers as unlike us in ways that underline their inferiority (cf. Powell & Menendian, 2016, p. 17). This raises a sense of uncanniness: why should we laugh, after all, and in what way?

To be fair, there are videos where parents seem to imitate their babies, or where imitation is ubiquitous. In one of the videos, a father, an infant and a dog inspire each other to howl. From a cultural perspective, we might assume that the funny actors are meant to be the dog and the infant rather than the adult. We laugh at them and with him, partly because adults constitute the "we-group" that set up the performance. "Adultism", or taking the adult as a norm while marginalising the child (Kennedy, 2006, p. 67), is probably at work here. Infants who imitate their parents are funnier than parents who imitate babies. The infant is the target, the object, not a subject.

In addition to mirroring general cultural norms and popular ideas, the videos seem to share certain characteristics with imitation theory, such as treating responsive acts and facial gestures separately from their larger context. Both imitation theory and the copycat videos combine a mechanical approach with a rationalising one: the baby as computer. In the videos, presenting infants' acts as funny underlines that the infant does not know what it does, but acts more or less mechanically in the way the adult does. Likewise, for imitation theory, the adult is the norm towards which the child strives. Finally, the videos and imitation theory seem to share an assumption of infants as less-than-(adult)-humans, perhaps even not-yet-human.

5   Play

If imitation theory is problematic, how can we construe an alternative explanation of responsive acts? According to imitation theory, the infant first identifies relevant body parts (mouth and tongue) and then performs the act. However, if we approach the situation as a lived event, the reaction can be described as more immediate: responding by gesture to gesture. We move, and we move with others. According to Jonathan Delafield-Butt (2018, p. 59) the "two psychological principles that drive human agency" are "I like to move it" and "I like to move it with you." Perhaps responding to another's act is more like play than imitation?

How does the infant know its body and recognise similar other bodies? From a phenomenological perspective, the movements and acts of foetuses in the womb, exploring their own body, is at the same time a temporal and spatial structuring of the world. The nose, the hand and the toe are not visually seen but haptically and kinaesthetically explored. To modify Merleau-Ponty's

(1992) observation of the two hands touching each other, with reciprocity and switch between which feels and which is felt: when foetuses or infants suck their thumb, attention can switch from the tongue exploring the thumb to the thumb exploring the mouth. Perceiving is multimodal: an exploration of forms and qualities that are recognisable through different sense modalities. Because the senses interact, a mouth that is seen as part of a face can be recognised based on earlier experiences of touching and feeling one's own face. There are the same forms, in the same constellation, doing similar things. Perhaps this is, or is at least part of, the supramodal framework Meltzoff (2005) assumes. Moreover, we can hardly overemphasise the importance of movement and rhythm in the life and development of foetuses and infants.[13] What the infant recognises in the adult's figure is not just static forms but a dynamic constellation of form and movement: animated flesh similar to myself, acting like me.

Moreover, a facial gesture such as tongue protrusion is an intentional act, not a mechanical or necessary reflex. The infant-person has the option of not responding with a similar gesture – which does not mean no response at all. In a typical situation, the adult holds the infant and they focus on each other's faces where minute movements form an overall expressive and dynamic texture. In addition, felt muscular tensions are part of the overall directedness of one's own and the other's body, that connect haptically and kinaesthetically with each other. When adults perform a facial gesture and new-borns respond, the situation of being held and attending to another is familiar while the gesture is new and contingent. Precisely this novelty, and the opportunity to engage in interaction, may be what stimulates, or interests, the infant.

The contingency of the act implies that meaning arises in the situation. This is the case with greetings, which are precisely reciprocal exchanges of similar gestures, vocal or physical. A greeting is a fundamental way of acknowledging another person as a person. Exchanging variations of facial gestures likewise establishes and affirms mutual recognition and the constitution of a we (not any persons); a minimal sub-culture where participants can be together while being different. The exchanges comprise a way of acting and being (a manner or style) but they also demand attention and willingness to reciprocate, to play, on each side.

The interaction, as a play of mutual response, establishes "ways-of-being-with" (Stern, 1985/2000, p. xv) construed by the two parties and established in the process (cf. Merleau-Ponty, 2003). Both of them learn. In my vignette, the newborn recognised me as the "tongue-showing one", and later took up the game with that particular person, not with others. I, the adult, had also learnt, in this case from research literature, that playing with the tongue is a possible form of interaction with infants. Instead of deferred imitation, suggesting mechanical causation, the infant's reason to initiate the game is probably curiosity, enjoyment, eagerness to establish a contact, or a mix of these – exactly like my own.

Playing with mutually responsive acts creates a tool for dialogue. Dialogue would not take place if the interaction were not a case of repeating differently, in other words a play that includes variation and improvisation. Infants are extremely sensitive to timing and nuances, and non-verbal dialogue is indeed about individual situations rather than generalised content, as suggested by the idea of comparing "felt event" and "seen event". Instead, the interactions are similar to arts of performance such as music or dance, especially when they involve improvisation and dialogue (cf. Stern, 2010). They are foundational for culture because they include freedom, choice, and variation, rather than mere repetition or imitation. The impossibility of strict imitation is a resource for communication, not a limitation.

A contingent gesture, which serves no particular function nor conveys any particular meaning, is a seed of shared aesthetic and intellectual explorations. This is precisely because it initially has no connection to physical needs and predetermined meaning. Rather, the exchange is performed for enjoyment, and for its own sake alone.[14] Mutual tongue protrusion, or other gestural exchanges that do not serve a particular goal, give rise to a new kind of intersubjectivity. The other is no longer just the one who takes care of me or the one who is taken care of by me, but someone interested in playing with me. The exchange of contingent gestures therefore opens a new and exciting dimension of subjectivity, related to the recognition of the other as another person, and a cultural subject.

6 Conclusions

Already in situations of early exchange, infants are capable of being culturally inventive, as my vignette shows. Without the initiative of the infant girl, our initial tongue protrusion might have remained a single occurrence, but she established it as a shared practice.

In the Introduction, I suggested a lacuna in the Convention when it comes to interaction and communication, which makes it hard to see how we can provide for infants' cultural rights. The cognitivist explanation of responsive acts does not help, as it largely misses the improvisational character of early interactions, where adjustments to the other person go on all the time. There is a serious limitation regarding infant subjectivity and intersubjectivity, and how they develop in interactions. The importance of this reaches beyond the academic world, for theories of infant development interest parents. Perhaps not surprisingly, the phenomenon of copycat babies show uncanny similarities to current cognitivist theories. While seemingly demonstrating what infants can do, they in fact often show situations with one-way, disconnected utterances. They maintain a gap between adult and infant, and between embodied gesture and mind.

Our beliefs of what infants can do and how they think influence our interactions with them. We treat them differently if we assume, they are only capable of imitation, as compared to how we treat them when we think of them as persons with interests and intentions. A strength of the existential approach is that it sees the infant as an individual in a certain situation, and does not take for granted categorical differences, for example in terms of intentionality, between infant and adult. The theories I have presented above as part of the existential approach also strongly acknowledge intersubjectivity, in fact in ways that challenge the traditional western ideal of a rational, autonomous subject.

The Convention's goals of education refer to the development the child's personality, in the spirit of respect and responsibility (29). We can only attain these goals if we treat the child in a like manner. Reciprocal, playful practices may be a critical ingredient of the ethical goals of education. Shared meaning, but also self and world are established and modified in these practices. Moreover, both parties are affected. The willingness to give of oneself and receive from the other is a key to human growth and culture. To get a mechanical response, we need not be fully attentive to the other, whereas play demands sensitivity and presence on both sides. An existential approach provides us with models and tools that can help understanding not just the infant, but also the adult of the relationship in more reflective ways.

Notes

1. This incident took place in October 2016 in Copenhagen.
2. From now on, I refer to it as the Convention. Reference numbers are to the Articles of the Convention.
3. The Convention includes one article (23) on disabled children – emphasising dignity, self-reliance and active participation – but this does not change the overall picture.
4. It also states "the right of the child to rest and leisure, to engage in play and recreational activities appropriate to the age of the child and to participate freely in cultural life and the arts" (article 31:1).
5. For a classical but still pertinent discussion of the limits of understanding what it is to be like someone radically different from oneself, see Nagel (1974).

6 This structure differs from the parallel minds that would come into play in "joint attention". However, to attend to something in the company of other people typically involves minute reactions that are perceptible to others. Even at a concert of classical music, where audience response is minimal, we are aware of the reactions of people in our vicinity, and especially of our companions.
7 Alloa and Jdey (2012) point out that for Merleau-Ponty, the body resembles a work of art exactly in this way. Relevant here is also Waldenfels' (2015, pp. 133–158) discussion of the aesthetic in Merleau-Ponty.
8 See Reddy's (2008, pp. 183–214) discussion of the sense of humour, or "funniness", in young children.
9 As studied by Piaget, the young child is an individual, even "egocentric", has no moral concepts and is unable to distinguish fantasy from reality. Development takes place through separate stages. For critical assessments of Piaget, see Merleau-Ponty (2001), Donaldson (1978), Trevarthen (2001), Reddy (2008). For critiques of cognitivism, see Reddy (2008, pp. 7–25) and Stock (2011).
10 Reddy (2008) and Trevarthen (2007, p. 12) both remind that the "theory of mind" is culture relative, not universal.
11 On the same page he writes: "Human acts are especially relevant to infants because they *look like* the infant feels himself to be and because they are events that infants can intend. When a new-born *sees* a human act, it may be meaningful: 'That *seen event* is like this felt event'" (hyphenation added). More recently, Meltzoff has studied touch and emphasised its importance for the body scheme and for social cognition. But to my knowledge, he has not revised the theory of imitation with a view to these themes.
12 Tongue protrusion as typical of Down's syndrome also comes up, but I shall put that aside.
13 Stern (2010) points out that the foetus moves before it has a brain, and Delafield-Butt (2018) suggests that there is a "brainstem self" with "basic self-consciousness" from 12-14 weeks of gestation.
14 The hallmark of the aesthetic, as traditionally defined, is precisely that its value is intrinsic and serves no exterior ends. It has also been described as "autotelic": having its end in itself.

References

Alloa, E., & Jdey, A. (2012). Du sensible à l'oeuvre. Sur le rapport entre Merleau-Ponty et les arts. In E. Alloa & A. Jdey (Eds.), *Du sensible à l'oeuvre. Esthétiques de Merleau-Ponty* (pp. 9–39). La Lettre volée.

Corsaro, W. A. (2018). *The sociology of childhood* (5th ed.). Sage Publications.

Delafield-Butt, J. (2018). "The emotional and embodied nature of human understanding: Sharing narratives of meaning." In J. Delafield-Butt, A.-W. Dunlop, & C. Trevarthen (Eds.), *The child's curriculum: Working with the natural values of young children* (pp. 59–84). Oxford University Press.

Donaldson, M. (1978). *Children's minds*. Fontana/Collins.

Gopnik, A. (2009). *The philosophical baby. What children's minds tell us about truth, love, and the meaning of life*. Farrar, Straus & Giroux.

Harris, P. L. (2000). *The work of the imagination*. Blackwell.

Huotilainen, M. (2012). "A new dimension on Foetal language learning". *Acta Paediatrica, 102*(2), 102–103. https://doi.org/10.1111/apa.12122

James, A., Jenks, C., & Prout, A. (1998). *Theorizing childhood*. Polity Press.

Kennedy, D. (2006). *The well of being. Childhood, subjectivity, and education*. State University of New York Press.

Malloch, S., & Trevarthen, C. (Eds.). (2009a). *Communicative musicality. Exploring the basis of human companionship*. Oxford University Press.

Malloch, S., & Trevarthen, C. (2009b). Musicality: Communicating the vitality and interests of life. In S. Malloch & C. Trevarthen (Eds.), *Communicative musicality. Exploring the basis of human companionship* (pp. 1–11). Oxford University Press.

Meltzoff, A. N. (2005). Imitation and other minds. The "like me" hypothesis. In S. Hurley & N. Chater (Eds.), *Perspectives on imitation: From neuroscience to social science* (Vol.2, pp. 55–77). The MIT Press.

Merleau-Ponty, M. (1992). *Phénoménologie de la perception*. Gallimard. (Original work published 1945)

Merleau-Ponty, M. (2001). *Psychologie et pédogogie de l'enfant*. Cours de Sorbonne 1949–1952. Verdier.

Merleau-Ponty, M. (2003). *L'Institution. La Passivité. Notes de cours au Collège de France (1954–1955)*. Belin.

Moon, C., Lagercrantz, H., & Kuhl, P. K. (2012). "Language experienced in utero affects vowel perception after birth: A two-country study". *Acta Paediatrica, 102*(2), 156–160. https://doi.org/10.1111/apa.12098.

Mühlhoff, R. (2015). Affective resonance and social interaction. *Phenomenology and the Cognitive Sciences, 14*, 1001–1019.

Nagel, T. (1974). "What is it like to be a bat?" *The Philosophical Review, 83*(4), 435–450.

Powell, J. A., & Menendian, S. (2016). The problem of othering: Towards inclusiveness and belonging. *Othering & Belonging. Expanding the Circle of Human Concern, 1*, 14–39. Retrieved September 15, 2019, from http://www.otheringandbelonging.org/the-problem-of-othering/

Reddy, V. (2008). *How children know minds*. Harvard University Press.

Stern, D. N. (2000). *The interpersonal world of the infant. A view from psychoanalysis and developmental psychology*. Basic Books. (Original work published 1985)

Stern, D. N. (2010). *Forms of vitality. Exploring dynamic experience in psychology, the arts, psychotherapy, and development*. Oxford University Press.

Stock, K. (2011). Unpacking the boxes. The cognitive theory of imagination and aesthetics. In E. Schellekens & P. Goldie (Eds.), *The aesthetic mind. Philosophy and psychology* (pp. 268–282). Oxford University Press.

Trevarthen, C. (2001). The neurobiology of early communication: Intersubjective regulations in human brain development. In A. F. Kalverboer & A. Gramsbergen (Eds.), *Handbook on brain and behavior in human development* (pp. 841–882). Kluwer.

Trevarthen, C. (2007). Wer schreibt die Autobiographie eines Kindes? In H. Welzer & H. J. Markowitsch (Eds.), *Warum Menschen sich erinnern können. Fortschritte der interdisziplinären Gedächtnisforschung* (pp. 225–255). Klett-Cott.

Trevarthen, C. (2011). The generation of human meaning: How shared experience grows in infancy. In A. Seemann (Ed.), *Joint attention. New developments in psychology, philosophy of mind, and social neuroscience* (pp. 73–114). The MIT Press.

Trevarthen, C. (2018). What young children give to our learning. In J. Delafield-Butt, A.-W. Dunlop, & C. Trevarthen (Eds.), *The child's curriculum: Working with the natural values of young children* (pp. 13–38). Oxford University Press.

UNCRC. (1989). *United Nations Convention on the Right of the Child*. Retrieved April 17, 2020, from https://downloads.unicef.org.uk/wp-content/uploads/2010/05/UNCRC_united_nations_convention_on_the_rights_of_the_child.pdf?_ga=2.259582415.454887985.1587459175-44770236.1585716747

von Bonsdorff, P. (2018). Children's aesthetic agency: The pleasures and power of imagination. In J. Delafield-Butt, A.-W. Dunlop, & C. Trevarthen (Eds.), *The child's curriculum: Working with the natural values of young children* (pp. 126–138). Oxford University Press.

Waldenfels, B. (2015). *Sinne und Künste in Wechselspiel. Modi ästhetischer Erfahrung.* Suhrkamp.

Zeedyk, M. S. (2012). Wired for communication. How neuroscience of infancy helps understanding the effectiveness of intensive interaction. In D. Hewett (Ed.), *Interaction. Theoretical perspectives* (pp. 55–71). Sage.

CHAPTER 4

Children with Severe, Multiple Disabilities: Interplaying Beings, Communicative Becomings

Kristin Vindhol Evensen

Abstract

According to the United Nations Convention on the Rights of the Child, being understood is a human right. This chapter focuses on children with severe, multiple disabilities and their transitions between interplay and communication, between embodiment and expressive skills, between subjectivity and objectivity, between expressivity and interpretation, and between being and becoming.

Through a literature review, I show that transitions between interplay and communication when children have severe, multiple disabilities are considered from three dominant perspectives.

Papers that describe communication as an objective technique describe technical possibilities when translating highly subjective expressions of children with severe and multiple disabilities into symbolic language. However, critical self-reviews by the authors of some of these papers indicate that their findings show that those technical communication skills are of restricted value if the relation between interplay and communication remains unproblematised.

Papers that describe the children's communication as a result of contextual impressions, and relational and interactional stimuli show that neither disability, nor the context alone can shape the child's potential abilities, or his or her wish to enter into interplay or to communicate. On the contrary, it seems that the quality of interplay that the participating children are *already* taking part in appears to be decisive when the children express their experiences to the people surrounding them.

Papers that describe expressions as causally connected to diagnostic phenotypes describe important objective features of medical diagnoses, yet, it appears that possibilities for interactions and communication are lost when movements are interpreted as results of medical conditions rather than as subjective expressions.

Keywords

children with severe – multiple disabilities – interplay – communication

1   Introduction

To be understood is a human right, also when symbolic communication is challenged. The United Nations Convention on the Rights of the Child (1989) states that no child shall experience discrimination because of their disability. In addition, the convention includes two articles that are specifically directed towards the right to freedom of opinion and expression. Article 12 (1) of the above Convention describes how states should assure that children who are capable of forming their own views have the right to express their views. In addition, this article states that these expressions shall be given the appropriate weighting in conformance with the child's age and maturity. In article 13 (1) of the Convention, the United Nations enhance that freedom of expression by including expressions that exceed verbal and symbolic expressions, in a spectrum including speech, artistic expressions or expressions of the child's own choice. Thus, being accredited as expressional is the right of every child, including children with severe, multiple disabilities. Skarstad (2018) demarcates the importance of accrediting persons with intellectual disabilities as expressive from a human rights perspective. She refers to the United Nations Convention on the Rights of Persons with Disabilities to pinpoint the importance of acknowledging interests, personality and lived experiences as keys to different kinds of expressiveness when intellectual disabilities make symbolic communication difficult.

Children with severe, multiple disabilities are typically subject to extensive use of technical assistive devices such as wheelchairs, standing and walking aids and orthoses. When a person experiences an application of external forces that limits freedom of movement, he or she is 'automatically forced from the circle of the proper' (Goffman, 2008, p. 93). When assistive aids, bows, Velcros and straps apply external forces that limit a person's freedom of movement and co-exist with internal forces such as intellectual disabilities, spasticity, epilepsy and loss of senses, children with severe, multiple disabilities might experience limitations in their possibilities to express their perspectives (Evensen, Ytterhus, & Standal, 2017; Hautaniemi, 2004; Horgen, 2006).

This chapter specifically focuses on how research describes children with severe, multiple disabilities as they move between non-intentional interplay and interpretive, intentional communication, between subjectivity and objectivity, between embodiment and skills, and between being and becoming, all against the backdrop of the phenomenology of perception as understood by Merleau-Ponty (2014).

2   Interplay and Communication

The German philosopher Habermas (as cited in Lorentzen, 2009) emphasises that the communicative human being intentionally wants to pass on a message. The task of those that communicate with each other is to explore a partner's ability for intentional communication, and thus to adapt to the attributes the other has at hand. Hence, communication will always include more than one person. For an expression to be detected, interpreted and included in further communication, the communication partner must also have the intention to communicate and must have sensing, looking, listening, feeling and smelling attributes to pay sensitive attention to what is uttered or gestured (Fröhlich, 1995; Horgen, 2006). When humans express their perspectives, listen to others and adapt to their communication partners, each person receives stimulation to communicate his or her perspectives in ways that do not depend on a shared symbolical language. Through intentional expressions and intentional sensing, communication turns dialogical, sequential and directed from the past, through the present towards the future (Toombs, 2001).

Intentionality is what makes a distinction between communication and interplay. The interplaying human is released from intentions and strategies. Being together and getting to know the perspective of each other is a goal by its own means, where I have to be open to getting to know your perspective in the same way as you have to be open to getting to know mine. This means that both of us have to give ourselves up in partly unpredictable situations because your perspective will always be different from mine and mine will be different from yours. These subjective perspectives can be – but are not necessarily – carried out through a shared, objective and intentional symbolic way of communicating. Thus, interplay will always have an uncertain outcome.

Being in interplay provides shared experiences. The French philosopher Merleau-Ponty (2014) describes how he, Maurice, and his friend Paul share the same focus, yet he acknowledges that they are two different persons, having two different points of departure. Still, they are connected through a shared experience. Maurice and Paul share details in a landscape when Paul points his finger towards a steeple. Maurice and Paul do not perceive the steeple from the same point of view. However, from that moment of shared attention, they share an experience and a story of a steeple in a landscape. Such stories of shared attention bridge different points of departure in human experience.

The non-strategical and unpredictable nature of interplay and shared attention is closely connected to the openness of play. Karoff (2013) describes how play takes place between play practices and play moods. To be in a play mood is to be open and ready for the possibilities of other persons producing meaning. Through layered reciprocal interplay, the ones in play are surrounded by a certain uncertainty depending on who is taking the next step. The players will experience reciprocal unpredictability when intensity changes the rhythm of interplay. The players will experience reciprocal shifts of tension, where they show who they are while being aware that they are being looked at by the other. Lastly, the players might experience euphoria caused by the possibility of their own and others' silliness, a silliness released when the illusion of controlling the situation is terminated (Karoff, 2013).

Through layering, changes of intensity, shifts of tension and possibilities of silliness, humans can harmonise with others in play practices. Play practices are actions undertaken when being in a play mood. Play moods are not instrumental, intentional or purposeful in the same way as play practices are. Play practices are play moods expressed through actions. In play practices, the playing humans express their moods through behaviours, the use of toys and objects and through the ways they move their bodies, all with an intention of sustaining the play. Thus, we can understand play moods to create the foundation of play practices in the same way as different subjects' shared interplay is foundational for communication to take place.

3   Children with Severe, Multiple Disabilities: Perspectives

Because of the complexity and severity of their diagnoses, limiting possibilities for symbolic communication and creating a need for other ways to understand and be understood, children with severe, multiple disabilities magnify the layered appearance of interplay and symbolic communication. The literature understands and describes the limitations and possibilities of children with severe, multiple disabilities in a wide range of perspectives.

From a medical, diagnostic perspective, severe multiple disabilities are understood as complex conditions where intellectual disabilities are combined with motor-, somatic- and health-related difficulties, and in some cases loss of senses such as sight or hearing.

From a socio-relational perspective, the complexity of conditions results in difficulties caused by mismatches between persons with severe, multiple disabilities and their socio-cultural environment. Continuous assessments of individual hallmarks, medical needs and social environments such as homes, kindergartens and schools, create frameworks for adaptations where significant other possibilities are sought to align the mismatch to a greater or lesser degree.

From a phenomenological perspective, persons with severe, multiple disabilities are considered to have subjective interests, different meanings and different social and experiential backgrounds. In this perspective, children with severe, multiple disabilities are acknowledged as full-worthy active and perceiving children who, when moving in space, in time with objects and in relations with other persons, live experiences with the same values as everyone else.

4 Children with Severe, Multiple Disabilities: Perceptional Phenomenology Challenges Normality

To find a relationship between medical knowledge, social expectations and phenomenological embodiment, I follow French philosopher Merleau-Ponty (2010, 2014) in examples where normality is challenged. Investigating expressiveness from a phenomenological perspective provides a possibility to overcome the dichotomy of being able or disabled, as it unfolds in medical and social perspectives. However, I make a sociological "Goffman" (2008) turn by including children who are severely limited in their embodied freedom to investigate interplay and communication. Goffman included persons who experienced internal or external embodied constraints into his research to investigate possibilities of general human relations. To explore how acknowledging various ways of expressiveness can be formative for a person's possibilities to be understood, I turned to an outpost of symbolic communication. Thus, children with severe, multiple disabilities, whose performance of symbolic language is either out of reach or requires thorough training, are main contributors to this investigation.

Interactions, whether through interplay or symbolic communication, are easily shaped by the asymmetry between interactional partners. I will argue that asymmetry contains possibilities to accredit and include embodied expressions of humans with severe, multiple disabilities into interplay in ways that create meaning for the parties involved. This approach is challenged by the phenomenology of perception. In the philosophy of Merleau-Ponty (2014), a whole world can be expressed when gestures, sounds, mimicry, body position, change of breathing or the gaze of an eye, are acknowledged as full-worthy expressions and are included in further interactions. Thus, I claim that accreditation of embodied expressivity is a path towards a balanced meeting that bridges gaps, even when relations are asymmetrical due to different persons' points of departure.

Interactions in pre-symbolic life are often carried out as highly asymmetrical and hierarchic, where values are communicated from the adult to the child. Hence, hierarchy is sustained when values are transferred from the person communicating symbolically to the person communicating pre-symbolically, to lead the latter to a more complex and credible level of communication. Merleau-Ponty held a position as chair of psychology and pedagogy at the University of Sorbonne from 1949 to 1952. In 'Child Psychology and Pedagogy. The Sorbonne Lectures 1949–1952' (2010), Merleau-Ponty's validation of students' notes on his lectures shows us that he criticises a pedagogical approach that leaves the child in a state of being an unfinished adult. However, Merleau-Ponty does not naively erase differences between adult and child to create an equilibrium. Even in objective discussions, Merleau-Ponty claims that it is alluring to be the one who is proved right (2010). He underlines the importance of being critically aware of the longing for being right and the asymmetry between adult and child.

> ... the triumph of reason is always felt as a personal triumph. Moreover, situations are rarely completely equal. Even if we make an effort to respect the autonomy of the other, even if we grant the other freedom, the other will never feel completely free since he receives his freedom in a partnership. (Merleau-Ponty, 2010, p. 83)

Merleau-Ponty also challenges the notion that the experience of disability is a state of being disabled towards a given standard of normality and ability. Thus, he dares us to consider whether having a disability includes an obligation to strive towards standards of what is considered to be able within the borders of normality:

> The desire for a healthy body or the refusal of the diseased body are not formulated for themselves; the experience of the amputated arm as present or of the diseased arm as absent are not of the order of the "I think that"
>
> This phenomenon – distorted by both physiological and psychological explanations – can nevertheless be understood from the perspective of being in the world. What refuses the mutilation or the deficiency in us is an I that is engaged in a certain physical and inter-human world, an I that

continues to tend toward its world despite deficiencies or amputations and that to this extent does not *de jure* recognize them. (Merleau-Ponty, 2014, p. 83, original emphasis)

To shed light on the possibility that humans have to acknowledge various states of being fully worthy of expressivity in a landscape between interplay and symbolic communication, I follow Merleau-Ponty's *Phenomenology of perception* (2014) and *Child Psychology and Pedagogy. The Sorbonne Lectures 1949–1952* (2010) to provide an alternative perspective that challenges the asymmetry that appears when pre-symbolic language is mainly presented as an unavoidable, mandatory transition towards future symbolic language. If we let go of the triumph of reason, asymmetrical relationships can persist above conflicts and the battle of being right is renounced (Merleau-Ponty, 2010).

5 Severe, Multiple Disabilities, Interplay and Communication in Research

In addition to Merleau-Ponty's philosophy and pedagogy, this chapter includes results from a literature overview investigating how research describes interplay and communication of children with severe, multiple disabilities. The perspectives of students with intellectual disabilities in general and students with severe, multiple disabilities in particular, are rarely subject to research, and when they are, the research approaches are either medical, social or behaviouristic (Evensen, 2018). These approaches to intellectual disabilities and movements in general, and movements of children with severe, multiple disabilities in particular, find resonance in the work of contemporary disability researchers Egilson, Ytterhus, Traustadóttir, and Berg (2015). They state that the dominant perspective in childhood disability research

> is framed within special education or rehabilitation, often taking a biomedical and individualistic approach. The dominant perspective has been medical, viewing disability as an abnormality of the individual child. There is an urgent need for an alternative to this narrow understanding of childhood disability that draws attention to and articulates the social relational views of disability which is currently considered the cornerstone of forward thinking in disability policy and which is also one of the foundations of the UNCRPD. There is also a need to develop understanding and knowledge about disabled children using social, cultural and human rights perspectives, especially research-based writings that

bring forward views and perspectives of disabled children and youth. (2015, p. 3)

To investigate the possibilities children with severe, multiple disabilities are given to express their views, I conducted a literature review that focused on interplay, interaction and communication, separated for analytical purposes, yet with the knowledge that these features are intertwined and hardly separable in subjective lived experiences.

The review revealed three main directions in previously published research. The most prominent direction describes interplay and communication of children with severe, multiple disabilities as pure technique. The second most prominent direction describes interplay and communication as a result of contextual impressions, and relational and interactional stimuli. The least prominent direction describes interplay and communicative expressions as causally connected to diagnostic phenotypes.

When connecting research literature to phenomenology, I will emphasise that pedagogical possibilities are inherent when recognising the subjectivity of interplay and interactions and objectivity of communication as intertwined, where one cannot fulfil its potential without the other being present (Lorentzen, 2009). However, paying attention to differences between playful, non-intentional interplay and intentional communication provides important knowledge when analysing expressions in daily life situations, in pedagogical contexts as well as in academic reading and writing.

6   The Literature Overview

During February 2018, I conducted a literature overview by searching the databases Web of Science, EBSCOHost, SPORTDiscus, ERIC and Oria. I included the concepts child*, young child*, communicat*, interact*, interplay* with severe* multiple* disabil*, and severe* multiple* impair*. The search produced a total of 454 papers. Reading headings and abstracts, I excluded papers that included humans older than 18 years of age, papers that included deaf children and children with blindness and autism spectrum disorders but without intellectual disabilities and papers that included parental communication in the supporting system.

Despite the challenges that children with severe, multiple disabilities face when expected to perform symbolic communication, the prominent research discourse has treated communication of children with severe, multiple disabilities as a skill that can be trained, as depending on contextual impressions, relations and interplay, or as causally related to diagnostic phenotypes. The findings in the overview are thematically presented in tables with a short phrase about each paper's contribution to the findings. Then, chosen examples are presented in a more elaborated way.

7 Literature Overview Findings Presenting Communication as a Technique When Children Have Severe, Multiple Disabilities

A total of 15 studies describe *communication* as *trainable, technical skills*. Four out of these contain critical discussions addressing whether technical skills alone provide access to the perspective of the child.

Out of the 15 papers concerning communication as technique, there are nine intervention studies where one child or three children test one or more assistive technical communication devices. Four studies are literature studies, one is a survey including perspectives of parents and professionals, and one study is a mixed-methods case study.

The majority of these 15 studies show that children who participate increase their technical communicational competence. They learn to use switches to make choices. They learn to point out symbols representing persons they want to be with, or objects they want to play with, when they use the graphic symbolic language BLISS, or when they use other augmentative and alternative communication techniques. For example, Lancioni, Singh, O'Reilly, and Bacani (2006) describe how the participating children learn to push switches that transform their subjective expressions when providing an affirmative response saying 'yes' – such as lifting the foot, and a negative response saying 'no' when turning the head – into symbolic language where their affirmative and negative responses are translated and spoken verbally by a canned voice machine.

Altogether, these 15 papers describe a large potential when it comes to translating subjective expressions of children with severe, multiple disabilities into symbolic language, thus making the expressions of the participating children more easily accessible for others who do not know their subjective expressions, wishes and needs. Meanwhile, critical studies show that technical communication skills are of restricted value if the relation between interplay and communication remains unproblematised. Suhonen, Nislin, Alijoki, and Sajaniemi (2015) give an example when they describe how children with severe, multiple disabilities do not necessarily increase their social competence even if they increase their technical communication skills. The children tend to fall outside play as a social field, even when they have developed technical communicational skills directed towards play participation. The children that acquired

TABLE 4.1   Communication as technique

Papers	Theme
Calculator, R. (2009)	Interventions involving the use of augmentative and alternative communication (AAC)
Campbell, P. H., Milbourne, S., Dugan, L. M., and Wilcox, J. M. (2006)	Assistive technology, switch-activation, computer use, AAC
Horn, E. and Kang, J. (2012)	Identification of each child's needs to provide the right AAC; critical discussion
Hummels, C., van der Helm, A., Hen-Geveld, B., Luxen, R., Voort, R., Van Balkom, H., and De Moor, J. (2007)	Development of an interactive and adaptive educational toy to stimulate language and communicative skills
Lancioni, G., O'Reilly, M., Singh, N., Oliva, D., Marziani, M., and Groeneweg J. (2002)	Assessment of microswitches versus interaction to receive benefits
Lancioni, G., Singh, N., O'Reilly, M., and Oliva, D. (2004)	Use of microswitches to choose an event
Lancioni, G., Singh, N., O'Reilly, M., Oliva, D., Monitroni, G., and Chierchie, S. (2004)	Use of a chin-controlled microswitch to provide a pleasant stimulation
Lancioni, G., Singh, N. O'Reilly, M., and Bacani, S. (2006)	Use of a microswitch to establish 'yes' and 'no' responses
Lancioni, G. Singh, N., and O'Reilly, M. (2017)	Use of a microswitch to choose activities
Mumford, L., Lam, R., Wright, V., and Chau, T. (2014)	Implementation of access technologies and response efficiency
Pilesjö, M. S. and Norèn, N. (2017)	Use of BLISS to create sequences of communication; critical discussion
Shull, J., Deitz, J., Billingsley, F., Wendel, S., and Kartin, D. (2004)	Adaptation of switch-operated devices on self-initiated behaviours
Stasolla, F., Caffo, A. O., and Damiani, R. (2015)	Assistive technology use to promote communication and leisure opportunities
Suhonen, E., Nislin, M., Alijoki, A., and Sajaniemi, N. (2015)	Communication abilities in playing in Finnish kindergarten; critical discussion
Wilder, J., Magnusson, L., and Hanson, E. (2015)	Blended learning networks to share knowledge of AAC; critical discussion

new communication skills appeared to withdraw from solitary play, social play, and rough and tumble play. These withdrawals entailed that they had fewer possible experiences with formative turn-taking, problem-solving, negotiating of perspectives and use of language adapted to the present situation than they had before the skill-focused communication rehearsal was implemented. Hence, it appears that their restricted possibilities to participate in play rest upon a lack of possible interplay founded on their premises, rather than on an apparent lack of communicative competence. Further, Suhonen et al. (2015) underline that it is of crucial importance that children with severe, multiple disabilities are subject to positive experiences regarding the social aspects of communication, such as social directedness towards others and non-symbolic expressions. To attend to these values, the authors underline the importance of adults who are sensitive and responsive towards the subjective expressions of the child by imitating the child's own expressions, by stimulating emergent symbolic expressions and by supporting the child's regulation of affections.

When turning back towards the distinction between the playful mood of interplay and the intentionality of symbolic communication, it appears that interplay is supported by personal traits rather than by skills, while communication to a larger degree is objective and accessible on a symbolic level. It is nevertheless of importance to recognise that there are uninterrupted transitions between what is considered interplay and what is considered communication. However, with an operationalisation and pedagogical awareness that makes it possible to detect what divides these two features, interplay and communication will be possible to detect, acknowledge and treat separately in analytical processes, aiming for both to stand out and co-exist in a variety of life-worlds. If so, both concepts are to be understood on their own premises, ensuring that one is not judged by the traits of the other.

8 Contextual Impressions as Substantive for Subjective Expressions When Children Have Severe, Multiple Disabilities

A total of 12 studies describe contextual impressions, relations and interplay as decisive for the children's possibilities to express themselves and thus to be understood. Three of these studies accredit subjective expressions of the children, whereas four focus on intersubjectivity. The studies include video observations, interventions, interviews with the child's significant others, literature reviews and mixed methods.

Altogether, the studies shed light on contextual impressions, relations and interplay as substantive for the expressions of the child. These studies show

TABLE 4.2   Communication as contextual impressions

Papers	Theme
Groark, C. J., Muhamedrahimov, R. J., Palmov, O. I., Nikiforova, N. V., and McCall, R. B. (2005)	Interventions to promote relationships and attachment between caregivers and children in Russian orphanages; intersubjectivity
Hautaniemi, B. (2004)	Describes how children relate emotionally to the world; subjective expressions
Lima, M., Silva, K., Amaral, I., Magalhaes, A., and de Sousa, L. (2013)	Assessing responsiveness to sensory stimuli
McFerran, K. S. and Shoemark, H. (2013)	The possibilities of relations in music therapy
Munde, V. S., Vlaskamp, C., Maes, B., and Ruijssenaars, A. J. (2014)	Assessment of stimuli and patterns of alertness
Nijs, S., Vlaskamp, C., and Maes, B. (2016)	Peer interaction and scaffolding of support workers; intersubjectivity
Olsson, C. (2006)	Use of communication and communicational partners; intersubjectivity
Perifano, A. and Scelles, R. (2015)	Identification of psychological distress; subjective expressions
Stensæth, K. (2013)	Investigation of net-based musical devices with multimedia capacities; intersubjectivity
Tunson, J. and Chandler, C. (2010)	Behavioural states in a multisensory environment
Young, H. (2016)	Experiences of loss
Wilder, J. and Granlund, M. (2003)	Existing interaction patterns as a foundation for planning communicative interventions; subjective expressions

that neither disability alone, nor the context alone shape the child's possibilities or wish to enter interplay or to communicate. On the contrary, it seems that the quality of interplay that the participating children already participate in appears to be decisive as to whether the children express their experiences to the people surrounding them. For example, Groark, Muhamedrahimov, Palmov, Nikiforova, and McCall (2005) describe how Russian orphanage children with severe disabilities increased their regulation of effects, and improved their language development, motor and social skills to a larger degree than children with minor disabilities, when the orphanage staff members were educated in how to give responsive, sensitive care. In addition, Wilder and Granlund (2003) describe the possibilities of children with severe, multiple disabilities to express their experiences as more closely connected to the caregiver's experience of the child as interplaying than to the child's objective communicative skills. Interplay thus appears to be foundational for the development of symbolic language.

Nijs, Vlaskamp, and Maes (2016) investigated interactions in adult–child relations as well as in child–child relations when the child had severe, multiple disabilities. They found that the children related to a significantly smaller degree to other children when an adult was present in the room. Using video observations, the researchers found that the children looked at each other more frequently, had a more active mimicry, increased use of voice and more frequent use of touch when alone in the child–child scenario than when there was an adult present. The only type of engagement that happened more frequently between children in the presence of an adult was seen as subject–object in the child's handling of things.

When research has paid attention to contexts, relations and interplay, findings underline the responsibility of the significant other. The quality of interplay is more foundational for expressivity than are the contextual factors and the disability itself. Further, the quality of interplay is more dependent on the adult's view of the interacting child than the child's acquired communicational skills. Without saying anything about the quality of interaction, Nijs, Vlaskamp, and Maes (2016) showed that child–child interactions increase in frequency when children with severe, multiple disabilities had the opportunity to relate to each other without an adult present in the room. Adapting to the child to promote quantitative as well as qualitative positive interplay is thus an adult responsibility. Acknowledging this responsibility is apparently more important for a holistic view of the child's learning than rehearsing communicative skills.

9 Communication as Causally Linked to Diagnoses When Children Have Severe, Multiple Disabilities

Four studies describe the children's expressions as causal results of their medical diagnoses. Cass et al. (1999) diverge from the others as they place communication at the lowest level in a hierarchical system. The researchers claim that

TABLE 4.3   Communication as causally linked to diagnoses

Papers	Theme
Cass, H., Price, K., Reilly, S, Wisbeach, A. & McConachie, H. (1999)	A hierarchical model for assessing problems
Derby, K., Fisher, W. & Piazza, K. (1996)	Responses enforce self-injurious behaviour
Mount, R. H., Hasting, S., Richard, P., Reilly, S., Cass, H. & Charman, T. (2001)	Behavioural phenotypes in Rett syndrome
Ryan, D., McGregor, F., Akermanis, M., Southwell, K., Ramke, M. & Woodyatt, G. (2004)	The amount of cuing to provide communication with children with Rett syndrome

objective knowledge about diagnostic hallmarks is a foundational premise for teaching the child communicative skills.

These studies approach expressions as causal results connected to the disability itself and include one study of literature, an intervention study, a case study and an observational study. Such causally inspired research literature may shed light on how severe, multiple disabilities can have objective, causal ends. For example, Mount, Hasting, Richard, Reilly, Cass, and Charman (2001) describe how behaviour such as stereotypic, repetitive movements of the hands, sleeping difficulties, teeth grinding and breathing difficulties in girls with Rett syndrome can be understood as genetic phenotypes related to the specific syndrome, or as expressions related to the complex and severe condition of the diagnosis.

Causally inspired research describes communication as objective behaviour closely tied to the child's basic needs, to genetics and to phenotypes. Self-injurious behaviour is not interpreted as expressions of an experienced unease, but as a negative appeal for attention. Cass, Price, and Reilly (1999) describe how weak communicative skills when children have severe, multiple disabilities, are to be placed in a hierarchical order where medical needs such as the function of eyesight, positioning of the body and questions regarding nutrition have to be addressed before communicational skills can be achieved.

Causally inspired research describes important objective features of severe, multiple disabilities, yet, it appears that possibilities for interplay and communication are lost when movements are credited as medical and behavioural cause and effect rather than as subjective, full-worthy expressions. When movements like repetitive hand-movements in girls with Rett syndrome are described as pure genetic phenotypes, possibilities to include hand-movements into shared interactions are hidden.

10 Ending

Communication and interplay with children with severe, multiple disabilities are subject to investigation within different scientific paradigms, and thus also through different methodological approaches ranging from quantitative surveys to hermeneutic phenomenology. Although research is carried out over a wide spectrum of approaches, it appears that intertwining between interplay and communication is partly accredited, partly wiped out and partly ignored in the research literature. The principal lines in the research literature show how researchers have emphasised communication as skills; intentional, independent and separate from interplay as existential human directedness. There is thus a disproportion that might make the schism between interaction and communication hard to understand to the child embedded in his or her lifeworld. The same might be said about the child's significant others, which in the words of Merleau-Ponty (2010) have a duty to keep the child safe in the world without encroaching on the child's values. As the encroachment takes place if the adult looks back towards 'past traumas' (Merleau-Ponty, 2010, p. 83), the solution might be paying attention to the child's present situation. If focusing too strongly towards the past or future, the present moment might slip out of the perceptional field of the adult and the possibilities inherent in the lifeworld of the child.

So, where does the intertwining between interplay and communication lead when children have severe, multiple disabilities? Research is situated in a wide range of paradigms and has provided a wide range of methodological approaches describing interplay and communication. Turning to how interplay and communication are divided for analytical purposes, the lived experiences of interplay and communication are embodied in the relation between the child with severe, multiple disabilities and the sensitive significant other, summing up techniques, contexts, relations and objective medical knowledge.

So, recognising how interplay and communication can be interwoven and given back to the world through movement, we find ourselves in families, circles of friends, at postnatal wards, in kindergartens, in classrooms and in schoolyards, in auxiliary housing, in hospitals, at playgrounds and in swimming pools, together with the child with severe, multiple disabilities. We turn to the research literature and gather important – sometimes vital – knowledge about well-being and pain, about life and death, about nutrition and medicine, about head switches and about technique, about alternative augmentative communication, about diagnoses, about developmental stages, about perceptional impressions and impressions that create expressions, and about causes and effects. Then, we meet the gaze, the gesture, the mimicry or the movements of the child, a child who is eager, tired, restless, impatient, calm, happy or sad, to, in the blink of an eye, realise that objective knowledge does not contain all that we need to know. How shall we act? From where and from whom shall we seek knowledge to build our decisions upon? The answer to these questions may be placed between objective research and the poetry of everyday life.

The late kindergarten teacher Roger Sivoll (1996) provides a glimpse of an answer in the poem 'Thinking'. 'Thinking' sums up the ambivalent relation between knowing, to know that one does not know, and the relief given by the experience when one discovers that parts of the answer are already given.

> So, all of a sudden, one finds oneself sitting, thinking
> if one has to know what one is doing
> to believe in what one is doing,
> or
> at least to believe that one knows what one is doing,
> or if it is enough
> to do what one believes to know
> – and usually, this is where it stops,
>
> but then a kid comes
> fragrant with heavy diapers,
> and then it is obvious
>
> SIVOLL (1996, p. 22, author's translation)

References

Calculator, R. (2009). Augmentative and Alternative Communication (AAC) and inclusive education for students with the most severe disabilities. *International Journal of Inclusive Education, 13*(1), 93–113.

Campbell, P. H., Milbourne, S., Dugan, L. M., & Wilcox, M. J. (2006). A review of evidence on practices for teaching young children to use assistive technology devices. *Topics in Early Childhood Special Education, 26*(1), 3–13.

Cass, H., Price, K., Reilly, S., Wisbeach, A., & McConachie, H. (1999). A model for the assessment and management of children with multiple disabilities. *Child Care, Health and Development, 25*(3), 191–211.

Derby, K., Fisher, W., & Piazza, K. (1996). The effects of contingent and noncontigent attention on self-injury and self-restraint. *Journal of Applied Behavior Analyses, 29*(1), 107–110.

Egilson, T., Ytterhus, B., Traustadóttir, R., & Berg, B. (2015). Introduction: Disabled children and youth in the nordic countries. In R. Traustadóttir, B. Ytterhus, S. T. Egilson, & B. Berg (Eds.), *Childhood and disability in the Nordic countries* (pp. 1–11). Palgrave McMillian.

Evensen, K. V. (2018). *Give me a thousand gestures. Embodied meaning and severe, multiple disabilities in segregated special needs education* (Doctoral dissertation). Norwegian School of Sport Sciences.

Evensen, K. V., Ytterhus, B., & Standal, Ø. F. (2017). "He is not crying for real": Severe, multiple disabilities and embodied constraint in two special-needs education units. *Society, Health & Vulnerability, 8(1)*, 1387474. doi:10.1080/20021518.2017.1387474

Fröhlich, A. (1995). *Basal stimulering [Basic stimulation]*. Ad Notam Gyldendal.

Goffman, E. (2008). *Interaction ritual. Essays in face-to-face behavior.* Aldine Transaction

Groark, C. J., Muhamedrahimov, R. J., Palmov, O. I., Nikiforova, N. V., & McCall, R. B. (2005). Improvements in early day care in Russian orphanages and their relationship to observed behaviors. *Infant Mental Health Journal, 26*(2), 96–109.

Hautaniemi, B. (2004). *Känslornas betydelse i funktionshindrade barns livsvärld [The meaning of emotions in the lifeworld of disabled children]* (Doctoral dissertation). Pedagogiska Instituten, Stockholms Universitet.

Horgen, T. (2006). *Det nære språket. Språkmiljø for mennesker med multifunksjonshemming [The close language. Language environment for humans with severe, multiple disabilities]*. Universitetsforlaget.

Horn, E., & Kang, J. (2012). Supporting young children with multiple disabilities: What do we know and what do we still need to learn? *Topics in early childhood special education, 31*(4), 241–248.

Hummels, C., van der Helm, A., Hen-Geveld, B., Luxen, R., Voort, R., Van Balkom, H., & De Moor, J. (2007). Explorascope: Stimulation of language and communicative skills of multiple handicapped children through an interactive adaptive educational toy. *Digital Creativity, 18*(2), 79–88.

Karoff, H. S. (2013). Play practices and play moods. *International Journal of Play, 2*(3), 76–86.

Lancioni, G., O'Reilly, M., Singh, N., Oliva, D., Marziani, M., & Groeneweg J. (2002). A social validation assessment of the use of microswitches with persons with multiple disabilities. *Research in Developmental Disabilities, 23*(5), 309–318.

Lancioni, G., Singh, N., & O'Reilly, M. (2017). Promoting functional activity engagement in people with multiple disabilities through the use of microswitch-aided programs. *Frontiers in Public Health, 5*(205).

Lancioni, G., Singh, N., & O'Reilly, M., & Bacani, S. (2006). Teaching 'yes' and 'no' responses to children with multiple disabilities through a program including microswitches linked to a vocal output device. *Perceptual and Motor Skills, 102*(1).

Lancioni, G., Singh, N., O'Reilly, M., & Oliva, D. (2004). A microswitch program including words and choice opportunities for students with multiple disabilities. *Perceptual and Motor Skills, 89*(1), 214–222.

Lancioni, G., Singh, N., O'Reilly, M., Oliva, D., Monitroni, G., & Chierchie, S. (2004). Assessing a new response-microswitch combination with a boy with minimal motor behavior. *Perceptual and Motor Skills, 2004, 98*(2), 459–462.

Lima, M., Silva, K., Amaral, I., Magalhaes, A., & de Sousa, L. (2013). Beyond behavioral observations: A deeper view through the sensory reactions of children with profound intellectual and multiple disabilities. *Child Care, Health and Development, 39*(3), 422–431.

Lorentzen, P. (2009). *Kommunikasjon med uvanlige barn [Communication with unusual children]*. Universitetsforlaget.

McFerran, K. S., & Shoemark, H. (2013). How musical engagement promotes well-being in education contexts: The case of a young man with profound and multiple disabilities. *International Journal of Qualitative Studies on Health and Well-Being, 8*(1), 20570.

Merleau-Ponty, M. (2010). *Child psychology and pedagogy. The Sorbonne Lectures 1949–1952.* Northwestern University Press

Merleau-Ponty, M. (2014). *Phenomenology of perception.* Routledge.

Mount, R. H., Hasting, S., Richard, P., Reilly, S., Cass, H., & Charman, T. (2001). Behavioural and emotional features in rett syndrome. *Disability and Rehabilitation, 23* (3–4), 129–138.

Mumford, L., Lam, R., Wright, V., & Chau, T. (2014). An access technology delivery protocol for children with severe and multiple disabilities: A case demonstration. *Developmental Neurorehabilitation, 17*(4), 232–242.

Munde, V. S., Vlaskamp, C., Maes, B., & Ruijssenaars, A. J. (2014). Catch the wave! Time-window sequential analyses of alertness stimulation in individuals with profound intellectual and multiple disabilities. *Child Care, Health and Development, 40*(1), 95–105.

Nijs, S., Vlaskamp, C., & Maes, B. (2016). The nature of peer-directed behaviours in children with profound intellectual and multiple disabilities and its relationship with social scaffolding behaviours of the direct support worker. *Child Care, Health and Development, 42*(1), 98–108.

Olsson, C. (2006). *The kaleidoscope of communication. Different perspectives on communication involving children with severe multiple disabilities* (Doctoral dissertation). Stockholm Institute of Education.

Perifano, A., & Scelles, R. (2015). Psychological distress of children with progressive diseases and multiple disabilities: A crossed analyses. *Archives de Pédiatrie, 22*(9), 916–923.

Pilesjö, M. S., & Norèn, N. (2017). Teaching communication aid use in everyday conversation. *Child Language Teaching and Therapy, 33*(3), 241–253.

Ryan, D., McGregor, F., Akermanis, M., Southwell, K., Ramke, M., & Woodyatt, G. (2004). Facilitating communication in children with multiple disabilities: Three case studies of girls with rett syndrome. *Disability and Rehabilitation, 26*(21–22), 1268.

Shull, J., Deitz, J., Billingsley, F., Wendel, S., & Kartin, D. (2004). Assistive technology programming for a young child with profound disabilities: A single-subject study. *Physical & Occupational Therapy in Pediatrics, 24*(4), 47–62.

Sivoll, R. (1996). *Blant enda flere unger* [*Among even more kids*]. Pedagogisk forum.

Skarstad, K. (2018). Ensuring human rights for persons with intellectual disabilities? *The International Journal of Human Rights, 22*(6), 774–800. doi:10.1080/13642987.2018.1454903

Stasolla, F., Caffo, A. O., & Damiani, R. (2015). Assistive technology-based programs to promote communication and leisure activities by three children emerged from a minimal conscious state. *Cognitive Processing, 16*(1), 69–78.

Stensæth, K. (2013). "Musical co-creation"? Exploring health-promoting potentials on the use of musical and interactive tangibles for families with children with disabilities. *International Journal of Qualitative Studies on Health and Well-being, 8*. doi:10.3402/qhw.v8i0.20704

Suhonen, E., Nislin, M., Alijoki, A., & Sajaniemi, N. (2015). Children's play behaviour and social communication in integrated special day-care groups. *European Journal of Special Needs Education, 30*(3), 287–303.

Toombs, S. K. (2001). Reflections on bodily change: The lived-experience of disability. In S. K. Toombs (Ed.), *Handbook of phenomenology and medicine* (pp. 247–261). Kluwer Academic Publishers.

Tunson, J., & Chandler, C. (2010). Behavioral states of children with severe disabilities in the multisensory environment. *Physical & Occupational Therapy in Paediatrics, 30*(2), 101.

United Nations. (1989). *The Convention on the Rights of the Child*. Retrieved February 16, 2018, from http://www.ohchr.org/EN/ProfessionalInterest/Pages/CRC.aspx

Wilder, J., & Granlund, M. (2003). Behaviour style and interaction between seven children with multiple disabilities and their caregivers. *Child Care, Health and Development, 29*(6), 559–567.

Wilder, J., Magnusson, L., & Hanson, E. (2015). Professionals' and parents' shared learning in blended learning networks related to communication and augmentative and alternative communication for people with severe disabilities. *European Journal of Special Needs Education, 30*(3), 367–383.

Young, H. (2016). Loss and profound intellectual disabilities: The significance of early separation responses. *Advances in Mental Health and Intellectual Disabilities, 10*(6), 315–323.

CHAPTER 5

Spaces for Transitions in Intergenerational Childhood Experiences

Czarecah Tuppil Oropilla

Abstract

This chapter focuses on exploring spaces given to children's voices in the discourse of intergenerational interactions through a review of literature done systematically. Particular focus is given to voices of young children – where are the children's voices in these interactions? How are they listened to? How are their voices collected?

The decision to focus on children's voices in the realm of intergenerational experiences draws from the UN Convention on the Rights of the Child (UNCRC, 1989) which upholds the view that children are competent, strong, active, participatory, meaning-makers, and fellow citizens that have a right to be involved in decisions affecting them and have the freedom to express their thoughts and opinions.

Literature on intergenerational interactions was reviewed systematically through a PRISMA-inspired workflow process. Specific inclusion and exclusion criteria were utilised for database searches. Content analysis of the methodologies used in identified literature was conducted to see analyse recurring themes, trends or issues. A matrix has been developed and presented to summarise results.

Results revealed potential spaces for transformations in intergenerational research to make a bigger space for younger children's voices to be heard. A promising trend observed through an increase in use of qualitative participatory methodologies seems to be venue where children's voices are acknowledged. This is a transitional and transformational space for intergenerational research *with* children, and not on or of them.

Keywords

intergenerational experiences – children's voices in research

1 Introduction

In exploring spaces given to children's voices in the realm of intergenerational interactions through a review of literature done systematically, this chapter will discuss recurring themes concerning interactions of older adults and young children. What do we already know, and what else do we need to know? What spaces are available for these intergenerational interactions to happen, flourish and prosper? What transitions and transformations occur in these spaces? Voices of young children is given focus – what transitions and spaces are available for children's voices to be acted upon?

2 Intergenerational Interactions in Popular and Social Media

The topic of intergenerational learning and experiences particularly between younger children and older adults is one that is gaining more attention in the recent years. Browsing through social media platforms like Facebook, YouTube and even in online newspapers and magazines like Nordre Aker Budstikke in Norway and Independent.co.uk, there have been numerous features of intergenerational interactions of younger children and older adults from all over the world. Basing on the number of likes, the amount of comments and the number of times these features have been shared, it can easily be said that it is a topic that interests general public viewers. In fact, because of interest in the topic, two television shows were produced and aired primarily in United Kingdom. These are Channel 4's Old People's Home for 4-year olds, and BBC's Toddlers Who Took on Dementia, which aired in 2017 and 2018 respectively.

TABLE 5.1 Experimental questions

Old people's home for 4-year olds[a]	Toddlers who took on dementia[b]
If four-year-olds and 84-year-olds work and play together, will it improve the health and happiness of the older group? Ten pre-schoolers welcome 11 pensioners into their classroom.	In a bold new experiment, a group of toddlers head to a dementia day-care centre to share three days of time and activities with adults in their 70s and 80s.

a Source: https://www.channel4.com/programmes/old-peoples-home-for-4-year-olds?fbclid=IwAR1RrSNp_jdZ5uJJGhwpiafVhTJD0TwvvoN_vk8a1s8aPsu9MxBLjmzzZ8U
b Source: https://www.bbc.co.uk/programmes/p067t39n

Both television shows have been conceptualised to answer experimental questions focusing on the well-being of older adults.

As the experimental questions (see Table 5.1) were stated in a way that called for children as variable and means to get the desired outcome and while older adult's health and well-being are as equally important, it would seem that children's voices are not given as much importance. Beyond being cute and entertaining for adults, where are the children's voices in these interactions? How are they listened to? How are their voices collected?

3   Intergenerational Interactions in Research

Growing interest in intergenerational interactions and experiences does not only exist in popular and social media. As part of their initiative to work towards achieving the 2030 Agenda and 17 Sustainable Development Goals (SDGs) set forth by their institution, United Nations has also included intergenerational work in their repertoire. Of the 17 SDGs, five are closely linked to intergenerational research: SDG 1 No Poverty, SDG 2 Zero Hunger, SDG 3 Good Health and Well-Being, SDG 4 Quality Education and SDG 16 Peace, Justice and Strong Institutions. With particular focus on the context families and family policies, these Sustainable Development Goals can be attained if different generations work with each other. Further, in the General Assembly resolution 73/144 adopted in 17 December 2018, it is explicitly stated that members states are encouraged to invest in inclusive, family-oriented policies and programmes, including early childhood development and education towards advancing social integration and intergenerational solidarity to support implementation of the 2030 Agenda.

4   Viewing Younger Children and the Older Adults

In searching for children's voices in this discourse, this review would like to highlight the young children's ability to participate in matters that involve them and their path on being to becoming. Congruently, the research would also like to recognise the younger adults' wisdom, strengths that they could contribute to the society, most especially to younger children. Both age groups are similar in that they have their own unique cultures that the other age group could benefit from, and that both age groups seek empowerment from their position as dependents of society (The TOY Consortium, 2013).

This review considers younger children and older adults to be in a sociocultural context where they prosper and make meaning through interactions with their environment and each other (James & Prout, 1990). Framed in a relational sociology of childhood, this chapter views children as active social agents, who participate in knowledge construction and daily experience of childhood (James & Prout, 1997a; James et al., 1998; Alanen & Mayall, 2001; Mayall, 2002; Alanen, 2009). In such a frame, children's points of views, opinions, perspectives, perceptions and aspirations are recognised and respected (Alanen, 2014). Further, in seeing children as more than just becoming, Uprichard (2008) has written about a perspective to view children as both 'being and becoming.' She wrote that "perceiving children as 'being and becoming' does not decrease children's agency, but increases it, as the onus of their agency is in both the present and future" (Uprichard, 2008, p. 311). In such a perspective, young children are viewed as agents who are deemed capable and are active authors of their own narratives and lived experiences (Garvis, Ødegaard, & Lemon, 2015).

For the purposes of this chapter, I will define some terminologies used. *Intergenerational experiences* refers to engagements between younger children and older adults and could be deemed as the stories lived and told by individuals as they are embedded within cultural, social, institutional, familial, political, and linguistic narratives (Clandinin, 2013). It also necessarily situates one in a social, cultural and historical situation with motives within activities and practices situated in traditions and cultures (Hedegaard & Fleer, 2008). Intergenerational experiences, then, from a narrative inquiry and cultural-historical points of views is an acknowledgement of the phenomenology of childhood – or childhoods, intentionally pluralised in order to highlight that there is no one universal childhood, but instead there are different social and cultural life worlds and experiences of individual children within that particular social space of childhood (Alanen, 2014). This terminology is used concurrently and alternatively with *intergenerational interactions* and *intergenerational activities*.

As this framework situates children in social, cultural and relational situations, settings and circumstances, and as such occurs naturally in a familial setting where generational ordering is necessarily in place, the discourse of intergenerational interactions of younger children and older adults is one that includes familial settings but also takes it further to include intentional non-familial intergenerational interactions. Accordingly, henceforth, *older adults* will refer to the members of the older generations, ages 50 years and above, regardless of their relationship with the younger children. This terminology was purposefully selected as it is deemed the more respectful term in reference to people of this age group (Walker & Gemeinschaften, 1993; UN High Commissioner for Human Rights, 1995; Falconer & O'Neill, 2007). On the other hand, *younger children* will refer to children in the earliest stage of the human life cycle and generational ordering, which typically includes children from birth until adolescence, encompassing early childhood and primary school years.

Particular to this study, we refer to *voice* as children's participation in intergenerational research where feedback was obtained from them and not just from adults. These voices can be oral/verbal but may also be in the form of body language captured in photos, drawings and video recordings during intergenerational interactions as represented in research.

5 Valuing the Various Ways Children Communicate

The decision to search for children's voices in the realm of intergenerational experiences draws from the UN Convention on the Rights of the Child (UNCRC, 1989). Ratified in most countries of the world, the UNCRC is a framework that has been the basis for changes in policy, research and practice in childhood studies. It plays a major role in how children are viewed and treated as there are stipulations as to what the role of the state, adults and of the children are (Hayes, 2002; Taylor, 2000).

Article 16 of the UNCRC calls for protection of children, chiefly as regards their privacy and protection. While this is an important discourse, the UNCRC also upholds the view that children as being competent, strong, active, participatory, meaning-makers, and fellow citizens as highlighted in Article 12 and 13 in particular. These articles state that children have a right to be involved in decisions affecting them and their freedom to express their thoughts and opinions, as well as to receive information that is allowed by the law (UNCRC, 1989). These Articles of the UN Convention on the Rights of a Child have the potential to serve as an agent for change and action at policy level to give children the opportunity and a voice within society (Hayes, 2002).

In line with the transitional force in the past 20 years that saw a reconceptualisation of childhood studies, particularly in early childhood, there is now a focus on children's voices in research to better investigate their lived experiences (Einarsdóttir, 2014; Clark & Moss, 2011; Clark, Clark, 2007, 2010, 2019; Harcourt & Mazzoni, 2012; Baird, 2013; Palaiologou, 2019). This transitional paradigm shift is particularly important especially since it has been noted that children continue to lack voice in policy and research contexts (Pascal & Bertram, 2009), and most times, children 'have been the invisible and voiceless objects of concern, and not understood as competent, autonomous persons who have a point of view' (Smith & Taylor, 2000, p. ix). And while children's viewpoints are being sought and respected particularly in Nordic research, children's voices are still underrepresented despite claims of otherwise (Emilson & Johansson, 2018).

Several systematic reviews of literature on intergenerational experiences have already been published. In 2013, a review of related literature was conducted by the Together Old and Young Consortium funded by the European Commission to examine intergenerational learning in seven European countries namely Ireland, Italy, Spain, Slovenia, the Netherlands, Poland and Portugal (The TOY Project Consortium, 2013). In their review, they discussed a phenomenon of growing separation between children and older adults, as well as the benefits intergenerational practices have for both young children and older adults. While their review included focus on interaction of younger children and older adults, there was not particular focus on children's voice. Rather, they described several intergenerational practices from the identified seven European countries.

Another group of researchers in Spain conducted a systematic review of related literature on the topic of intergenerational experiences. They focused primarily on the effectiveness of various intergenerational programmes by evaluating empirically based interventions, which they find have scarcely been done in the intergenerational context (Canedo-García et al., 2017). While their review methodology was largely variable analysis of intergenerational programmes, part of their findings encourage development and implementation of these programmes that would meet users' needs, break down communication barriers between generations and break down social isolation of age groups (Canedo-García et al., 2017).

Another review was published in 2017 to examine the benefits of intergenerational volunteering in long-term care (Blais et al., 2017). Their review framed interactions of youth volunteers, from high-schools and colleges, and older adults, and the perceived benefits and challenges of intergenerational volunteering in long-term-care homes in Canada. Another article in JIR sought a literature search on intergenerational learning programmes that follow conditions of the intergroup contact theory to reduce prejudice and achieve positive effects (Gendron et al., 2018). They found 10 programmes to analyse within the intergroup contact theory, which they deem is an appropriate theoretical framework to develop intergenerational programmes.

A review of different intergenerational care models that may inform the process of putting up an intergenerational care programme in Australia has also been published. They looked at a specific type of programme that involves caring for older adults and young children in a shared setting under the supervision of a formally trained caregiver where both the younger and older generations are receiving programmed care in an environment where activities and resources are shared between them, in Australia (Radford et al., 2016). They defined 'younger generations' as being 0–5 years old, while the 'elderly' were people 65+ years of age. Through the use of Preferred Reporting Items for Systematic Reviews and Meta-Analyses (PRISMA) guidelines (Liberati et al., 2009), they set forth criteria for their review and found three major intergenerational care model types – visitations, co-located, and single site (Radford et al., 2018). *Visitations* refer to intergenerational programmes across two separate institutions, typically with the younger group visiting the older group. For this type of programming to work in term of cost-effectiveness, the two institutions should be within close proximity with each other. The *co-located* type of intergenerational programming, on the other hand, can be further divided into two categories: *co-located visitation,* referring to care institutions that do not have specific and identified areas where intergenerational interactions can happen, and *co-located shared space,* where there are specific physical space as part of their facilities for intergenerational interactions to happen. These type of intergenerational programming benefits institutions in terms of shared overhead costs. However, Radford et al. (2016) pointed out that although there may be specific spaces allocated for unstructured intergenerational interactions, there is still a need for intentional and structured activities for more meaningful interactions to happen. The third type the review has identified is *single-site,* where intergenerational care is delivered in a single setting without a formal and structured [educational] programme underpinning interactions of the older and younger groups. Homes with groups or families of different generations can be considered part of this type. However, while this type of intergenerational setting offers practical solutions for care of both older and younger age-group, educational benefits are lost without formal, intentional and structured intergenerational programmes (Radford et al., 2016).

Another relevant systematic review of literature was conducted by a team in Torino, Italy summarising the effects of intergenerational programs and activities on both elderly and children (Gualano et al., 2018). They have considered papers reporting data about intergenerational programs involving older adults and children in the early years and in primary school. They have done their search in the PubMed and Scopus databases and summarised 10 studies discussing effects on children, and 17 studies discussing effects on the elderly. Their general conclusion yielded a positive impact on both the children and the elderly.

While all mentioned literature reviews have added important knowledge in the realm of intergenerational studies, most intergenerational reviews focus on intergenerational programmes – the development, effectiveness and types and models. A gap is seen in terms of intentionally seeking out a space for the end-users of these programmes as no review has focused on finding out spaces for children's voices to be heard. As such, in the succeeding portion of this chapter, there will be a discussion on a review of related literature done systematically focusing on these concerns.

6 Methodology

Focused on finding young children's voices in the discourse of intergenerational research as an identified space for transformation, this review set forth a process for selecting studies to review. In order to make the selection process be systematic, inspiration was taken from the work-flow of Preferred Reporting Items for Systematic Review and Meta-Analyses (PRISMA). Although primarily used in the medical field for reporting systematic reviews particularly for randomised medical trials or interventions, the proponents of PRISMA have created a checklist and a flow diagram focused on transparent reporting of systematic reviews and meta-analyses that can be used for systematic reviews in other academic fields (Liberati et al., 2009). They have prescribed a work-flow for selecting studies into the review that has four parts – identification, screening, eligibility towards a decision for final inclusion. This work-flow allows for systematic sifting through the resources leading to the decision of which studies to include or not.

6.1 *Databases*

Databases used for searching literature for this review have been selected based on Creswell's (2014) list of suggested databases. Additionally, search from these databases have been conducted with the guidance of a university research librarian for appropriate search terms and techniques. As such, databases hosted by EBSCO have been utilised which include the following: ERIC, Medline, Teacher Reference Center, CINAHL, SocIndex, Academic Search Elite. The databases searched were a mix of sources for pedagogy and health care.

6.2 *Key Terms for Identification*

As above, with the guidance of a university research librarian, the following key terminologies and search strategies have been used for initial identification of articles:
- S1: intergeneration*

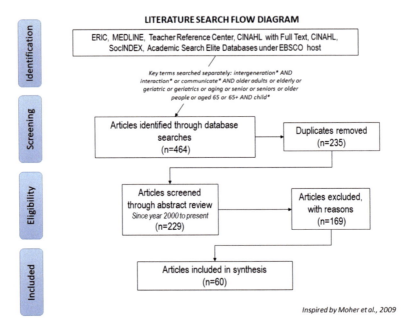

FIGURE 5.1   PRISMA-inspired work flow (based on Moher et al., 2009)

- S2: interaction*
- S3: communicate*
- S4: S2 or S3
- S5: S1 and S4
- S6: older adults or elderly or geriatric or geriatrics or aging or senior or seniors or older people
- S7: S5 & S6
- S8: child*
- S9: S7 and S8
- S10: limited to date published from 2000 to 2019

Search from the databases using these terminologies brought back 464 articles (see Figure 5.1). The database automatically removed duplicates (n = 235). Afterwards, these articles were further screened for eligibility through an abstract review (n = 229). This step excluded n = 169 articles for reasons enumerated below. A total number of n = 60 articles were included for content analysis of the methods of listening to children's voices.

6.3   *Inclusion and Exclusion Criteria for Screening*

Databases used for searching literature for this review have been selected based on Creswell's (2014) list of suggested databases. Additionally, search from these databases have been conducted with the guidance of a university research librarian for appropriate search terms and techniques. As such, databases hosted by EBSCO have been utilised which include the following: ERIC, Medline, Teacher Reference Center, CINAHL, SocIndex, Academic Search Elite. The databases searched were a mix of sources for pedagogy and health care.

Articles that have been included in the synthesis (n = 60) had to have the following:
- Presence of interaction between children (early years until primary years) and older adults.
- Voices of the children were documented through their reported methodologies.

Initially, literature that had primary school children interacting with older adults were excluded in hopes to make the systematic review more focused in the early childhood years, to the voices of the youngest children. However, upon further consideration and realisation that early childhood is often lumped together in just one category, then literature with children ages 0–13 to also include primary school aged children as part of young children. This decision was brought on from the position that these literature would still prove to be relevant because childhood is an element of social structure according to their ages (Qvortup, 1987, as cited in Alanen, 2009) which positions children as a separate social category that is interrelated to other social categories (Alanen, 2009). Further, not taking childhood as one social category may be difficult especially since there is a system of social ordering that pertains to children as a specific social category circumscribed in particular social locations from which they act and participate (Alanen, 2009). Including this social category is important as it is a nod to children's involvement in the daily construction of their own lives through their relationships with other people.

A total of 169 articles were excluded from being synthesised for the following reasons:
- While children were involved in interactions, only voices of the older adults, institution staff, older adolescents, teenagers, college students, parents, young adults were sought. Articles that have included voices of older children in highschool and college have been excluded to concentrate on the voices of the youngest children.
- Program profiles, program planning and their benefits were highlighted – children were present, but their voices were not sought.
- Some articles have been written in languages other than English have also been excluded because of the author's incapability to read Chinese, Japanese, French, Portuguese and Spanish.

6.4 Data Analysis

Upon having identified which research to include in the synthesis of related literature through the process described above, content analysis mainly of the methodologies used was conducted to see whether or not there are recurring themes, trends or issues. In order to summarise data from all the reviews of related literature, the matrix below has been developed to include the data seeking out young children's voices in the discourse of intergenerational relationships (see Table 5.2).

6.5 Limitations of the Study

Although the researcher has taken a PRISMA-inspired workflow as the methodological process used to find and select studies in the hope to reduce bias and have results that are more likely to produce reliable and accurate conclusions, this study acknowledges some limitations. First, this study is not a systematic review of related literature. As such, there may be databases including pertinent journal articles that have not been covered by the search criteria. Second, choices in the databases used for the search only yields journals included within their archives. Third, book chapters and other academic texts such as theses and dissertation manuscripts have not been included as a delimitation in the search criteria. Because of these limitations, this study does not claim to be a conclusive and in no way can be considered generalizable. Rather, it can be viewed as a preliminary review done systematically.

7 Results

7.1 Younger Children's Voices

As the search for children's voices in the discourse of intergenerational experiences was conducted through a literature review, the first paradox jumped out from the article selection process. Despite having 464 journal articles to review, only 60 articles (13%) have reported including children's voices. The 60 journal articles that were included in the review were synthesised into the matrix as shown in Table 5.2.

7.2 Profile of Child Respondents: Age, Country, Kind of Setting

While the data shows that the age range of children who participated in the reviewed articles were from two until 24 years of age, the most common age range was from six to 12 years old for both quantitative and qualitative methodologies. Three researches included two year-olds as their participants (Davis

TABLE 5.2 Results matrix

Year of publication	Authors	Research title	Country/ continent	Kind of setting	Age of children respondents	Methodology	Methods	Topic	Journal field of study
2000	Chowdhary et al.	Intergenerating Activities and Aging Appreciation of Elementary School Children	USA	Primary school	8–10 years old	Mixed methods, mostly quantitative	Questionnaires, drawings	Children's perceptions on aging	Educational Gerontology
2002	Middlecamp & Gross	Intergenerational Day Care and Preschoolers' Attitudes about Aging	USA	Day care	3–5 years old	Mixed methods	CATE, Children's Attitudes Toward the Elderly Word Associations and Activity Scale	Children's attitudes about aging	Educational Gerontology
2003	Hayes	An Observational Study in Developing an Intergenerational Shared Site Program	USA	Shared site	3–4 years	Qualitative	Videos Observation Researcher journal notes	Children's reactions to intergenerational program	Intergenerational Relationships
2004	Boström	Intergenerational Learning in Stockholm County in Sweden: A Practical Example of Elderly Men Working in Compulsory Schools as a Benefit for Children	Sweden	Primary school	School aged	Quantitative	Questionnaires	Children's perceptions of granddad's job in school	Intergenerational Relationships

(*cont.*)

TABLE 5.2   Results matrix (cont.)

Year of publication	Authors	Research title	Country/continent	Kind of setting	Age of children respondents	Methodology	Methods	Topic	Journal field of study
2004	Orel, Dupuy & Wright	Auxilliary Caregivers	USA	Home	7–17 years old	Qualitative	Interviews	Caregiving tasks and reflections	Intergenerational Relationships
2005	Okoye	Young Children's Perception of the Elderly	Nigeria	Primary school	10–11 years old	Quantitative	Child-Adolescent facts on Aging Quiz (CAFAQ)	Children's perceptions of older adults	Intergenerational Relationships
2006	Macdonald	Intergenerational Interactions Occurring within a Shared Reading Program	Canada	Kindergarten	5–6 years old	Qualitative	Videos observation researcher journal notes Interviews	Intergenerational shared reading sessions	Intergenerational Relationships
2006	Agate et al.	An Intergenerational Approach for Enriching Children's Environmental Attitudes and Knowledge	USA	Primary school	5th and 6th graders	Mixed methods	Questionnaires (Children's Environmental Attitudes and Knowledge Scale); experimental intervention	Children's Environmental Attitudes and Knowledge	Intergenerational Relationships

(cont.)

TABLE 5.2 Results matrix (cont.)

Year of publication	Authors	Research title	Country/ continent	Kind of setting	Age of children respondents	Methodology	Methods	Topic	Journal field of study
2006	Epstein & Boisvert	Let's Do Something Together: Identifying the Effective Components of Intergenerational Programs	USA	Shared site	Infants to 6 years	Mixed methods	Intergenerational Program Quality Assessment (I-G PQA)/The High-Scope Intergenerational Program Quality Assessment (Observations of Interactions)	Program quality observed through behavior	Intergenerational Relationships
2006	Kaplan, Kiernan, James	Inter generational Family Conversations and Decision Making about Eating Healthfully	USA	Single site	10–13 years old	Qualitative	Focus group discussions	Decisions about eating healthfully	Nutrition Education and Behavior
2007	Lynott & Merola	Improving the Attitudes of 4th Graders toward Older People through a Multidimensional Intergenerational Program	USA	Primary school	8–10 years old (4th grade)	Mixed methods	17 item questionnaire	Children's attitudes about older people	Educational Gerontology

(cont.)

TABLE 5.2 Results matrix (cont.)

Year of publication	Authors	Research title	Country/ continent	Kind of setting	Age of children respondents	Methodology	Methods	Topic	Journal field of study
2007	Heydon	Making Meaning Together: Multi-Modal Literacy Learning Opportunities in an Inter-Generational Art Programme	Canada	Single site	Children mean age is 4 years old	Qualitative	Naturalistic: videos of sessions, observer field notes, informal discussions	Children's voices (utterances) through interactions with older adults	Curriculum Studies
2007	de Souza & Grundy	Intergenerational Interaction, Social Capital and Health: Results from a Randomised Controlled Trial in Brazil	Brazil	Single site	12–18 years old	Mixed Methods	Randomized control trial; questionnaires, interviews	Social capital, family relationships, and self-rated health	Social Science and Medicine
2008	Hall & Batey	Children's Ideas about Aging before and after an Intergenerational Read-Aloud	USA	Primary school	3rd graders	Mixed methods	Word association test and informal interviews	Ideas about aging	Educational Gerontology

(cont.)

TABLE 5.2 Results matrix (cont.)

Year of publication	Authors	Research title	Country/ continent	Kind of setting	Age of children respondents	Methodology	Methods	Topic	Journal field of study
2008	Davis et al.	"I Wish We Could Get Together": Exploring Intergenerational Play across a Distance via a 'Magic Box'	Australia	Home	2–10 years old	Qualitative	Interviews Magic Box activity	Intergenerational play in the family context	Intergenerational Relationships
2008	Davidson, Luo & Fulton	Stereotyped Views of Older Adults in Children from the People's Republic of China and from the United States	China and USA	Primary school	6–11 years old	Quantitative, experimental	Stereotype Assessment Task in experiment format	Children's biases toward older adults	Intergenerational Relationships
2008	Hannon & Gueldner	The Impact of Short-Term Quality Intergenerational Contact on Children's Attitudes toward Older Adults	USA	Summer camp	6–12 years old	Quantitative, experimental	Questionnaire including Newman's Children's Views of Aging and Polizzi's Semantic Differential	Children's attitudes toward older adults	Intergenerational Relationships

(cont.)

TABLE 5.2　Results matrix (cont.)

Year of publication	Authors	Research title	Country/ continent	Kind of setting	Age of children respondents	Methodology	Methods	Topic	Journal field of study
2008	Heyman & Gutheil	"They Touch Our Hearts": The Experiences of Shared Site Intergenerational Program Participants	USA	Shared site	not specified but attends day care	Qualitative	Focus group discussions	Intergenerational activities	Intergenerational Relationships
2009	Chorndunhan & Casadonte	Children's Attitudes and Classroom Interaction in an Intergenerational Education Program	USA	Primary school	Primary and junior high students	Mixed methods	Children's View on Aging survey	Children's attitudes and classroom interaction	Educational Gerontology
2009	Saito & Yasuda	An Empirical Study of the Frequency of Intergenerational Contacts of Family Members in Japan	Japan	Home	not specified but attends primary school	Quantitative	Survey questionnaires	Frequency of intergenerational contact	Intergenerational Relationships
2009	Kinoshita	Charting Generational Differences in Conceptions and Opportunities for Play in a Japanese Neighborhood	Japan	Community	10–12 years old	Qualitative, participatory	Participatory map making Interviews	Play spaces in the neighborhood	Intergenerational Relationships

(cont.)

TABLE 5.2 Results matrix (cont.)

Year of publication	Authors	Research title	Country/ continent	Kind of setting	Age of children respondents	Methodology	Methods	Topic	Journal field of study
2010	Hurme, Westerback & Quadrello	Traditional and New Forms of Contact between Grandparents and Grandchildren	Finland	Home	11–13 and 16–17 years old	Quantitative	New technologies questionnaire	Forms of contact between grandparents and grandchildren	Intergenerational Relationships
2010	McNair & Moore	The Effects of Intergenerational Programs on Individuals with Alzheimer's Disease or Dementia	USA	Shared site vs preschool	Adolescents, preschoolers	Mixed methods	Children's Views on Aging (CVOA) pre and posttest; drawings and an interview	Children's Perceptions of the Elderly; Gerontologic Care; Psychiatry/ Psychology	Therapeutic Recreation
2011	Belgrave	The Effect of a Music Therapy Intergenerational Program on Children and Older Adults' Intergenerational Interactions, Cross-Age Attitudes, and Older Adults' Psychosocial Well-Being	USA	Retirement living facility	4th graders collectively	Mixed methods	CATE, Children's Attitudes Toward the Elderly, observations videotaped	Children's attitudes about older people	Music Therapy

(cont.)

TABLE 5.2 Results matrix (cont.)

Year of publication	Authors	Research title	Country/ continent	Kind of setting	Age of children respondents	Methodology	Methods	Topic	Journal field of study
2011	Kamei et al.	Six Month Outcomes of an Innovative Weekly Intergenerational Day Program with Older Adults and School-Aged Children in a Japanese Urban Community	Japan	Single site	Elementary school children	Mixed methods	Participant observations and interviews, semantic differential scales in questionnaires	Children's perceptions of older adults	Nursing Science
2011	Carson, Kobayashi, Kuehne	The Meadows School Project: Case Study of a Unique Shared Site Intergenerational Program	Canada	Shared site	10–12 years old	Qualitative	Audio of individual semistructured interviews, reflective journal entries on project experiences, field researcher notes	Exploring potential health and educational impacts of the program	Intergenerational Relationships
2011	Kleinspehn-Ammerlahn et al.	Dyadic Drumming across the Lifespan Reveals a Zone of Proximal Development in Children	Germany	Single site	5 and 12 year olds	Experimental, quantitative	Dyadic drumming	Observation of children's drumming with partners	Developmental Psychology

(cont.)

SPACES FOR TRANSITIONS IN INTERGENERATIONAL CHILDHOOD 93

TABLE 5.2 Results matrix (cont.)

Year of publication	Authors	Research title	Country/ continent	Kind of setting	Age of children respondents	Methodology	Methods	Topic	Journal field of study
2011	Roos	The Generational Other: The Cultural Appropriateness of an Intergenerational Group Reflecting Technique	South Africa	Community centre	3–13 years old	Mixed methods	Intergenerational group reflecting technique (IGRT), individual interviews, focus group discussions	How grandparents communicate important information	Intergenerational Relationships
2011	Heyman, Gutheil & White-Ryan	Preschool Children's Attitudes toward Older Adults: Comparison of Intergenerational and Traditional Day Care	USA	Kindergarten	3–5 years old	Quantitative	Drawings to elicit response Children's Attitudes Toward the Elderly (CATE) measure	Children's attitudes toward older adults	Intergenerational Relationships
2012	Luchesi, Dupas & Pavarini	Evaluation of the Attitudes of Children Living with Seniors toward Aging	Brazil	Community centre	7–10 years old	Mixed methods	Interviews; Todaro Scale for the assessment of attitudes of children toward the elderly	Children's attitudes about living with older people	Nursing Science
2012	Xie et al.	Connecting Generations: Developing Co-Design Methods for Older Adults and Children	USA	Single site	6–9 years old	Qualitative, co-design	Co-design activities, conversations	Children gave feedback on co-designing process	Behaviour and Information Technology

(cont.)

TABLE 5-2 Results matrix (cont.)

Year of publication	Authors	Research title	Country/ continent	Kind of setting	Age of children respondents	Methodology	Methods	Topic	Journal field of study
2013	Morita & Kobayashi	Interactive Programs with Preschool Children Bring Smiles and Conversation to Older Adults: Time-Sampling Study	Japan	Single Site	5–6 years old	Mixed methods	Video, observations, behavior time sampling	Observations of changes in visual attention, facial expression, engagement/ behaviour, and intergenerational conversations with older adults	Geriatrics
2013	Larkin, Wilson & Freer	Images of Old: Teaching about Aging through Children's Literature	USA	Kindergarten	5–10 years old	Qualitative	Observations Teacher's journal reflections Participatory Venn diagram activity	Teaching aging though storybooks	Intergenerational Relationships
2013	Mann, Khan, Leeson	Variations in Grandchildren's Perceptions of Their Grandfathers and Grandmothers: Dynamics of Age and Gender	UK	Home	4–18 years old	Quantitative	Questionnaire, completed with parents	Children's perceptions of their grandparents	Intergenerational Relationships

(cont.)

TABLE 5.2　Results matrix (cont.)

Year of publication	Authors	Research title	Country/ continent	Kind of setting	Age of children respondents	Methodology	Methods	Topic	Journal field of study
2014	Gamliel & Gabay	Knowledge Exchange, Social Interactions, and Empowerment in an Intergenerational Technology Program at School	Jerusalem	Primary school	Children aged 11–12	Mixed methods	Closed-ended feedback questionnaires, quantitative data were collected from face-to-face interviews, qualitative data were collected via two hours per week of observations and unstructured interviews	Feedback for IG tech program	Educational Gerontology
2015	Low et al.	Grandfriends, an Intergenerational Program for Nursing-Home Residents and Preschoolers: A Randomized Trial	Australia	Shared site	4 years old	Quantitative	Children's Attitudes to the Elderly Interview (CATI)	Children's biases toward older adults	Intergenerational Relationships

(cont.)

TABLE 5.2   Results matrix (cont.)

Year of publication	Authors	Research title	Country/ continent	Kind of setting	Age of children respondents	Methodology	Methods	Topic	Journal field of study
2015	Jirata	Intergenerational Continuity and Change in Conceptualization of the "Child" among Guji People of Ethiopia	Ethiopia	Community	Not specified but part of the Guji children population	Qualitative	Participant observation, narrative interview, ethnograpic methodology	Conceptualization of being a child	Intergenerational Relationships
2015	Tafere	Intergenerational Relationships and the Life Course: Children-Caregivers' Relations in Ethiopia	Ethiopia	Community	8–15 years old	Qualitative	Drawings; interviews	Family life in Ethiopia	Intergenerational Relationships
2016	Babcock; MaloneBeach & Woodworth-Hou	Intergenerational Intervention to Mitigate Children's Bias against the Elderly	USA	Primary school	10–11 years old	Quantitative	Child-Age Implicit Association Test (IAT)	Children's biases toward older adults	Intergenerational Relationships

(cont.)

TABLE 5.2 Results matrix (cont.)

Year of publication	Authors	Research title	Country/ continent	Kind of setting	Age of children respondents	Methodology	Methods	Topic	Journal field of study
2016	Yasunaga et al.	Multiple Impacts of an Intergenerational Program in Japan: Evidence from the Research on Productivity through Intergenerational Sympathy Project	Japan	Single site	Children in the first to sixth grade	Quantitative	Survey questionnaire; program effect testing	Informing effects of the REPRINTS program	Geriatrics and Gerontology
2016	Lane	"Are You Going to Come and See Us Again Soon?" An Intergenerational Event between Stroke Survivors and School-Children	England	Primary school	6–7 years old	Qualitative	Field notes of observations of writing, hand-tracing and talking about pictures	Increase the citizenship experience of young children and their awareness of what it means to live with stroke	Ageing and Older Adults

(cont.)

TABLE 5.2 Results matrix (cont.)

Year of publication	Authors	Research title	Country/ continent	Kind of setting	Age of children respondents	Methodology	Methods	Topic	Journal field of study
2016	Burgman & Mulvaney	An Intergenerational Program Connecting Children and Older Adults with Emotional, Behavioral, Cognitive or Physical Challenges: Gift of Mutual Understanding	USA	Primary school	5–14 years old	Quantitative	Children's attitude toward the elderly test	Children's attitudes toward older adults	Intergenerational Relationships
2016	Babcock et al.	Development of a Children's IAT to Measure Bias against the Elderly	Germany	Primary School	8–12 years old	Quantitative	Child-Age Implicit Association Test (Child IAT)	Children's biases toward older adults	Intergenerational Relationships

(cont.)

TABLE 5.2 Results matrix (cont.)

Year of publication	Authors	Research title	Country/ continent	Kind of setting	Age of children respondents	Methodology	Methods	Topic	Journal field of study
2016	Cerruti, Shepley, & Oakland	The Effects of Spatial Enclosure on Social Interaction between Older Adults with Dementia and Young Children	USA	Shared site	2–5 years old	Mixed Methods	Video observations; photographic stimulation; quasi-experiment and semi-structured interviews; elder-child social interaction (ECSI) observation instrument	Intergenerational shared spaces	Health Environments
2017	Weckström	Steps Together: Children's Experiences of Participation in Club Activities with the Elderly	Finland	Single site	4–12 years old	Qualitative	Observations and interviews	Children's experiences of participation in club activities with the elderly	Intergenerational Relationships
2017	Whiteland	Claymation for Collective Intelligence and Intergenerational Learning in an Educational Environment	USA	Single site	8–11 years old	Qualitative, participatory	Questionnaires; interviews	Intergenerational activities	Intergenerational Relationships

(cont.)

TABLE 5.2 Results matrix (cont.)

Year of publication	Authors	Research title	Country/ continent	Kind of setting	Age of children respondents	Methodology	Methods	Topic	Journal field of study
2017	Senior & Green	Through the Ages: Developing Relationships between the Young and the Old	Australia	Primary school	10–11 years old	Quantitative	Children's Perceptions of Aging and Elderly (CPAE) test	Intergenerational activities	Intergenerational Relationships
2017	Chien & Tann	Study of a Multigenerational Learning Program in Taiwan	Taiwan	Single site	Primary school children lumped with university students (younger group)	Mixed methods	Observations and unstructured interviews with questionnaires	Awareness of MLP benefits and the feedback from participants	Educational Gerontology
2018	Bertram et al.	Generations Learning Together: Pilot Study for a Multigenerational Program	USA	Shared site	4 years old	Qualitative	Interviews	Setting up a multigenerational program	Intergenerational Relationships
2018	David et al.	Connecting the Young and the Young at Heart: An Intergenerational Music Program	Canada	Primary school	Elementary students collectively	Qualitative	Discussions post workshop	Accounts about the intergenerational music program	Intergenerational Relationships

(cont.)

TABLE 5.2 Results matrix (cont.)

Year of publication	Authors	Research title	Country/ continent	Kind of setting	Age of children respondents	Methodology	Methods	Topic	Journal field of study
2018	Belgrave & Keown	Examining Cross-Age Experiences in a Distance-Based Intergenerational Music Project: Comfort and Expectations in Collaborating with Opposite Generation through Virtual Exchanges	USA	Community centre	9–14 years old	Qualitative	Reflective journals to answer three writing prompts after viewing each "virtual" video-recorded exchange	Cross-age comfort, preconceived notions, and expectations as part of feasibility study	Medicine
2018	Agate et al.	'Roots and Wings': An Exploration of Intergenerational Play	USA	Home	7–10 years old	Qualitative, participatory	Drawings questionnaire with open-ended questions	Intergenerational play	Intergenerational Relationships
2018	Bates	Grillin' with My Grandchild©: Multigenerational Programming for Grandfathers and Grandchildren	USA	University	9–18 years old	Qualitative, participatory	Interviews Electronic memory book (videos, photographs, images)	Intergenerational activities	Intergenerational Relationships

(cont.)

TABLE 5.2 Results matrix (cont.)

Year of publication	Authors	Research title	Country/ continent	Kind of setting	Age of children respondents	Methodology	Methods	Topic	Journal field of study
2018	Hanmore-Cawley & Scharf	Intergenerational Learning: Collaborations to Develop Civic Literacy in Young Children in Irish Primary School	Ireland	Primary school	9–10 years old	Quantitative, mixed methods	Questionnaires checklists	Civic literacy and leadership in interactions	Intergenerational Relationships
2018	Babcock, MaloneBeach & Salomon	A Quantitative and Qualitative Evaluation of the Impact of an Intergenerational Program on Children's Biases Toward Older Adults	USA	Primary school	10–11 years old	Quantitative	Child-Age Implicit Association Test (Child IAT)	Children's biases toward older adults	Intergenerational Relationships
2018	Cucinelli et al.	Intergenerational Learning through a Participatory Video Game Design Workshop	Canada	Primary school	7 years old onwards	Qualitative, participatory	Workshop interviews	Video game co-designing	Nutrition Education and behavior
2018	Johnston	Linking Generations in Northern Ireland: Age Friendly School Project	UK	Primary school	8–10 years old	Qualitative	Interviews	Intergenerational activities	Intergenerational Relationships

(cont.)

TABLE 5.2 Results matrix (cont.)

Year of publication	Authors	Research title	Country/ continent	Kind of setting	Age of children respondents	Methodology	Methods	Topic	Journal field of study
2018	Santini et al.	Intergenerational Programs Involving Adolescents, Institutionalized Elderly, and Older Volunteers: Results from a Pilot Research-Action in Italy	Italy	Shared site	Adolescents (mean age: 14 years old)	Qualitative	Focus group and interviews	Insights for intergenerational programming	BioMed
2018	Pace & Gabel	Using Photovoice to Understand Barriers and Enablers to Southern Labrador Inuit Intergenerational Interaction	Canada	Community	8–24 years old	Qualitative, participatory	Photography interviews, photo exhibit	Barriers and enablers to intergenerational interaction	Intergenerational Relationships

(cont.)

TABLE 5.2   Results matrix (cont.)

Year of publication	Authors	Research title	Country/ continent	Kind of setting	Age of children respondents	Methodology	Methods	Topic	Journal field of study
2019	Mosor et al.	An Intergenerational Program Based on Psycho-Motor Activity Promotes Well-Being and Interaction between Preschool Children and Older Adults: Results of a Process and Outcome Evaluation Study in Austria	Austria	Single site	2 to 7 years old	Mixed methods	Mixed methods	Intervention – intergenerational contact through psychomotor activity	Public Health

et al., 2008; Cerruti, Shepley, & Oakland, 2016; Mosor et al., 2019) thoroughly mostly observations, although in Davis et al. (2008), they were reported to have more participatory roles with their siblings and grandparents for exploring intergenerational play even though they live distances apart from each other through the Magic Box activity. On the other hand, the 24-year olds were clustered with the younger group than the older group for the Photovoice methodology (Pace & Gavel, 2018).

The review features articles from 18 countries – Australia, Canada, China, Ethiopia, Finland, Germany, Ireland, Japan, Nigeria, Sweden, United Kingdom, Taiwan, South Africa, Jerusalem, Italy, Brazil and USA. Twenty-six of the articles were from the USA, six came from Canada, five came from Japan, three from Australia and the UK. Brazil, Ethiopia, Finland, and Germany each had two articles, and the rest of the countries were represented by one article each.

Most of the data in the reviewed articles were collected single-sites where intergenerational interactions occurred for the reports but does not have an institutionalised intergenerational program in place. Primary schools are part of this group, making up 55% of the 60 articles included in the review. This finding is congruent to the most common age-range of the child respondents. The second most common research locale were shared-sites (23%), where intergenerational interaction happens intentionally. Community and home made up 12% and 10% of the articles respectively.

7.3 *Year of Publication and Methodologies*

While there has been at least one article that includes children's voices in intergenerational interactions per year, it is noteworthy that the most significant increase in number of articles to include children's voices was observed in 2018. It also noticeable that although both quantitative and qualitative methodologies were used since 2000 until the present, 2018 also saw an increase in the use of qualitative methodologies, particularly of participatory approaches, to listen to children's voices. This also shows the increasing trend for this type of research, especially with young children.

Upon closer look on the methods used to include children's voices, it has been found that questionnaires, checklists were the most common, particularly for primary school children.

Different kinds of tests have been conducted, some of which are experimental in nature. These include the following:
- Child-Adolescent facts on Aging Quiz (CAFAQ),
- Questionnaire including Newman's Children's Views of Aging and Polizzi's Semantic Differential,
- Children's Attitudes to the Elderly Interview (CATI),

Row Labels	2000	2002	2003	2004	2005	2006	2007	2008	2009	2010	2011	2012	2013	2014	2015	2016	2017	2018	2019	Grand Total
Mixed Methods		1				2	2	1	1	1	3	1	1	1		1	1		1	17
Qualitative			1	1		2	1	2			1		1		2	1	1	5		18
Qualitative, co-design												1								1
Qualitative, participatory									1								1	4		6
Quantitative				1	1				1	1	1		1		1	4	1	1		13
Quantitative, experimental								2												2
Experimental, Quantitative											1									1
Mixed Methods, mostly quantitative	1																			1
Quantitative, mixed methods																		1		1
Grand Total	1	1	1	2	1	4	3	5	3	2	6	2	3	1	3	6	4	11	1	60

FIGURE 5.2   Year of publication and methodologies

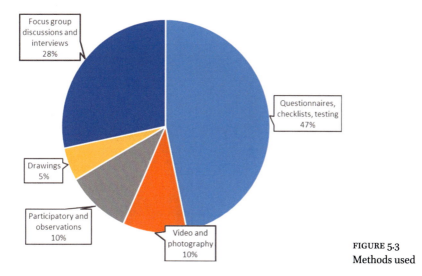

FIGURE 5.3
Methods used

- Implicit Association Test (IAT),
- Children's Perceptions of Aging and Elderly (CPAE) test,
- Child-Age Implicit Association Test (Child IAT),
- Children's Attitudes Toward the Elderly (CATE),
- Questionnaires developed by the authors themselves.

Another interesting finding of the data collected from the literature review was the field of study of the journals where they have been published. It is very noticeable that majority of the publications came from allied health medical professions and geriatric studies rather than from education and pedagogy. This finding confirms that intergenerational interactions has had a long history in the field of gerontology as discussed by Brownell and Resnick (2005) as they dissected the terminology's its etymology as against 'multigenerational.' Both terminologies are frequently used in the context of the study of old age, or the processes concerning older adults and ageing, intergenerational interactions involve discussions of understanding generational differences in an effort to bring generations together.

In the realm of social studies and pedagogy, the concept of 'generational ordering' (Alanen, 2001, 2009) may be used more frequently as regards childhood studies in relation to the older generations. The concept of generational ordering and its derivatives (generationing, generational order), is rooted in the premises of the new sociology of childhoods (Alanen, 2019). Effectively, literature that uses these terminologies and concepts, put children's voice and views in high regard, but also works with concepts of children's agency, and power relations. As such, this concept is more often than not applied in studying childhood cultures because it is seemingly focused on distinctions between

TABLE 5.3   Journal field of study

Journal field of study	
Intergenerational Relationships	36
Educational Gerontology	7
Nursing Science	2
Nutrition Education and Behavior	2
Ageing and Older Adults	1
Behaviour and Information Technology	1
BioMed	1
Curriculum Studies	1
Developmental Psychology	1
Geriatrics	1
Geriatrics and Gerontology	1
Health Environments	1
Medicine	1
Music Therapy	1
Public Health	1
Social Science and Medicine	1
Therapeutic Recreation	1
Grand total	60

childhood and adulthood – what makes the generations separate and different from each other. However, intergenerationality is a concept of the shared and of intersectionality – finding meaning in the experiences coming about from interactions of generations. It is, therefore, a conscious decision that the terminology '*intergenerational*' was chosen to frame the search of children's voices because it is in a field dominated by discourses often coming from perspectives concerning the well-being of older adults. This is an identified transitional and transformational space for childhood culture, the new relational sociology of children and phenomenology of childhoods to be analysed and make an impact to transform further research.

8   Discussion: The Way Forward

Overall, the results seem to indicate the following points and paradoxes, leading to potential spaces of transformations for children's voices to be heard in the discourse of intergenerational experiences.

8.1   On Landscapes and Places

Intergenerational experiences happen all over the world, as reflected by the different countries, contexts and settings included in this review. While there are more publications coming from one country, which is the USA, this does not discount articles coming from other countries. This is an indication of more potential countries for voices, particularly of young children, to be sought and be heard. Future research from different countries and contexts, and hence interactions in landscapes and global and local, or glocal artefacts, would add to this existing pool of knowledge. Glocal artefacts is part of the conceptualisation that though there may be globalisation discourse in place in a landscape, it does not necessarily penetrate every aspect of the local culture, traditions and views (Ødegaard, 2016).

8.2   On Making Bigger Space

There is space for young children to be heard in intergenerational experiences. Currently, the review seems to indicate that space seeking out young children's voices in the intergenerational research arena is not as substantial and popular as seeking out older children and adult voices. But there is a space, and with more research focusing on seeking out young children's voices in the intergenerational field would be a transitional and transformational move towards a bigger space for participation of children in a discourse dominated by adults.

8.3   Repercussions for Pedagogical Practices

Additionally, there is space for the intergenerational discourse within pedagogy. Seeing as intergenerational interactions are mostly discussed within the field of allied health professions, it is a space that practitioners in childhood institutions such as schools, communities and the home can participate in. It is a concept that is seemingly often taken for granted because families and homes are naturally multi-generational in nature, but intergenerational interactions would necessarily go beyond the closest institutions around children's lives, such as the school and community centres. There is a need to talk about repercussions of having intentional intergenerational interactions in pedagogical practices.

8.4   On Methodologies, and Research WITH and Not ON Them

While there are still various tests, questionnaires and checklists being developed to examine children's attitudes, biases and responses, the increase in use of qualitative participatory methodologies in 2018 seems to be an indication of a transitional and transformational space where children's voices are acknowledged not just through the more traditional methods of listening (e.g. interviews, focus group discussions), but also through emerging multi-modal approaches such as through mapping, and the use of photography and videos. The use of a multi-modal methodologies such as narrative inquiry and visual methodologies in intergenerational experiences of younger children acknowledges the many different ways the younger children and even the older adults can communicate to fully understand their lived experiences and shed light to relationships and interactions (Garvis & Pramling, 2017). Particular to listening to younger children's voices, the visual narrative methodology has been applied by a number of researchers to hear infants' and children's voices (Ridgway, Li, & Quinones, 2016; Sikder & Fleer, 2015; White, 2011; Sumsion et al., 2014). White (2015) has utilised this methodology and described it in length in her book titled Introducing Dialogic Pedagogy Provocations for the Early Years. Inspired by Bakhtinian principles to dialogism, she speaks of the importance of engaging with polyphonic videos alongside transcripts of the conversations because meaning-making and language is always concerned with the social space between people and artefacts (White, 2015). There is potential to this methodology in intergenerational experiences as it is a nod towards the direction of intergenerational research *WITH* children, and not just *ON* and *OF* them. Another possibility is for younger children and older adults to engage in co-creative activities such as collaborative narratives where older adults can build on children's interest and experiences are by engaging them in co-narrating conversations (Ødegaard & Pramling, 2013). In doing so, both are engaged in a linguistic and cultural tool for meaning making, as well as empowering children to become agents of their own learning (Ødegaard & Pramling, 2013; Garvis, Ødegaard, & Lemon, 2015). Engaging in intergenerational experiences and activities is a matter of participation – of something that they have a right to voice out and be involved in as it directly affects them (UNCRC, 1989).

Another approach to listening to young children was born as a response to the call for social researchers to use research methodologies that aid in listening to young children's voices and to understand their lived experiences and that is the Mosaic Approach (Clark & Moss, 2011). This approach is an integrated way of listening that acknowledges both children and adults as co-constructors of meaning through a combination of visual and verbal methods (Clark & Moss, 2011). It is particularly helpful for doing research with younger children because it is a framework that uses different methods in recognition of the different languages and voices of children through the use of participatory activities to highlight the children's role as experts and agents in their lives (Clark & Moss, 2011). The Mosaic Approach regards children as having an active role in research and pedagogy. Clark (2005) discusses this shift in the view of children as she discusses the conception of the Mosaic Approach through the use of child-friendly methodologies to listen to children acknowledges their role and part in the society. Such methodologies also give children a venue to voice their concerns and participate in a wider context that has been dominated by adults far too long.

8.5   On Matters That Affect Them

As also observed from the synthesis of the review, topics within the intergenerational research seeking out children's voices are varied. There are articles focused on planning out intergenerational programs, some discuss potential intergenerational activities and play. Children's perceptions, attitudes and biases against older adults were also observed to be of interest to researchers. However, some topics are results of emerging discourses in intergenerational experiences. Alongside discussions of global phenomenon that have affected and transformed lives of people, particularly of childhoods, all over the world such as industrialisation, digitalisation, migration, technology for communication emerge topics like kinship care, frequency of intergenerational contact, possible intergenerational play despite being physically distant, the need to make use of digital tools to communicate with each other. Even changes in play spaces in the neighbourhood have been explored to find out just how different physical spaces for play are throughout the years. Repercussions from this finding is the realisation that as these topics are often too complex for just one field of expertise to make light of, and hence intergenerational research would benefit from interdisciplinarity.

8.6   Space for Empirical Research

Ultimately, the data collected from this review speaks of a space for explorative and possibly transitional and transformative empirical research that would pave a bigger discourse of intergenerationality in institutions beyond the home, in different contexts, and through the use of multi-modal creative methodologies to listen to children's and older adults' voices. Doing so would also push forth UN's 2030 Sustainable Development Goals and Agenda in local and global contexts.

9   Conclusion

To conclude, this chapter has described and discussed the process and results of conducting a review of related literature done systematically focusing on children's voices in intergenerational experiences. It was deemed necessary to give this review a space in the research project because of a lack of recent systematic reviews of research particularly focused on the intergenerational experiences of younger children. In addition to this, it was important to synthesise what is currently known regarding the topic because of evidence of growing interest in this topic in different social media platforms all over the world. Results of the review speak of potential spaces of transformations in intergenerational research to make a bigger space for younger children's voices to be heard.

References

Agate, J. R., Agate, S. T., Liechty, T., & Cochran, L. J. (2018). 'Roots and wings': An exploration of intergenerational play. *Journal of Intergenerational Relationships, 16*(4), 395–421. doi:10.1080/15350770.2018.1489331

Alanen, L. (2009). Generational order. In J. Qvortrup, W. Corsaro, & M. S. Honig (Eds.), *The Palgrave handbook of childhood studies* (pp. 159–174). Palgrave Macmillan.

Alanen, L. (2014). Childhood and intergenerationality: Toward an intergenerational perspective on child well-being. In A. Ben-Arieh, F, Casas, I. Frønes, & J. Korbin (Eds.), *Handbook of child well-being: Theories, methods and policies in global perspective* (pp. 131–160). Springer.

Alanen, L. (2019). Generational order: Troubles with a 'travelling concept'. *Children's Geographies*, 1–3.

Alanen, L., & Mayall, B. (Eds.). (2001). *Conceptualizing child-adult relations*. Psychology Press.

Babcock, R. L., MaloneBeach, E. E., Hannighofer, J., & Woodworth-Hou, B. (2016). Development of a children's IAT to measure bias against the elderly. *Journal of Intergenerational Relationships, 14*(3), 167–178. doi:10.1080/15350770.2016.1195245

Babcock, R. L., MaloneBeach, E. E., & Salomon, H. M. (2018). A quantitative and qualitative evaluation of the impact of an intergenerational program on children's biases toward older adults. *Journal of Intergenerational Relationships, 16*(1–2), 123–138. doi:10.1080/15350770.2018.1404423

Babcock, R. L., MaloneBeach, E. E., & Woodworth-Hou, B. (2016). Intergenerational intervention to mitigate children's bias against the elderly. *Journal of Intergenerational Relationships, 14*(4), 274–287. doi:10.1080/15350770.2016.1229542

Baird, K. (2013). Exploring a methodology with young children: Reflections on using the mosaic and ecocultural approaches. *Australasian Journal of Early Childhood, 38*(1), 35–40.

Bates, J. S. (2018). Grillin' with my grandchild©: Multigenerational programming for grandfathers and grandchildren. *Journal of Intergenerational Relationships, 16*(3), 339–345. doi:10.1080/15350770.2018.1477437

BBC. (2018). *The toddlers who took on dementia.* Retrieved April 26, 2019, from https://www.bbc.co.uk/programmes/b0b3kk1h

Belgrave, M. J. (2011). The effect of a music therapy intergenerational program on children and older adults' intergenerational interactions, cross-age attitudes, and older adults' psychosocial well-being. *Journal of Music Therapy, 48*(4), 486–508.

Belgrave, M. J., & Keown, D. J. (2018). Examining cross-age experiences in a distance-based intergenerational music project: Comfort and expectations in collaborating with opposite generation through "virtual" exchanges. *Frontiers in Medicine, 5*, 214. https://doi.org/10.3389/fmed.2018.00214

Bertram, A. G., Burr, B. K., Sears, K., Powers, M., Atkins, L., Holmes, T., ... Kuns, J. B. (2018). Generations learning together: Pilot study for a multigenerational program. *Journal of Intergenerational Relationships, 16*(3), 243–255. doi:10.1080/15350770.2018.1477402

Blais, S., McCleary, L., Garcia, L., & Robitaille, A. (2017). Examining the benefits of intergenerational volunteering in long-term care: A review of the literature. *Journal of Intergenerational Relationships, 15*(3), 258–272.

Boström, A. (2004). Intergenerational learning in Stockholm County in Sweden. *Journal of Intergenerational Relationships, 1*(4), 7–24. doi:10.1300/j194v01n04_02

Brownell, P., & Resnick, R. P. (2005). Intergenerational-multigenerational relationships: Are they synonymous? *Journal of Intergenerational Relationships, 3*(1), 67–75.

Bulman, M., & Hoddinott, H. (2018). *'It's a lovely awakening': Elderly people and children sing and dance together in UK's first intergenerational care home.* Retrieved April 26, 2019, from https://www.independent.co.uk/news/uk/home-news/elderly-children-intergenerational-care-home-nightingale-house-a8271876.html

Burgman, C. B., & Mulvaney, E. A. (2016). An intergenerational program connecting children and older adults with emotional, behavioural, cognitive or physical challenges: Gift of mutual understanding. *Journal of Intergenerational Relationships, 14*(4), 353–359. doi:10.1080/15350770.2016.1229536

Canedo-García, A., García-Sánchez, J. N., & Pacheco-Sanz, D. I. (2017). A systematic review of the effectiveness of intergenerational programmes. *Frontiers in Psychology, 8*, 1882.

Carson, A. J., Kobayashi, K. M., & Kuehne, V. S. (2011). The Meadows school project: Case study of a unique shared site intergenerational program. *Journal of Intergenerational Relationships, 9*(4), 405–417. https://doi.org/10.1080/15350770.2011.618369

Cerruti, M., Shepley, M., & Oakland, K. (2016). The effects of spatial enclosure on social interaction between older adults with dementia and young children. *HERD: Health Environments Research & Design Journal, 9*(3), 63–81.

Channel 4. (2017). *Old people's home for 4 year olds*. Retrieved April 26, 2019, from https://www.channel4.com/programmes/old-peoples-home-for-4-year-olds?fbclid=IwAR1RrSNp_jdZ5uJJGhwpiafVhTJDoTwvvoN_vk8a1s8aPsu9MxBLjmzzZ8U

Chien, H. J., & Tann, D. B. (2017). Study of a multigenerational learning program in Taiwan. *Educational Gerontology, 43*(12), 619–629.

Chorn Dunham, C., & Casadonte, D. (2009). Children's attitudes and classroom interaction in an intergenerational education program. *Educational gerontology, 35*(5), 453–464.

Chowdhary, U., Schultz, C. M., Peter, Hasselriis, Kujath, H. A., Penn, D., Henson, S. (2000). Intergenerating activities and aging appreciation of elementary school children. *Educational Gerontology, 26*(6), 541–564.

Clandinin, D. J. (2013). *Engaging in narrative inquiry*. Routledge.

Clark, A. (2007). Views from inside the shed: Young children's perspectives of the outdoor environment. *Education, 35*(4), 3–13.

Clark, A. (2010). Young children as protagonists and the role of participatory, visual methods in engaging multiple perspectives. *American Journal of Community Psychology, 46*(1), 115–23.

Clark, A. (2019). 'Quilting' with the Mosaic approach: Smooth and striated spaces in early childhood research. *Journal of Early Childhood Education Research, 8*(2), 236–251.

Clark, A., & Moss, P. (2011). *Listening to young children: The mosaic approach*. Jessica Kingsley Publishers.

Creswell, J. W. (2014). *Research design – Qualitative, quantitative, and mixed methods approaches* (4th ed.). Sage Publications.

Cucinelli, G., Davidson, A., Romero, M., & Matheson, T. (2018). Intergenerational learning through a participatory video game design workshop. *Journal of Intergenerational Relationships, 16*(1–2), 146–165. doi:10.1080/15350770.2018.1404855

David, J., Yeung, M., Vu, J., Got, T., & Mackinnon, C. (2018). Connecting the young and the young at heart: An intergenerational music program: Program profile. *Journal of Intergenerational Relationships, 16*(3), 330–338.

Davidson, D., Luo, Z., & Fulton, B. R. (2008). Stereotyped views of older adults in children from the people's republic of China and from the United States. *Journal of Intergenerational Relationships, 5*(4), 6–24. doi:10.1300/j194v05n04_02

Davis, H., Vetere, F., Francis, P., Gibbs, M., & Howard, S. (2008). "I wish we could get together": Exploring intergenerational play across a distance via a 'magic box'. *Journal of Intergenerational Relationships, 6*(2), 191–210. doi:10.1080/15350770801955321 de Souza, E. M., & Grundy, E. (2007). Intergenerational interaction, social capital and health: Results from a randomised controlled trial in Brazil. *Social Science & Medicine, 65*(7), 1397–1409.

Einarsdóttir, J. (2014). Children's perspectives on play. In L. Brooker, M. Blaise, & S. Edwards (Eds.), *The Sage handbook of play and learning in early childhood* (pp. 319–329). Sage.

Emilson, A., & Johansson, E. (2018). Values in Nordic early childhood education: Democracy and the child's perspective. In A. Ben-Arieh, F. Casas, I. Frønes, & J. Korbin (Eds.), *International handbook of early childhood education* (pp. 929–954). Springer.

Epstein, A. S., & Boisvert, C. (2006). Let's do something together: Identifying the effective components of intergenerational programs. *Journal of Intergenerational Relationships, 4*(3), 87–109.

Falconer, M., & O'Neill, D. (2007). Out with "the old," elderly, and aged. *BMJ: British Medical Journal, 334*(7588), 316.

Gamliel, T., & Gabay, N. (2014). Knowledge exchange, social interactions, and empowerment in an intergenerational technology program at school. *Educational Gerontology, 40*(8), 597–617.

Garvis, S., Ødegaard, E. E., & Lemon, N. (2015). *Beyond observations: Narratives and young children*. Sense Publishers.

Garvis, S., & Pramling, N. (2017). *Narratives in early childhood education: Communication, sense making and lived experience*. Routledge.

Gendron, T. L., Rubin, S. E., & Peron, E. P. (2018). Making the case for transgenerational learning. *Journal of Intergenerational Relationships, 16*(1–2), 139–145.

Hall, K. W., & Batey, J. J. (2008). Children's ideas about aging before and after an intergenerational read-aloud. *Educational Gerontology, 34*(10), 862–870.

Hanmore-Cawley, M., & Scharf, T. (2018). Intergenerational learning: Collaborations to develop civic literacy in young children in Irish primary school. *Journal of Intergenerational Relationships, 16*(1–2), 104–122. doi:10.1080/15350770.2018.1404421

Hannon, P. O., & Gueldner, S. H. (2008). The impact of short-term quality intergenerational contact on children's attitudes toward older adults. *Journal of Intergenerational Relationships, 5*(4), 59–76. doi:10.1300/j194v05n04_05

Harcourt, D., & Mazzoni, V. (2012). Stand points on quality: Listening to children in Verona, Italy. *Australasian Journal of Early Childhood, 37*(2), 19–26.

Hayes, C. L. (2003). An observational study in developing an intergenerational shared site program. *Journal of Intergenerational Relationships, 1*(1), 113–132. doi:10.1300/j194v01n01_10

Hayes, N. (2002). *Children's right – Whose right? A review of child policy development in Ireland* (Studies in Public Policy, Vol. 9). The Policy Institute, Trinity College.

Hedegaard, M., & Fleer, M. (2008). *Studying children: A cultural-historical approach*. McGraw-Hill Education (UK).

Heydon, R. M. (2007). Making meaning together: Multi-modal literacy learning opportunities in an inter-generational art programme. *Journal of Curriculum Studies, 39*(1), 35–62.

Heyman, J. C., & Gutheil, I. A. (2008). "They touch our hearts": The experiences of shared site intergenerational program participants. *Journal of Intergenerational Relationships, 6*(4), 397–412. doi:10.1080/15350770802470726

Heyman, J. C., Gutheil, I. A., & White-Ryan, L. (2011). Preschool children's attitudes toward older adults: Comparison of intergenerational and traditional day care. *Journal of Intergenerational Relationships, 9*(4), 435–444. doi:10.1080/15350770.2011.618381

Hurme, H., Westerback, S., & Quadrello, T. (2010). Traditional and new forms of contact between grandparents and grandchildren. *Journal of Intergenerational Relationships, 8*(3), 264–280. doi:10.1080/15350770.2010.498739

James, A., Jenks, C., & Prout, A. (1998). *Theorising childhood*. Polity Press.

James, A., & Prout, A. (Eds.). (1997a). *Constructing and reconstructing childhood: Contemporary issues in the sociological study of childhood*. Falmer Press.

James, A., & Prout, A. (Eds.). (1997b). Re-presenting childhood: Time and transition in the study of childhood. In A. James & A. Prout (Eds.), *Constructing and reconstructing childhood, contemporary issues in the sociological study of childhood* (pp. 230–250). Falmer Press.

Jirata, T. J. (2015). Intergenerational continuity and change in conceptualization of the "child" among Guji people of Ethiopia. *Journal of Intergenerational Relationships, 13*(2), 104–117. doi:10.1080/15350770.2015.1026242

Johnston, L. (2018). Linking generations in Northern Ireland: Age-friendly school project. *Journal of Intergenerational Relationships, 16*(1–2), 184–189. doi:10.1080/15350770.2018.1404860

Kamei, T., Itoi, W., Kajii, F., Kawakami, C., Hasegawa, M., & Sugimoto, T. (2011). Six month outcomes of an innovative weekly intergenerational day program with older adults and school-aged children in a Japanese urban community. *Japan Journal of Nursing Science, 8*(1), 95–107. https://doi.org/10.1111/j.1742-7924.2010.00164.x

Kaplan, M., Kiernan, N. E., & James, L. (2006). Intergenerational family conversations and decision making about eating healthfully. *Journal of Nutrition Education and Behavior, 38*(5), 298–306.

Kinoshita, I. (2009). Charting generational differences in conceptions and opportunities for play in a Japanese neighborhood. *Journal of Intergenerational Relationships, 7*(1), 53–77. doi:10.1080/15350770802629024

Kjelstrup, K. (2019). *Hjertevarm video med livsgledebarna og de eldre*. Retrieved May 6, 2019, from https://nab.no/hjertevarm-video-med-livsgledebarna-og-de-eldre/ 19.18753

Kleinspehn-Ammerlahn, A., Riediger, M., Schmiedek, F., von Oertzen, T., Li, S. C., & Lindenberger, U. (2011). Dyadic drumming across the lifespan reveals a zone of proximal development in children. *Developmental Psychology, 47*(3), 632.

Lane, K. (2016). "Are you going to come and see us again soon?" An intergenerational event between stroke survivors and school-children. *Quality in Ageing and Older Adults, 17*(4), 246–252.

Larkin, E., Wilson, G. P., & Freer, M. (2013). Images of old: Teaching about aging through children's literature. *Journal of Intergenerational Relationships, 11*(1), 4–17. doi:10.1080/15350770.2013.755068

Liberati, A., Altman, D. G., Tetzlaff, J., Mulrow, C., Gøtzsche, P. C., Ioannidis, J. P. A., et al. (2009). The PRISMA statement for reporting systematic reviews and meta-analyses of studies that evaluate health care interventions: Explanation and elaboration. *PLoS Med, 6*(7), e1000100. https://doi.org/10.1371/journal.pmed.1000100

Low, L., Russell, F., McDonald, T., & Kauffman, A. (2015). Grandfriends, an intergenerational program for nursing-Home residents and preschoolers: A randomized trial. *Journal of Intergenerational Relationships, 13*(3), 227–240. doi:10.1080/15350770.2015.1067130

Luchesi, B. M., Dupas, G., & Pavarini, S. C. I. (2012). Evaluation of the attitudes of children living with seniors toward aging. *Revista gaucha de enfermagem, 33*(4), 33–40.

Lynott, P., & Merola, P. (2007). Improving the attitudes of 4th graders toward older people through a multidimensional intergenerational program. *Educational Gerontology, 33*(1), 63–74. https://doi.org/10.1080/03601270600864041

Macdonald, M. (2006). Intergenerational interactions occurring within a shared reading program. *Journal of Intergenerational Relationships, 3*(4), 45–61. doi:10.1300/j194v03n04_04

Malaguzzi, L. (1993). No way. The hundred is there. In C. Edwards, L. Gandini, & G. Forman (Eds.), *The hundred languages of children: The Reggio Emilia approach to early childhood education.* Ablex Publishing.

Mann, R., Khan, H. T., & Leeson, G. W. (2013). *Variations in grandchildren's perceptions of their grandfathers and grandmothers: Dynamics of age and gender. Journal of Intergenerational Relationships, 11*(4), 380–395. doi:10.1080/15350770.2013.839326

Mayall, B. (2002). *Towards a sociology for childhood: Thinking from children's lives.* Open University Press.

McNair, B. A., & Moore, K. S. (2010). The effects of intergenerational programs on individuals with Alzheimer's disease or dementia. *Annual in Therapeutic Recreation, 18,* 141–156. http://search.ebscohost.com/login.aspx?direct=true&db=c8h&AN=105237408&site=ehost-live

Middlecamp, M., & Gross, D. (2002). Intergenerational daycare and preschoolers' attitudes about aging. *Educational Gerontology, 28*(4), 271–288.

Moher, D., Liberati, A., Tetzlaff, J., & Altman, D. G. (2009). Preferred reporting items for systematic reviews and meta-analyses: The PRISMA statement. *Annals of Internal Medicine, 151*(4), 264–269.

Moher, D., Pham, B., Lawson, M. L., & Klassen, T. P. (2003). The inclusion of reports of randomised trials published in languages other than English in systematic reviews. *Health Technol Assess, 7*(41), 1–90.

Morita, K., & Kobayashi, M. (2013). Interactive programs with preschool children bring smiles and conversation to older adults: Time-sampling study. *BMC Geriatrics, 13*, 111. https://doi.org/10.1186/1471-2318-13-111

Mosor, E., Waldherr, K., Kjeken, I., Omara, M., Ritschl, V., Pinter-Theiss, V., ... Stamm, T. (2019). An intergenerational program based on psycho-motor activity promotes well-being and interaction between preschool children and older adults: Results of a process and outcome evaluation study in Austria. *BMC Public Health, 19*(1), 254.

Ødegaard, E. E. (2016). 'Glocality'in play: Efforts and dilemmas in changing the model of the teacher for the Norwegian national framework for kindergartens. *Policy Futures in Education, 14*(1), 42–59.

Ødegaard, E. E., & Pramling, N. (2013). Collaborative narrative as linguistic artifact and cultural tool for meaning-making and learning. *Cultural-Historical Psychology, 2*, 38–44.

Okoye, U. O. (2005). Young children's perception of the elderly. *Journal of Intergenerational Relationships, 3*(3), 6–24. doi:10.1300/j194v03n03_02

Orel, N. A., Dupuy, P., & Wright, J. (2004). Auxiliary caregivers. *Journal of Intergenerational Relationships, 2*(2), 67–92. doi:10.1300/j194v02n02_05

Pace, J., & Gabel, C. (2018). Using photovoice to understand barriers and enablers to Southern Labrador Inuit intergenerational interaction. *Journal of Intergenerational Relationships, 16*(4), 351–373. doi:10.1080/15350770.2018.1500506

Palaiologou, I. (2019). Going beyond participatory 3 ideology when doing research with young children. *Using Innovative Methods in Early Years Research: Beyond the Conventional, 31*.

Pascal, C., & Bertram, T. (2009). Listening to young citizens: The struggle to make real a participatory paradigm in research with young children. *European Early Childhood Education Research Journal, 17*(2), 249–262.

Radford, K., Oxlade, D., Fitzgerald, A., & Vecchio, N. (2016). Making intergenerational care a possibility in Australia: A review of the Australian legislation. *Journal of Intergenerational Relationships, 14*(2), 119–134.

Ridgway, A., Li, L., & Quinones, G. (2016). Visual narrative methodology in educational research with babies: Triadic play in babies' room. *Video Journal of Education and Pedagogy, 1*(1). https://doi.org/10.1186/s40990-016-0005-0

Roos, V. (2011). "The generational other": The cultural appropriateness of an intergenerational group reflecting technique. *Journal of Intergenerational Relationships, 9*(1), 90–97.

Saito, Y., & Yasuda, T. (2009). An empirical study of the frequency of intergenerational contacts of family members in Japan. *Journal of Intergenerational Relationships, 7*(1), 118–133. doi:10.1080/15350770802629180

Santini, S., Tombolesi, V., Baschiera, B., & Lamura, G. (2018). Intergenerational programs involving adolescents, institutionalized elderly, and older volunteers: Results from a pilot research-action in Italy. *BioMed Research International, 2018*.

Senior, E., & Green, J. (2017). Through the ages: Developing relationships between the young and the old. *Journal of Intergenerational Relationships, 15*(3), 295–305. doi:10.1080/15350770.2017.1329600

Smith, A., & Taylor, N. (2000). Introduction. In A. Smith, N. Taylor, & M. Gollop (Eds.), *Children's voices: Research, policy and practice* (pp. ix–xiii). Pearson Education New Zealand.

Sumsion, J., Bradley, B., Stratigos, T., & Elwick, S. (2014). 'Baby cam' and participatory research with infants: A case study of critical reflexivity. In *Visual methodologies and digital tools for researching with young children* (pp. 169–191). Springer.

Tafere, Y. (2015). Intergenerational relationships and the life course: Children-caregivers' relations in Ethiopia. *Journal of Intergenerational Relationships, 13*(4), 320–333. doi:10.1080/15350770.2015.1110511

The TOY Project Consortium. (2013). *Intergenerational learning involving young children and older people*. The TOY Project.

United Nations. (1989). *Convention on the rights of the child*. Retrieved March 26, 2019, from http://www.unicef.org/crc/files/Rights_overview.pdf

United Nations Committee on Economic, Social and Cultural Rights. (1995). *The economic, social and cultural rights of older persons*. UN High Commissioner for Human Rights.

Uprichard, E. (2008). Children as 'being and becomings': Children, childhood and temporality. *Children & Society, 22*(4), 303–313.

Walker, A., & Gemeinschaften, G. B. E. (1993). *Age and attitudes: Main results from a Eurobarometer survey*. Commission of the European Communities.

Weckström, E., Jääskeläinen, V., Ruokonen, I., Karlsson, L., & Ruismäki, H. (2017). Steps together: Children's experiences of participation in club activities with the elderly. *Journal of Intergenerational Relationships, 15*(3), 273–289.

White, E. J. (2011). 'Seeing' the toddler: Voices or voiceless? In E. Johansson & E. J. White (Eds.), *Educational research with our youngest* (pp. 63–85). Springer.

White, E. J. (2015). *Introducing dialogic pedagogy: Provocations for the early years*. Routledge.

Whiteland, S. (2017). Claymation for collective intelligence and intergenerational learning in an educational environment. *Journal of Intergenerational Relationships, 15*(4), 411–418. doi:10.1080/15350770.2017.1368358

Xie, B., Druin, A., Fails, J., Massey, S., Golub, E., Franckel, S., & Schneider, K. (2012). Connecting generations: Developing co-design methods for older adults and children. *Behaviour & Information Technology, 31*(4), 413–423. https://doi.org/10.1080/01449291003793793

Yasunaga, M., Murayama, Y., Takahashi, T., Ohba, H., Suzuki, H., Nonaka, K., ... Fujiwara, Y. (2016). Multiple impacts of an intergenerational program in Japan: Evidence from the research on productivity through intergenerational sympathy project. *Geriatrics & Gerontology International, 16*, 98–109. https://doi.org/10.1111/ggi.12770

CHAPTER 6

Managing Risk and Balancing Minds: Transforming the Next Generation through 'Frustration Education'

Ida Marie Lyså

Abstract

Societal transformations in China during the last decades have been accompanied by changes in the perceived challenges for children in contemporary and future Chinese society. For the urban Chinese middle class, children's experiences radically differ from prior generations, both in everyday life and in life opportunities such as education and work. Simultaneously, middle-class urban childhoods are increasingly more isolated and privatised in comparison to past generations. The family planning policies that came into force in the late 1970s, aiming to regulate the family composition of urban Han Chinese to one child per family, has played a significant role in this changing social landscape. However, there is concern that the family scenario where four grandparents and two parents place all their attention onto one child has created a generation of emotionally spoiled 'little emperors'. Based on ethnographic fieldwork in an urban Chinese kindergarten, this chapter exemplifies how this perceived challenge was dealt with, through an educational strategy called frustration education, during a kindergarten day trip to an army school. The chapter explores how the kindergarten staff used frustration education to strengthen children's emotional balance in an attempt to transform the 'little emperors' into resilient citizens. Alongside concerns about how future competitive scenarios for these children place particular expectations on academic and artistic competencies from an early age, frustration education is interpreted as a way of managing and meeting concerns of future and contemporary risk. Frustration education is thus conceived of as a practice aligned with the principle of the 'best interest' (Article 3, UNCRC) of children in contemporary urban China.

Keywords

China – childhood – kindergarten – frustration education – UNCRC

1 Introduction

It is early morning and children are arriving, dressed in army uniforms, wearing camouflage trousers, army jackets and caps with red stars. Proud parents and grandparents with cameras in hand fill the street and kindergarten yard, surrounding large drums and cymbals brought in for the occasion, waiting to send off their children on a kindergarten daytrip.

As parents and grandparents wait outside, the children walk around in their classrooms, excited about the trip. Teacher Ma is sitting next to one of the tables, putting small tomatoes in plastic bags and the children go over to her and receive one bag each. All the adults are given a water bottle and two cucumbers. Everyone apart from my interpreter and me are dressed in camouflage army uniforms, including the teachers, the principal and the nurses. The children are told to sit in their seats, their bags behind their backs, and sing an army song (lyrics: happy song flying in the air, fly to Beijing, now chairman Mao is very happy to hear it). The teacher checks off a list for attendance and offers practical information. Loud sounds come in from outside – the sound of large drums. The teacher tells the children to go pee and reminds them to fasten the buttons well on the uniform, and to not turn the brim on their caps upwards; it should be flat. Teacher Liu is sitting next to us, she says that this is part of the play curriculum for this kindergarten. It is a collective activity. She says that the police and the army are children's heroes.

The drums and cymbals are getting louder. The sound is not constant but reaches a climax every time a group of children go outside. The song the children were singing in the classroom is also coming out of the speaker. We follow the children through a sea of parents and grandparents, from the kindergarten building to the gate. The parents are smiling and taking pictures. As we approach the gate, we can feel the parents pushing behind us. The guard yells at the parents that they must wait and not push, but they keep pushing. The children enter the bus, smiling and waving to the parents and grandparents standing outside on the pavement, taking pictures and waving back as the children put their seatbelts on. (Excerpt fieldnotes,[1] May 2012)

The 11-month fieldwork in Shanghai was coming to an end, and two weeks before departure I accompanied 'big class' children in the kindergarten on a trip to an army school. It was a special day and the atmosphere in the kindergarten prior to leaving was one of celebration and excitement. This army school trip would teach me about a practice that has become increasingly popular in Chinese society the last decades called 'frustration education'.[2] This is an educational method aiming to tackle a perceived negative trend in Chinese society that had followed in the footsteps of the family planning policies in the late 1970s, namely the problem of emotionally frail or 'spoiled' children. Alongside other changes in the historical, economic, social and political landscape, particularly in Chinas urban areas, this chapter will explore this perceived problem through the lens of generational and societal transformation – emphasising both how everyday experiences of children in contemporary China are subject to different concerns than prior generations, as well as how such concerns translates into a particular form of practice, aiming to shape a stronger and more resilient future generation of Chinese citizens. Using Ulrich Beck's notion of the risk society (1992, 2000), such practices are interpreted as part of reflexive modernity in the Chinese context, through exploring how contemporary and future risks and uncertainties of individual children are perceived and dealt with.

The global aspirations of the UN Convention on the Rights of the Child to set international norms and universal standards of childhood has been contested (Kaime, 2009; Twum-Danso Imoh, 2013). China ratified the UNCRC in 1992 with a reservation made to Article 6, the right to life and development; a reservation made in connection to family planning and the Constitution of the People's Republic of China.[3] Not only has this reservation been controversial because children's rights, like human rights, are interrelated, interdependent and indivisible (Burr & Montgomery, 2003), thus of equal value and weight; some articles are furthermore emphasised as *guiding principles* of the UNCRC, Article 6 being one of these, together with Article 2 (principle of non-discrimination), Article 12 (principle of children's participation) and Article 3 (the 'best interest' principle).[4] China's reservation against Article 6 has been subject of critique from the UNCRC Committee (2013) and can in some ways be seen to compromise the core essence of the Convention, thus serving as an illustrative example of the intricacies and complexities inherent to the UNCRC as a global child rights document. The UNCRC has been said to contain a particular historical and cultural construct, namely that of a secure, carefree and happy childhood, a notion that is linked to the capitalist countries of Europe and North America (Boyden, 1997). The rights-bearing autonomous individual is seen in this concept from an emancipatory and individualistic lens (Liebel & Saadi, 2012), and includes specific norms and values regarding what can be considered a 'good' childhood. In this chapter, Article 3 and the principle of the 'best interest' of the child forms a backdrop for the discussion, as this article exemplifies potential tensions between global documents and local conceptions and convictions (Alston, 1994). Article 3 is complex because its meaning can be interpreted in very diverse ways, which may result in practices thought of as adequate and beneficial in one context but perhaps not in another. The following pages provide one example of how beliefs of the 'best interest' of children finds contextual form in an urban Chinese kindergarten.

2 Contemporary Urban Chinese 'Spoiled' Childhoods

China has gone through massive economic, political and social changes in the last few decades, which have transformed Chinese society in different ways, including the ways in which children and childhood are perceived (Jing, 2000b; Watson, 2000). For a large part of China's urban child population, changes in life conditions have been attributed to a betterment of living standard and educational facilities, but also to an increasingly private and isolated lifestyle (Naftali, 2010). Combined, such factors present life circumstances that differ greatly from prior generations, not only in terms of access to resources, entertainment and material assets, but also to life opportunities, education and work. Historical events such as the Sino-Japanese war, the Chinese civil war, and the Cultural Revolution in the 20th century saw periods of great economic difficulty, lack of resources and intense hardships for children (Yuhua, 2000). In the later parts of the 20th century, China's increased global outreach and engagement with multi-national capitalism, transitions to a market system, rapid economic growth and urbanisation, has seen immense changes in children's position in the family (Watson, 2000) and children's decisional power in families (Jing, 2000b), and such extreme differences in childhood experiences across generations is said to have created a generation gap (Yuhua, 2000). Societal changes in Chinese society have furthermore taken place within an increasingly scientifically oriented child-rearing scenario, in which parents heavily rely on and seek advice from 'objective' scientific sources such as biology, psychology, sociology and educational theories (Naftali, 2007). The role and authority of grandparents in the context of child-rearing has to some degree diminished (Ho, 1989; Zhu, 2010), although it is still common that grandparents care for grandchildren, particularly those below kindergarten age (children under three).

For the expanding middle class in urban metropoles such as Shanghai, children's daily life experiences are believed to have changed in particular ways over the last few decades, which has left a certain concern in educational and societal circles that urban Chinese children are 'spoiled little emperors' (Hsueh & Tobin, 2003; Jing, 2000a). The family planning policy, sometimes referred to as the single-child-policy, introduced in 1979, has been significant for the changing social position of children.[5] Beyond regulating the family composition to one child per urban (Han) Chinese family, these policies are said to have had an unintended consequence: The excessive amount of attention paid to one child by parents and two sets of grandparents, labeled the '4-2-1 family syndrome', has led to a generation of 'spoiled' children (Hsueh & Tobin, 2003; Jing, 2000b). Other labels used, such as the 'six-pockets syndrome' or the '4-2-1 indulgence factor' (French & Crabbe, 2010, p. 144), further underlines the perceived problems with these familial relationships. In this chapter, it is the perceived psychological consequences of emotional indulgence that is of concern, as it is considered to prevent children from coping well with (future) adversity.

There is a strong focus on enhancing children's qualifications, particularly in an academic sense but also in terms of artistic skills and competences, because it is considered important in preparing children for their competitive future lives (Naftali, 2007; Tobin, Hsueh, & Karasawa, 2009). In the kindergarten, such concerns were manifest in the emphasis on learning, as well as in the busy afternoon and weekend schedules of many children, where they engaged in extra-curricular activities to learn languages, storytelling or calligraphy, sports or other cultural activities (Lyså, 2018). Seeing that most of these single children are alone in carrying the future well-being of their families, such pressures might take on an additional strong meaning. In the kindergarten however, these pressures were not emphasised as problematic in children's everyday lives; rather, the excessive spoiling accompanying their status as single child was in focus.

3 Ethnographic Fieldwork in a Shanghainese Kindergarten

The empirical material in this chapter is from an ethnographic fieldwork in two kindergartens in Shanghai, China, during the fall of 2011 and the spring of 2012, as part of a doctoral project in interdisciplinary childhood research. I stayed close to one semester at each location, with children attending their last year in kindergarten before starting school, observing everyday routines and engaging with children and staff in their daily endeavors. I was accompanied by an interpreter three days a week, which greatly facilitated my understanding of the dialogues and practices among children and staff in the kindergartens.[6] Alongside an adjusted form of participant observation, I also conducted qualitative interviews with children and teachers towards the end of my stay in both kindergartens, with the interpreter. The doctoral project was concerned with exploring disciplinarian practices in urban Chinese kindergartens, theorised as a relational form of practice, where children and teachers in daily interaction reinforce and reproduce practices of discipline and control (Lyså, 2018). The topic of this chapter, frustration education, was a related form of educational practice, which directly spoke to the explicit concerns for children's contemporary and future well-being. In this chapter, I explore how such practices can also be understood as managing perceived future risks and concerns, relating increased individualisation in society and the increased significance of scientific authority to ways of approaching children in educational institutions such as the kindergarten (Beck, 1992).

The kindergarten represented in this chapter was an institution with many resources and a good reputation. Children and teachers could be considered of fortunate socioeconomic backgrounds, and the kindergarten was located in a relatively upscale area. There were around 30 children in the class, with equal gender representation, and two kindergarten teachers and some assistants staying with the children, often dividing the class in two groups. The kindergarten emphasised both individual children's emotional, academic and creative skills and abilities, as well as the 'collective grace' of belonging to the group, kindergarten and Chinese society. Such an emphasis reflected the contemporary societal aim of fostering individually strong and resilient children, while simultaneously stressing the significance and value of a relational sense of belonging (Lyså, 2018). Such values were manifest in everyday schedules and routines, such as morning calisthenics in the front yard, detailed lunch routines for mealtimes, or the rigorous practicing of sitting, standing and walking in straight lines. These practices were given great care and attention, providing a space for embodied knowledge and experience in values and ideals of order and control, correctness, evaluation and the public character of discipline (Lyså, 2018). This kindergarten also had a special ceremony each week, where the older children in the kindergarten, together with teachers and staff, would stand still and straight in lines and rows, respecting Chairman Mao and the flag of the People's Republic of China. Everyday routines, practices, values and concerns in the kindergarten mirror the larger societal and historical context in which it is located, a context whose transformations over the last few decades have also led to concerns for the contemporary and future well-being of China's urban child population. The following section will begin to explain how Ulrich Beck's theory of *risk society* (1992, 2000) connects with such concerns, how they can be understood as ways of managing future risk, and how they closely connect to historical change and the emergence of reflexive modernity and increased individualism in the Chinese context.

4   Chinese Individualism and Urban Risk Society

Ulrich Beck's theory of risk society is generally attributed to Western societies, but as will be demonstrated, processes of individualisation as a result of modernisation are also significant in China (Beck & Beck-Gernsheim, 2010; Hansen & Svarverud, 2010; Yan, 2010a). According to Beck, "in advanced modernity the social production of *wealth* is systematically accompanied by the social production or *risks*" (1992, p. 19, original emphasis). Through techno-economic developments and 'releasing' human beings from traditional constraints, an increasing amount of energy and time is spent into managing, controlling and dealing with risk, created by the very condition of modernity (Beck, 1992). Risk can be defined as "a systematic way of dealing with hazards and insecurities induced and introduced by modernization itself" (Beck, 1992, p. 21); or said differently, the 'unintended consequences' of the logic of control that dominates modernity (Beck, 2000, p. 215). In the case of contemporary Chinese urban childhoods and the following analysis, these 'unintended consequences' are connected to the problem of 'little emperors'.

Using a comparative perspective, Beck and Beck-Gernsheim (2010) explore variations of individualisation, stressing how the European form of individualisation is not a template, an authentic or original form that should be translated into all other contexts, but rather one amongst many varieties of such processes. Individualisation is a process parallel to modernisation, which is connected to three dimensions: economic production and reproduction, sociocultural integration and politics (Beck & Beck-Gernsheim, 2010, pp. xv–xvi). In China, processes of individualisation are not embedded in democracy, welfare state thought or human rights philosophy such as in some European contexts; the close state-individualisation connection is of a different kind (Beck & Beck-Gernsheim, 2010, p. xvii). In the Chinese context, individualism is not about emancipation, but rather about earning your rights, relating to collectivity, saving the nation and building a strong nation state (Yan, 2010b, pp. 29–31). Yan (2010a) emphasises how China's state-sponsored quest for modernity since the mid-20th century has led to the rise of the individual and processes of individualisation. According to Yan, party-state loyalty has replaced the role of family and kin to individuals, and Maoist socialism has thus (ironically) introduced a partial and collective kind of individualisation in Chinese society (2010a). Yan shows how a transformation in the individual-ancestor/family axis to an individual-state axis provided a party-state to which an individual' sense of belonging and becoming was strengthened (Yan, 2010a). In this chapter, the project of analysing and managing individual children's (contemporary, but perhaps particularly future) emotional state was at the core of practices aiming to create resilient children. Such a focus can exemplify how cultural definitions leave their imprint on risks, as risks directly or indirectly relate to contextual standards of what should be considered tolerable or intolerable in a given context (Beck, 2000); in our case, in an urban Chinese kindergarten in Shanghai.

Risks are not necessarily visible for the human eye, but rather identified by and accessed through theory and science; i.e. risk is part of a "*scientized* consciousness, even in the everyday consciousness of risks" (Beck, 1992, p. 28, original emphasis). It is the not-yet-knowing and relying on expert rationality, which is significant in risk society, as societies of knowledge and risks open up a space of uncertainty (Beck, 2000). The power of and ways of coping with risk, lies in the power of *knowledge* and thus *awareness* of the hazards; it is connected to potentiality and judgements about probabilities (Beck, 2000, p. 213). The *perception* of threat and risk determines how risk concern is manifest in thought and action (Beck, 2000, p. 213). Frustration education can be explored as one such 'scientised consciousness'; as an increased concern with children's resilience in the urban Chinese context, connected to the strengthened role of scientific perspectives in childrearing in China (Naftali, 2007).

According to Beck, the concept of risk reverses the relationship of past, present and future – rather than the past determining the present, it is the future – something yet to occur, or something that could occur were we not to change course – which is the determining factor for present action (Beck, 2000). In addition, processes of individualisation have in some sense disentangled the individual from being mainly determined by class distinctions, leading to an *individualisation of social risk* whereby social problems and inequalities that exist are explained in terms of individual traits and inadequacies and psychological dispositions (Beck, 1992, p. 100). Such matters will be exemplified below, through how frustration education engages in practices that speak directly to the analysis of individual children's emotional health and well-being.

5 Frustration in the Barracks and the Analysis of Tears

Frustration education was an educational strategy used in everyday situations and interactional processes in the kindergarten, where teachers would make a game a little more difficult or present an obstacle in children's activities, for them to learn to cope with hardship. The kindergarten leadership emphasised how this was related to changes in focus. Previously their kindergarten focused 'too much on talking' and teaching children about moral education and collective concepts. The focus now was rather to educate the children 'in context', as 'natural education'. Teachers were trained to leave space for the children, to let them do things themselves. Letting children feel free, engage in self-help, was considered a way of protection. The training in the army school was also included in such discussions and the kindergarten leadership had also made sure the experience was shaped in certain ways, such as asking for male coaches and guides, as there as mostly female teachers in the kindergarten – as well as asking that primary school children were kept in separate areas at the army school premises, to create a better context for training for the children.

Although the kindergarten had traveled to the army school several times, visiting army schools was not common practice for kindergartens in Shanghai; rather something primary school children would experience. The kindergarten made this trip for several reasons; it was part of the kindergarten play curriculum, where role play (simulation) was both valued for educational purposes as well as considered fun for the children. In addition, the experience would teach the children about responsibility and self-discipline, which was also connected to the kindergarten-school transition. The idea of *frustration education* furthermore constituted a significant part of the trip. Frustration education was about putting the child in a position where she or he faced something new and unexpected and see how he or she would cope. The trip itself was also part of this, as the children did not usually go on trips without their parents.

While at the army school, the children engaged with different military activities, such as marching or following orders for different movements, watching a small rocket launch, running and climbing a large wooden obstacle, gun practice and having lunch in the canteen. After lunch, they were subject to frustration education. Children and teachers walked together to the army barracks (where soldiers sleep), and small groups of children were placed in rooms together with an army coach. The rooms were equipped with six steel bunk beds alongside the walls, each containing thin mattresses and green-grey colored pillow and sheets, and the children sat down at the lower beds. The children were then informed that they would stay in these rooms instead of returning to their parents.[7] The children were then informed of where the toilets were, after which the doors were closed and the teachers left the hallway and gathered outside the building at the opposite side of the house. The teachers stood outside for around five minutes, after which they returned to the hallway. A lot of activity followed, with teachers opening and closing the doors of the rooms, telling children how long they would stay, asking if anyone cried, telling them to not cry, but also saying that those who cried because they missed their parents could go home, and then the teachers closed the doors again. There was a lot of commotion during this time, and several children were crying. The children were asked to be brave, be good army people, and not cry. The analysing and explaining of the children's tears was the focus for teachers in the aftermath of the frustration education.

After the frustration education in the barracks, everybody gathered in a large room to have a group song contest, organised by the army instructor. The children were sitting in lines on the floor, while the teachers were sitting on chairs behind them. *Do you regret crying*? an army instructor asked the children. *Yes, a man should be brave*, someone answered. The principal, vice principal and teacher Liu were sitting in front of us, and we proceeded to talk about the frustration education. The principal said: *The children used to say 'blood, sweat and no tears', but in context they cried*. She emphasised that if the children had cried because they were nervous, this was considered normal and good. The kindergarten staff explained how it was good for the children to cry, to have tears, because they needed the *release*. Although some children might experience challenges in their daily lives, which could help them get this 'release', this was not the case for every child. Rather, many children had a general *lack* of frustration in their life because of their life situation – being single children with four to six people (parents and grandparents) to take care of them. She further explained that there could be several reasons for why the children would *not* cry; first, mature children could treat the experience as not being real, not believing that they had to spend time there alone, and therefore did not cry. These children had a mature approach to the situation of frustration, which informed the teachers that they coped well with the challenging situation they found themselves in. Second, some children might have considered it as a task that they had to finish and accept this. This was also considered positive, as these children's approach was also mature. The third reason for why a child would not cry was because they do not know how to release their emotions, and this was considered problematic and something the teachers had to pay attention to. In such ways, the teachers would analyze the children's reactions, find out why the children would cry or not and what this could tell them about the children's psychology and emotional state. The presence or absence of tears was not the issue – rather, individual children's reactions and tears were individually assessed.

The trip to the army school had been debated and discussed by the kindergarten leadership prior to taking place. They expressed strongly that the goal was never to make children cry or play tricks on them. Rather, the experience the children gain during this trip was considered valuable for them; just like the activities the children engage in during role play in the kindergarten, the army trip would let children engage with the reality of army life. The kindergarten staff explained: *this happens in the army every day, it is real life. It is not easy for the army uncles, they miss their parents too, it is not easy for them*. Another kindergarten staff added that she had disagreed to do the dormitory activity in the beginning before realising that it was frustration education. *She continued: The army life is that way, army men must live far away from their parents, and kids will know that army life is not easy for the men. This is simulation.*[8] Simulating real life situations through role play or army activities, boys and girl in the kindergarten would get experiences they might also encounter in the 'outside' world, which would give them a stronger basis from which they could meet future life challenges and experiences. The frustration education experience was thus a psychological experience or test that would both help the teachers understand the children better, as well as provide useful life experiences for the children. A scholarly psychological explanation, simulation, was offered by kindergarten staff to explain the significance and meaning behind frustration education. Scholarly authority thus informed the practice, shaping the 'scientised consciousness' regarding child well-being for the kindergarten staff.

From the children's point of view, the army day contained both fun and exciting, as well as negative experiences. Several children talked about how it was very exciting to do the gun exercise, the army training and climbing experience, as well as watching the rocket launch. Several children talked in negative terms about the food options, expressing that the soup 'tasted like something from the river'. There was some discussion regarding who had cried or not during the frustration education, but most children did not want to talk much about that part of the day. The general feedback was however that they did not want to go back, and one explicitly said the children would be unhappy if they had to stay there.

6 Balancing (Future) Minds through Frustration Education

The urban Chinese *risk society* is manifest in practices such as 'frustration education', where success in life is connected to individual accomplishments. In the kindergarten children's well-being and emotional state were subject to concern, due to future uncertainties and beliefs that life would offer many hardships and strong competition. To combat the potential failures of individual children, their emotional state became subject for attention and analysis. In this context, childhood comes to signify and encompass other challenges and concerns than prior generations, as the unintended consequences of modernity had presented novel challenges for this generation of children.

From the 1970s and onwards, the rise of – and changing possibilities for – the individual, as well as structural changes from institutional reforms policy and the impact of the market economy, has led to an individualisation of the social structure in China (Yan, 2010a). Such changes include the opening up of the labor market, labor migration and rural-urban mobility, privatisation of housing, marketisation of education and medical care – all forcing individuals to take more responsibility for own lives, be actively engaged with market-based competition, assume more risks and be more reflexive (Yan, 2010a).

Furthermore, rights awareness and rights movements have contributed to changing the "balance in the structured relations among the individual, social groups and institutions" (Yan, 2010a, p. 501). This has increased the significance of individual choice and the workings of 'the Chinese dream', where notions of hard work and networks can help individuals be whoever they want to be, as well as engage in the individual pursuit of happiness (Yan, 2010a). Reformation of the self and search for individual identity have been celebrated and negotiated in the public space, and this has enabled the presence of a more proactive self who works towards success, but who may simultaneously still be patriotic and nationalist (Yan, 2010a).

In the kindergarten, the careful attention towards individual children's 'psychology' is illustrative of the effort made to build strong individuals. Although the assessments and analysis of the children's reactions to frustration education was in many ways meant to help children to be prepared for the future and cope with difficulties, there was also a strong emphasis on the group and the collective. This parallel focus illustrates the relational nature of individualism in context. As stressed by the kindergarten staff, frustration education does not just meet the personality needs of children, but also offers space for 'collective grace' and collective emotion. The 'single family' was mentioned by kindergarten staff as something that had to be emphasised when talking about Chinese childhoods; a group of children for which emotional ability was particularly important to develop, alongside strengthened partner relation and collective interaction. The future competition in life for these single children, which also includes their future responsibility for their families, demands action according to the kindergarten staff to safeguard *both* individual children's and families' futures. Social risk in this situation is about individual *pathology,* since successes and failures rest on and in the individual.

Frustration education has been a popular educational method in China in the 21st century, as illustrated in (translated) book titles of educational literature such as *To Give Children the Best Setback Education*[9] and *Setback Education Excellent Children Come from Adversity,*[10] *Frustration Education (Educational Method),*[11] as well as in discussions taking place on online resource portals in China.[12] The main message is that we inevitably will experience setbacks. Children who do not suffer hardship and learn how to cope with it, become like 'flowers' in a greenhouse, unable to adapt, and individuals who cannot cope with frustration are bound to be unsuccessful. According to Wang, "society is a school and setback is the best teacher" because it enables learning about striving, struggling, maturing, simultaneously fostering knowledge, wisdom and persistence, as well as optimism and happiness (2016, p. 247). More than only being considered an educational method or a sort of test, it can also be considered a way of "teaching people how to break through adversity and overcome difficulties" (Wang, 2016, p. 247). This educational method is not the same as tradition and parents' experience, but another kind of 'unconscious' education (Wang, 2016); a novel form of education aimed at the intangible, the risks associated with lack of suffering in daily life, which is not necessarily visible to the human eye, and which can create hardships in the future. This is perceived to improve people's tolerance of suffering and make them more relaxed, and is seen to be needed in schools as well as family education, but it is important that it is accompanied by proper psychological guidance (Wang, 2016). Setback or frustration education is thus emphasised as not only teaching children and individuals to become stronger, but also cultivating happiness.

There are also counter-voices to the method of setback- or frustration education, arguing that this method is harming the children of China.[13] For the kindergarten staff on the other hand, frustration education is considered a strong and positive educational method, particularly useful and valuable for the single children in urban China who are emotionally spoiled by their surrounding adults. The amount of attention children receive from parents and grandparents requires a need to emphasise more on children's emotional state, to avoid that parents 'drown their children with love' (Fung, 1999; Wu, 1995) and create 'greenhouse flowers' that are bound to fail in real life. The kindergarten staff used scholarly conclusions and understandings to engage reflexive practices that responded to future concerns; the uncertainty of the future in this way informed current practices. Frustration education therefore serves as an example of how perceptions of risks are directly related to cultural understanding and considerations of what is considered a good and proper life situation (Beck, 2000) such as having a balanced mind, where both pleasure and pressure are considered valuable in order to create fuller human beings who can cope well with challenges in life. Frustration education could thus be understood as a method for creating resilient and strong 'flowers' that can survive and thrive outside the walls of greenhouses, i.e. in Chinese society at large.

7   Conclusion

This chapter demonstrates how an urban Chinese kindergarten deals with one of the unforeseen consequences of the family planning policy and the societal transformation and socioeconomic developments among its urban population in a well-to-do neighborhood in Shanghai. While the family planning policies with one child in each family was thought to create balance in society, it has created children with 'unbalanced' and 'spoiled' minds. Using the notion of risk, I explored how the practice of frustration education was used to manage uncertainties and securing success in the future lives of individual children and consequently the nation state of China. According to the kindergarten staff, who also engaged in research activities themselves, due to better living standards and the excessive attention received by older generations, single children were emotionally spoiled or fragile, and this was something they needed to deal with and respond to. The kindergarten staff engaged with practices of frustration education with the purpose of strengthening children's emotional balance, in order to prepare the children for contemporary and future difficulties in their lives, and in such ways engage in processes of transforming the generation of 'emotionally spoiled little emperors' to resilient citizens in Chinese society.

Since its conception, the UNCRC is a result of compromise, and its global reach requires a certain openness and flexibility for the possibilities of member states to engage with and interpret the articles (Alston, 1994). The Convention already contains inherent internal tensions, for example between articles promoting caretaking or liberation, i.e. the need to protect children and the need to let children participate with their perspectives in matters concerning them (Archard, 1993). Cultural variation and interpretation furthermore add to the expanded and varied meanings that the articles contain in different contexts. As demonstrated in this chapter, frustration education is considered an adequate way to work towards safeguarding the future success of children, whose life experiences are seen to rob them of important life lessons. This form of practice is thus made with children's best interest in mind, considered a responsible action made towards the unintended consequence of the so-called one-child policy. For the kindergarten staff, the best interest of the child is to be strong individuals who can cope with challenges that will come and be better prepared for future risks. It is through experiencing hardship and frustration, and through balancing out children's emotions, that this can best be done.

Notes

1 This chapter is based on fieldwork (2011–2012) conducted for a PhD project resulting in the dissertation entitled *Duties and Privileges: an Ethnographic Study of Discipline as Relational Practice in two Urban Chinese Kindergartens* (Lyså, 2018). Chapter 11 in the dissertation particularly relates to the phenomenon of frustration education.
2 Chinese translation of frustration education is 挫折教育 (cuo zhe jiao yu). 'Setback education' is sometimes used as the 'foreign name' of this educational method.

3   United Nations Treaty Collection, Status of Treaties, Convention on the Rights of the Child. Member states overview. Status as at 6 April 2020. https://treaties.un.org/Pages/ViewDetails.aspx?src=IND&mtdsg_no=IV-11&chapter=4&clang=_en#EndDec (accessed 7 April 2020).
4   Four guiding principles of the UN Convention on the Rights of the Child https://www.unicef.org.uk/what-we-do/un-convention-child-rights/ (accessed 9 April 2020).
5   Since 2016, this policy has changed, and couples are now encouraged to have two children.
6   See Lyså (2018) for an elaboration on the complexities inherent to practices of translation in a research encounter, as well as the potential benefits and intricacies that such practices might entail.
7   See Lyså (2018) for a more detailed reconstruction of the event in the army barracks.
8   *Simulation* (mónǐ, 模拟).
9   *To Give Children the Best Setback Education* is written by Zhang Duanran (2013), Qingdao Publishing Group (Chinese edition). Information found on https://www.amazon.in/Give-Children-Best-Setback-Education/dp/7543651084 (accessed 18 October 2019).
10 *Setback education excellent children come from adversity* written by Ma Li Qin (2009), Blossom Press (Chinese edition). Information from https://www.amazon.com.mx/Setback-education-excellent-children-adversity/dp/7505421093 (accessed 18.10.2019).
11 *Frustration education* (educational method), written by Luo Ming (2009) Chaohua Publishing House published books (Chinese edition). Information found on https://baike.baidu.com/item/%E6%8C%AB%E6%8A%98%E6%95%99%E8%82%B2/3907 (accessed 18 October 2019).
12 Such as for example the web portal Sina parent-child center http://baby.sina.com.cn/cuozhe/ (accessed 18 October 2019).
13 *Setback Education. The Parenting Fad Harming China's Kids*, by Zeng Qifeng, psychoanalyst in Wuhan, China. https://www.sixthtone.com/news/1001083/setback-education-the-parenting-fad-harming-chinas-kids (accessed 18 October 2019).

References

Alston, P. (1994). The best interest principle: Towards a reconciliation of culture and human rights. In P. Alston (Ed.), *The best interest of the child: Reconciling culture and human rights* (pp. 1–25). Oxford University Press.

Archard, D. (1993). Liberation or caretaking? In D. Archard (Ed.), *Children: Rights and childhood* (pp. 64–79). Routledge.

Beck, U. (1992). *Risk society. Towards a new modernity*. Sage.

Beck, U. (2000). Risk society revisited: Theory politics and research programmes In B. Adam, U. Beck, & J. Van Loon (Eds.), *The risk society and beyond. Critical issues for social theory* (pp. 211–229). Sage Publications.

Beck, U., & Beck-Gernsheim, E. (2010). Foreword: Varieties of individualization. In M. H. Hansen & R. Svarverud (Eds.), *iChina: The rise of the individual in modern Chinese society* (pp. xiii–xx). NIAS Press.

Boyden, J. (1997). Childhood and the policymakers: A contemporary perspective on the globalization of childhood. In A. James & A. Prout (Eds.), *Constructing and reconstructing childhood: Contemporary issues in the sociological study of childhood* (pp. 184–210). Falmer Press.

Burr, R., & Montgomery, H. (2003). Children and rights. In M. Woodhead & H. Montgomery (Eds.), *Understanding childhood. An interdisciplinary approach* (pp. 135–169). The Open University.

Concluding observations on the combined third and fourth periodic reports of China, adopted by the Committee at its sixty-fourth session (16 September–4 October 2013). (2013).

Convention on the Rights of the Child, 20 November 1989. (1989). https://www.refworld.org/docid/3ae6b38f0.html

French, P., & Crabbe, M. (2010). *Fat China. How expanding waistlines are changing a nation*. Anthem Press.

Fung, H. (1999). Becoming a moral child: The socialization of shame among young Chinese children. *ETHOS, 27*(2), 180–209.

Hansen, M. H., & Svarverud, R. (2010). *iChina: The rise of the individual in modern Chinese society* (Vol. 45). Marston Book Services.

Ho, D. Y. F. (1989). Continuity and variation in Chinese patterns of socialization. *Journal of Marriage and the Family, 51*(1), 149–163.

Hsueh, Y., & Tobin, J. (2003). Chinese early childhood educators' perspectives. On dealing with a crying child. *Journal of Early Childhood Research, 1*(1), 73.

Jing, J. (2000a). *Feeding China's little emperors. Food, children, and social change*. Stanford University Press.

Jing, J. (2000b). Introduction: Food, children, and social change in contemporary China. In J. Jing (Ed.), *Feeding China's little emperors. Food, children, and social change* (pp. 1–26). Stanford University Press.

Kaime, T. (2009). The foundations of rights in the African Charter on the rights and welfare of the child. A historical and philosophical account. *African Journal of Legal Studies, 3*(1), 120–136.

Liebel, M., & Saadi, I. (2012). Cultural variations in constructions of children's participation. In M. Liebel (Ed.), *Children's rights from below* (pp. 162–182). Palgrave Macmillan UK.

Lyså, I. M. (2018). *Duties and privileges: An ethnographic study of discipline as relational practice in two urban Chinese kindergartens* (PhD dissertation). Norwegian University of Science and Technology, Trondheim.

Naftali, O. (2007). *Reforming the child: Childhood, citizenship, and subjectivity in contemporary China* (Doctoral dissertation). University of California, Santa Barbara.

Naftali, O. (2010). Caged golden canaries: Childhood, privacy and subjectivity in contemporary urban China. *Childhood, 17*(3), 297–311.

Tobin, J. J., Hsueh, Y., & Karasawa, M. (2009). *Preschool in three cultures revisited: China, Japan and the United States.* University of Chicago Press.

Twum-Danso Imoh, A. (2013). Children's perceptions of physical punishment in Ghana and the implications for children's rights. *Childhood, 20*(4), 472–486.

Wang, D. (2016). *The missing and return of current setback education.* Paper presented at the 3rd International Conference on Education, Lanugage, Art and Inter-Cultural Communication (ICELAIC 2016).

Watson, J. L. (2000). Food as a lens: The past, present and future of family life in China. In J. Jing (Ed.), *Feeding China's little emperors. Food, children, and social change* (pp. 199–212). Stanford University Press.

Wu, D. Y. H. (1995). Drowning your child with love: Family education in six Chinese communities (The 8th Barbara Ward Memorial Lecture). *The Hong Kong Anthropologist, 8,* 2–12.

Yan, Y. (2010a). The Chinese path to individualization. *The British Journal of Sociology, 61*(3), 489–512.

Yan, Y. (2010b). Introduction: Conflicting images of the individual and contested process of individualization. In M. H. Hansen & R. Svarverud (Eds.), *iChina: The rise of the individual in modern Chinese society* (pp. 1–38). NIAS Press.

Yuhua, G. (2000). Family relations: The generation gap at the table. In J. Jing (Ed.), *Feeding China's little emperors. Food, children, and social change* (pp. 94–113). Stanford University Press.

Zhu, J. (2010). Mothering expectant mothers: Consumption, production, and two motherhoods in contemporary China. *ETHOS, 38*(4), 406–412.

CHAPTER 7

Children's Food Choices during Kindergarten Meals

Hege Wergedahl, Eldbjørg Fossgard, Eli Kristin Aadland and Asle Holthe

Abstract

The aim of the present study was to examine children's food choices during lunch in a small case study, and how the food choices contributed to children's dietary intake.

The case study was carried out at two kindergartens in Norway. Data was collected through individual interviewing of principals, focus-group interviewing of staff, observations of the lunchtime meal and individual registration of 40 children's dietary intake during lunch.

The two kindergartens offered lunch predominantly as a cold meal involving open sandwiches and various types of toppings, vegetables and milk or water. The principal and the staff decided which food to put on the table, and children's food choices were limited by the availability and accessibility of the food items available during mealtimes. The children helped themselves during lunch or expressed their food choices in various ways. The freedom of the children to choose the food they wanted, kindergarten staff's mild influence on children's food choices and stricter regulation of children's food intake were all observed in the two kindergartens. Half of the children in the study experimented with various combinations of sandwich toppings on the bread, some of which could be considered part of a typical Norwegian diet, but others not. Children's freedom to choose their own food and their experimentation with food items could all be seen as steps toward a transformation of children into independent food consumers, and as respect for children's views in line with article 12 in the United Nations Convention on the Rights of the Child.

Keywords

food consumers – freedom to choose – food choice – children's diet – transformation

1 Introduction

Most children aged 1–5 in Norway spend much of their time in kindergarten, viz. in 2020 92% of children attend kindergarten – most of them full-time (Statistics Norway, 2020). It is common for children to eat open sandwiches for lunch at kindergartens in Norway. According to the national survey of food and meals in Norwegian kindergartens from 2012 (Norwegian Directorate of Health, 2012), most kindergartens served wholemeal bread, vegetable margarine and sandwich toppings such as liver pâté, fish, cheese and meat cuts. Sweet sandwich toppings such as jam were less common. The national survey reported that the food offered in kindergartens was generally of a good nutritional quality (Norwegian Directorate of Health, 2012), though there were some challenges, one of the most important of which was the low number of kindergartens serving vegetables daily. Correspondingly, results from national dietary surveys of children aged 1, 2 and 4 showed that their diets were mostly consistent with the dietary guidelines (Kristiansen, Andersen, & Lande, 2009; Øverby, Kristiansen, Andersen, & Lande, 2009). However, challenges were also reported, the most prominent ones being a low intake of vegetables and vitamin D and a high intake of saturated fat. Correspondingly, similar dietary challenges have been reported for older children, and for these children a low intake of fish and a high intake of added sugar were also reported (Hansen, Myhre, Johansen, Paulsen, & Andersen, 2015).

Food consumed in kindergarten constitutes a substantial part of the children's daily food intake, as they usually eat three meals daily there (breakfast, lunch and afternoon meal), five days a week. Evidence from longitudinal studies has suggested that eating behaviors established in childhood are likely to persist into adulthood (Craigie, Lake, Kelly, Adamson, & Mathers, 2011; Mikkilä, Räsänen, Raitakari, Pietinen, & Viikari, 2004), and this makes kindergartens important settings for children's diets and meal practices. According to socio-ecological models (Sallis, Owen, & Fisher, 2008), the physical and social environment we live in influences our health-related behavior. In kindergarten social factors could, for instance, be the staff's knowledge, attitude and behaviors, and physical factors could, for instance, be the food served for lunch.

The kindergarten staff may influence children's food choices and food consumption during meals by using various feeding styles (Gubbels, Gerards, & Kremers, 2015; Gubbels et al., 2010; Ward, Belanger, Donovan, & Carrier, 2015; Ward et al., 2017). These feeding styles include authoritarian, authoritative and permissive behaviors. Hughes et al. (2007) describe the authoritative feeding style as staff having adequate control over children's eating through reasoning and involvement. An authoritarian feeding style, on the other hand, was characterised by extensive external control with high use of restrictive behavior and power-assertive directives. Lastly, a permissive feeding style was described, in which little or no structure was provided. Nicklas et al. (2001), Ward et al. (2017) and Dev, McBride, Speirs, Donovan and Cho (2014) used similar descriptions of various feeding styles in studies of childcare providers' influence on children's food consumption at kindergartens.

The food environment at the kindergarten defines what food is available and accessible to the children. Availability is related to the physical presence of food, for instance the food served in the kindergarten. Accessibility, on the other hand, is defined as food being available in a form and location that facilitate their consumption (Story, Kaphingst, Robinson-O'Brien, & Glanz, 2008). Availability and accessibility of food are associated with children's dietary behavior (Pearson, Biddle, & Gorely, 2009; Rasmussen et al., 2006). There is an interplay between the various levels of factors affecting an individual's dietary behavior (Kremers et al., 2006). The physical factors may be influenced by individual factors, e.g. food preferences and social factors, for instance the feeding styles mentioned above. The aim of this study was to examine children's food choices during lunch in a small case study of two kindergartens, and how the food choices contributed to children's dietary intake. The study will provide new insight into how children's food intake is affected by a combination of physical and social regulations within the kindergarten and of children's own opinions and expressions of food choices. Respect for children's views and opinions in matters affecting them, and in accordance with his or her age and maturity, is stated in United Nations Convention on the Right of the Child, article 12 (United Nations, 1989).

2   Methods

2.1   *Study Design*

The study used a case design with an exploratory approach (Yin, 2003) in two kindergartens with departments for the youngest children (ages 1–2) and for older children (ages 3–5) that offered lunch every day, mainly as cold lunchtime meals based on open sandwiches. The study was conducted in accordance with the Helsinki Declaration, and the protocol was approved by the Norwegian Centre for Research Data. Prior to commencement of the study, kindergarten staff and parents were informed of the study in writing. Written informed consent was obtained from parents of the participating children, and oral consent was given by the kindergarten staff during the interviews.

2.2 Case Description

The two kindergartens were located in a municipality in Western Norway and were run by the municipality. Kindergarten A consisted of two departments, one of the departments having 10 children aged 1–2 and three employees, the other department having 14 children aged 3–5 and four employees. Kindergarten B consisted of two departments with 10–15 children aged 1–2 and three to four employees per department, and two departments with 15–20 children aged 3–5 and three employees per department. Lunch was offered in both kindergartens. During lunch the children were placed at 2–3 tables in each department, and the food and beverages were presented on the tables.

2.3 Dietary and Meal Registration

Dietary registration and observation of the meal in each kindergarten were conducted in one department with children aged 1–2 and in another department with children aged 3–5. Individual food and beverage intake were registered during lunch. Dietary intake was registered for a total of 40 children, and during three visits to each of the kindergartens within a period of seven months. The goal was to register the dietary intake of each child three times, but because of illness and other absences some children were registered once or twice. A total of 93 individual dietary registrations were performed (Table 7.1).

TABLE 7.1 Informants and number of participating children at the two kindergartens

	Kindergarten A	Kindergarten B
	Occupation, department (Interview code)	
Interviews		
Focus-group interviews	Assistant, ages 3–5 (A2)	Pedagogical leader, ages 3–5 (B2)
	Assistant, ages 1–2 (A3)	Pedagogical leader, ages 1–2 (B3)
	Student, ages 3–5 (A4)	Assistant, ages 1-2 (B4)
Individual interviews	Principal (A1)	Assistant principal (B1)
	Number of children	
Participating children	19	21
Dietary registrations		
Registration No. 1	13	18
Registration No. 2	14	19
Registration No. 3	13	15

Food and beverage intake was recorded continuously for each child on a semi-structured dietary registration form. The number and type of different food items served at each department were recorded immediately prior to the start of the dietary registration. The weight of slices of bread, vegetables and sandwich toppings as well as the volume of drinking glasses were recorded in order to improve the accuracy of the dietary registration. One child ate food brought from home at one of the three dietary registration days, and this registration was omitted from further analyses. The staff's interactions with the children were noted throughout the meal. Pilot testing of the observation form was conducted before data collection, and some changes were made based on the pilot test.

2.4 Interviews

One individual interview of the principle and one focus-group interview of three employees were performed in each kindergarten (Table 7.1). Semi-structured interview guides were used for both types of interview, with questions related to the lunch and the food served during lunch. Pilot testing of the interview guides was performed prior to data collection, resulting in a few changes to the interview guides.

2.5 Data Analysis

The interviews were transcribed by the authors. The data was analysed using case-oriented analysis (Miles & Huberman, 1994). Analysis of the qualitative data comprised data reduction, preparation and comparison of the kindergartens or kindergarten departments. Dietary intake was analysed using the diet tool *Kostholdsplanleggeren* (Dietary Planner) (Norwegian Food Safety Authority), and calculated using Microsoft Office Excel 2010 and SPSS Statistics, Version 24 (SPSS-Inc.). Triangulation was performed by comparing data from interviews, observations and dietary registration when appropriate.

2.6 Strengths and Limitations

The present study has strengths and weaknesses that need consideration when interpreting the data. The small sample of kindergartens was a limitation of the study. Strengths of the study were the combination of dietary registrations, observations and interviews, and the fact that different informants participated in the interviews. The study could be further strengthened by interviewing children. The findings cannot be generalised, but the study contributes knowledge on the social and physical influences on children's food choices during lunch at kindergarten.

3 Results

3.1 Decisions on What Food to Put on the Table

As regards *who* decided which type of food to offer in the kindergarten, there was consensus in the two kindergartens amongst the staff (principal, pedagogical staff and assistants). However, during the interviews it was obvious that the children also had some influence: "We have also asked the children what they like" (B1). The staff also pointed out that they observed what the children were fond of and took that into consideration when deciding which food to serve.

As regards *why* they offered the specific food items at lunch, perceptions of healthiness seemed to be of importance to the staff in both kindergartens. However, daily routines and the staff's own preferences and opinions also seemed to affect the types of food served at lunch.

> What determines things is our own daily routine and our own perception of what is healthy to eat. And we think it is important that there are vegetables, i.e. tomato, sweet pepper, cucumber, although they may not always eat it. My opinion of what one should eat affects my choices. I would not have chosen white bread; I think that is more like candy. (A2)

In Kindergarten B the staff for children aged 1–2 expressed that the most important consideration was that the children should eat.

> In our department, with small children, it is very important that they get enough food. Many of them are small and flimsy and need a lot of fat. We want the children to get the nutrients their body needs. (B3)

Furthermore, the staff at both kindergartens seemed to think that it was important for the children to have a variety of food items to choose from during lunch, as well as variations in their food intake. "A variety of sandwich toppings, within reasonable limits. Meat, cheese, a regular lunch table" (B2).

3.2 Children's Expression of Food Choices

Observations in both kindergartens revealed that the meal started by sending the basket of bread around the table so the children could help themselves. The staff asked the children several times during the meals to send the basket of bread or plates of sandwich toppings around the table for them to help themselves. During lunch the children prepared the open sandwiches by themselves. The staff at both kindergartens expressed during the interviews that the children would get help if they needed to, but that the children first tried to manage by themselves. The youngest children were also allowed to try to manage by themselves, or the staff asked them what they wanted to eat: We then ask "Do you want any cheese?" to be absolutely sure they will get what they want on the slice of bread (B3). We observed that the staff asked the youngest children several times during the meals what type of sandwich topping they wanted on the slice of bread, whether they wanted more food or more to drink, and whether they had finished eating.

The youngest kindergarten children expressed their food preferences in various ways. According to the staff at both kindergartens, understanding what the youngest children wanted to eat was not a problem. The staff explained that the children expressed themselves by pointing at the food or nodding/shaking their head. Crying could also be a sign of a small child not getting his or her needs satisfied. Pointing, nodding, gesticulation, yes/no answers, noises and crying were also noted during observation of the meals as part of the youngest children's expressions of food preferences. In these situations we observed that the staff asked the children if they had understood correctly, whereupon they responded. For instance, in Kindergarten B one of the youngest girls pointed at the tube of mackerel in tomato sauce and responded by nodding when one of the staff asked if she wanted mackerel on the slice of bread.

3.3 The Staff's Influence on Children's Food Choices

The interviews indicate that the staff wanted to influence the children's food choices during the meals by encouragement.

> They are allowed to choose, of course, but we often ask: don't you want to try that? You cannot know if you like it or not if you haven't tried it, you know. But we do not force anyone to eat sausage if they tell us all the time that they want cheese. We just don't do that. Because we do not think that is our task. But we can encourage, and we do that. (A2)

The staff also tried to influence the youngest children's food choices by asking if they wanted certain food items: "Then you ask them, just as you do with the older children, but you point and ask: don't you want that on (the bread)?" (A3).

Observations were in line with results from the interviews. For instance, during an observation in one of the departments for children aged 1–2 one of the staff helped the children put sandwich toppings on the bread slices, and continually asked if they wanted mayonnaise. Luring was also used as a strategy to encourage the youngest children to eat the food. For example, adding extra mayonnaise to the last part of the slice of bread to encourage the child to finish the meal, or comments like "eat the bread – it will give you strong teeth" when the child preferred to eat only the sandwich topping. The staff also encouraged some of the children to try sandwich toppings on the slice of bread other than the ones they usually ate, or to take a bite of the bread before they started to drink milk. There did not seem to be any consistency about commenting on a child for eating or not eating all the food on the plate, as we observed both practices during our observations in the two kindergartens.

Although the staff expressed that they encouraged the children to try different food items and that they wanted the children to be independent, they also wanted to regulate the intake of some food items. Several times during the observations we noticed that the staff commented when a child added too much sandwich topping on a slice of bread. One example was observed in Kindergarten A, when one of the staff told a child "Enough!" when he put too much cream cheese on the slice of bread. The child also wanted egg slices on top of the cream cheese and was allowed to add the egg. When the child wanted even more egg on the bread, the staff told him "I think it is enough because there is no more room on top of the slice of bread." This form of regulation was also expressed during the interviews:

> We encourage the children to be as independent as possible. There may be too much butter or too little butter (on the slice of bread), they are allowed to have a little control. But of course, we limit it, we don't let them add butter as thick as the bread slice. (B2)

Some children turned to the staff for help on decisions regarding the amount of sandwich topping to put on the slices of bread after the staff had commented on it, as exemplified by a short conversation in Kindergarten B: Now you have far too much margarine on the slice of bread (staff). How much should I remove? (child). Almost everything (staff). Like this? (child). Yes, now it is fine (staff).

More strict regulation of the food choices was observed during the meals in the departments of 1- to 2-year-olds. Examples are one child who wanted crispbread instead of the slice of bread, but was told that she first had to eat the slice of bread, or comments like "You must eat the slice of bread before you get milk." Furthermore, comments like "Take one more slice of bread" and "Eat your food" occurred several times during the observations.

3.4 *Presence of Food Items and Children's Food Choices*

The two kindergartens offered differing numbers of food items for lunch, and at Kindergarten A the number of different food items was almost twice that at

Kindergarten B (Table 7.2). The difference in availability of food items at the two kindergartens resulted in a difference in the number of food items chosen by the children, as shown in Table 7.3.

TABLE 7.2   Types of food item registered at lunch during four observations at each kindergarten

	Kindergarten A								Kindergarten B							
	Ages 3–5				Ages 1–2				Ages 3–5				Ages 1–2			
	Registration No.								Registration No.							
	1	2	3	4	1	2	3	4	1	2	3	4	1	2	3	4
Bread																
Bread, coarse flour	x	x	x	x	x	x	x	x	x	x	x	x	x	x	x	x
Crisp bread, wholemeal flour[a]	x	x	x	x	x	x	x	x								
Spread																
Margarine	x	x	x	x	x	x	x	x	x	x	x	x	x	x	x	x
Mayonnaise	x	x	x	x	x											
Meat-based sandwich fillings																
Cured mutton sausage	x	x	x	x	x				x	x		x				
Salami sausage	x	x		x	x					x				x		x
Bologna sausage									x	x	x	x	x			
Ham (turkey or pork)[a]	x		x	x	x		x									
Liver pâté (pork or chicken)[a]	x	x		x		x		x	x	x	x	x	x	x	x	x
Sausage	x															
Dairy-based sandwich fillings																
Cheese, hard	x	x	x	x	x	x	x	x	x	x	x	x				x
Whey cheese, hard[a]	x	x	x	x	x		x	x	x	x	x	x	x	x	x	x
Whey cheese, spread	x	x	x	x	x		x	x								
Cheese spread[a]	x	x	x	x	x		x		x	x		x	x	x	x	x
Seafood-based sandwich fillings																
Mackerel fillets in tomato sauce	x	x	x	x	x		x	x	x	x	x	x	x	x	x	x
Cod-roe spread	x	x	x	x	x	x		x	x	x	x	x	x	x	x	x
Eggs	x	x		x	x	x	x									

(cont.)

TABLE 7.2   Types of food item registered at lunch during four observations at each kindergarten (*cont.*)

	Kindergarten A								Kindergarten B							
	Ages 3–5				Ages 1–2				Ages 3–5				Ages 1–2			
	Registration No.								Registration No.							
	1	2	3	4	1	2	3	4	1	2	3	4	1	2	3	4
Jam	x	x	x	x	x											
Vegetables																
Tomato		x	x	x		x	x	x	x	x		x				
Cucumber	x	x	x	x	x	x	x	x	x			x				
Sweet pepper	x	x	x	x	x	x		x		x						
Carrot	x	x	x	x	x	x		x								
Broccoli	x	x		x	x											
Beverage																
Milk, semi-skimmed	x	x	x	x	x	x	x	x	x	x	x	x	x	x	x	x
Water	x	x	x	x	x		x		x	x	x		x	x	x	
Total	23	22	19	23	22	11	11	17	14	15	10	13	10	10	9	10

a 1–2 different types of food items

TABLE 7.3   Number of food items eaten and availability of various food items for each individual child at lunchtime at the two kindergartens

	Kindergarten A (n = 19)	Kindergarten B (n = 21)	
Food items during lunch	Mean ± SD[a]	Mean ± SD	p-value[b]
Eaten	6.7 ± 1.8	5.5 ± 1.2	0.017
Available	21 ± 3.7	12 ± 1.4	0.001

a The mean and the SD were calculated from the average of up to three lunches for each individual child.
b Independent t-test.

Sandwich toppings served during lunch on all observation days were chosen by a higher percentage of children at the two kindergartens than were toppings served on only one or two of the observation days (Figure 7.1A). Sandwich

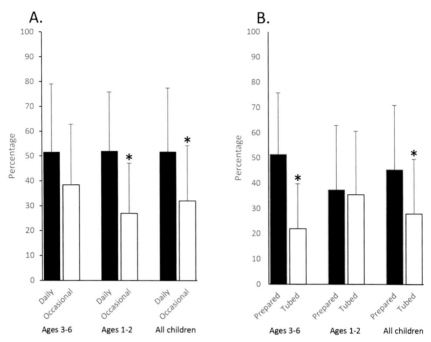

FIGURE 7.1 Effect of availability and accessibility on food-item intake. The data is shown as mean ± standard deviation of the percentage of children who chose the food items

toppings that were prepared in one way or another were chosen more often than those in a tube (Figure 7.1B).

The prepared food items could be slices of various types of meat and hard cheese on plates, whey-cheese spread, jam and margarine in small bowls and slices of various types of vegetable on plates. Unprepared sandwich fillings could be mayonnaise, various types of cheese spread and cod-roe spread, all from tubes, and mackerel fillets in tomato sauce from a tin or a tube. The proportion of children who chose prepared food items was different to the proportion who chose unprepared food items amongst 3- to 5-year-olds, but not amongst 1- to 2-year-olds (Figure 7.1B).

Fifty percent of the children experimented with combinations of various sandwich toppings on the slice of bread on one or more of the observation days. The combination of sandwich toppings was more common in children aged 3–5 than in children aged 1–2 (Table 7.4).

Furthermore, experimentation with various combinations of sandwich toppings on the slices of bread was more common at Kindergarten A than at

TABLE 7.4 Combination of toppings and spreads on the slices of bread for different age groups at the two kindergartens

	Kindergarten A		Kindergarten B	
Age group	Combinations (n)	Children (n)	Combinations (n)	Children (n)
Ages 3–5	10	12	6	13
Ages 1–2	4	7	0	8

Note: The data shows the number of children combining toppings and spreads on one or more of the observation days at the two kindergartens.

TABLE 7.5 Combination of toppings and spreads on the slices of bread at the two kindergartens

	White cheese (hard)	Whey cheese (hard, spread)	Meat (cured mutton sausage, ham, salami)
Jam	4	1	5
Fish spread	3	4	3
White cheese		2	3
Whey cheese	2		8
Meat	3	8	
Egg	3	1	3
Mayonnaise		4	1

Note: The data shows the number of combination of toppings and spreads chosen by the children during three observations at each of the two kindergartens.

Kindergarten B. The various combinations of sandwich toppings are shown in Table 7.5.

For instance, jam is normally added to cheese in Norway, but not to meat toppings. For children in the present study it was just as normal to combine jam with meat as to combine it with cheese. Furthermore, it is considered normal to combine meat with white cheese but not with whey cheese. The children in the present study, however, combined meat with whey cheese more often than with white cheese. Norwegians also normally combine egg or mayonnaise with meat, but not with cheese. For the children in the present study it was more common to combine egg or mayonnaise with cheese than with meat. The children also combined fish spread with cheese or meat, although these combinations are not considered part of a typical Norwegian diet. In addition, vegetables were included on top of the sandwiches by some of the children, but this data was not included in the analysis of combinations of sandwich toppings.

3.5 Dietary Challenges: Vegetables, Fish and Jam

Kindergarten A served 3–5 different types of vegetable at each of the registered lunchtime meals (cucumber, sweet pepper, tomato, carrot, broccoli), whilst Kindergarten B served two vegetables at two of the three registered lunchtime meals at Kindergarten B (tomato, cucumber or sweet pepper), and only for children in the age group 3–5 (Table 7.2). Table 7.6 shows the average dietary intake of various sandwich fillings, including vegetables. The average daily vegetable intake was 16.6 g for children that had access to vegetables for lunch, and 28.5 g for children that consumed vegetables.

TABLE 7.6 Dietary intake of various sandwich fillings from the lunch at two kindergartens

	Intake in children who ate the sandwich fillings (g)	Intake in all children offered the sandwich fillings (g)
Meat-based sandwich fillings	15.5 ± 13.5	9.9 ± 12.6
Dairy-based sandwich fillings	14.7 ± 8.7	10.1 ± 10.0
Seafood-based sandwich fillings	15.5 ± 10.1	5.5 ± 9.5
Jam	10.8 ± 3.5	3.9 ± 5.7
Vegetables	28.2 ± 47.6	16.6 ± 38.9

Note: Data is shown as mean ± standard deviation in 40 children for up to three dietary registrations for each child.

The availability of various vegetables was higher at Kindergarten A than at Kindergarten B. The children seemed to have similar preferences as regards types of vegetable in the two kindergartens (Figure 7.2). Carrot, cucumber and sweet pepper were preferred to tomato and broccoli at Kindergarten A, and cucumber and sweet pepper were preferred to tomato at Kindergarten B.

In Norway, cod-roe spread and mackerel fillets in tomato sauce are common as sandwich toppings. The children in Kindergarten A and Kindergarten B had access to both cod-roe spread and mackerel fillets in tomato sauce for lunch on

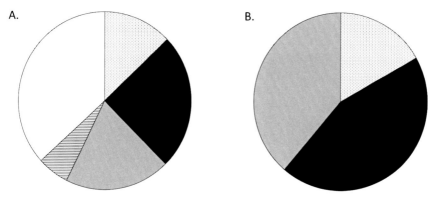

FIGURE 7.2 Distribution of vegetable intake when offered at Kindergarten A (A) and Kindergarten B (B)

all observation days, with one exception: children aged 1–2 in Kindergarten A had access to one or two of the fish products. Children consumed more dairy- and meat-based sandwich fillings than fish products at lunch (Table 7.6).

In Kindergarten A children aged 3–5 had access to jam on all observation days (Table 7.2). Six of the 12 children aged 3–5 ate jam on all or most of the observation days, corresponding to 10.8 g jam per day (Table 7.6), whilst the other children in that age group did not eat any jam at all. Children aged 1–2 had access to jam on one of the observation days, but none of the children ate jam during that observation day. Kindergarten B did not offer jam for lunch on any of the observation days.

3.6 *Nutrient Intake and Nutritional Challenges*

As shown in Table 7.7, lunch contributed to 24% of the daily energy requirement for children aged 2–5. A large part of the energy intake was through fat, especially saturated fat and polyunsaturated fat. When the intake of fat is presented as an energy percentage of the meal (E%), the data shows that a large amount (42E%) of the energy intake was in the form of fat, and that the intake of saturated fat was high during lunch (16E%). Although the average intake of sugar during lunch was low (Table 7.7), some of the children ate jam on all observation days, thereby contributing to an elevated intake of added sugar for these children.

The average intake of vitamins and minerals was generally at least 24% of the daily recommendations (data not shown). The dietary intake of vitamin D and of sodium during lunch is shown in Table 7.7. Vitamin D intake was only 11% of the daily requirement. The dietary intake of sodium, however, was high, and the children in our study consumed an average of 42% of their daily recommended intake of sodium at lunch alone (Table 7.7).

TABLE 7.7   Intake of nutrients during lunch at two kindergartens

	Amount	Percentage of daily need (%)	E% in the meal
Energy, KJ	1283 ± 506	24 ± 10	
Protein, g	11.5 ± 4.2	29 ± 11	16 ± 3
Fat, g	15.0 ± 7.0	30 ± 14	42 ± 7
– saturated fat, g	5.5 ± 2.6	36 ± 17	16 ± 3
– monounsaturated fat, g	3.9 ± 1.7	20 ± 9	11 ± 1
– polyunsaturated fat, g	4.2 ± 2.6	37 ± 22	12 ± 5
Carbohydrate, g	29.5 ± 11.7	18 ± 7	42 ± 6
– added sugar, g	1.1 ± 1.3	3.7 ± 4.3	2 ± 5
Dietary fiber, g	4.0 ± 1.8	25 ± 11	
Sodium, mg	545 ± 263	42 ± 20	
Vitamin D, µg	0.79 ± 0.56	11 ± 7	

Note: Data is shown as mean ± standard deviation in 40 children. The mean of up to three dietary registrations for each child was used in the calculations. The percentage of the daily requirement was calculated in accordance with the recommended daily nutrient requirement of children aged 2–5 (Norwegian Directorate of Health, 2014).

4   Discussion

In the present study we aimed to examine children's food choices during lunch in a small case study of two kindergartens, was well as how the food choices contributed to children's dietary intake. We found that the children expressed their food choices and had varying degrees of freedom to make their own food choices and experiences during lunch. However, the availability or accessibility of the food items at kindergarten limited these choices. Differences were found at the two kindergartens regarding the variability of food items served during lunch, including vegetables. Children's food choices were therefore based on a framework set by the adult staff at the kindergartens.

Our results showed that the pedagogical staff and the principals decided together what food to put on the table. Although these decisions were influenced by the children's requests, other aspects were more influential, e.g. the healthiness of the food offered, the routines at the kindergarten and the staff's personal preferences. In addition to deciding what type of food was to be offered at the kindergarten, thereby affecting children's food choices at a physical level, the staff also influenced children's food choices at a social level.

This was seen to different degrees, and the results can be seen in connection with the emerging literature on different feeding styles (authoritative, authoritarian and permissive). The staff's influence on children's food choices generally appeared to be in line with an authoritative feeding style, i.e. a feeding style whereby the staff have adequate control of children's eating through reasoning and involvement (Hughes et al., 2007). For instance, the staff in the departments for children aged 3–5 allowed the children to serve themselves, and helped them if necessary. Giving the children freedom to decide which sandwich topping to choose and letting them prepare the sandwiches by themselves was pointed out by one of the staff at Kindergarten B as a way of making the children more independent.

The staff frequently used encouragement in an attempt to influence children's food choices, and they sometimes guided the children on how much sandwich topping to put on the slice of bread. The authoritative feeding style was observed amongst the staff in the departments for the youngest children, for instance when the children were asked about what they wanted on the slice of bread and were encouraged to eat/try something new, and so on. However, more strict influences on the children's food choices were also observed, e.g. when the staff told the children to eat one type of food before they could get another type – which could be interpreted more as an authoritarian feeding style (Hughes et al., 2007).

The staff did not comment when the children experimented with several layers of toppings on the slices of bread. Children being allowed to experiment with different combinations of sandwich toppings on the slices of bread without any regulations could be seen as a permissive feeding style, i.e. a feeding style without any structure, whereby the children can eat whatever they want (Hughes et al., 2007). However, this experimentation with combinations of sandwich toppings could be part of children's exploration of taste and texture and could also be interpreted as growth of the child's autonomy. This experimentation was more common amongst children aged 3–5 than amongst children aged 1–2, which could partially be explained by the more regulated feeding style observed by the staff of the departments for the youngest children.

Some of the combinations of sandwich toppings were considered normal in a Norwegian diet. However, for the children in our study it was just as normal to try combinations not considered part of a typical Norwegian diet, and children and adults may have different views on what are considered proper food choices (Karrebæk, 2012). Although the data on combinations of sandwich toppings on the slices of bread only involved 20 children, it shows a tendency of the children to be creative and combine sandwich toppings irrespective of whether or not they form part of a typical Norwegian diet. Andersen and Holm

(2013) argue that it is important for the staff to show children confidence and respect their way of doing things, even though it is different from the way an adult would do it. Whether or not children's decisions and experimentation with various food items are in line with national recommendations for food and meals at kindergartens (Norwegian Directorate of Health, 2018) is dependent on the availability and accessibility of healthy food for lunch.

The availability of food at kindergarten is an important physical factor that may affect children's food choices during lunch. Our study revealed that the two kindergartens displayed different variabilities of food items available during lunch, and there was also a difference between the departments for the youngest and the oldest children within the same kindergarten. The differences in food variety affected children's food choices, as a higher number of different food items available during lunch resulted in consumption of a higher number of different food items. It is recommended that the food served at kindergartens be in accordance with national recommendations on food and meals at kindergarten (Norwegian Directorate of Health, 2018), i.e. the food should be healthy and in line with the national food guidelines (Norwegian Directorate of Health, 2014). Children who are offered a variety of healthy foods from early childhood onward appear to have healthier diets throughout childhood (Cooke, 2007). Thus, both the healthiness and the variability of the food offered in kindergartens contribute to formation of the child's future food choices. The lower variability for various food items for 1- to 2-year-olds than that for 3- to 5year-olds found in our study should be taken into consideration. Exposure to a variety of food items early in life could help prevent reluctance to try new foods (food neophobia) – something that emerges at around two years of age and is associated with lower dietary quality and variety (Helland, Bere, Bjornara, & Overby, 2017).

The frequency of the various food items offered during lunch is also of importance. Our study showed that sandwich toppings served during lunch on all observation days were chosen by a higher percentage of children than toppings served on only one or two of the observation days. These results seem to be in line with Cooke (2007), who argues that the most important determinant of a child's liking for a particular food seems to be the extent to which it is familiar. That is, children prefer the food that is familiar to them. It is reasonable to suggest that the children in our study were familiar with the food items served daily. However, caution should be exercised in interpreting the data, as we do not know whether the results were caused by the familiarity of the sandwich toppings or whether the kindergarten served some sandwich toppings less often because they experienced that they were less popular amongst the children.

Not only availability but also accessibility may affect children's food choices. In our study the accessibility of the various sandwich toppings seemed to be a factor in food choices amongst the older children, aged 3–5, but not amongst the younger children, aged 1–2. Tubed sandwich toppings may appear less accessible to children serving themselves than toppings prepared on plates. However, the lack of differences between the more easily accessible food items and the tubed/canned food items in the departments for children aged 1–2 may be due to the staff helping these children during lunch.

Our study showed that the two kindergartens and the different departments within the same kindergarten displayed differing frequencies of and variation in vegetables served for lunch. The frequency of and variation in serving vegetables is important for vegetable intake, and two recent review articles showed that repeated exposure to vegetables increased children's vegetable consumption (Hodder et al., 2018; Holley, Farrow, & Haycraft, 2017). Advocating daily serving of a variety of vegetables at kindergarten is in line with studies showing that vegetable consumption in childhood is associated with lower rates of non-communicable diseases in adulthood (Maynard, Gunnell, Emmett, Frankel, & Smith, 2003; Ness et al., 2005). However, in our study the amount of vegetables consumed in relation to the total amount of food ingested during lunch did not seem to be affected by the variability of vegetables offered, but the sample of our study was small. Our results are in contrast to recent studies showing that an intervention at kindergartens, focusing on availability and accessibility of vegetables, encouragement and role modelling, was successful in increasing children's consumption of vegetables (Kristiansen et al., 2019). The vegetable intake in our study, were, however, higher than has been reported in a Dutch study serving lunch based on open sandwiches (Gubbels et al., 2015).

A few nutrients will be highlighted in the following discussion. National surveys in Norway have reported that the intake of saturated fat is higher than that recommended for both adults (Totland et al., 2012) and children of various ages (Hansen, Myhre, & Andersen, 2016; Hansen et al., 2015; Kristiansen et al., 2009; Øverby et al., 2009). Also, in our study the relative amount of saturated fat in the food was high. When comparing the nutrient intake to the percentage daily requirement, or calculating it as E% in the meal, it is obvious that the lunchtime meal in our study contributed to a high quantity of saturated fat. Our findings were also higher than has been reported in other European studies (Gubbels et al., 2010; Gubbels, Raaijmakers, Gerards, & Kremers, 2014; Sepp, Lennernas, Pettersson, & Abrahamsson, 2001). There is scope to reduce the intake of saturated fat at the kindergartens in our study. One strategy could be to reduce the availability of meat with a high content of saturated fat, e.g. cured mutton sausage, salami sausage and bologna sausage, and to replace it with less saturated fat-containing alternatives. Ham of chicken, turkey or pork contains much lower amounts of fat, but this sandwich topping was only served in one of the kindergartens. Cured mutton sausage and salami sausage also contain high amounts of sodium. Our data showed that sodium intake was high during lunch, and contributed to over 40% of the maximum recommended daily sodium intake (Norwegian Directorate of Health, 2014). This constitutes an additional reason to find alternatives to these meat-based sandwich toppings. High sodium intake by children has also been found in other European studies (Huybrechts & De Henauw, 2007; Korkalo et al., 2019; Moreira et al., 2015). However, cod-roe spread is also a source of sodium that contributes substantially to the sodium intake in our study. Cod-roe spread is one of the common fish products served at Norwegian kindergartens along with mackerel fillets in tomato, in line with the results of our study. The kindergarten staff are thus torn between the dietary recommendation that fish and seafood intake be increased and the recommendation that sodium intake be reduced (Norwegian Directorate of Health, 2014). It is questionable whether kindergarten staff have the requisite nutritional expertise to juggle these recommendations, as there has been scant emphasis on food, meals and nutrition in kindergarten teacher education (Norwegian Ministry of Education and Research, 2006, 2012) and the framework plan for kindergartens in Norway (Norwegian Ministry of Education and Research, 2006). Serving additional types of fish product suitable for a sandwich-based lunch, e.g. fish burgers, with a high fish content and a low sodium content could be a strategy to increase the consumption of fish at kindergartens.

Adequate vitamin D intake has been a challenge for the Norwegian population – both children (Hansen et al., 2015, 2016; Kristiansen et al., 2009) and adults (Totland et al., 2012). Vitamin D intake was also low in our study when the data was analysed as a percentage of the daily requirement, and much lower than what was reported in a Finnish study in which hot lunches were served (Korkalo et al., 2019). A simple change that kindergartens could make is replacement of semi-skimmed milk with semi-skimmed milk containing vitamin D.

Although the average intake of added sugar is within the recommended maximum intake for children aged 1, 2 and 4, and is less than in earlier surveys (Hansen et al., 2016; Kristiansen et al., 2009; Øverby et al., 2009), the intake is still higher than that recommended for older children (Hansen et al., 2015) in Norway. It is therefore important to continue to try and limit the intake of added sugar in early childhood. Our study showed that if jam was offered during lunch, as was the case on all observation days in one of the departments of

Kindergarten A, half of the children aged 3–5 chose to eat jam. A strategy could be to avoid offering jam at kindergarten, as was the case at Kindergarten B.

5 Conclusion

This study was conducted as a case study at two kindergartens in Norway, with the aim of examining children's food choices during lunch, as well as how these food choices contributed to children's dietary intake. The findings demonstrate that differences in the variability of food items served during lunch resulted in differences in children's food choices and thus their dietary intake. We recommend daily serving of a variety of sandwich toppings for all children at kindergarten, with a special emphasis on vegetables and various fish products. An effort should be made to ensure that the youngest children, aged 1–2, also get a wide variety of food items for lunch. We observed varying degrees of freedom for children to make their own food choices and experiences during lunch, mostly in line with an authoritative feeding style. Feeding styles whereby children could make their own decisions, be encouraged to expand their food repertoire and be allowed to experiment with several layers of sandwich toppings may potentially empower the children and contribute toward transforming them into independent food consumers. It is also in line with United Nations Convention on the Rights of the Child, article 12, regarding children's rights to express their views.

Acknowledgement

We are grateful to the staff and the children who participated in the study.

References

Andersen, S. S., & Holm, L. (2013). *Maddannelse, madmod og madglæde. Hvilken betydning har daginstitutioners madkultur og måltidspædagogik?* [*Food bildung, food courage and food enjoyment. What is the significance of kindergarten food culture and meal pedagogy?*]. Retrieved April 16, 2020, from https://raadetforsundmad.dk/wp-content/uploads/2020/01/06-01-2013-maddannelsesrapport.pdf

Cooke, L. (2007). The importance of exposure for healthy eating in childhood: A review. *Journal of Human Nutrition and Dietetics, 20*(4), 294–301. doi:10.1111/j.1365-277X.2007.00804.x

Craigie, A. M., Lake, A. A., Kelly, S. A., Adamson, A. J., & Mathers, J. C. (2011). Tracking of obesity-related behaviours from childhood to adulthood: A systematic review. *Maturitas, 70*(3), 266–284. doi:10.1016/j.maturitas.2011.08.005

Dev, D. A., McBride, B. A., Speirs, K. E., Donovan, S. M., & Cho, H. K. (2014). Predictors of head start and child-care providers' healthful and controlling feeding practices with children aged 2 to 5 years. *Journal of the Academy of Nutrition and Dietetics, 114*(9), 1396–1403. doi:10.1016/j.jand.2014.01.006

Gubbels, J. S., Gerards, S. M., & Kremers, S. P. (2015). Use of food practices by childcare staff and the association with dietary intake of children at childcare. *Nutrients, 7*(4), 2161–2175. doi:10.3390/nu7042161

Gubbels, J. S., Kremers, S. P., Stafleu, A., Dagnelie, P. C., de Vries, N. K., & Thijs, C. (2010). Child-care environment and dietary intake of 2- and 3-year-old children. *Journal of the Academy of Nutrition and Dietetics, 23*(1), 97–101. doi:10.1111/j.1365-277X.2009.01022.x

Gubbels, J. S., Raaijmakers, L. G., Gerards, S. M., & Kremers, S. P. (2014). Dietary intake by Dutch 1- to 3-year-old children at childcare and at home. *Nutrients, 6*(1), 304–318. doi:10.3390/nu6010304

Hansen, L. B., Myhre, J. B., & Andersen, L. F. (2016). *UNGKOST 3. Landsomfattende kostholdsundersøkelse blant 4-åringer i Norge, 2016* [*UNGKOST 3. National dietary survey among 4 year olds in Norway, 2016*]. Retrieved October 15, 2019, from https://fhi.no/globalassets/dokumenterfiler/rapporter/2016/rapport-ungkost-3-landsomfattende-kostholdsundersokelse-blant-4-aringer-i-norge-2016.pdf

Hansen, L. B., Myhre, J. B., Johansen, A. M. W., Paulsen, M. M., & Andersen, L. F. (2015). *UNGKOST 3. Landsomfattende kostholdsundersøkelse blant elever i 4. og 8. klasse i Norge, 2015* [*UNGKOST 3. National dietary survey amound pupils in 4. and 8. grade in Norway, 2015*]. Retrieved October 15, 2019, from https://www.fhi.no/globalassets/dokumenterfiler/rapporter/2016/ungkost-rapport-24.06.16.pdf

Helland, S. H., Bere, E., Bjornara, H. B., & Overby, N. C. (2017). Food neophobia and its association with intake of fish and other selected foods in a Norwegian sample of toddlers: A cross-sectional study. *Appetite, 114*, 110–117. doi:10.1016/j.appet.2017.03.025

Hodder, R. K., O'Brien, K. M., Stacey, F. G., Wyse, R. J., Clinton-McHarg, T., Tzelepis, F., ... Wolfenden, L. (2018). Interventions for increasing fruit and vegetable consumption in children aged five years and under. *Cochrane Database Systematic Review, 5*, CD008552. doi:10.1002/14651858.CD008552.pub5

Holley, C. E., Farrow, C., & Haycraft, E. (2017). A systematic review of methods for increasing vegetable consumption in early childhood. *Current Nutrition Reports, 6*(2), 157–170. doi:10.1007/s13668-017-0202-1

Hughes, S. O., Patrick, H., Power, T. G., Fisher, J. O., Anderson, C. B., & Nicklas, T. A. (2007). The impact of child care providers' feeding on children's food consumption. *Journal of Developmental and Behavioral Pediatrics, 28*(2), 100–107. doi:10.1097/01.DBP.0000267561.34199.a9

Huybrechts, I., & De Henauw, S. (2007). Energy and nutrient intakes by pre-school children in Flanders-Belgium. *British Journal of Nutrition, 98*(3), 600–610. doi:10.1017/S000711450773458X

Karrebæk, M. S. (2012). "What's in your lunch box today?" Health, respectability, and ethnicity in the primary classroom. *Journal of Linguistic Anthropology, 22*(1), 1–22.

Korkalo, L., Nissinen, K., Skaffari, E., Vepsalainen, H., Lehto, R., Kaukonen, R., ... Erkkola, M. (2019). The contribution of preschool meals to the diet of Finnish preschoolers. *Nutrients, 11*(7). doi:10.3390/nu11071531

Kremers, S. P., de Bruijn, G. J., Visscher, T. L., van Mechelen, W., de Vries, N. K., & Brug, J. (2006). Environmental influences on energy balance-related behaviors: A dual-process view. *International Journal of Behavioral Nutrition and Physical Activity, 3,* 9. doi:10.1186/1479-5868-3-9

Kristiansen, A. L., Andersen, L. F., & Lande, B. (2009). *Småbarnskost 2 år. Landsomfattende kostholdsundersøkelse blant 2 år gamle barn* [Småbarnskost 2 year. National dietary survey among 2 year old children]. Norwegian Directorate of Health.

Kristiansen, A. L., Bjelland, M., Himberg-Sundet, A., Lien, N., Holst, R., & Andersen, L. F. (2019). Effects of a cluster randomized controlled kindergarten-based intervention trial on vegetable consumption among Norwegian 3–5-year-olds: The BRA-study. *BMC Public Health, 19*(1). doi:10.1186/s12889-019-7436-3

Maynard, M., Gunnell, D., Emmett, P., Frankel, S., & Smith, G. D. (2003). Fruit, vegetables, and antioxidants in childhood and risk of adult cancer: The Boyd Orr cohort. *Journal of Epidemiology and Community Health, 57*(3), 218–225. doi:10.1136/jech.57.3.218

Mikkilä, V., Räsänen, L., Raitakari, O. T., Pietinen, P., & Viikari, J. (2004). Longitudinal changes in diet from childhood into adulthood with respect to risk of cardiovascular diseases: The cardiovascular risk in young finns study. *European Journal of Clinical Nutrition, 58*(7), 1038–1045. doi:10.1038/sj.ejcn.1601929

Miles, M. B., & Huberman, A. M. (1994). *Qualitative data analysis: An expanded sourcebook.* Sage.

Moreira, T., Severo, M., Oliveira, A., Ramos, E., Rodrigues, S., & Lopes, C. (2015). Eating out of home and dietary adequacy in preschool children. *British Journal of Nutrition, 114*(2), 297–305. doi:10.1017/S0007114515001713

Ness, A. R., Maynard, M., Frankel, S., Davey Smith, G., Frobisher, C., Leary, S. D., ... Gunnell, D. (2005). Diet in childhood and adult cardiovascular and all cause mortality: The Boyd Orr cohort. *Heart, 91*(7), 894–898. doi:10.1136/hrt.2004.043489

Nicklas, T. A., Baranowski, T., Baranowski, J. C., Cullen, K., Rittenberry, L., & Olvera, N. (2001). Family and child-care provider influences on preschool children's fruit, juice, and vegetable consumption. *Nutrition Reviews, 59*(7), 224–235. doi:10.1111/j.1753-4887.2001.tb07014.x

Norwegian Directorate of Health. (2012). *Måltider, fysisk aktivitet og miljørettet helsevern i barnehagen. En undersøkelse blant styrere og pedagogiske ledere* [*Meals, physical activity and environmental health care in kindergarten. A survey among heads of kindergartens and pedagogical leaders*] (IS-0345). Norwegian Directorate of Health.

Norwegian Directorate of Health. (2014). *Anbefalinger om kosthold, ernæring og fysisk aktivitet* [*Norwegian guidelines on diet, nutrition and physical activity*] (IS-2170). Norwegian Directorate of Health.

Norwegian Directorate of Health. (2018). *Nasjonal faglig retningslinje for mat og måltider i barnehagen* [*National guideline for food and meals in kindergarten*] (IS-2783). Norwegian Directorate of Health.

Norwegian Food Safety Authority. *Kostholdsplanleggeren*. Retrieved October 15, 2019, from https://www.kostholdsplanleggeren.no/

Norwegian Ministry of Education and Research. (2006). *Rammeplan for barnehagens innhold og oppgaver* [*Framework plan for the content and task of kindergartens*]. Norwegian Ministry of Education and Research.

Norwegian Ministry of Education and Research. (2012). *Nasjonale retningslinjer for barnehagelærerutdanning* [*National guidelines for kindergarten techer education*]. Norwegian Ministry of Education and Research.

Øverby, N. C., Kristiansen, A. L., Andersen, L. F., & Lande, B. (2009). *Spedkost 12 måneder. Landsomfattende kostholdsundersøkelse blant 12 måneder gamle barn* [*Spedkost 12 months. National dietary survey among 12 month old children*] (IS-1635). Norwegian Directorate of Health.

Pearson, N., Biddle, S. J., & Gorely, T. (2009). Family correlates of fruit and vegetable consumption in children and adolescents: A systematic review. *Public Health Nutrition, 12*(2), 267–283. doi:10.1017/S1368980008002589

Rasmussen, M., Krolner, R., Klepp, K. I., Lytle, L., Brug, J., Bere, E., & Due, P. (2006). Determinants of fruit and vegetable consumption among children and adolescents: A review of the literature. Part I: Quantitative studies. *International Journal of Behavioral Nutrition and Physical Activity, 3*, 22. doi:10.1186/1479-5868-3-22

Sallis, J. F., Owen, N., & Fisher, E. B. (2008). Ecological models of health behavior. In K. Glanz, B. K. Rimer, & K. Viswanath (Eds.), *Health behavior and health education: Theory, research and practice* (pp. 465–482). Jossey-Bass.

Sepp, H., Lennernas, M., Pettersson, R., & Abrahamsson, L. (2001). Children's nutrient intake at preschool and at home. *Acta Paediatrica, 90*(5), 483–491. https://doi.org/10.1111/j.1651-2227.2001.tb00786.x

SPSS-Inc. SPSS Statistics (Version 19). IBM.

Statistics Norway. (2020). *Barnehager* [*Kindergartens*]. Retrieved April 16, from https://www.ssb.no/utdanning/statistikker/barnehager

Story, M., Kaphingst, K. M., Robinson-O'Brien, R., & Glanz, K. (2008). Creating healthy food and eating environments: Policy and environmental approaches. *Annual Review of Public Health, 29*, 253–272. doi:10.1146/annurev.publhealth.29.020907.090926

Totland, T. H., Melnæs, B. K., Lundberg-Hallén, N., Helland-Kigen, K. M., Lund-Blix, N. A., Myhre, J. B., ... Andersen, L. F. (2012). *Norkost 3. En landsomfattende kostholdsundersøkelse blant menn og kvinner i Norge i alderen 18–70 år, 2010–11* [*Norkost 3. A national dietary survey among men and women in Norway at age 18–70 year, 2010–11*] (IS-2000). Norwegian Directorate of Health.

United Nations (1989). *The Convention on the Rights of the Child.* Retrieved April 16, 2020, from https://www.ohchr.org/Documents/ProfessionalInterest/crc.pdf

Ward, S., Belanger, M., Donovan, D., & Carrier, N. (2015). Systematic review of the relationship between childcare educators' practices and preschoolers' physical activity and eating behaviours. *Obesity Review, 16*(12), 1055–1070. doi:10.1111/obr.12315

Ward, S., Belanger, M., Donovan, D., Vatanparast, H., Muhajarine, N., Engler-Stringer, R., ... Carrier, N. (2017). Association between childcare educators' practices and preschoolers' physical activity and dietary intake: A cross-sectional analysis. *BMJ Open, 7*(5), e013657. doi:10.1136/bmjopen-2016-013657

Yin, R. K. (2003). *Case study research: Design and methods.* Sage.

CHAPTER 8

Children, Food and Digital Media: Questions, Challenges and Methodologies

Karen Klitgaard Povlsen, Stinne Gunder Strøm Krogager, Jonatan Leer and Susanne Højlund Pedersen

Abstract

To research digital media use is not a simple project. Contrary to 'traditional' audience studies it is difficult even for well-educated grown-ups to describe their actual uses of digital media, for instance what they do, when they 'just google' (Povlsen, 2016). It might be even more difficult for children to explain to others what they do on their ipads or smart phones and why and how they select and trust the results they do. Not least in relation to everyday routines and practices such as food. But if we want to take UNCRC's children's right to express themselves in all matters seriously, it is also important to understand their media practices – not least related to everyday matters such as food.

From the 1930s studies on children's media uses have been dominated by didactical concerns and by fear of new media, often termed as 'media panics' (Drotner et al.). The concerns from this tradition have been radicalized in the digital revolution. Much research has focused on 'vulnerable' audiences that have to be protected. In contrast, audience studies from the 1970s and onwards focus on the negotiations among active audiences. This contrast is also radicalized by digital media, because they are everywhere. An important question therefore is, what methods are suitable? How can we experiment to overcome the special challenges with personal uses of individual digital devices such as smart phones and ipads? The chapter will discuss the pros and cons of different methods for different ages and contexts, giving examples of our Danish research.

Keywords

home economics – cross-disciplinary – collaborative research design – UNCRC article 12 – children's agency

© KAREN KLITGAARD POVLSEN, STINNE GUNDER STRØM KROGAGER, JONATAN LEER AND SUSANNE HØJLUND PEDERSEN, 2021 | DOI: 10.1163/9789004445666_008
This is an open access chapter distributed under the terms of the CC BY 4.0 License.

1   Introduction

This chapter will present the methodological reflections on an emergent iterative research design in a series of interventions in Danish schools in the 6th and 7th grade home economic classes. The research group is cross-disciplinary with two scholars of media studies, one scholar of anthropology, and one of cultural and gender studies. The aim is to present our process towards a collaborative research design, inviting children to participate as co-designers, co-workers, co-producers of data, and creative producers of a first analysis of their experiences in 3-minute YouTube videos. In the project, we position ourselves as researchers in the paradigm of new childhood studies based on ethnographic participative observations of children's competences and agency from the 1990s (James & Prout, 2015), a tradition that has been strong in the Nordic countries after the 1990s (Solberg, 2015). It is also a position that often – as we do here – has focused on the intersections between formal learning in institutions and schools and informal activities in the home with media entertainment and media productions (Drotner, 1995; Povlsen, 1999). The digital media offer new possibilities of inviting children to express their views freely as the article 12 of the UNCHR proposes. Here we experiment with diverse possibilities of communication in an everyday context such as the home economy class. The data produced by the children might give researchers new insights in the explicit and implicit views and experiences, but the digital media productions also pose new challenges.

The book has traditionally been accepted as a media, fitted for learning, but digital and entertaining media might be prohibited or only given limited access in some schools. This media perspective might be especially relevant in the Nordic countries where digital media and curriculum are implemented to a higher degree than in other parts of the world (Eurostat, 2017), but it is also a general challenge for research in matters that involve practices that exist in school and leisure. The schooling systems in the five Nordic countries differ and they differ from the systems in many other parts of the world, but a common trait in the Nordic countries is still a high degree of democracy, participation and problem-based learning. Choosing three different schools in regard to pedagogics, media tolerance and home economics teaching, we will reflect and discuss the most important methodological – as well as empirical – challenges in an iterative, interventional and explorative research design process.

Following the tradition for researching the intersections between formal and informal learning in school and leisure, we wanted to explore the explicit and implicit competences and literacies from routines in children's everyday life, not least in relation to food and media (Potter & Goldsmith, 2017; Shade et al., 2015) and the relations between the two fields. This is too big a field to explore, so an intrinsic question is, how to establish a real-life 'research laboratory' that gives us the possibility to collaborate among four researchers and make a research design together with children in well-known and habitual circumstances. In this chapter, we will focus especially on how we were inspired by iterative research design processes that invite users of software to participate creatively in the design processes until a soft- or hardware can be designed and produced. Our 'production', however, is not a model or the development of a fixed research design; it is the iterative research design process itself.

2   Background and Purpose

The interventions were created as a result of our common interest in taste and cooking. All four of us take part in an externally funded research project: Taste for Life (Nordea Foundation, 2014–2018). The big collaborative project (app. 50 participants) focuses on taste education and competencies among children and young people in schools, on festivals and special events etc. (www.smagforlivet.dk). The field of taste and cooking practices therefore was our common point of departure and an obligatory theme for our interventions. We wanted to explore if and how this field of practice may interact with the field of media practices. Both fields are parts of the everyday lives of most children and young people. Food and cooking are a basic human field of experience and practice. Access to media such as books, newspapers, magazines etc. has for hundreds of years been part of children's school and leisure life. Today, access to digital media allows children and young people to search for information or to entertain them. Digital media also allows them from an early age to take an active cultural role as producers and distributors on social network media platforms such as Facebook, Snapchat, Instagram, Twitter and in this case YouTube. Digital media – and food – are accessible everywhere if a digital device is accessible. Both are also publicly debated, and many homes and schools have strict rules for sugar and unhealthy food as they have for smart phones and tablets. Both fields are relevant to all spheres of daily life and both fields are contested in relation to corporeal and mental health, to obesity and stress and depression. Both fields are the subjects of teaching activities and both are fields, where all children might be able to contribute. Which is exactly why we found the possible patterns of relations between the two fields important to explore as an example of how we can investigate the complex relations between practice fields by inviting people – in this case – children – to create and collaborate with us in practices that are limited in time and space.

## 3	Practice Theory across Two Fields

In media sociology, the methodological tradition and the research design considered 'best practise' is a pre-planned methodological design (e.g. Schrøder et al., 2003, Schrøder, 2003), inspired by classical sociology (Bryman, 2016). Contrary to this, cultural and visual anthropology has developed traditions of participant or non-participant observations, field studies etc., where the researcher constantly adapts her or his methods to situations and people (Mills, Durepos, & Wiebe, 2010). In recent years, the argument has been made that we need to apply a broader practice-oriented perspective if we wish to understand the role that media play in people's everyday lives (Couldry, 2004; Coudry & Hepp, 2013). Digital media that give access to many traditional media are used seamlessly interwoven with the daily routines and rituals and practices such as for instance cooking. In a medialized society, it makes sense to adapt fluid methodologies from anthropology into media sociology or audience studies and study media-use as part of the wide range of other everyday practices it is normally seamlessly embedded into:

> Mediatization is extended into everyday life, at work, at home, and in between. We are still listeners, readers and viewers as we continue to select our individual set of audiences from a more differentiated set of service providers, among them old media, but we are also able to be senders, writers, printers, and producers as part of daily communication, thereby establishing the individual, social, and public connections form our own audiences. (Finnemann, 2011, p. 84)

This is also true for children in the 6th and 7th grade. In our perspective, this has important implications. The interventions we make in the home economic class constitute a setting within which we initiate and partly participate in practices: cooking and video production. We observe and participate in the ways the participants perform these practices through sayings and doings (Reckwitz, 2002; Schatzki, 2008). We make ad hoc interviews and we take photos and videos; we partake in the children's practices and enact our own practices as researchers, observed by the children that observe and interview us on what we are doing. Working with practices in research gives us an indication of how everyday practices intersect (Orlikowski, 2010; Halkier, 2009), and initiating food and media use/production practices opens up to a vast range of sayings and doings within the fields of food, cooking, taste, media use, competencies, literacy etc. Thus, we work from an understanding that it is not possible to study one practice isolated from other practices – let alone media practices (or research-practices). In a society vastly mediatized it is seldom possible to study media use isolated from the everyday life that it is part of. Similarly, it is not possible to separate everyday practices or routines from their joining with media practices. Andreas Hepp uses the notion of amalgamation to describe this development: "Amalgamation means that media-related and non-media related acting increasingly merge and mingle" (Hepp, 2012, p. 4). Our study is an example of how we initiate a situation (an intervention) with this amalgamation of media practices and cooking practices – which could be any other non-media related practice. Our purpose is to explore what happens in this imagined and collaborative 'laboratory' that mirrors everyday situations but is limited in time and space.

In our perspective, this has two major implications. (1) We must rethink how media studies, anthropology, and other parts of cultural studies intersect methodologically. One the one hand, media use is a not a practice detached from other social and cultural practices, but an element in all of these. On the other hand, anthropology and cultural studies have to integrate media into their field, because media use and production often are part of everyday routines. (2) Therefore, studying childhood in the age of digitalisation raises methodological challenges and we have to experiment with new methodological designs that can explore complex and diverse intersections between cooking (or other practices) and media-productions among children in contemporary culture.

Our response to the second implication has been to initiate a participatory design, which is collaboratively developed and changed and refined during the research process. An abductive process took place, alternating between induction (in the fields) and deduction (pre-planning and theoretical pre-understandings, i.e. of which media formats that the children might know). We had to attune the intervention to diverse contexts: the three schools were not just located in different areas of Denmark, the surroundings within the school and particularly in the home economics class were more diverse than imagined. The schools had different perspectives on teaching and using media in learning processes, and the teachers had distinctive ways of interacting with their pupils and us. Also, the children's media literacy (Drotner & Erstad, 2014; Drotner & Kobbernagel, 2014) and culinary capital (Naccarato & LeBesco, 2012) differed. Last but not least, the groups of children were different in relation to number, gender patterns, ethnicity and class. Thus, many factors and dynamics varied from school to school and most of them we had no chance of predicting or preparing for. If we want to understand the complexity of contemporary children's lives – and not just think about cause-effect, but go deeper into the complex criss-cross relations between media and social lives in children's lives – we need to work in ways that are flexible and open for change in the processes, we initiate.

The emerging research design described in this article offers a step in this direction. Some of the ambitions of the design and some of the thoughts behind it are relevant to developers of new methodological approaches within childhood studies. Particularly: (1) the aspiration to think research designs as an iterative process, not as a fixed and inflexible manual, (2) the ambition to go beyond the traditional interview (sayings), or observations studying children's practices and discourses (sayings and doings) at a distance. We need to accept the children as agents, collaborators and participants at all levels, including an accept of their suggestions of how we should make changes in our pre-plans for the interventions, and include their video-productions in not only our data-set but also as part of our analytical results.

3   Case-Studies and Iterative Methodologies

To explore the two fields of practices, competences and possibly intersections: cooking and media, we choose to have multiple cases, because case studies are suitable for an empirical enquiry about a contemporary phenomenon (e.g. a 'case'), set within its real world context – especially when the boundaries between phenomenon and context are not clearly evident (Yin, 2011, p. 4). Case studies are especially relevant when you want to "analyze complex social interactions, to uncover 'inseparable' factors that are elements of the phenomena" (VanWynsberghe & Khan, 2007, p. 84).

The complexity and embeddedness of social interactions was exactly what we wanted to explore. We did not expect to be able to explain the causes and effects of the relations between cooking and media competences and the social relations in the classroom, but we hoped to be able to uncover essential 'inseparable' factors in the field. In our pre-understanding (Gadamer, 2007) two inseparable factors were likely to be cooking skills and media information competencies or even more general media literacies (Drotner & Erstad, 2014; Drotner & Kobbernagel, 2014; Livingstone, 2010). We hoped to produce data that allowed for an 'extendability', but not necessarily for generalisations as more quantitative studies would allow us (VanWynsberghe & Khan, 2007; Flyvbjerg, 2013).

Our three qualitative cases of interventions were chosen among several contacts for maximum diversity (Yin, 2011): one urban, one suburban and one city school each with their specific didactic profile. Which means that we are not able to compare the cases one to one. As already mentioned, taste and cooking was our common point of departure. One of the media researchers had done a pilot study among boys aged 12–14, confirming that they were fond of food television, and especially liked the format Masterchef in the American and Australian versions and the Danish junior version with children aged between 11–15. Furthermore, in 2016, Den store Bagedyst, a BBC-format, had huge ratings among Danish girls and women from 11 and upwards. An interest in cooking and competition – at least as television entertainment – seemed to exist in the age group. Therefore, we decided to borrow elements from the two formats and present the children for a 'reality' cooking-competition in school. We hoped they would find it funny to mimic the television-formats and be able to 'play' together with us in a kind of recognised scenario (Schön, 1983). We established competing groups, each consisting of boys and girls working together, because gender issues might be at stake here in relation to cooking as well as in relation to the knowledge of the television-formats. We knew that DIY videos on YouTube were popular in the age group, so we encouraged the groups of children to make their own cooking video on tablets with software they already knew how to use. This was our basic idea, which we tried in the first – rural – school. But we did not know if the children wanted to participate and what would happen in class. We were open for change and surprises.

We will use the term iterative research design for our procedure. Iterative means repetitive or repeated processes. Iterative design is a term originally used for societal planning design that experienced a crisis in the 1960s' open societal systems, where problems were not that easily to find or define. One had to understand the field extensively to know if a problem or a complex of problems exist (Rittel & Webber, 1973, pp. 160–161). Therefore, repeated investigations alike and not so alike were made, involving citizens that often were not satisfied with traditional linear, effective planning initiatives as co-creators. In our case, we were not problem-oriented, but we wanted to explore in some depth, what is going on between the two fields cooking and media use in a school-context. If we could understand some of the relations between cooking and media use and between accepted competences in school and in leisure – gendered or not – we would be able to argue for how to incorporate cooking and eating in school in new ways, and for how to make the media competences acquired in leisure and home fruitful in a school context and vice versa. We knew that each case is essentially unique and that its particularity might be bigger than its commonalities with other cases (ibid., pp. 164–165). Which means that we had to repeat the interventions, as if we never did it before and accept the changes and challenges posed by the particular pupils and teachers in the particular school. Iterative research design thus is by nature nonlinear and often progresses in circles or spirals: it is an exploratory process that is repeated over and over again (Brown, 2009, IDEO). Pragmatically, we choose to have only three cases of home economic classes.

Similar procedures are also called co-design (Pedersen, 2015). It has been developed in relation to design of ITK hardware, computer programs and software when it comes to develop problem based digital software (Pedersen, 2015). The basic idea is an open and co-creative research design, as for instance a scenario that encourages collaborative work practices and user-centered approaches like our interventions before the design of a prototype. To start over and over again as many times as you can afford in a collaborative and participatory process until you have a joint idea of a design that can explain or solve a problem (Brandt & Messeter, 2004). Our product is not a design object but a prototype of research design.

We repeated the intervention three times, but we could have done it many more times in many more schools. We used the same fundamentals: (1) introduction of the intervention to the class, we showed a funny food video as an example. (2) Cooking of food items, that we brought to the school. Parallel to this the groups and the researchers filmed. The researchers participated, observed and interviewed. (3) A board of judges tasted the food and a winner was elected. (4) Eating, taste discussions and a break. (5) The films were edited in iMovie. (6) A film-festival with the participating children as judges gave a prize to the best film. (7) Brief evaluation with the teacher and in the research group.

We were open for changes in all three interventions, but some of the changes surprised us. We invited the children in the classroom as co-designers and co-producers of our three cases and the qualitative data set. But in the second intervention we decided to ask the teacher not to involve herself as much as she would have liked to. So, we actually excluded her as co-designer. None of the teachers took part in cooking or in filming, so they also excluded themselves. The collaborative process thus was performed between the children and the four researchers that were present. We did not reflect upon the role of the teachers in the process, but if we do the interaction a fourth time, the role of the teacher, as co-producer would need to be in more focus. We would try to invite the teacher as a co-producer on par with the children and with the researchers. We do not know what would happen. But it is a good example on how to work iteratively: to repeat but to change focus in the repetition, because we found a blind spot – or a problem behind the problem (Rittel & Webber, 1973, pp. 158–160).

The research-group was stable in all interventions. We had worked together before, but we are trained in different qualitative methods and have different research strengths even though all of us for years have published on children and adolescents in school or institutional contexts. It surprised us, how much our divergences in methods mattered. All of us were present during all interventions. The anthropologist took the lead in taking field notes. But after the first intervention, it was obvious, that the notes, photos, videos and interviews we had made were very diverse. The ethnographer looked at cooking skills, the media researchers listened for references to media formats, genres and technologies. The cultural studies person looked for boys doing masculinity. For the second intervention, we therefore planned to have each our focus: media uses, gender-roles and hand skills. This also resulted in very diverse observations and we were not able to keep our foci, because the children acted differently, the teacher was more dominant – but also because the children in the second, suburban school had previously had researchers in the classroom. They invited us into their reflections and doings and asked us questions, that explicitly made us part of joint productions in the classroom. In the third, private school the classroom was small and crowded. Most of the children here felt on par with us and participated in the collaboration as equals – or even as superiors. They invited us to participate with them and took the lead, especially when it came to tasting and cooking skills, demonstrating high competences, broad knowledge of international chefs and high self-esteem. The teacher was passive, reluctant towards media use and took the role of a facilitator in the situation.

The pupils and the school context in the three interventions thus actually co-produced our research design as an iterative process. We started over again three times because the three different classes, schools and teachers acted differently and made us act differently and take ad hoc decisions about what to do. Such as to ask one teacher to take a more discrete role or to become more involved with the children than planned. Our observations were more or less participatory; the relations between the researcher and the pupils were more or less on par etc. We succeeded in getting the children to co-operate in the design process and to co-produce parts of our data, but in other ways, than we had thought originally. The role of the teachers only occurred to be a problem to us after all three interventions.

Our research roles also changed: the anthropologist began to look for media use and the media researcher began to look for how ethnicity was constructed in the classroom. The conclusion is that when you decide to have an iterative process of repeating and then changing the methodology, you must be prepared to start more or less all over again with each case, and you have to accept to have your research plans redefined and to change your own skills as a researcher. If you work in a cross-disciplinary team, you must be ready to learn from other disciplines in the process. Thus, an iterative research design is an on-going process with an unknown end or goal. Unlike in other qualitative designs, where the ultimate idea would be to continue until nothing new is found (Kvale & Brinkmann, 2011/2015), an iterative design keeps repeating the exploratory proceedings – and changing them – until the problems behind the problem may occur. In this case we had to take a pragmatically decision and stop after three interventions because of our research frame: time and money expired.

Qualitative methodology is often explained as a series of steps proceeding from one phase to another. If we take Bryman's model as an example, he suggests six steps:
1. The general research questions
2. Selection of relevant sites and subjects
3. Collection of relevant data
4. Interpretation of data
5. Conceptual and theoretical work
6. Writing up findings or conclusions

In this case, our research question was explorative: We were looking for possible relations and intersections between cooking and media use and –productions. Secondly, we were looking for intersections of competences retrieved in formal learning processes at school and informal learning in leisure and home. As a means we created real life participatory interventions to enact collaborative practices in and across the two fields: cooking and media-uses. In Bryman's model we were at step 1,2,3,4 at the same time: in search for a precise research question, we made interventions in three cases to collect data and we collaboratively in the research group started to interpret the data with the children's data-interpretation in their videos.

This is not easy to show in a model, because it is all messed up. Figures 8.1 and 8.2 are two examples of how software-designers visualize the iterative process towards developing a prototype – in this case a prototype for iterative research design methodology.[1]

The second model (Figure 8.2) looks chaotic but describes our explorative methodology: we started at the same point: presenting ourselves to the class and bringing bags with food items to the schools. From this starting point, a collaborative process of research practices and cooking and media practices took over, again and again and again: iteratively. The research methodology concept/prototype is still a work in progress.

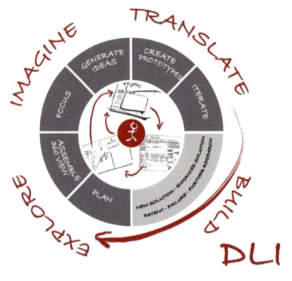

FIGURE 8.1 SAP Design Led Innovation (DLI) process

FIGURE 8.2 The process of Design Squiggle by Damien Newman (thedesignsquiggle.com), licensed under a Creative Commons Attribution – No Derivative Works 3.0 United States License (https://creativecommons.org/licenses/by-nd/3.0/us/)

4   Data and Results

We produced a rich data set consisting of the 12 videos, of our photos and videos, of observation- and field notes and ad hoc interviews during the day. Most children in all three schools instantly recognized the popular television-format that we imitated in the set up. But they all negotiated the format differently. None of the teachers or school managers seemed to know the format and none of them reflected explicitly upon it. The practices in the home economics classes gave room for the children's creativity in relation to cooking and video co-productions and most of them thought the interventions simply to be fun. They invited us to repeat the intervention.

The interventions produced demonstrated questions, that would often not have possible to ask or to answer in an ordinary interview setting, because they were actualized in the specific practices, enacted by specific children in a specific classroom in a specific school-setting. For instance, we were surprised by the complexity of the differences between the school contexts and in the social backgrounds of the children. We were surprised by cooking practices (urban school) and skills and also surprised by media skills – or the lack of them (urban school). Thus, we left the schools with insights and new questions: The intersections between cooking skills and media skills and literacies were not as simple as we had imagined. We began to think in cross-over models instead of relational models. It had been a good idea with a meeting with the class after the intervention to reflect together with the children and their teacher and to invite them to further co-analyse our joint data and discuss the different models of understanding the data with us The next step in an iterative design-process thus would have been to start all over again at a fourth school, etc.

To sum up, we argue that we need to give space for and consider our informants, the children, as co-producers of the research design and knowledge and 2) new media offer easily accessible possibilities for innovative research designs which can give us insight into the children's social lives, their media competencies and cooking practices as a supplement to well-known methods such as interview, textual analysis and observations. Gubrium and Harper (2016) stress that participatory and collaborative research with children means, that all are involved all the way through the process as co-investigators, co-writers and co-analysers. This proved difficult to do in the strict sense, but the videos the children produced and that we analyse as part of our data are in themselves a first analyses or narratives of how the children summed up the intervention.

5   New Childhood Studies Revisited

Collaborative research with children has been done since the 1990s. James and Prout's (1990/2015) seminal anthology on Constructing and Reconstructing Childhood suggested a new paradigm for the sociology of childhood. In a Nordic context, Solberg (2015) proved important for looking at children as agents in and for their own lives and as products of historical social relations in and outside families and societal institutions such as Kindergarten and school.

Christensen and James (2008) developed the idea of participatory research with children in psychological research and pointed to important ethical dilemmas. They also stressed the importance of open-mindedness towards the diversities of childhoods, which our three school-cases confirm the relevance of. It is in this tradition our interventions have been created. We acknowledge the importance of ethics, when we work together with children, but in our case, we were interested in the joint skills and competences in the groups we formed in the class, not in the individual child. Our collaboration with the children was 'at a distance' and our ethical concerns were related to the schools, which is why we are not specific about which schools we visited. We choose not to use the real names of the children, but we have a lot of videos and photos showing their faces.

Much research has been done on children's productions such as narratives, photos, drawings, collages and scrapbooks, lego and other visual materials (Bragg & Buckingham, 2008; Buckingham, 2009; Krogager, 2012, 2016). In line with this research, we do not claim to tell the 'truth' about the approximate 65 children and the three schools. Any intervention is situated in a specific time and at a specific place among humans that participate in a co-production of research and data. Our cases and data are negotiated co-productions in a specific situation. We can report what happened in this specific situation among a specific group and we can understand and argue that some of the 'happenings' are 'extendable' to other situations where the same 'inseparable' factors are said or done, such as gender roles, competences and literacies. What we can conclude, however, is that experimental and iterative methodologies are of great importance when we want to explore relations and intersections between two or more fields of practices.

Our iterative design experiences are relevant for new methodological approaches within childhood studies. Particularly: (1) the aspiration to think research designs as an iterative process, not as a fixed and un-flexible manual, (2) the ambition to go beyond the traditional interview (sayings), or observations studying children's practices and discourses (sayings and doings) at a distance.

The gains of doing research this way is many. The participants collaborate in different practical processes that we can observe, get involved in and ask them about. We are in the front row to the numerous negotiations and compromises that take place as part of the practical enactment with the media (i-Pad) and the food. Hence, this collaborative and co-productive method is resourceful at many levels: it works differently than traditional interviewing and conventional observation because the participants show us their media and cooking practices whilst discussing and negotiating with their peers – and with us as researchers. If we ask the participants questions about their 'doings' in the intervention the retrospective element is less dominant than when making interviews (Reckwitz, 2002; Schatzki, 2008; Warde, 2005).

Certainly, there are challenges and pitfalls to this way of doing research too. Particularly, the lack of control and consequently also the absence of a systematic procedure that we can rely on and repeat pose a challenge. The context (and the many factors that it involves e.g. the school kitchen, the attitude and handling of tablets, the different role of the teachers etc.) is defining for what takes place during the day and that makes it difficult draw parallels between the three interventions. Also, practical matters as data storage has posed a challenge.

However, there is no turning back. Iterative research design with children offer new possibilities for researchers to see and hear children's views and experiences. In a quickly developing and complicated world, researchers must continually adjust and develop their approaches to doing research. Childhood experiences in a digital era is indeed a challenging object of study which demands an agile and creative researcher and participating children. We hope this article's methodological reflection might inspire further creativity and agility within Nordic childhood studies.

Note

1 See www.hci.Stanford.edu

References

Bragg, S., & Buckingham, D. (2008). Scrapbooks as a resource in media research with young people. In P. Thomson (Ed.), *Doing visual research with children and young people.* Routledge.

Brandt, E., & Messeter, J. (2004). Facilitating collaboration through design games. *Proceedings Participatory Design Conference.* ACM 1-58113-85/-2/04/07

Brown, T. (2009). *Change by design. How design thinking transforms organizations and inspires innovation.* Harper Collins.

Buckingham, D. (2009). Creative visual methods in media research. *Media, Culture and Society, 31*(4), 633–652.

Buckingham, D. (2009). The future of media literacy in the digital age: Some challenges for policy and practice. In EuroMeduc (Ed.), *Media literacy in Europe: Controversies, challenges and perspectives* (pp. 13–24). European Union.

Christensen, P., & James, A. (2008). *Research with children. Perspectives and practices*. Routledge.

Couldry, N. (2004). Theorising media as practice. *Social Semiotics, 14*(2), 115–132.

Couldry, N., & Hepp, A. (2013). Conceptualizing mediatization: Contexts, traditions, arguments. *Communication Theory, 23*(3), 191–202.

Drotner, K. (1995). *At skabe sig selv. Ungdom, æstetik, pædagogik*. Gyldendal.

Drotner, K., & Erstad, O. (2014). Inclusive media literacies: Interlacing media studies and education studies. *International Journal of Learning and Media, 4*(2), 19–34.

Drotner, K., & Kobbernagel, C. (2014). Toppling hierarchies? Media and information literacies, ethnicity, and performative media practices. *Learning, Media and Technology, 39*(4), 409–428. doi:10.1080/17439884.2014.964255

Eurostat. (2017). *Key figures on Europe*. Publications Office of the European Union.

Facer, K. L., Furlong, V. J., Furlong, R., & Sutherland, R. J. (2001). What's the point of using computers: The development of young people's computer expertise in the home. *New Media and Society, 3*(2), 199–219.

Finnemann, N. O. (2011). Mediatization theory and digital media. *Communications, the European Journal of Communication Research, 36*(1), 67–89.

Flyvbjerg, B. (2013). Fem misforståelser om casestudiet. In S. Brinkman & L. Tangaard (Eds.), *Kvalitative metoder* (pp. 463–487). Reitzels Forlag.

Garcia-Ruiz, R., Ramirez-Garcia, A., & Rodriguez-Rosell, M. M. (2014). Media literacy: Education for a new Prosumer citizenship. *Communicar, 22*(43), 15–23.

Gauntlett, D. (2008). *Creative explorations*. Routledge.

Gubrium, A., & Harper, K. (2016), *Participatory visual and digital methods*. Routledge.

Hepp, A. (2012). Mediatization and the 'moulding force' of the media. *Communications, the European Journal of Communication Research, 37*(1), 1–28.

Hoechsmann, M., & Poyntz, S. R. (2012). *Media literacies: A critical introduction*. Blackwell Publishing. doi:10.1002/9781444344158

James, A., & Prout, A. (2015). *Constructing and reconstructing childhood*. Routledge. (Original work published 1990)

Livingstone, S. (2010). Media literacy and media policy. In B. Bachmair (Ed.), *Medienbildung in neuen Kulturräumen*. VS Verlag für Sozialwissenschaften/GWV Fachverlage GmbH Wiesbaden. doi:10.1007/978-3-531-92133-4_2

Mills, A. J., Durepos, G., & Wiebe, E. (Eds.). (2010). *Encyclopedia of case study research*. Sage Publications.

Naccarato, P., & LeBesco, K. (2012). *Culinary capital*. Berg Publishing.

Orlikowski, W. (2010). Practice in research: Phenomenon, perspective and philosophy. In D. Golsorkhi, L. Rouleau, D. Seidl, & E. Vaara (Eds.), *Cambridge handbook of strategy as practice*. Cambridge University Press.

Pedersen, J. (2015). War and peace in CoDesign. *International Journal of CoDesign*. doi:10.1080/15710882.2015.1112813

Potter, A., & Goldsmith, B. (2017). Reality's children. Young people and factual entertainment. *Media International Australia*, *164*(1), 44–55.

Povlsen, K. K. (1999). *Beverly Hills. Ironi, 'soaps' og danske unge*. Klim.

Povlsen, K. K. (2016). I (never) just Google: Food and media practices. In J. Leer & K. K. Povlsen (Eds.), *Food and media: Practices, distinctions and heterotopias* (pp. 129–148). Routledge.

Prensky, M. (2001). Digital natives, digital immigrants part 1. *On the Horizon*, *9*(5), 1–6. https://doi.org/10.1108/10748120110424816

Reckwitz, A. (2002). Toward a theory of social practices. *European Journal of Social Theory*, *5*(2), 243–263.

Shade, D. D., Kornfeld, S., & Oliver, M. B. (2015). The uses and gratifications of media migration. *Journal of Broadcasting and Electronic Media*, *59*(2), 318–341.

Schatzki, T. R. (2008). *Social practices: A Wittgensteinian approach to human activity and the social*. Cambridge University Press.

Schön, D. (1983), *The reflective practitioner: How professionals think in action*. Basic Books.

Schrøder, K. (2003). Generelle aspekter ved mediereception? – Et bud på en multidimensional model for analyse af kvalitative receptionsinterviews. *MedieKultur, 35*. doi:http://dx.doi.org/10.7146/mediekultur.v19i35.1236

Schrøder, K., Drotner, K., Kline, S., & Murray, C. (2003). *Researching audiences: A practical guide to methods in media audience analysis*. Bloomsbury Academic.

Solberg, A. (2015). Negotiating childhood: Changing constructions of age for norwegian children. In A. James & A. Prout (Eds.), *Constructing and reconstructing childhood contemporary issues in the sociological study of childhood* (pp. 110–127). Taylor and Francis.

VanWynsberghe, R. & S. Khan. (2007). Redefining case study. *International Journal of Qualitative Methods*, *6*(2). https://journals.sagepub.com/doi/full/10.1177/160940690700600208

Warde, A. (2005). Consumption and theories of practice. *Journal of Consumer Culture*, *5*(2), 131–153.

Yin, R. K. (2011). *Applications of case study design*. Sage.

CHAPTER 9

'Children at Risk' in Public Health Policy: What Is at Risk?

Jorunn Spord Borgen, Gro Rugseth and Wenche S. Bjorbækmo

Abstract

This chapter investigates how the concept of 'children at risk' is produced as a problem within public health policy. Globally and nationally, political authorities are concerned with what they consider risk factors, connected to the population's health and well-being. One of the most common long-term health concerns is non-communicable diseases, related to sedentary behaviour and a reduced level of physical activity. Such diseases are considered by international organisations, such as the World Health Organization (WHO) and the Organisation for Economic Cooperation and Development (OECD), to be the most challenging public health concerns of our time. This chapter examines how children's future health risk is produced and transformed in the Nordic context and investigate how the concept of 'children at risk' is produced as a problem in two health policy documents. The results indicate that the focus of children at risk changed in four years from kindergarten children to youth. These findings suggest various interpretations of the term 'in the best interest of the child', article 3, and challenge the understanding of children as active agents, article 12, in the UNS convention on the Right of the Child (United Nations, 1989). We discuss how 'risk reduction' tends to become 'risk production' through the creation of new problems, such as standardisation, variation and exclusion.

Keywords

children – youth – risk – public health policy – kindergarten – school

1 Introduction

According to the British sociologist Nikolas Rose, political authorities, in alliance with stakeholders and others, have taken responsibility for the management of life in the name of the well-being of the population and of each of its living creatures (Rose, 2001, p. 1). Political authorities, nationally and internationally, engage in what is considered responsible activities for managing certain risk factors, which are considered to be connected to the population's health and well-being. Drawing on Foucault's (1997) concept of biopolitics, Rose sees the concept of risk as bound up with the desire to control, especially to control the future (Rose, 2001). Although the future is unpredictable, ideas about and hopes for possible futures are currently present and historically constituted and formative in society (Koselleck, 1985). The concept of risk reflects the social constructions of risk shared by a particular culture at a particular time in history, and the construction of risk brings into play the tensions between the future and the present. Ulrich Beck (1992) defined risk society as a society that has "systematic ways of dealing with hazards and insecurities induced and introduced by modernization itself" (Beck, 1992, p. 21), and Anthony Giddens (1999) declared that modern societies are increasingly preoccupied with the future and safety. He sees risk as a key aspect of modernity. In offering new conceptualisations of risk, these authors enhance, extend, combine and critique many existing disciplinary perspectives and theoretical approaches to risk (Ekberg, 2007). According to Skinner (2002), no concept can have a single definition or a standard meaning or conceptualisation. For instance, risk, as it relates to society and children, must be understood through context. Analysis of the rhetorical use of concepts is a way of linking political language to political action.

2   Policies to Address Future Risks

Ideas about future risk shape the organisation of children's everyday lives (Biesta, 2014) and the activities and practices that take place in kindergartens and schools (Christensen & Mikkelsen, 2008; Ingulfsvann, Engelsrud, & Moe, 2020; Malone, 2007). Defining and managing risk factors for young children's current and future health have become central elements in policy documents, curricula, didactic tools, pedagogical theories, and commercial offerings on early childhood care and education (Qvortrup, 2009). The political activities of surveillance, discipline and control of children's present circumstances to reduce their risk of future bad health challenge the UNCRCs understanding of children as active agents (United Nations, 1989, article 12). These activities also suggest various interpretations of the term 'in the best interest of the child' (United Nations, 1989, article 3).

Noncommunicable diseases, also referred to as lifestyle diseases, which are increasingly prevalent across the world are among the most common concerns.

Lifestyle diseases, which are connected to sedentary behaviour, reduced levels of physical activity, unhealthy eating, smoking, alcohol and other risky behaviours, are considered to be the most challenging public health concerns of our time by international organisations such as the World Health Organization (WHO) (WHO, 2018) and the Organisation for Economic Co-operation and Development (OECD) (OECD, 2016). However, the implementation of public health policy targeting these behaviours as processes has not been widely studied (Langøien et al., 2017; Muellmann et al., 2017). Health policy initiatives related to noncommunicable diseases are especially directed at children and youth in kindergarten and schools. In its global recommendations on physical activity for health (WHO, 2010), the WHO advises one hour of moderate to vigorous physical activity every day for children and youth. It is thought that physical activity for health lowers the risk of illness and earlier death (WHO, 2010) and, thus, benefits society. Advocates of this understanding of health adopt a lifelong perspective and argue that physical activity should be prioritised in kindergartens and schools for the benefit of children and the future health and well-being of youth (Borgen, 2018a, 2018b; Cigman, 2012). Within the field of health research, there is a substantial body of intervention studies and randomised controlled trials that seek evidence of the benefits of physical activity for children and youth (Adab et al., 2018; Kriemler et al., 2010; Skrede, 2019). Within education research, Thomas Popkewitz (2018) identified a paradox whereby the good intention to eliminate risks for all children excludes and abjects those who do not make the right choices:

> The liberal hope of school research is to produce an inclusive society. This hope is embodied in making children as particular kinds of people, sometimes called problem-solvers and lifelong learners for that future society. But for all these good intentions, the hope of future inscribes double gestures in reform-oriented research. The hope for making kinds of people embodies fears about the dangers and dangerous populations that threaten that desired future. These 'other' kinds of children are distinguished as students who 'lack motivation' or are classified as 'at-risk'. (Popkewitz, 2018)

Researchers tend to objectify differences for classification purposes, such as to determine who is at risk, and what kinds of risks must be addressed. When researchers describe someone as engaging in healthy behaviour, the antitype is those who do not engage in such behaviour (Popkewitz, 2018). Children and youth are objectified as 'becomings' (Uprichard, 2008) in these health policy initiatives. However, such initiatives also grant importance to decision making and agency to enable children and youth to become independent learners capable of taking responsibility for themselves in school and in broader society (Aarskog, Barker, & Borgen, 2018). This is an instance of the educational paradox (Løvlie, 2008). In a report on the benefits of physical education and physical activity in schools for a better future for everyone, the OECD (2019) regards the school setting as a context for health policy. However, school is also a place for students to develop agency and individual responsibility:

> Schools are not just places where students go to pursue academic achievement: schools should be nurturing environments that develop the whole child, including their social, emotional, physical and mental well-being. If children and young people are to become responsible, productive and happy members of society, they need a holistic education that prepares them not just for cognitive tasks, but for the broad gamut of personal, social and professional opportunities, challenges and duties in life. (OECD, 2019, p. 3)

State-organised or state-supported initiatives in the interests of the health of the population have played a role in politics in many liberal democratic societies in the twentieth century (Rose, 2001, p. 6). In Nordic countries – which have small populations, the highest global quality of life rankings, and a "paradoxical blend of social democracy and liberalism" (Tin, Telseth, Tangen, & Giulianotti, 2019) global health policies and recommendations influence everyday life and physical culture in kindergarten and schools.[1] In Norway, risk-reducing public health policies are described in white papers (Meld. St.), which are presented to the Storting (parliament) to explain the work being conducted in a particular field and guide future policy-making. These white papers and discussions of them in the Storting often form a basis for a draft resolution or bill. They are accompanying documents that describe the aims of policies, norms and recommendations and are seen as guidelines for local practice.

This article examines the research question: How is the concept of the future health risks of children and youth presented in two recent Norwegian public health white papers, which were produced by the same government within four years? (Ministry of Health and Care Services, 2015, 2019). We are interested in the similarities and differences between these policy documents, which were published within a relatively short period. The documents are as follows:
– Document A: Folkehelsemeldingen. Mestring og muligheter (Meld. St. 19 (2014–2015)). [Public Health White Paper. Mastering and Possibilities].
– Document B: Folkehelsemeldinga. Gode liv i eit trygt samfunn (Meld. St. 19 (2018–2019)). [Public Health White Paper. Good Lives in a Safe Society].

3   What Is the Problem – What Is at Risk?

According to Carol Bacchi (1999), how we perceive or think about something will affect what we think ought to be done, and, at its most basic, this insight is commonsensical. She suggests that every political call for action or solutions inevitably and in various ways defines a problem to be solved (Bacchi, 1999). One example of what Bacchi (2016) calls 'mainstream health policy theorizing' can be found in the WHO's (2015) *Health in All Policies Manual*, which defines four stages of policy-making: agenda-setting (e.g. identification of the problem), policy formation, policy implementation and policy review (e.g. monitoring, evaluation, and reporting) (Bacchi, 2016, p. 4). The white papers on public health policy analysed here have this structure. Bacchi (2016) argues for an alternative approach. She advocates examining policy proposals and policy instruments, such as childcare or health policies, to uncover problem representations. She reminds us that the banal and vague notions of 'the problem' and its partner 'the solution' are heavily laden with meaning (Carson, 2018). Bacchi starts from the position that problems are not given but instead are social constructions and, therefore, contextual. She challenges the idea that governments react to pre-existing problems and instead argues that they are active in creating problems. For Bacchi, focusing on problematisations rather than problems sheds light on the role problems play in governing processes. Bacchi's approach to analysing policies aimed at addressing social problems is the 'What's the Problem Represented to be?' (WPR) approach and is guided by six questions.[2] First, it is necessary to consider what the problem is represented as in the policy or policy proposal that is being studied (e.g., children's risk of developing bad health) and what presuppositions or assumptions underpin this representation of the problem. It is also worth considering how the representation of the problem has come about and what is left unproblematised in that representation. The effects produced by the representation of the problem and how this representation of the problem has been produced, disseminated and defended is important for identifying solutions that may be unintentionally harmful. According to Bacchi's Foucauldian poststructuralist approach to policy analysis, the WPR approach is a methodological approach to studying policy (Bacchi, 2016, p. 1). It goes beyond the question of what the subject of politics is and asks how something has become the subject of politics.

Inspired by the critical question 'what is the problem?' (Bacchi, 1999), we draw on Bacchi's WPR methodology and qualitative content analysis (Hsieh & Shannon, 2005) to answer the research question. Our study includes both quantitative and qualitative content analysis of the two policy documents. First, we conducted a summative content analysis, which involved counting words selected by the authors to represent the categories derived from the text data in the two documents for the purpose of comparison. This was followed by an interpretation of the underlying context. According to Bacchi (2016, p. 10), a summative content analysis of how problems are conceptualised within policy documents is useful for a WPR analysis. We then conducted a qualitative conventional content analysis (Hsieh & Shannon, 2005) of the two documents. Categories were derived directly from the text data in accordance with the WPR approach. The white papers were examined for content on physical activity in relation to children and adolescents, the risks related to this subject, and future prospect for children and youth. By focusing on these topics in our initial examination of the documents, we sought to reveal a possible narrative about physical activity, children, youth and health in these documents. We focused on what the problem was represented as in the white papers and asked what presuppositions or assumptions underpinned this representation of the problem. In other words, we began by looking for the proposed solution(s) and derived from these ask what the problem was represented as. In dialogue with the critical literature on risk society, we read and re-read the documents to identify the assumptions behind their understanding of the problem that could be solved by the proposed solution or activity. In the next section, we present our summative content analysis, followed by a textual analysis of a selection of excerpts from the documents being investigated.

4   Risk as an Element of Politics

First, we conducted a count of words in the two policy documents (A and B) to identify consistencies and changes between 2015 and 2019 in public health policy messages between 2015 and 2019 (see Table 9.1). We defined two categories, 'children' and 'risk', and, informed by recent health policy research, searched for words connected to those categories.[3]

4.1   *Change of Scope from Children to Youth*

The word 'child', either alone or in combination with an institution or service (e.g. child welfare, child policy initiatives), is mentioned 908 times in Document A and 726 times in Document B (see Table 9.1). By contrast, the word 'youth', either alone or in combination with an institution or service, is mentioned more often in Document B (564 times) than in Document A (490 times). In Norwegian, the phrase 'children and youth' refers to the UNCRC definition of children (0–18 years) and is used more often in Document B than in Document A. As an institutional context, 'kindergarten' is mentioned more often in

TABLE 9.1   Words related to public health policy in two Public Health White papers (Documents A and B)

Words	Document A	Document B
	Mestring og muligheter (St meld nr 19 (2014–15)) [*Mastering and Possibilities*. Public Health White Paper]	Gode liv i eit trygt samfunn/ (St meld nr 19 (2018–19)) [*Good Lives in a Safe Society*. Public Health White Paper]
Ansvar/*Responsibility*	109	183
Risiko/*Risk*	186	193
Barn/*Child* (*all variations including barn/child*)	368 (908)	351 (726)
Unge/*Youth* (*all variations including unge/youth*)	289 (490)	334 (564)
Voksne/*Adults*	71	58
Familie/*Family* (*familien/the family*)	11 (29)	6 (17)
Valg/*Choice* (*individual*)	34	13
Livskvalitet/*Quality of life*	57	152
Livsstil/*Lifestyle*	53	17
Helse/*Health*	2316	2690
Tidlig/*Early* (*effort, death, intervention, etc*)	153	141
Død/*Death*	136	84
Smittsom/*Contagious*	22	45
Sykdom/*Illness*	321	1
Barnehage/*Kindergarten*	47	20
Skole/*School*	57	71

Document A than in Document B, whereas 'school' is mentioned more often in Document B than in Document A. However, the compound phrase 'kindergarten and school' is mentioned in combination with services (e.g., health services and policy initiatives) in both documents. While 'family' is only occasionally mentioned, kindergartens, schools, public institutions and services are frequently mentioned as instruments for health policy in these documents. The more frequent mention of 'child' in Document A than in Document B indicates that the policy proposed in Document A is aimed at young children.

Some words were used infrequently but, when they were used, were associated with strong normative and often leading statements, whereas some frequently mentioned words were used in weak statements. For instance, in Document A, 'choice' is mentioned 34 times, and 'health-friendly choices', which we consider making a strong statement about what individuals do or should do, is mentioned 13 times. In Document B, we find 'choice' once in the phrase 'responsible choices of life' and 12 times in the phrase 'health-friendly choices'. We consider 'choices of life' to make a strong statement due to the context within which it is mentioned, that is, the new Norwegian curriculum reform in compulsory education, which is being launched in 2020. The topic of public health and life mastery is one of three priority interdisciplinary topics in this new curriculum, which, according to Document B, "will help students gain competencies that promote good mental and physical health, and that gives them the power to make responsible choices of life" (p. 31). Thus, children of kindergarten age are the target of the health policy in Document A, while the policy in Document B appears to target children and youth of school age. Another example is the phrase 'quality of life', which is mentioned three times more frequently in Document B than in Document A. However, the compound phrase 'quality of life and well-being' is used in Document A only, while 'health and quality of life' is used most frequently in relation to statements about the objectives for the health policy in Document B. 'Illness' is a frequently used word in Document A (occurring 321 times) in statements about problems that health policy initiatives should solve, whereas 'illness' is mentioned only once in Document B.

The word counting exercise revealed distinct differences in scope between the two documents. Document A frequently mentions 'child' in connection with a wide range of institutional contexts and policy initiatives, whereas the term is used within a narrower context in Document B. The term 'youth' is mentioned more frequently in Document B than in Document A, while children and youth appear to be given equal emphasis in Document B in terms of the frequency with which they are mentioned. Compared to Document A, Document B appears to grant more attention to structural framework conditions (e.g., meta-concepts such as quality of life and early interventions for children and youth) and less attention to individual choices and action. Although risk appears to be an element of politics common to the two documents, the two documents reveal a considerable change of scope within four years.

4.2 *From Individual Action to Structures and Arenas*

For the initial conventional content analysis of the two policy documents, categories were derived directly from the Norwegian text data. The excerpts (our translation) are presented in block quote, while our analysis is presented in plain text.

4.2.1 A Negative Trend about What?

> The population, which includes children, is less physically active now than before and does not meet the health recommendations for physical activity. About 2.5 million people do not meet the health recommendations for physical activity. Adults spend an average of nine hours of their waking time at rest. Sitting for extended periods is a risk factor for illness and health problems. (Document A, p. 14)

Children are included in this overview of a negative trend of insufficient physical activity. Within a physical activity–health paradigm, activity level and health are considered to be causally related. To be less active means to be less healthy. In the given context of the above statement, characterising physical activity among children as 'less than before' constructs or creates a problem based on weak evidence, general assumptions and unsubstantiated opinions. Data is lacking on previous levels of activity among children, as this type of measurement has only been conducted in recent years and only occasionally, not systematically. In contrast to the assertion made above, the Norwegian Institute of Public Health (NIPH) reported in 2017 that most children (as much as 80–90%) in Norway were physically active in line with governmental recommendations. This means that the problem is considered to be that children are becoming less active. However, if less is still enough for the vast majority of the child population, what is the problem? By reporting that children do not meet government recommendations, the document portrays children as problems in themselves. The implied narrative is that the authorities recommend that the population, including children, increase their level of physical activity level, but the population, children included, do not follow this recommendation. They do not make the right choices. Are children ignorant, unwilling or unable to be sufficiently physically active? What, according to the authorities, is the problem with not being sufficiently physically active?

4.2.2 Why Is Physical Activity Such a Concern?

> Non-communicable diseases are the main cause of early death and early loss of quality of life. The solutions to this problem include physical activity, a healthy diet, a smoke-free environment and moderation in alcohol consumption. (Document A, p. 14)

> To create more quality years of life and increase life expectancy, the government, in line with the WHO's global goals, will continue its efforts to reduce the incidence of premature death and health problems due to noncommunicable diseases. (Document B, p. 105)

As these excerpts indicate, physical activity is seen as a vital risk-reducing behaviour. It is implied that the risks of future disease, loss of quality of life and early death can be addressed by engaging in healthy behaviour and sufficient levels of physical activity during childhood. Physical activity is seen as a tool and as part of a dose-response framework that will yield calculated results in the future on both an individual level and a public health level. However, proposing the risk of future disease as a reason for physical activity constitutes an oversimplification of the solution. It suggests that one risks acquiring these kinds of diseases if one does not engage in certain behaviours, such as being sufficiently physically active and eating healthy food. According to Document B, the work will continue as recommended by WHO.

4.2.3 Society Must Take Responsibility

> A society that facilitates good health choices is a prerequisite for enabling individuals to take responsibility for their own health. The government will work to ensure that healthy choices are simple and natural choices for everyone. Organisation of physical activity is important and must take place within all sectors. (Document A, p. 9)

> Being able to make good health choices is a prerequisite for the good health of the individual. The government aims to expand its work of facilitating health-friendly choices by promoting increased physical activity, a better diet and less use of tobacco and intoxicants. Society must make healthy choices easy choices. More emphasis should be placed on how to make information on health-friendly choices available to everyone. It is important for the individual to make informed choices. (Document B, p. 20)

The above statements imply that the population does not take responsibility for its own health, at least not when it comes to being physically active. Thus, the health authorities deem it necessary to take charge to ensure that the population itself can take such responsibility by facilitating increased physical activity in all sectors of society. Once this is achieved, the responsibility lies with the people themselves. More organised opportunities for physical activity appear to be the solution to the problem – a problem represented as people failing to take responsibility for their health by not being sufficiently physically active. The implication is that if there are enough opportunities to participate in physical activity, the population will make use of these opportunities and take responsibility for their health, both now and in the future.

4.2.4   Responsibility for What?

> All children and adolescents must be given opportunities for mastery and development. These opportunities include good living and upbringing conditions that promote mental health, opportunities for a healthy diet, physical activity in kindergartens and schools, and tobacco-free surroundings. The foundations for good health and good health habits are laid early and remain important throughout a person's entire lifetime. (Document A, p. 12)

> A balance must be struck between community responsibility for the health of inhabitants and the individual's responsibility for their own health. At the same time, there must be a balance in the instruments that are used, so that one respects the freedom of the individual. (Document B, p. 143)

Children and adolescents, as segments of the population, are of special interest. Since ways of living and living habits are decided during childhood, encouraging healthy habits in this period of life is seen as crucial for producing healthy adults. To ensure good health habits during the early years of life, health authorities emphasise the importance of upbringing conditions. The upbringing conditions in focus are mental health, healthy diet, physical activity and smoke-free surroundings. It is implied that these are of vital importance if children and youth are to establish healthy habits and be capable of taking care of themselves and taking responsibility for their own health as adults. However, it is also stressed that children and young people must be given the opportunity to experience mastery and development. How is this to be understood in relation to the focus on upbringing conditions that promote good mental health, a healthy diet and adequate physical activity? Could it be that eating properly, being sufficiently physically active and keeping their mood up or looking on the bright side of life enables children to feel that they can master various challenges in life and, thereby, develop in a positive direction to become healthy adult citizens?

If the solution is a healthy diet, sufficient physical activity and smoke-free surroundings, enabling children to achieve mastery and development and, thereby, become healthy individuals, the problem might be understood as a problem with children and young people's development, that is, that they do not develop in the 'right way'. The assumption underlying these solutions appear to suggest that environmental conditions (e.g. the actions of parents and other guardians) are the fundamental prerequisites for healthy development during childhood and into adulthood. However, the role of the family is not mentioned. Rather, it is implied that the responsibility for making the right choices is that of the individual and is portrayed as an expression of the freedom of the individual.

5 Discussion

We have asked the following questions: What do the documents say? What is the problem? What is at risk? What problematisation can be revealed? Here, we elaborate on the results of the textual analysis, focusing on the solutions to the represented problem of children being at risk offered in the documents. We consider the implied or unquestioned presuppositions that underlie the problem represented and explore the effects that might result from this representation of the problem. Using a WPR approach, we read the documents that constituted our material in this study with the purpose of discerning how the problem was represented within the documents and subjecting this problem representation to critical scrutiny. In accordance with the WPR method, we posed the six questions of our material and of ourselves as researchers.

5.1 *Political Vigour*

Public health policy attempts to exhibit political vigour by drawing a rather gloomy picture of the future. In this picture, most people are unable to live their lives so that they become financially productive without political pressure. A modern society without social and normative guidelines will result in fat, sick and lazy adults in the future. Education is aimed at making children and young people into useful citizens in the future. In Document A, the future is manifest in the kindergarten child. Children are not physically active enough and move too little to become the healthy adults that political authorities portray as ideal. Children are a focus area, and kindergarten is presented as the main arena in which risk-reducing practices can be employed. To eliminate unhealthy and risk-producing practices, kindergartens should be guided to establish new standards for physical activity and meals. It is through these institutions and policy initiatives that the government will facilitate good health choices.

The message in Document B is that children in kindergarten are the most physically active segment of the population. Thus, what was described as a major public health problem in Document A might not be a problem in Document B (i.e., four years later). In Document B, it is young people who are the targets for new measures to increase physical activity, and they are the ones who should make good health choices. Did Document A create a problem that was not yet there? Does 'risk reduction' tend to become 'risk production' by creating new problems, such as standardisation, variation and exclusion? For instance, the measures to increase physical activity among children in kindergartens described in Document A as necessary to prevent the health risk problem have already been initiated and have become standard in Norwegian kindergartens (Grorud District, 2014).

5.2 *What Is too Little?*
The concrete claims in both documents are that today's children and youth are not active enough and are less active than before. This generates a norm of what children should be and indicates what they should not be. The documents convey the message that this issue (citizen health) is out of control. This is an expression of the educational paradox: children and young people should have freedom of choice but must be guided to make the right choices to reach the prescribed level of health in the future. In Document A, kindergarten children are ordered to move in specific ways chosen by adults. In Document B, the youth should make good choices themselves. We could characterise this as a health education paradox (cf. Løvlie, 2008).

5.3 *How Has This Representation of the Problem Come About?*
Today, access to "big data" has increased. These data provide grounds for associations between phenomena and are interpreted as explanatory conditions. Researchers and politicians can problematise both one and the other as problems and use data to problematise in new ways. Access to these new data changes how we view problems and enables us to discover new problems that were not apparent before. Time is interesting here. The past is somewhat unclear. We do not know what has happened before, and instead, we predict risks on the basis of which we act in the present for the future.

5.4 *What Is Silently Understood?*
The child, here and now, is silently understood as a future adult. The responsibility to act in the present to become a good citizen in the future is placed on

the individual. Physical activity is represented as an instrumental force. The child is equated to their physical activity and the amount of that activity. This objectification of the child is far from the UNCRC's concept of the child as an individual who has a right to express their views freely in all matters affecting them and whose views should be given due weight in accordance with their age and maturity (article 12) (United Nations, 1989). The child is understood as a future adult who is healthy and not sick. It is taken for granted that action here and now will provide future gains. However, the WHO's (2010) recommendation is aimed at children aged between 5 and 17. It remains unchallenged whether these recommendations for older children are useful for children aged between 1 and 5, which is the age of kindergarten children in Norway.

This health policy paradox places responsibility on children and youth, while at the same time prescribing that the adults must do something about the problem and control the children and young people. The policy is silent on how adults decide on the benefits of certain activities for children and youth. It seems unclear whether the problem lies with the children and youth or with society. Politicians and bureaucrats can propose measures, which are implemented as practices in kindergarten and schools. This must be operationalised within specific contexts. People must do new things, and this creates new economies and practices, for instance physical activity experts and physical activity programs in kindergarten and schools. The concerns for the sick adult are paradoxical. We do not know whether the measures targeting schools and kindergartens will lead to healthier adults.

5.5   How Can the Represented Problem Be Challenged, Disrupted and Replaced?

Children are movement-oriented, and we are all moving beings (Sheets-Johnstone, 2011). How, then, do we regulate movement in society? Is it a cause for concern that children are moving less than before? What do we end up with if children are less physically active than before? There is silence regarding what the children can use their new-found time for or what they might gain by moving less. Such gains could include rest, artistic experience, environmental awareness, social participation and the development of citizenship and democratic competencies.

In the two public health policy documents examined in this study, physical activity is presented as similar to health; this health concept is instrumental and behaviourally understood. Physical activity is understood as a double benefit for children insofar as it benefits them both in the present and the future. However, if it is linked to risk, its non-occurrence becomes a deficiency. Reports on physical activity and health have an instructive character. When they are translated and operationalised within local contexts, the linguistic implications are expressed through practitioners attempts to translate documents into practices, with the result that practices are categorical and standardised, rather than adapted to contexts.

6   Conclusion

What is at risk? Childhood as a purpose and not a goal in and of itself becomes the basis for action. When children and youth are projected as objects rather than actors and reduced to their quantified behaviour, they are understood as becomings and not as beings of becomings (Uprichard, 2008). This perspective contradicts that of the UNCRC, which regards children as active agents, capable of reflecting upon and speaking about their own situation and of being entitled to speak freely about it (article 12) (United Nations, 1989). It may also contradict society's view of health. Society does not see health solely in terms of disease and a future synonymous with the risk of illness and early death. It does regard future health as inseparable from history and the present (Koselleck, 1985). In a Nordic – and, more specifically, Norwegian – cultural context, children's present and future well-being and health are seen as deeply connected to their access to privacy, free play and freedom to spend time away from adult surveillance and discipline. Norwegian public health policy, which is highly influenced by the WHO's policy (2010, 2015), is based on a precautionary principle that appears to be very effective. In this public health policy, variation among children and youth is represented as a problem and provides a ground for continuous linking of political language to political action (Skinner, 2002).

The Norwegian government's management of life in the name of the well-being of the population (Rose, 2001), as a translation of the WHO's global health policy, appears to lose sight of the fact that although they live in the best of societies, large groups of the population are projected as the antitype of those who engage in healthy behaviour (Popkewitz, 2018) and make judicious life choices. Peters (2018) argues that global challenges, such as climate change, food insecurity, massive migration, refugee crises and emerging and re-emerging diseases, are mutually reinforcing and cause the greatest harm to the most vulnerable populations. When policy-makers focus on the physical activity and individual choices of children and youth and when more global challenges, such as the covid-19 pandemic in 2020, remain on the periphery of public health policy-making, it is clear that considerable changes in our dialogue relating to risks and health policy nationally and globally are required.

Notes

1. To provide some context for Norwegian public health policy concerning children and youth, Statistics Norway (ssb.no) has reported that 70% of women participate in work life in Norway, and 92% of all children aged 1–5 years attend kindergarten. All children start in school during the calendar year in which they turn 6 years old and have a statutory right to 13 years of compulsory education. In Norway, 92% of the 16–18-year olds are pupils, apprentices or trainees in upper secondary education, and 93% of these attend public schools (ssb.no).
2. Question 1: What's the 'problem' of represented to be (constituted to be) in a spesific policy or policies? Question 2: What presuppositions – necessary meanings antecedent to an argument – and assumptions underlie this representation of the 'problem'? Question 3: How has this representation of the 'problem' come about? Question 4: What is left unproblematic in this problem representation? Where are the silences? Question 5: What effects (discursive, subjectification, and lived) are produced by this representation of the 'problem'? Question 6: How and where has this representation of the 'problem' been produced, disseminated, and defended? How has it been and/or can it be questioned, disrupted, and replaced? See Bacchi (2016, p. 9).
3. The Norwegian word for kindergarten is 'barnehage', and 'barn' is also the Norwegian word for child and children (both singular and plural). The Norwegian word 'skole' means 'school', which is the educational context for children aged 6–18. However, the Norwegian word for the period of compulsory education from level 8 to level 10 is 'ungdomsskole', which includes the word 'ung', often translated to 'youth' in English. We took these language variations into account when developing the selection criteria for the summative analysis.

References

Aarskog, E., Barker, D., & Borgen, J. S. (2018). What were you thinking? A methodological approach for exploring decision-making and learning in physical education. *Sport, Education and Society*. https://doi.org/10.1080/13573322.2018.1491836

Adab, P., Pallan, M., Lancashire, E. R., Hemming, K., Frew, E., Barret, T., ... Cheng, K. K. (2018). Effectiveness of a childhood obesity prevention programme delivered through schools, targeting 6 and 7 year olds: Cluster randomised controlled trial (WAVES study). *BMJ* 2018, 360. https://doi.org/10.1136/bmj.k211

Bacchi, C. (1999). *Women, policy and politics: The construction of policy problems*. Sage Publications. http://dx.doi.org/10.4135/9781446217887.

Bacchi, C. (2016). *Problematizations in health policy: Questioning how 'problems' are constituted in policies*. Sage Open. https://doi.org/10.1177/2158244016653986

Beck, U. (1992). *Risk society: Towards a new modernity*. Sage.

Biesta, G. J. J. (2014). *The beautiful risk of education*. Paradigm Publishers.

Borgen, J. S. (2018a, June 28). *Monitoring of quality PE – From a Norwegian perspective: Realities and perspectives*. Paper presented at the meeting of the Conceil Europeen des Rescherches en Education Physique et Sportive (CEREPS) 2018, Workshops, University of Lisbon, Lisbon, Portugal.

Borgen, J. S. (2018b). *International comparative review of physical education. OECD education 2030 in-depth analysis of Physical Education (PE) in 12 countries* [Report prepared under the auspices of the OECD Future of Education and Skills 2030 project]. Norwegian School of Sport Sciences.

Carson, L. (2018, February 13). *The politics of the problem: How to use Carol Bacchi's work.* Power to Persuade. http://www.powertopersuade.org.au/blog/the-politics-of-the-problem-using-carol/12/2/2018

Christensen, P., & Mikkelsen, M. R. (2008). Jumping off and being careful: Children's strategies of risk management in everyday life. *Sociology of Health & Illness, 30*(1), 112–130. https://doi.org/10.1111/j.1467-9566.2007.01046.x

Cigman, R. (2012). We need to talk about well-being. *Research Papers in Education, 274*(4), 449–462. https://doi.org/10.1080/02671522.2012.690238

Ekberg, M. (2007). The parameters of the risk society: A review and exploration. *Current Sociology, 55*(3), 343–366. https://doi.org/10.1177/0011392107076080

Foucalt, M. (1997). The birth of biopolitics. In P. Rabinow (Ed.), *Michel Foucault, ethics: Subjectivity and truth* (pp. 73–9). The New Press.

Giddens, A. (1998). Risk society: The context of british politics. In J. Franklin (Ed.), *The politics of risk society order.* Polity Press.

Grorud District. (2014). *The Grorud standard for public health work in kindergarten.* Grorud District.

Hsieh, H.-F., & Shannon, S. E. (2005). Three approaches to qualitative content analysis. *Qualitative Health Research, 15*(9), 1277–1288. http://journals.sagepub.com/doi/10.1177/1049732305276687

Ingulfsvann, L. S., Engelsrud, G., & Moe, V. F. (2020). Tensions and tractions of moving together and alone in physical education. *Sport, Education and Society*. https://doi.org/10.1080/13573322.2020.1712654

Koselleck, R. (1985). *Futures past: On the semantics of historical time.* Columbia University Press.

Kriemler, S., Zahner, L., Schindler, C., Meyer, U., Hartmann, T., Hebestreit, H., ... & Puder, J. J. (2010). Effect of school based physical activity programme (KISS) on fitness and adiposity in primary schoolchildren: Cluster randomised controlled trial. *BMJ, 340,* c785. https://doi.org/10.1136/bmj.c785

Langøien, L. J., Terragni, L., Rugseth, G., Nicolaou, M., Holdsworth, M., Stronks, K., Lien, N., & Roo, G. (2017). Systematic mapping review of the factors influencing physical activity and sedentary behaviour in ethnic minority groups in Europe: A DEDIPAC study. *International Journal of Behavioral Nutrition and Physical Activity, 14*(99), 1–24. https://doi.org/10.1186/s12966-017-0554-3

Løvlie, L. (2008, March 28). *The pedagogical paradox and its relevance for education.* Paper presented at The Philosophy of Education Society of Great Britain (PESGB)

Annual Conference, Oxford. https://www.researchgate.net/profile/Lars_Lovlie2/publication/242678544_The_Pedagogical_Paradox_and_its_Relevance_for_Education/links/56a6183d08ae2c689d39d060.pdf

Malone, K. (2007). The bubble-wrap generation: Children growing up in walled gardens. *Environmental Education Research, 13*(4), 513–527. https://doi.org/10.1080/13504620701581612

Muellmann, S., Steenbock, B., De Cocker, K. De Craemer, M., Hayes, C., O'Shea, M. P., ... Pischke, C. R. (2017). Views of policy makers and health promotion professionals on factors facilitating implementation and maintenance of interventions and policies promoting physical activity and healthy eating: Results of the DEDIPAC project. *BMC Public Health, 17*(932), 1–17. https://doi.org/10.1186/s12889-017-4929-9; doi:10.1186/s12889-017-4929-9

Norwegian Institute of Public Health (NIPH). (2017). *Physical activity in Norway. Public Health report*. Norwegian Institute of Public Health. https://www.fhi.no/nettpub/hin/levevaner/fysisk-aktivitet/

OECD. (2016). *The future of education and skills. Education 2030* (Position paper). Author. https://www.oecd.org/education/2030/E2030%20Position%20Paper%20(05.04.2018).pdf

OECD. (2017). *PISA 2015 results: Students' well-being, PISA* (Vol. III). http://dx.doi.org/10.1787/9789264273856-en

OECD. (2019). *OECD future of education 2030. Making physical education dynamic and inclusive for 2030. International curriculum analysis*. https://www.oecd.org/education/2030-project/contact/OECD_FUTURE_OF_EDUCATION_2030_MAKING_PHYSICAL_DYNAMIC_AND_INCLUSIVE_FOR_2030.pdf

Peters, D. H. (2018). Health policy and systems research: The future of the field. *Health Research Policy and Systems, 16*(84). https://doi.org/10.1186/s12961-018-0359-0

Popkewitz, T. (2018, September 6). *The paradox of research: The good intentions of inclusion that excludes and abjects*. Keynote presented at European Conference on Educational Research (ECER) 2018 Conference, Bolzano. https://eera-ecer.de/ecer-2018-bolzano/whats-on/keynote-speakers-keynote-panel/thomas-popkewitz/

Qvortrup, J. (2009). Childhood as a structural form. In J. Qvortrup, W. A. Corsaro, & M. S. Honig (Eds.), *The Palgrave handbook of childhood studies* (pp. 21–33). Palgrave Macmillan.

Ministry of Health and Care Services. (2015). *Folkehelsemeldingen. Mestring og muligheter* (Meld. St. 19 (2014–2015)) [Mastering and possibilities. Public Health White Paper 19 (2014–2015)]. https://www.regjeringen.no/no/dokumenter/meld.-st.-19-2014-2015/id2402807/

Ministry of Health and Care Services. (2019). *Folkehelsemeldinga. Gode liv i eit trygt samfunn* (Meld. St. 19 (2018–2019)) [Good lives in a safe society. Public Health White Paper 19 (2018–2019)]. https://www.regjeringen.no/no/dokumenter/meld.-st.-19-20182019/id2639770/

Rose, N. (2001). The politics of life itself. *Theory, Culture and Society, 18*(6), 1–30.

Sheets-Johnstone, M. (2011). *The primacy of movement* (exp. 2nd ed.). John Benjamins Publishing.

Skinner, Q. (2002). *Visions of politics: Regarding method* (Vol. 1). Cambridge University Press. https://doi.org/10.1017/CBO9780511790812

Skrede, T. (2019). *Prospective associations between sedentary time, physical activity and cardiometabolic risk factors in children: The active smarter kids study* (Unpublished doctoral dissertation). Norwegian School of Sport Sciences.

Tin, M. B., Telseth, F., Tangen, J. O., & Giulianotti, R. (Eds.). (2019). *The Nordic model and physical culture.* Routledge.

United Nations (1989). United Nations Convention on the Right of the Child (UNCRC). Retrieved April 21, 2020, from https://downloads.unicef.org.uk/wp-content/uploads/2010/05/UNCRC_united_nations_convention_on_the_rights_of_the_child.pdf?_ga=2.259582415.454887985.1587459175-44770236.1585716747

Uprichard, E. (2008). Children as beings and becomings: Children, childhood, and temporality. *Children and Society, 22*(4), 303–313.

WHO. (1990). *Prevention in childhood of adult cardiovascular diseases: Time for action. Report of a WHO Expert Committee* (Technical report series, World Health Organization). Author.

WHO. (2010). *Recommendations on physical activity for health.* Author.

WHO. (2015). *Health in all policies: Training manual.* Author. https://www.who.int/social_determinants/publications/9789241507981/en/

WHO. (2018). *Factsheet: Physical activity and young people.* Author. http://www.who.int/dietphysicalactivity/factsheet_young_people/en/

CHAPTER 10

'Childish' beyond Age: Reconceptualising the Aesthetics of Resistance

Susanne C. Ylönen

Abstract

This chapter explores the concept of 'aesthetic sublation' – a performative mode of meaning making that seeks to degrade its object (Ylönen, 2016; Korsmeyer, 2011). Here, the phenomenon of aesthetic sublation is discussed as a form of resistance. Moreover, it is related to intergenerational negotiations through cases in which the labels of 'childish' and 'horrific' or 'nasty' converge. The chapter offers a review of how resistance is conceptualized in, for example, childhood studies, aesthetics and research on popular culture and it asks what can be gained by reconceptualising these instances as aesthetic sublation.

Keywords

children's culture – resistance – aesthetics – childish – nasty

1 Introduction

Let us consider some examples related to the consumption and creation of so-called 'low' culture: The enjoyment and creation of content deemed inappropriate or insulting or dirty and trash. Turning high standards into corrupted, humorous interpretations that entertain a selected group. Managing awesome, overpowering things and the fear or admiration that they cause by a willful lowering and concretising. These are examples of activities that humans in general and children in particular engage in. In them, things that are not under an individual's power are managed and controlled through reinterpretations, aesthetically. But how do we conceptualize this form of aesthetic control or management?

This article explores the methodological potential of concepts through a discussion of the concept of 'aesthetic sublation' – a performative mode of meaning making that seeks to control its object via a willful lowering (Korsmeyer, 2011; Ylönen, 2016). Here, the phenomenon is discussed as a form of resistance. Moreover, it is related to intergenerational negotiations through cases in which the labels of 'childish' and 'horrific' or 'nasty' converge. The questions addressed range from a broader "Why do we need to discuss and to revise concepts?" to more specific ones, such as "What *new* does the concept of aesthetic sublation (as a conceptualisation of resistance) offer in relation to concepts such as the grotesque and the abject, or less well-known terms such as stuplimity and ket aesthetics?".

The approach of the paper is rooted in research on horror in children's culture. Horror is often controlled through aestheticisation (beautification) and cutification (cute-making) in adult-produced children's culture. Children themselves, however, often resort to a carnivalising or an aesthetically sublating approach that seeks to control possibly frightening experiences through interpretations and re-iterations that focus on disgust and humor. This approach resists aestheticisation and counters the practice of cutsification, and it does not adhere to discourses that label unwanted content 'trash' either. Rather, it is the playful appropriation of trashy things in a socially meaningful and perhaps 'childlike' (as in open to new interpretations in a positive sense) manner. As such it is also associated with lack of respect and resistance to social norms and, thus, negative 'childishness'. This same label of 'childishness' is also used to discredit similar approaches in adult culture or culture in general.

The dichotomy between childishness and childlikeness mirrors the discourses on what is suitable for children or desirable behavior in children or adults. As such, it directly relates to the UNCRC's Article 31, which states the child's right to engage in play and recreational activities as long as they are "appropriate to the age of the child" (United Nations, 1989). This appropriateness is, of course, under constant negotiation in day-to-day interactions between children and their caretakers and it naturally gives rise to many acts of resistance. Not all of this resistance is aesthetic, but some of it is. In order to outline the phenomenon, it is useful to look at the terminology used in relation to it.

When describing age and generation related resistance, people often talk of the terrible two's, of teenage rebellion, and of whole generations that embrace certain countercultural aesthetics. In the field of aesthetics, resistance may also be described through, among others, terms such as carnivalism, and the embracing of abject and grotesque content and expression - with case examples ranging from offensive humor to punk aesthetics. I claim that there are similarities between the above-mentioned forms of age and generation related resistance and the aesthetic concepts applied to things that are considered nasty and distasteful. I also argue that we need a new concept to discuss the aesthetics of resistance. Many of the available concepts are too heavily bound to certain theories, fields or cases to sufficiently bridge disciplinary borders and to fully encompass the whole richness of the aesthetics of resistance. I am conscious of the fact that the concept that I am suggesting has its drawbacks as well, but I would like to offer the ideas discussed in this paper as an example of conceptual work that still needs attention within aesthetics more broadly and the study of children's culture in particular.

Content-wise, this article traces points in which aesthetic value statements related to disgust and disapproval co-occur with age-related categorisations and alternative peer-cultural meaning making. It is somewhat like a review article that looks at how resistance is conceptualized in childhood studies, aesthetics and research on popular culture and it asks what can be gained by reconceptualising these instances as aesthetic sublation. The examples brought forth in the paper thus include references to (1) previous research focusing on resistant, aesthetic behavior within childculture studies, (2) references to conceptualisations of resistance within developmental-psychology and counterculture research and (3) examples of the methodological framing that I undertook in my own research of child cultural horror.

2 Developing New Concepts

Concepts may be understood as units of knowledge or as mental representations (Blunden, 2014; Margolis & Laurence, 2014), tools that people use to communicate ideas. They 'look like words' and are used to 'facilitate discussion' (Bal, 2002, pp. 22–23) and most research guidebooks would advise the graduate student or aspiring researcher to define the concepts in use in a clear and, if possible, unambiguous manner – or, at least to offer a 'working definition' of the concepts in use. As Geoffrey Harpham notes:

> As a practical matter we commonly adhere to several tacit assumptions about ideas: that they can be clearly expressed; that they have kernels or cores in which all is tidy, compact and organized; and that the goal of analysis is to set limits to them, creating sharply defined, highly differentiated, and therefore useful concepts. We assume that, however complex an idea may be, it is essentially coherent and that it can most profitably be discussed in an orderly way. (Harpham, 2006, pp. xxi–xxii)

Whereas some words, like 'childhood' or 'children's culture' may be used as both concrete time-, space- or material-related everyday words and as abstract, theoretical concepts, others are created from the start as theoretical tools, as generalisations of observations or theoretical work that has been done in relation to certain phenomena (Metsämuuronen, 2011, pp. 50–52; Hirsijärvi et al., 2009). The concept of agency, for example, is a purely abstract or theoretical notion and the same applies to the notion of resistance - or, indeed the idea of aesthetics. And of course even seemingly arbitrary concepts can be deconstructed and theorised in ways that produce fruitful conversations and even paradigm shifts (as the field of childhood studies - deconstructing the notion of childhood - exemplifies) (James & Prout, 1997). Concepts, thus, have methodological potential beyond their common or working definitions.

The concept of aesthetic sublation is an example of the more abstract kind. It denotes a process of degradation and control, but it also designates the serious, philosophical potential that disgusting matters have. The concept 'sublate' was first used in relation to aesthetics by Carolyn Korsmeyer in her 2011 book *Savoring disgust: The foul and the fair in aesthetics*. For Korsmeyer, the negative experience of disgust can be turned into the positive experience of the 'sublate' just as the negative experience of terror can be turned into positive awe in the experience of the sublime. Borrowing the term from the field of alchemy, where it denotes the transition of matter from gaseous to solid form, Korsmeyer argues that the concept 'sublate' can be regarded as the opposite of sublimation (or the sublime) also in a metaphorical sense. Hence, the term sublate can be taken to refer to the magnetic pull that death and decay exercise over us, although they are disgusting (Korsmeyer, 2011, pp. 130–135).

When writing my doctoral dissertation, I found Korsmeyer's account of the sublate promising, as I was, at the time, trying to understand the lure of the nasty and ridiculous kinds of horror entertainment. These kinds of horror narratives were not pleasing in the simple, pleasurable sense of the beautiful (as, for example, aestheticised violence), nor did they fit into the category of the sublime (the lofty, philosophical, awe-inspiring over-whelmingness of things beyond the grasp of our senses). Rather, they were affiliated with the grotesque and the ugly, or with what has been theorised as abject in the wake of Julia Kristeva's influential account in her book *Powers of Horror* (Kristeva, 1982). Yet none of the established concepts such as the grotesque or the abject really seemed like the perfect counterpoint to the beautiful and the sublime. Perhaps this was due to the fact that the grotesque, to me, was too bound up with the literary and the art historical to be easily applied to the everyday production and consumption of disgusting entertainment (especially its performative aspects), while the abject was too heavily indebted to a psychoanalytical framework. Furthermore, I felt like I could not select one of these concepts over the other, as they both have their advantages - and using both would have unnecessarily divided the category that I saw as the third part of the three-partite heuristic model of sublime-beautiful-nasty.

This is why I decided to adopt the term 'sublate' - or my own, corrupted version of it as 'aesthetic sublation'. As I saw it, this new, relatively unqualified term promised to be more malleable and, importantly, free from the heavy theoretical baggage that accompanies more established terms like the grotesque or the abject. Since I was leaning on Korsmeyer, I did not wholly invent the new term, but I did turn it into a more performative form, that emphasised the making-of aspect of deeming something disgusting. To me, the notion of aesthetic sublation exemplified how something like horror can be made 'dirty' and yet promising, discursively.

However, working with not-yet-established terms has its drawbacks as well. One of the most obvious problems with using newly produced terms and concepts is the fact that no one will know what you speak about if you do not provide an elaborate definition or description of the concepts while you use them. This can distract the reader from any analysis that you attempt to make while using the concept. In the case of 'aesthetic sublation' one may, furthermore, run the specific risk of people confusing the term with the Hegelian concept of 'Aufhebung', which often gets translated as 'sublation' in English. To Korsmeyer, this confusion does not seem dangerous, as the Hegelian concept of Aufhebung refers to two contrasting things or ideas being resolved by a new idea that both preserves and transcends them (Korsmeyer, 2011, pp. 130–131; "Aufhebung", n.d.), which resonates with Korsmeyer's understanding of the sublate as something philosophically productive. Yet, if one wants to read the process of aesthetic sublation as a willful lowering or degradation of things that might otherwise be experienced as beautiful or frightening, the conflation with Aufhebung (which carries connotations of lifting up and suspending) might not be as desirable.

A further, more general danger is the fact that by coming up with a new term, one might actually just be referring to the same things as before by a new name, without actually providing new or significant insights to the matter. After all, the sublate is not the first term to appear in theoretical musings as a counterpoint to the sublime. Victor Hugo already famously claimed that the grotesque provided respite from the beautiful and the sublime that had previously dominated the field of art (Hugo, 1827/2001). And in 2005 Sianne Ngai suggested that the term 'stuplimity', a synthesis of boredom and shock, could be used as 'twentieth-century mutation' of the affect of the sublime (Ngai, 2005, pp. 5, 9, 248–297). This is probably why all textbooks on methodology warn one from getting too creative in the process of academic writing.

Yet there are fields in which reinventions of vocabulary, or corruptions/alterations of existing terms, are more common than in others. The field of philosophy is a good example. Some texts produced within the field of philosophy are nearly untranslatable, because the language in them has been cleverly manipulated to evoke new ideas by twists of words that do not evoke the same ideas in another language. Martin Heidegger's philosophical use of the term *Dasein* presents a case in point, as has been noted by Risto Niemi-Pynttäri (2000) who tackles the problems of translation in relation to this particular concept in his text 'Kuinka Dasein kääntyy?' (How to translate Dasein?). And of course new concepts are invented in any field, whenever developments in science or our understanding of the world call for a renewed vocabulary. What seems important for the success of a new concept, is that it should be evocative enough to 'stick' affectively (Ahmed, 2004; Heath & Heath, 2007). Following Dan and Chip Heath's ideas on stickiness (Heath & Heath, 2007), one could argue that a sticky concept is one that evokes the right connotations and meets the right needs (turns up in the right place at the right time) and that is thus taken into use on a larger scale by people who feel that they need it. This does not mean that the concept needs to be clear or well-defined. In fact, a somewhat indefinite or vague concept may prove more sticky, as its level of abstractness might cover a greater area.

But how could one evaluate the potential of a new concept before applying it? To answer this question, I will go back to my own dissertation process and to the expectations that I had in regard to the new concept of the 'sublate'.

3   Dreaming up the Concept of Aesthetic Sublation

What I was searching for, at the time of my dissertation project, was a term that could serve as a third point in a heuristic model that would express the different approaches that people may adopt when creating and evaluating horror. I had characterised the other two parts as a sort of being-overwhelmed in the tradition of the sublime and as a sort of beautification or cutsification in the tradition of the aestheticisation of violence, but I was lacking a conceptualisation for the sort of control that comes in the form of ridicule and degradation. To speak of 'grotesque-making' or 'uglifying' seemed unhandy as none of these terms encompassed the peer-cultural promise of the phenomenon, and to resort to 'abjecting' seemed to evoke the motion of rejecting or casting away, while there was definitely a sense of enjoyment and appropriation to this kind of behavior in the social valorisation of the bad and the nasty forms of horror that I had witnessed. 'Carnivalisation', in turn, did not fulfill the need, as it strongly connects to the celebratory, which was not always the case in approaches that resorted to this kind of ugly-making. Some of the ugly-making that I witnessed was definitely quite everyday and did not encompass the social role-inversions inherent in the carnivalesque, as the case of labeling some cultural products 'trash' exemplifies.

The sublate, then, came to me at a moment when I was looking for a tool, a concept that would help me built a theoretical and methodological framework for my study. Like the idea of aestheticisation, aesthetic sublation seemed to me a way of controlling the frightening. Yet, it also curiously overlapped with the sublime (or aesthetic sublimation, not to be confused with the Freudian definition of sublimation), in that it could tip into a direction that might be interpreted as frightening or alarming, which makes it a practice that can be used to shock 'outsiders'. As an example, one can refer to the peer- or subcultural appropriation of things considered 'trashy' or inappropriate by the mainstream (such as adults, or other more conventional people, people not part of a certain peer-, sub- or counterculture). This kind of appropriation can be observed in, for example, horror fandom (Hills, 2005) and the consumption of weird candies observed in children's culture (James, 1998). In both cases, a line can be drawn according to differing tastes: horror fans will attest to a taste for the nasty or the horrific, and children may prefer candies that toy with the improper (cannibalistic consumption of skull-shaped candy or eyeballs, or, the enjoyment of lollipops dipped in toilet-shaped containers of tasty powder). Next to these even the practice of drawing horns, moustaches or spectacles on celebrities and models in magazines may be considered as an example of aesthetic sublation. But how have these approaches been conceptualised in the above-mentioned fields of study: child and peer cultures?

4   Forms of Resistance in and around Children's Culture

As said, the process of expressing enjoyment in the face of products that insult mainstream taste has been characterised as an act of resistance in both subcultures and children's culture. This can be explained by the Foucauldian notion of power relations, as resistance, for Foucault, was a way of self creation (Butin, 2001, p. 169). The link between resistance as self creation and aesthetics as a field devoted to taste can be exemplified by punk aesthetics. Like shock art, a punk attitude can be described as a manner of puncturing "conformity's protective balloon" (Wilson, 2002, p. 71), but it is notable, that this attitude often takes form in clothing and music - that is, aesthetics. When trying to relate this aesthetic stance to children's culture, one might thus follow the ideas of Roger Scruton, who aptly notes that aesthetic judgement (which to him related to the beautiful) can be 'experienced as an affliction', 'an intolerable burden' of ideals and aspirations that are in sharp contrast to the 'tawdriness of our improvised lives'. According to Scruton, child cultural appreciation of disgusting things can be explained by a desire to turn the expectations of niceness around:

> The desire to desecrate is a desire to turn aesthetic judgement against itself, so that it no longer seems like a judgement of us. This is what you see all the time in children – the delight in disgusting noises, words, allusions, which helps them to distance themselves from the adult world that judges them, and whose authority they wish to deny. (Hence the appeal of Roald Dahl.) (Scruton, 2009, p. 184)

This delight that children take in trash has inspired some research, although none of it is very recent. In his article "'Trash' as a Barrier against the Adult World" Kaspar Maase (2002) discusses children's movie screenings in pre World War I Germany. He suggests that children of the time used the emergent media constellations of 'trash mag' series and film as well as pop music to "mark out a territory in which they temporarily – liberated themselves from the duties and constraints of the adult world" and in which they evaded adult control and middle-class protection. In the pre WWI context studied by Maase, 'filth' denominated things that were not forbidden, but that were considered obscene, lewd or erotic and which thus represented a danger for the unsophisticated masses under the title 'Volk' (Maase, 2002, pp. 153–154). Margareta Rönnberg (1990) takes up this same theme in a 1990's Finnish context her book on the child cultural appropriation of trash, or, not-so-good children's culture. Her argument can be placed in the context of the 1980's TV violence debate and it represents an attempt to defend children's rights and agency in an atmosphere of moral panic and amongst calls to protective measures that seemed to overlook children's rights and agency. In short, she questions the adult ability to decide which child cultural products are good or bad while arguing that children have the right to determine what is good and interesting to them. Allison James's term ket aesthetic, which she used to describe the above mentioned consumption of sweets, has likewise been recycled/re-used in discussions of the values of child cultural products such as the dislike that some parents faced in the case of Barney the purple dinosaur (Thompson,

2005), which proves that the phenomenon of culturally negotiating between children's and adults' differing tastes is itself a somewhat 'sticky' a theme, even if the concepts used to describe the aesthetics of resistance related to it do not really 'stick' enough to become big mainstream concepts.

In order to understand how large the variety of concepts applied to child cultural resistance actually is, one would, however, also have to look at how resistance itself has been theorised. The Oxford Living Dictionary defines 'resistance' as "the refusal to accept or comply with something" attaching it to more or less open power-play such as the use of force or violence or a "secret organisation resisting authority" ("Resistances", n.d.). On a general definitional level, resistance is, hence, seen as a reaction to oppression and as a mode of defiance directed at dominant cultural norms and hierarchies, whether these be gender, class, race or age related (Leblanc, 1999). Within (or in relation to) children's culture, the phenomenon has been described as rebellion, inappropriate behavior and opposition or counteraction, next to which we also speak of 'childish antics', defiance and noncompliance (Stolp, 2011; Dix et al., 2007; Lickenbrock et al., 2013). Following a developmental framework, people also speak of 'the terrible twos' or of 'teenage rebellion' assigning the defiance of adult rules and norms to certain more oppositional life phases that one is supposed to grow out of.

It is fairly easy to find examples of child cultural resistance, but as the multitude of terms used about the phenomenon indicates, the conceptualisation of the phenomenon itself is rather uneven and scattered. In fact, conceptual aspects are largely left undiscussed in many of the empirical studies on the subject. Research on (or related to) child cultural resistance tends to focus on conflicts around food, media consumption and clothing, or, more exactly, on (1) disagreements around sugar and other unhealthy products, (2) disputes on sexual and violent media contents and (3) generational battles around (foul) language and neat or sloppy dressing (Fuhs, 2017, p. 58; O'Connell & Brannen, 2014; Jenkins, 2006; Rönnberg, 1990; Martsola & Mäkelä-Rönnholm, 2006; Goode & Ben-Yehuda, 1994; Leblanc, 1999), but while the acts of children and young people within these conflicts are often categorised as resistance, the conceptualisation of the term itself remains vague. Furthermore, the terms used to describe the phenomenon seem to be field-specific. The search word 'noncompliance' will, hence, not yield any research results within sociologically oriented journals such as *Childhood*, while it does produce hits when used within journals like *Infant and Child Development*. 'Resistance', which is more commonly used throughout the different child culture related research fields, may thus seem like a better term. It is, however, a "rather loose concept, one open to many interpretations" as Lauraine Leblanc, writing on girls within the punk subculture, notes. In youth or subculture research, it has been read into the 'construction of sartorial style'. Feminist studies, in turn, have located it in, for example, "subversive interpretations of texts" (Leblanc, 1999, p. 14; see also Lurie, 1990). Searches with the search word 'resistance' are thus likely to produce many hits, but not many of the found studies will provide helpful definitions of the concept itself.

One of the few attempts at discussing the phenomenon of child cultural resistance through its various conceptualisations is provided by Marleena Stolp (2011), who examines the phenomenon and the different terms that can be applied to it within and in relation to a theater project prepared and executed with 6-year-old children. In the project, the screenwriter-actor-children defied the adult researcher-directors by showing no interest in rehearsing, by clogging the toilet minutes before the show and by using unplanned props on stage as well as by altering the storyline ad hoc, while performing. While the toilet episode can be described as an overt prank, the refusal to rehearse may be conceptualised as a more obtuse, less flashy, form of defiance (related to the silences discussed by Spyrou, 2016) and the altering of the storyline may be interpreted as a form of losing oneself in imaginative play while forgetting that the event is supposed to be a scripted performance (which is not necessarily an act of defiance at all). According to Stolp, the terms that we choose to describe the phenomenon matter, in that each of them carries different connotations. Using a term like 'rebellion' associates the act with the seriousness of historical uprisings. Talking about it as 'fooling around', 'pranking' or 'playfulness', in turn, links it to the idea of 'mere' childishness or even a more positive childlikeness. As Stolp notes, the terms that we use are indicative of the position that we choose or represent in what comes to the unequal power relations between children and adults (Stolp, 2011).

Other terms that have been applied in the study of child cultural resistance include the idea of interpretive reproduction, as well as terms such as hybridisation and bricolage. Following the by now paradigmatic idea of children's own agency and input in the shaping of their own cultural environments, these terms highlight the way in which children are no longer seen as passive recipients of cultural input, but as active producers and recyclers of cultural content (Corsaro, 1985, 1997; Thompson, 2005, 2007; Tam, 2012). Interpretive reproduction addresses the way in which children operate both within adult culture and within their own, independent cultures, borrowing, preserving and changing or mixing aspects of both of these overlapping worlds/cultures. It emphasises children's creativity and focuses on their participation in the shaping of cultural realities. As such, it undermines ideas of linear, top-down socialisation and indicates the importance of peer cultures in the creation of, for example, routines and values. This has made it instrumental in the development of the 'new' sociologically oriented childhood studies and its focus on children's agency (Corsaro, 2012).

Po Chi Tam (2012), writing about children's cultural resistance within the practise of sociodramatic play, offers some examples about how children in a Hong Kong kindergarden used hybridisation and bricolage as means of cultural resistance against play frames constructed by the teacher. Instead of reproducing the teacher-prescribed play frame, the children that Tam observed also broke the prescribed play frame in more or less visible ways, resorting to tactics that Tam has titled 'disarray', 'disguise' and 'invalidation'. Examples that Tam discusses include "degrading the heroic and serious task of fire fighting into a mundane housekeeping theme which even includes a whimsical and comic storyline of killing cockroaches" and turning a fishing scene supposed to train their fine-motor skills into "a rhythmic and bizarre cooking game" (Tam, 2012, p. 256). Similar research has been conducted in Finland by Suvi Pennanen (2009), who has observed, that children react to discourses of risk and protection by openly playing media related content despite the teacher's disapproval or by hiding or camouflaging non-proper content. A further Nordic example is provided by Ingvild Åmot and Borgunn Ytterhus (2013) who describe a scene of bodily resistance or rebellion in a Norwegian daycare center. They observed a situation in which a group of children peed their pants in order to get indoors during 'outdoor time', an action termed 'sneaky' by the caretakers, but conceptualised as "a response to the misrecognition of children's rights in the name of institutional logic" by the researchers.

5 The Aesthetics of Resistance, Reconceptualised

In my own research, I have made observations similar to the ones described above. In my study of child cultural horror, resistance was visible in both the production of exceptional or more daring picture books that defied the norms of children's literature in one way of the other (child culture -related resistance by adult producers) *and* in the manner in which some of the children that I interviewed, in particular moments, purposefully misinterpreted the books that we were reading (or the general subject of the discussion - the theme of horror). In the children's case, the acts of resistance included a humoristic misreading of a violent happening (the hair of a girl catching fire after she plays with matches in the 1845 picturebook *Slovenly Peter*) as 'cool hairdo', which would follow the subversive interpretations of texts as described by Leblanc in relation to feminist studies. The resistance that I identified in this case was, hence, directed at hegemonic discourses and conventions or practices of how to talk about horror *to* children and *as* children. In the first case, the actors engaging in the act of resistance were adults in charge of the production of children's culture and the manner of defiance was visible in the punk-like aesthetic and the embracing of a violent or physical solution (boxing) to the mastering of fear in a picture book. In the second case, the case of the children, resistance, in turn, took the form of subversive interpretations.

What the above presented examples have in common is that they are all rather bodily, messy, bizarre and cheap (as in sneaky) instances of rebellion - instances easily considered more or less nasty or disrespectful by adults. Terms that have so far taken the aesthetic aspects of such behaviour most fully into account are the concept of carnivalism and the idea of 'ket aesthetics'. The term 'ket aesthetic', already brought up above, was introduced to the field of child culture studies by Allison James, who used it to describe the consumption of cheap candy. James noted that the term 'ket', which had, in old English, been used to describe animals, whose meat was sold although they had died of natural causes (James, 1998, p. 394), was used by children in (which area of Britain?) in reference to cheap candies popular among them, but not valued by adults. James observed that consuming kets was marked by the breaking of regular eating times and customs. Not considered 'proper' food, kets were consumed in between regular meals. Practices like taking an already sucked-on candy out of the mouth and passing it on to the next child can likewise easily be considered improper and disgusting. Next to this, James noted that many of the kets had names that connected them to humans or items, evoking ideas of cannibalism and surrealism (James, 1998).

As said, the notion of ket aesthetics has since been used by other researchers in relation to undesired childish consumption whether this be related to food or popular culture (Thompson, 2005; Ruckenstein, 2014; Campbell Galman, 2017). Yet none of this research develops the aesthetic side of the 'kets' further and the term itself has not encountered wider following beyond the field of child culture research.

In the field of literature and visual art, the preferred term for discussing acts of word-image-based resistance, is the grotesque. Here, the reference point is most often Mikhail Bahtin's work on the carnivalesque and its subversive power (Bakhtin, 1968/1984). In a sense, the rebellious aspect of carnivalism can be equated with the idea of profanation, which, according to Paul Bouissac signifies the challenging of the limits that "determine normalcy and decency in the culture in which it occurs" (Bouissac, 1997). Scatalogy, blasphemy and obscenity can thus be related to each other and used as a means to resist the pressure of social norms. Yet this usage is, as Bakhtin has argued, not merely abusive, but can also be interpreted as a representation of irrepressible vitality and freedom. Hence, it may be argued that, while "subversion often takes the form of so-called perversion" (Hutcheon, 1983, p. 88), this perversion is fruitful and meaningful in that attacks the powerful from below, creating a lowbrow laughter that is easily equated with the laughter of the common folk, the uneducated masses, the down-trodden and the less powerful. Consequently this kind of rebellion has also been labeled 'childish', as the same custodial stance that marks attitudes toward childishness has also been applied to various other groups from the common folk to women and colonial subjects.

What is missing in the bigger picture, is a study that would draw together all these notions, made in the different fields of developmental philosophy, childhood studies and studies of children's culture, anthropology and aesthetics. Such a study could produce a more encompassing description of how the aesthetics of resistance draw on the disgusting in order to demarcate the lines between us and them. While an attempt to provide such an all-encompassing theory is beyond the scope of this article, the discussion provided here hopefully exemplifies why conceptual work is still needed in this area.

The terms that we choose to describe resistant behavior do not just reflect our ideas and positioning in what comes to child-cultural resistance. They also affect the way in which we view the people participating in such behavior. As Sally Galman (2017) remarks in her article "Brave is a dress: Understanding 'good' adults and 'bad' children through adult horror and children's play", play that is considered bad by adults may taint the materials and even the players themselves faulty in the adults' eyes. Hence, if we term resistant behavior that we consider 'low' 'childish', we end up promoting attitudes that relate children and childish tastes to 'lower' forms of culture. This is a colonialist, custodial stance. Hence it is not surprising that Sarah Ahmed has chosen to exemplify her intersectional discussion of willfulness and collective histories of struggle with the Grim Brother's fairy tale of the willful child. While willfulness as a diagnosis is often regarded a negative, problematic trait (related to spoiling and disobedience at least in the case of children (Ahmed, 2014, 59–96)), she notes that it may also be seen as positive, especially when connected to the idea of a strong will. A strong will is, furthermore, "bound up with a normative decision about what directions are forces that should be resisted" (Ahmed, 2014, p. 81).

Like willfulness, childishness could, then, also be re-appropriated in a more positive sense if its connection to the more desirable 'childlikeness' was emphasised more. As a solution we might also want to develop a vocabulary that takes into account the wider applications of 'lowering' forms of attributing value. The development of the concept of aesthetic sublation as a tool for discussing aesthetic 'lowering' is one such attempt, but its stickiness has yet to be tested outside of the case study that focusing on child cultural horror.

6 Conclusion: Sticky, Muddy and Confusing – Promises and Pitfalls of Using New Concepts

While clarity is considered a virtue that science should aspire towards, a focus on concepts often ends up blurring the subject and causing confusion. The fact that we speak of 'working definitions' reveals that most concepts used in research are far from coherent and clear. Geoffrey Harpham, continuing the line of thought quoted in the beginning, and relating it to his research on the grotesque, observes, that:

> The grotesque places all these assumptions [of clarity and neatness] in doubt. Whether considered a pattern of energy or as a psychological phenomenon, it is anything but clear. Whereas most ideas are coherent at the core and fuzzy around the edges, the grotesque is the reverse: it is relatively easy to recognize the grotesque "in" a work of art, but quite different to apprehend the grotesque directly. (Harpham, 2006, pp. xxi–xxii)

In research constellations aiming to capture the children's own voices, obstructive behaviour that seeks to deflect or complicate the action by resorting to, for example, silence or mocking carnivalisation, is often discussed as a methodological problem. Yet as Stolp and Spyrou both claim, it is essential that researchers take instances of obtrusive, resistant behaviour seriously as a comment. Taking resistant behavior seriously as a comment adheres to the UNCRC's statement of a child's right to participate in cultural life, even if it at the same time questions the appropriateness clause within this statement. Brushing such behavior off as mere disinterest, boredom or non-compliance fails to ask what else might be communicated or achieved by it (Spyrou, 2016; Stolp, 2011, p. 18; United Nations, 1989, Article 31). When applying the concept of aesthetic sublation to examples or observations, one must, hence, of course, also ask what gets sublated in these instances and why.

All in all, the fuzziness of concepts and the fuss we make about concepts shows that concepts are enormously powerful. At best, new concepts may create interest in a previously under-researched phenomenon or provide new angles to an already much discussed issue. The development of concepts also serves to highlight the researcher's own thought processes and methodological journey, which may be considered a sign of maturity in comparison to a copy-paste method. While the invention of new terms is risky – especially in some research fields and especially when practiced by young, not well-established researchers, it is quite common in other fields, and more accepted when practised by well-established intellectuals. The question of how much liberties one can take in relation to concept-building is thus discipline-related and dependent on one's social positioning.

References

Ahmed, S. (2004). Collective feelings: Or, the impressions left by others. *Theory, Culture Society, 21*(2), 25–42.
Ahmed, S. (2014). *Willful subjects*. Duke University Press.
Åmot, I., & Ytterhus, B. (2013). 'Talking bodies': Power and counter-power between children and adults in day care. *Childhood, 21*(2), 260–273.
Aufhebung. (n.d.). *Oxford living dictionaries*. Retrieved February 24, 2019, from https://en.oxforddictionaries.com/definition/aufhebung
Bakhtin, M. (1984). *Rabelais and his world*. Indiana University Press. (Original work published 1968)
Bal, M. (2002.) *Travelling concepts*. University of Toronto Press.
Blunden, A. (2012.) *Concepts: A critical approach*. Brill.
Bouissac, P. (1997). The profanation of the sacred in circus clown performances. In R. Schechner & W. Appel (Eds.), *Means of performance: Intercultural studies of theater and ritual*. Cambridge University Press.
Butin, D. W. (2001). If this is resistance I would hate to see your domination: Retrieving Foucault's notion of resistance within educational research. *Educational Studies, 32*(2), 157–176.
Campbell Galman, S. (2017). Brave is a dress: Understanding "good" adults and "bad" children through adult horror and children's play. *Childhood*, 1–14.
Corsaro, W. (1985). *Friendship and peer culture in the early years*. Ablex.
Corsaro, W. (1997). *The sociology of childhood*. Pine Forge Press.
Corsaro, W. (2012). Interpretive reproduction in children's play. *American Journal of Play, 4*(4), 488–504.
Dix, T., Stewart, A. D., Gershoff, E. T., & Day, W. H. (2007). Autonomy and children's reactions to being controlled: Evidence that both compliance and defiance may be positive markers in early development. *Child Development, 78*(4), 1204–1221.
Fuhs, B. (2017). Kindergeschmack. Überlegungen zu Ästhetik und Bildung in der Kindheit. In S. Schinkel & I. Herrmann (Eds.), *Ästhetiken in Kindheit und Jugend: Sozialisation im Spannungsfeld von Kreativität, Konsum und Distinktion* (pp. 55–75). Transkript Verlag.

Goode, E., & Nachman, B. (1994). *Moral panics: The social construction of deviance*. Blackwell Publishing.

Harpham, G. G. (2006). *On the grotesque: Strategies of contradiction in art and literature*. The Davies Group Publishers.

Heath, C., & Heath, D. (2007). *Made to stick: Why some ideas survive and others die*. Random House.

Hills, M. (2005). *The pleasures of horror*. Continuum.

Hirsijärvi, S., Remes, P., & Sajavaara, P. (2009). *Tutki ja kirjoita*. 15. painos. Tammi.

Hugo, V. (2001 [1827]). Preface to Cromwell. In *Famous prefaces. The Harvard classics. 1909–1914*. Retrieved February 8, 2019, from https://www.bartleby.com/39/40.html

Hutcheon, L. (1983). The Carnivalesque and contemporary narrative: Popular culture and the erotic. *University of Ottawa Quarterly, 53*(1), 83–94.

James, A. (1998). Confections, concoctions and conceptions. In H. Jenkins (Ed.), *The children's culture reader* (pp. 394–405). New York University Press.

James, A., & Prout, A. (1997). *Constructing and reconstructing childhood: Contemporary issues in the sociological study of childhood*. New York, NY: Routledge Falmer.

Jenkins, H. (2006). The war between effects and meanings: Rethinking the video game violence debate. In *Fans, bloggers and gamers: Exploring participatory culture* (pp. 208–221). New York University Press.

Kristeva, J. (1982). *Powers of horror: An essay on abjection*. Columbia University Press.

Korsmeyer, C. (2011). *Savoring disgust: The foul and the fair in aesthetics*. Oxford University Press.

Leblanc, L. (1999). *Pretty in punk: Girls' gender resistance in a boys' subculture*. Rutgers University Press.

Lickenbrock, D. M., Braungart-Rieker, J. M., Ekas, N. V., Zentall, S. R., Oshio, T., & Planalp, E. M. (2013). Early temperament and attachment security with mothers and fathers as predictors of toddler compliance and noncompliance. *Infant and Child Development, 22*, 580–602.

Lurie, A. (1990). *Don't tell the grown-ups: The subversive power of children's literature*. Back Bay Books.

Maase, K. (2002). "Trash" as a barrier against the adult world. In F. Mouritsen & J. Qvortrup (Eds.), *Childhood and children's culture* (pp. 155–171). University Press of Southern Denmark.

Margolis, E., & Laurence, S. (2014). Concepts. In E. N. Zalta (Ed.), *The Stanford encyclopedia of philosophy*. https://plato.stanford.edu/archives/spr2014/entries/concepts/

Martsola, R., & Mäkelä-Rönnholm, M. (2006). *Lapsilta kielletty: kuinka suojella lasta mediatraumalta*. Kirjapaja.

Metsämuuronen, J. (2011). *Tutkimuksen Tekemisen Perusteet Ihmistieteissä: E-book Opiskelijalaitos*. International Methelp, Booky.fi.

Ngai, S. (2005). *Ugly feelings*. Harvard University Press.

Niemi-Pynttäri, R. (2000). Kuinka "Dasein" kääntyy? *Niin & Näin,* 2/00, 12–13.

O'Connell, R., & Brannen, J. (2014). Children's food, power and control: Negotiations in families with younger children in England. *Childhood, 21*(1), 87–102.

Pennanen, S. (2009). Lasten medialeikit päiväkodissa. In L. Alanen & K. Karila (Eds.), *Lapsuus, lapsuuden instituutiot ja lasten toiminta* (pp. 182–206). Tampere.

Resistance. (n.d.). *Oxford living dictionaries.* Retrieved February 24, 2019, from https://en.oxforddictionaries.com/definition/resistance

Rönnberg, M. (1990) *Siistiä!: Ns. Roskakulttuurista* (A. Tamminen, Trans.). Like kustannus.

Ruckenstein, M. (2014). *Lapsuus ja talous.* Gaudeamus.

Scruton, R. (2009). *Beauty.* Oxford University Press.

Spyrou, S. (2016). Researching children's silences: Exploring the fullness of voice in childhood research. *Childhood, 23*(1), 7–21.

Stolp, M. (2011). "Nyt joku on tehnyt jotain tosi, tosi, tosi tuhmaa": Vastustus ja käsitteellistäminen 6-vuotiatten teatteriprojektissa. *Kulttuurintutkimus, 4,* 17–30.

Tam, P. C. (2012). Children's Bricolage under the gaze of teachers in sociodramatic play. *Childhood, 20*(2), 244–259.

Thompson, C. M. (2005). The ket aesthetic: Visual culture in childhood. *The International Journal of Arts Education, 3*(1), 68–81.

Thompson, C. M. (2007). The culture of childhood and the visual arts. In L. Bresler (Ed.), *International handbook of research in arts education.* Springer.

United Nations. (1989). *Convention on the Rights of the Child.* Retrieved March 24, 2020, from https://www.ohchr.org/en/professionalinterest/pages/crc.aspx

Wilson, R. R. (2002). *The Hydra's tale: Imagining disgust.* University of Alberta Press.

Ylönen, S. (2016). *Tappeleva rapuhirviö: Kauhun estetiikka lastenkulttuurissa.* Jyväskylä Studies in Humanities, University of Jyväskylä.

CHAPTER 11

Approaching Agency in Intra-Activities

Liv Torunn Grindheim

Abstract

The 1989 United Nations Convention on the Rights of the Child that legalise children's right to express their views, underlines that children have relevant perspectives and agency. This approach has been an enormous gift to the field of social childhood studies. In our contemporary, transforming, and rapidly changing society, the time has come to move forward with this concept and to challenge the dichotomy between agency and structure. Supporters of the 'material turn' claim that their way of thinking makes room for the expansion of agency as an enactment, something that someone or something has, toward agency as 'doing'/'being' in its intra-activity. Intra-action reformulates the traditional notion of causality and opens up a relatively large space for material–discursive forms of agency. To understand and take into account this larger space for material–discursive forms of agency, an outline of methods for tracing the actors involved in intra-activities is needed. The chapter is therefore structured around the question: How can emerging actors be traced in an intra-activity? Thus, discursive formation due to the materials involved and hegemonic ideas can be depicted. The actors are traced in an activity involving Polydron, a building toy. The research method has a participatory and explorative design, and the relevant actors emerge throughout the research process. Polydron, children, teachers, families, the economy, play, learning, and the position of mathematics in education: these all emerge as actors. Accordingly, a range of actors that intra-act in the presented activity is depicted through networks of connection and disconnection, and paves the way for a continuum of practices to emerge. Thus, the space for agency between actors and structures can be recognised and widened.

Keywords

early childhood education – agency – exploration – intra-activity – actors

1 Introduction

The UN Convention on the Rights of the Child that legalise children's right to express their views (United Nations, 1989, art. 12), underlines that children have relevant perspectives and agency. Approaching children's agency has been an enormous gift to the field of social childhood studies (James, 2009). Ethnographic and anthropological research designs studying children in their everyday life have revealed how children are actors and constructors of their experiences and their everyday life. Interpreting agency in this way points to interesting research that depicts the necessity of understanding children's development culturally (Nsamenang, 2008, p. 219); it reveals how agency can be recognised as more than spoken language (Colegrove & Adair, 2014, p. 131); and it claims that children's agency should be given greater acceptance, for example, in ways of assessing children (Buzzelli, 2015, p. 210). Despite these valuable contributions obtained by creating childhood as a phenomenon within sociological discourse, Prout (2011) argues that the increasing complexity and ambiguity of childhood as a contemporary, destabilised phenomenon are not confronted, since the space for 'childhood' was created largely by the terms of modernist sociology. Prout (2011) claims that one aspect of this problem is apparent in the reproduction of the dichotomised oppositions between children's agency and childhood as a social construct within the sociology of childhood – the same goes for such dichotomies as nature and culture, and children as being and becoming.

As a way of dealing with these challenging dichotomies, Prout (2011) points to the 'excluded middle' as a way of meeting the increasing complexity and ambiguity of childhood as a contemporary, destabilised phenomenon. He points to Latour's (1993) 'actor-network theory' and to the 'rhizome' metaphor found in Deleuze and Guattari (1988). In these approaches, attention is drawn to the materials and practices from which an endless stream of new phenomena, including distinctions and dichotomies, are generated and emerge. In line with emphasising the excluded middle, I call for expanding the understanding of agency by involving more than humans and language by outlining material–discursive elements to discover formation and agency, inspired by Latour (2008) and Barad (2003). Thereby, I take departure from what is often referred to as the 'material turn'. The material turn indicates that more than humans (i.e. artifacts, architecture) are to be taken into consideration when exploring agency.

Supporters of the material turn claim that their way of thinking makes room for the expansion of agency as an enactment, something that someone or something has, toward agency as 'doing'/'being' in its intra-activity (Barad,

2003, p. 827). Since intra-action reformulates the traditional notion of causality and opens up a space, it creates a relatively large space for material–discursive forms of agency. To understand and take into account this larger space for material–discursive forms for agency, an outline of methods for tracing actors involved in an intra-activity is needed. The chapter is therefore structured around the question: *How can emerging actors be traced in an intra-activity?* Thereby, discursive formation due to the materials involved and hegemonic ideas can be depicted. My overall aim is to broaden the possibility for agency to emerge in networks/ensembles in early childhood education (ECE). My contribution could pave the way for teachers and researchers to take into consideration that there will always be several actors involved when a child comes forward as competent or incompetent, not meeting the standards of what is expected for a child, or not meeting the expected aims for activities in ECE. Pointing to several actors in a network provides a wider repertoire for what to challenge or 'mend', rather than fixing an individual child's ability to act.

The involved actors are traced from an activity where children are playing with a building toy called Polydron in light of my understanding of Barad's (2003) outlines of intra-activity (intra-action) and agency, and Latour's (2008) outlines of actor-network theory. The research method has a participatory and explorative design in which relevant material for analysis emerges throughout the research process. Polydron, children, teachers, families, economic, play, learning, and the position of mathematics in education: these all emerge as actors that intra-act in the presented activity and in the research process. Thus, a range of actors that intra-act are depicted and, therefore, the space for agency in the network of actors can be recognised and widened.

2   Theoretical Concepts

There seems to be an emerging interest for reconceptualising agency in ECE (Esser et al., 2016). Spyrou (2018) states that the need for reconceptualisation emerges from the apparent 'notion of agency' that "as property of self is theoretically limiting for the field. An understanding of agency which rests in the knowledgeable, self-reflexive, independent, and autonomous individual child finds its conceptual limits in light of social life's relationality, connectedness, and interdependence" (p. 147). Several researchers contribute in this area (e.g. Bordonaro & Payne, 2012; Lee, 2001; Leonard, 2016; Valentine, 2011; Mizen & Ofosu-Kusi, 2013; Payne, 2012). As several authoritative researchers in early childhood research have done, I turn to Latour (2005) and Barad (2003,

p. 2007) when trying to capture the actors in a network that are emerging from a specific activity in ECE.

There is an academic expectation to carefully explain newer ontologies and to show weaknesses with the former ontologies – which, in my case, is the sociology of childhood – and how and who has challenged these approaches, and their suggestions for how to meet these weaknesses. This expectation serves as an explanation for the long and detailed theoretic parts in the presentation of posthumanistic research. In contract to this expectation and practice, I simply and briefly point to the research field. Therefore, the rest of the theoretical part of this article is limited to presenting concepts that have room for unpredictability and instability and that have become relevant for how I traced the actors in an intra-activity that involved exploration. These concepts are exploration, intra-activity, actors and agency.

Exploration: Materials is emphasised in several ontological approaches like phenomenology, semiotics, and cultural-historical theories. In these approaches, the humanistic subjects are most often presented as related to materiality and to the world without being a part of it. Materials are viewed as tools for the conscious, rational humanistic subject (Hultman & Lenz Taguchi, 2010, p. 539). According to Sandvik (2015), humanistic understanding of the subject leaves material–discursive elements such as non-human materials (e.g., room, furniture, nature, toys, etc.) in the shadows. Therefore, post humanistic approaches aim to challenge the humanistic approach that is taken for granted, whereby language and ways of thinking are presented as the main ways to understand and learn. It is claimed that new insight into agency can be obtained by taking interest in materials.

From the material approach, the importance of understanding everyday practices as open processes and the need to let go of control have been revealed as well as the benefits of understanding pedagogical practices as something that is coming into present (Sandvik, 2015), as performativity (Barad, 2003; Srinivasan, 2018) or as flight pathways (Myhre, Myrvold, Joramo, & Thoresen, 2017). In addition, the advantage of improvisation is underlined to balance the known and the unknown, freedom and structure, and to improve practices and distribute power (Leirpoll, 2015). There is an outspoken aim to open up to complexity, contradictions, and disruptions (Kummen, 2014). Pedagogical practices are characterised by concepts such as 'letting go of control,' 'coming into present,' 'improvisation,' and 'performativity'. I use the concept of exploration to conceptualise emerging pedagogical practices that open up to the known and the unknown, freedom and structure, complexity, contradictions and disruptions.

Intra-activity: Researchers that place themselves in the material turn have depicted insight in intra-active processes among actors (Barad, 2003; Latour, 2008). Barad (2003, p. 810) calls it "agential realism". In this approach, materials, humans, discourses, and context are viewed as intra-active actors. Hence, for example, materials and humans are more than interrelated. Interrelation indicates that there are limits between those that are involved in an activity. In contrast, intra-active processes indicates that it is impossible to know where one starts and the other one ends; in an ongoing situated practice, all actors are intra-related. According to Barad (2003, p. 802), we need to move toward alternatives to representationalism and "shift the focus from questions of correspondence between descriptions and reality to matters of practices/doing/actions". I therefore aim to look for intra-activity in an ongoing practice.

Actors: The actor-network theory (ANT) aims to destabilise the subject and thereby allows the consideration of both humans and non-humans as participants in practice (Latour, 2005). According to Lafton (2015), the idea of how human agency is habitually assumed can therefore be reconsidered, and this allows recognition of the forces working between humans and non-humans within a network. According to Latour (2005), an actor can be anything that modifies other actors through a series of actions. An actor makes others act. The action is of main interest, and it will often differ from what was expected. The act is intra-woven in a network of actors, which is not stable and represents a source for insecurity. To trace the actors, I look for what can be seen as destabilising the practice at the present moment. It is not the same as explaining why things happen; it is done with the objective of mapping some of the networks of actors that are woven together.

Agency: The traditional understanding of causality is often outlined from a one-dimensional understanding of someone who acts and then this act leads to a change. Therefore, the ones who act are the ones who realise the action, and they possess/have agency. In contrast to this understanding, Barad (2003) outlines that:

> agency is about the possibilities and accountability entailed in reconfiguring material–discursive apparatuses of bodily productions, including the boundary articulations and exclusions that are marked by those practices in the enactment of a causal structure. Particular possibilities for acting exist at every moment, and these changing possibilities entail a responsibility to intervene in the world's becoming, to contest and rework what matters and what is excluded from mattering. (p. 827)

Barad (2003, p. 826) describes intra-activities as providing the conditions for an open future. Therefore, intra-actions are constraining but not determining, and neither a matter of strict determinism nor unconstrained freedom. Since intra-action reformulates the traditional notion of causality and opens up a space, it opens up a relatively large space for material–discursive forms of agency (Barad, 2003, p. 826). If several actors are involved in the act, then the act will not be fully known beforehand. The intentional human loses control. I find interest in identifying some of the actors that constitute the act, even if they are changing all the time. A network of actors makes a larger room for agency, since the activity does not emerge only from the effort of what the conscious human intended to do, but rather it starts a new beginning. I therefore look for agency as something that emerges among actors when a larger room for a variety of activities and ways of understanding is depicted.

3   Method

The experiences that form the basis for my analysis come from a study done in collaboration with teachers and children at an ECE institution in Norway from April 2016 to August 2017. The institution is located in an urban area on the west coast of Norway. During the period of this research, sixty-three children from 1 to 6 years of age were attending the institution. They were divided into four age-specific groups. The staff comprised seven teachers and included the manager and an extra teacher, who took care of the children with special needs, and nine assistants.

Five teachers at this ECE institution made videotapes to illustrate children's activities that they found to be of special interest and value. I visited their institution to pick up the videos and interview the teachers who recorded the activities, meeting one teacher at a time as well as the children in the particular video(s). I visited the institution eleven times, spending between 2 and 4 hours to do the interviews. Altogether, I obtained thirteen videotapes of activities that ranged in length from 1:11 minutes to 10 minutes, and all were followed by comments from the teachers who made the recordings. Seven videos also included comments from the involved children. Although the videos contained activities that took place over the period of one year and involved different teachers, children, activities, and places, they were all from the same institution.

The Norwegian Centre for Research Data approved the project. The teachers who made the recordings signed an agreement form as data processors; all the staff and the parents of the children who were recorded gave their written informed consent to participate in the study and they had the opportunity to withdraw from the study at any time. In addition, the involved children had the opportunity to withdraw from being recorded or watching the video.

Following my first analysis, which evoked more questions about the teachers' values and motives for the activities they found of specific value and interest, their opinions about play, and the conditions and demands they meet in their daily practices, I did a group interview (about 90 minutes) with four of the five teachers who had made the videotapes. In addition, I participated in two staff meetings (1 hour each): the first to introduce and discuss my aims and research interest; the second, to present and discuss my findings.

This participatory design is close to an ethnographical approach (Hammersley & Atkinson, 2007), and offered me, as a researcher, an unfamiliar position that could broaden the variety of topics or objects of research, topics or objects that the researcher would not be aware of in the first place, such as materiality. My awareness of materiality stemmed from an interview with one of the teachers. In the activities she had chosen to videotape, the children's play seems to be strongly influenced by the playthings. Most of the toys I saw were familiar to me, but in one of the videos, there was a toy that was new to me, and that aroused my curiosity. The toy was called Polydron, and asking about it generated even more curiosity. It seems to be very popular with both children and teachers. The awareness of this material made me contact a sales representative from a company that promotes and sells toys to ECE institutions in order to obtain more information about Polydron and about what kinds of toys are most popular for purchase by ECE institutions. This expanding of materials for analysis, through openness for what might emerge in research, is also in line with my engagement in exploration and which forms a basis for both the research and the content of my research. This is in line with Jackson's (2013) outlines of posthumanist data analysis, and it is my attempt to locate agency as an entanglement of constitutive human and non-human elements. The entanglement makes what Pikering (1993) conceptualises as the 'mangle,' where both non-humans and humans are constantly coming into being, fading away, moving around, and changing places with one another (Pickering, 1993, p. 563). The aim is to avoid the "trap of representation of a stable 'real'" (Jackson, 2013, p. 743). Thus, agency is not located in human intention but in a mangled or emerging practice. This constant emerging practices and actors are impossible to capture, since they are constantly changing and moving. That means that the actors that I trace through my analysis are not stable representations; it is a 'frozen' moment that indicates an awareness for space for agency in an evolving network of actors. The frozen moment provides insight into room for agency that comprises a range of actors that, despite their shifting and emerging positions, are involved and can be challenged – actors that might be left in the shadows if we were to leave out all actors other than humans.

My analysis to trace emerging actors in an intra-activity involving children and material/toys begins with an activity that was recorded in a video (1:23 minutes) of children playing with Polydron, followed by an interview with their teacher (about 1 hour) to investigate why this recorded play was of specific interest for the teacher. In addition, the material in my analysis also includes comments from the children in the video in dialogue with their teacher and the researcher, the group interview with the teachers in my cooperating ECE institution, and an interview with a sales representative from a company that promotes and sells toys to ECE institutions, and descriptions of the material (Polydron) from various websites.

4   Tracing Emerging Actors

To trace the emerging actors in the intra-activity involving children and Polydron, I start by presenting the videotape that aroused my interest in the first place. The next steps are in line with the emergence of several actors to inform my research question: the surprising new material, what was made with the material, the teachers' and the children's comments, the parents' interest, the understanding of good play, the history and the ontological meaning of the concept of polydron, the position of mathematics in education, structural learning, political interest in ECE, economy, and profit.

4.1   *The Exploring Activity and Comments about It*

Drawing on the emphasis on activities in the material turn, I start by presenting the activity in the video:

> The activity is performed on and around a table. On the table there is a play material called Polydron that woke my interest. In spite of my common visits in ECE institutions – bot as a researcher and as a teacher for ECE teacher students – this toy was unknown to me. At this video three boys are eagerly involved playing with Polydron. They are making a garage for cars. First, they make a one-dimensional road of square-shaped Polydron and place many cars in a line upon it. Then they extend the road and carefully wrap the cars in the connected Polydron pieces. It seems to be a challenge to know how many Polydron pieces are needed to cover the cars and how to connect the pieces of Polydron in 'open air'. The first time in the video, they do not succeed. The pieces of Polydron fall apart and the cars fall off the road. "No problem", one of the boys said,

placing the car upon the Polydron again, putting the pieces of Polydron together again, and carefully covering the cars with Polydron, using both hands. He had to place the two ends of the so far one-dimensional connected Polydron on the cars, to find a grip for 'clicking' the magnetic Polydron together and thereby make a roof and a garage, a three-dimensional building. "This is a big one", he commented, and he asked the teacher to take a photo of it for their parents. On the table where the activity was taking place, there was already a garage of the same kind. It was even longer. That obvious proof for their ability to make such a garage was thereby present, and further explained the boy's confidence that the breakdown of their garage was not a problem.

In the interview with the teacher who recorded the video, we started by talking about this toy, Polydron. The teacher told me that "Polydron can be used in multiple ways – and in unexpected ways. It is popular with both girls and boys. The bricks are used to make crowns for princesses, garages, balls, and so on". She recorded this video because, as she says,

> Polydron was recently purchased for my kindergarten, it is popular with the children, and they play with it daily. The boys are 3 years of age and often play together, and I see them as equals when playing together. I find this activity to be good play. They had been engaged in the activity for a while before I started to record their play.

The children in the video had a lot of fun when watching it together with their teacher and me. They laughed and tried to teach me how to pronounce Polydron. They told me, "We are best friends" and "Polydron can be used for any purpose". I also followed up on the comment from the boy who asked their teacher to take a photo of what they had built. He told me that the picture was taken. Their teacher found an album that contained many pictures of a variety of things made with Polydron. The album was also available for parents to view.

The children, their teacher, and I – and probably the parents as well – seem to be amazed by this new material. At first glance – that is obvious in my transcription of the video – polydron comes forward as a material for the use of conscious, rational humans. After talking to the teacher and the children, I realised that the material can serve as a starting point for a range of different activities, and thereby as an actor. It is hard to know where the children as exploring actors ends and the material starts when it comes to what is made – it appears to be an intra-activity. Polydron also intra-acts in a variety of practices in different children's play, in the choice of the teacher for what to record for our research, in the interview, and even, by the photos, extending to the families of the children. The exploring intra-activity seems to involve actors, including Polydron, children, photos, parents, teachers, understanding of good play, and me, in a network. All the actors made something happen – we made each other act.

4.2   *Polydron*

To understand why and how materials are intra-active actors in the practices of ECE, it is interesting to follow their history and the ontological meaning of the concept that labels the toys, that is, "Why is the toy Polydron called Polydron?" The website[1] explains the concept of polydron as follows:

> in geometry, a polyhedron (plural polyhedra or polyhedrons) is often defined as a three-dimensional object with flat, polygonal faces and straight edges. In this sense, it is a three-dimensional example of the more general structure called a polytope, which can have any number of dimensions. Cubes, prisms, and pyramids are examples of polyhedra.
>
> A polyhedron surrounds a bounded volume in three-dimensional space; sometimes this interior volume is considered to be part of the polyhedron, sometimes only the surface is considered, and occasionally only the skeleton of edges. A polyhedron is said to be convex if its surface (comprising its faces, edges, and corners) does not intersect itself and the line segment joining any two points of the polyhedron is contained in the interior and surface. A regular polyhedron is one in which the faces are regular polygons that are all congruent (exactly alike) and assembled in the same way around each vertex (corner). More generally, in mathematics and other disciplines, the term *polyhedron* is used to refer to a variety of related constructs, some geometric and others purely algebraic or abstract.

From this text, I conclude that the toy Polydron might have inherited its name from the shape of the pieces, and from the interest in teaching children mathematics. From reading the text, I suggest that Polydron is intra-active to actors such as mathematics and education. The emphasis on mathematics in education made the act where children intra-act. In addition, traces of intra-activity can be observed from the description; it "does not intersect itself". Thus, it seems to be hard to separate the toy from actors such as mathematics, education, and humans. The way children use the material (intersect it) – and build shapes with the ability to join the polarity of the material – can be seen as intra-active when children explore this material in their play. Thereby, a space for agency among mathematics, education and humans is depicted.

Space for agency when Polydron is present can also be traced from the web.[2]

> Edward Harvey, who, in the 1970s, made these squares and triangles that were possible to pull together and separate again, did not initiate these squares for making a worldwide pedagogical toy. According to the website, Polydron is paving the way for children to learn mathematics, geometry, numbers, and density while they are building things, such as houses for play, and can be used both inside and outside. (Translated into English by the author)

Despite the text's presentation of the toy as interrelated to humans – as a tool for learning mathematics, geometry, numbers, and density – traces of intra-action can also be found, for example, the surprise of the inventor for the huge interest and expansion of the toy. This exemplifies Barad's (2003) description of the missing singular causality between intention, and how activities come into existence. Polydron as a non-human actor that, in an intra-activity with children's exploration, provides room for agency distributed among the children, Polydron, an understanding of education, mathematics, and good play.

4.3 *Materiality, Profit, Politics, Play, and Learning in ECE*

According to the sales representative of materials for ECE and schools, "'basic toys,' such as cars, dolls, and equipment for play kitchens, are frequently sold to ECE institutions". These toys have a long history in ECE institutions. Despite this traditional approach to toys, Magnetic Polydron "has been the most popular toy in sales over the last five years", according to the seller. In line with the teacher's comments, he emphasises that "it can be used in multiple ways, and it conditions mathematical understanding". He said that "new toys for sale are most often connected to more than play". He continued, stating that "ECE institutions ask for materials that can be used in more formal learning activities, to meet the demands for more formal learning in ECE that is outlined in the Framework Plan for the content and task for Kindergartens". At his company's website, there is a specific link labelled *learning*, where many of these new products are presented. It is often material for concentration and construction. The sales representative emphasised, "Toys that stimulate mathematics are of special interest. In addition, products that stimulate activity and bodily movements, both indoors and outdoors, are also welcomed". Expected intra-activities involving play, learning, mathematics, and physical training are emerging. Moreover, economic profit emerges as an actor; what is offered and elaborated for sale has to provide income for the company that sells toys. The sales representative refers to the framework plan for ECE in Norway (UDIR, 2017), which has an emphasis on more structural learning. Therefore, the framework plan emerges as an actor, making it easier to sell toys that cover more than play (i.e. learning).

The group interview, as with the interview with the sales representative, turned out to be a discussion about play and learning, as it obviously would be about play, since I was bringing up questions about play. What is more interesting is that when we talked about play, learning became a part of the discussion. The relationship between play and learning was discussed whenever play was mentioned. Further, when asked about how to condition the play that was preferred by the teachers, a variety of conditions were mentioned, including: the competences and abilities of the staff, how to validate play – because of the learning potential, real-life experiences, follow-up on children's interests – including media-based interests, architecture, how to split children into groups, time, play materials (such as Duplo blocks, equipment for playing doctor and so on), flexibility when it comes to tidying-up time, and room for a variety of types of play, including play that refers to violence.

The references to learning while discussing play was even touched upon when discussing how to condition play, and may indicate that an understanding of the need for more structural learning is emerging. The material aspect can also be traced by the teachers' references to architecture, Duplo blocks, and equipment for playing doctor. Hence, more than relationships and language are at the core, even though the conditions are mostly presented as a tool for play. In contrast, the teachers also mentioned the importance of "valuing the golden moments of eagerness, exploring, and the importance of conditioning children's possibilities to find new and unexpected answers". These utterances may be understood as resistance to the actor of more structural learning that is coming to the fore in their practices. In addition, actors such as politics emerge. They are traced from such comments as "children need time and space for play"; "their activities should not be limited to sitting down and learning"; "play is more than learning"; "we must avoid politicians that change ECE into an arena for pre-defined goals of learning". Politicians, the framework plan, structural learning, companies that sell with aims for economic profit, and golden moments emerge as actors in a network that constitutes practices in ECE.

When tracing emerging actors in my material in light of the outlined concepts of exploration, intra-activity, actors, and agency, several actors are found: Polydron, the position of play, the position of mathematics in education, the contemporary emphasis on more structural learning in ECE, the framework plan, economic profit, politics, children, teachers, parents, and me as the researcher. Therefore, instead of limiting agency to the involved children, a range of actors traced from a short video recording of an activity in the everyday life of ECE, can be traced. Thus, a relatively large space for agency is emerging.

5 Summary

The web presentations, the activity seen in the video, the teachers' comments on the activity, the children's comments, the discussions from the group interview, and the interview with the sales representative exemplify the lack of coherence between human intentions and the agency that emerges in the presented intra-activity. Pickering (1993) states that actors are continually coming into being, since performativity is temporarily emergent in practice. The contours of human and material actors are never fully known in advance; instead, they emerge in real time, in real practices. In this presentation of intra-activity in exploration, Polydron is easily radically changed or is continually coming into being, in different shapes. This intra-activity can turn into a variety of activities that can be both play and learning. Polydron, which is presented as a tool for learning mathematics, can even be involved in a game of princesses. The shapes and the multifactorial opportunities of the material pave the way for a continuum of practices to emerge. This challenges not only anthropocentric approaches to agency, but also the idea that humans can control practices.

My limited analysis of the children's exploration involving Polydron depicts how agency emerges. Materials, children, teachers, materialised heritage of play, materialised heritage of structural learning, the framework plan, mathematics, available materials from producers and sellers of material for ECE, teachers, children, and parents: all intra-act. This can serve as an example for agency as something other than something or someone has, toward agency as 'doing'/'being' in its intra-activity. Therefore, the conventional dichotomies of play and learning, humans and materials, and child-initiated and teacher-initiated activities are challenged. It is interesting that my aim of widening space for agency in ECE through destabilising children and humans, appears as a contrast to the heritage of the sociology of childhood that, in the first place, depicted children as something else than adults, but still in a position to influence, and thereby gave room for children's agency. Children came forward as beings and not only becomings. These steps have been important for children's position in society. Again, ambiguity and contradictions occur. That might indicate that the increasing complexity and ambiguity of childhood can be met by approaches that emphasise ambiguity, contradictions, and disruptions. To provide opportunities for children's lives, several actors can be challenged, especially when more than a child's ability to act forms room for agency.

Notes

1 See http://web.newworldencyclopedia.org/entry/Polyhedron
2 See https://www.lekeakademiet.no/pl/Merker-Varemerker-Polydron_96906.aspx

References

Barad, K. (2003). Posthumanist performativity: Toward an understanding of how matter comes to matter. *Signs: Journal of Women in Culture and Society, 28*(3), 801–831.

Barad, K. (2007). *Meeting the universe halfway: Quantum physics and the entanglement of matter and meaning.* Duke University Press.

Bornardo, L., & Payne, R. (2012). Ambiguous agency: Critical perspectives on social interventions with children and youth in Africa. *Children's Geographies, 10*(4), 365–372.

Colegrove, K. S.-S. & Adair, J. K. (2014). Countering deficit thinking: Agency, capabilities and the early learning experiences of children of Latina/o immigrants. *Contemporary Issues in Early Childhood, 15*(2), 122–132.

Deleuze, G., & Guattari, F. (1988). *A thousand plateaus: Capitalism and schizophrenia II.* Althlone.

Esser, F., Baader, M. S., Betz, T., & Hungerland, B. (2016). Reconceptualising agency and childhood an introduction. In F. Esser, S. Meike, T. B. Betz, & B. Hungerland (Eds.), *Reconceptualising agency and childhood. New perspectives in childhood studies* (pp. 1–16). Routledge.

Hammersley, M., & Atkinson, P. (2007). *Ethnography: Principles in practice.* Routledge.

Hultman, K., & Taguchi, H. L. (2010). Challenging anthropocentric analysis of visual data: A relational materialist methodological approach to educational research. *International Journal of Qualitative Studies in Education, 23*(5), 525–542.

Jackson, A. Y. (2013). Posthumanist data analysis of mangling practices. *International Journal of Qualitative Studies in Education, 26*(6), 741–748.

James, A. (2009). Agency. In J. Qvortrup, W. A. Corsaro, & M.-S. Honig (Eds.), *The Palgrave handbook of childhood studies* (pp. 34–45). Palgrave.

Kummen, K. (2014). *Making space for disruption in the education of early childhood educators* (Ph.D. thesis). University of Victoria.

Lafton, T. (2015). Digital literacy practices and pedagogical moments: Human and non-human intertwining in early childhood education. *Contemporary Issues in Early Childhood, 16*(2), 142–152.

Latour, B. (1993). *We have never been modern.* Harvester/Wheatsheaf.

Latour, B. (2005). *Reassembling the social: An introduction to actor-network-theory.* Oxford University Press.

Lee, N. (2001). *Childhood and society: Growing up in an age of uncertainty.* Open University Press.

Leirpoll, B. (2015). En åpenhet for hendelser som kommer – om å plugge teori inn i – og dermed improvisasjonens mulighet for andre innganger til – barnehagelærerens etiske praksis. In A. M. Ottestad & A. B. Reinertsen (Eds.), *Metodefestival og øyeblikksrealisme – eksperimenterende kvalitative forskningspassasjer* (pp. 103–132). Fagbokforlaget.

Leonard, M. (2016). *The sociology of children, childhood and generation.* Sage.

Mizen, P., & Ofosu-Kusi, Y. (2013). Agency as vulnerability: Accounting for children's movement to the streets of Accra. *The Sociological Review, 61*(2), 363–382.

Myhre, C. O., Myrvold, H. B., Joramo, U.-W., & Thoresen, M. (2017). Stumbling into the 'kitchen island': becoming through intra-actions with objects and theories. *Contemporary Issues in Early Childhood, 18*(3), 308–321.

Nsamenang, A. B. (2008). Agency in early childhood learning and development in Cameroon. *Contemporary Issues in Early Childhood, 9*(3), 211–223.

Payne, R. (2012). Extraordinary 'survivors' or 'ordinary lives'? Embracing 'everyday agency' in social interventions with child-headed households in Zambia. *Children's Geographies, 10*(4), 399–411.

Pickering, A. (1993). The mangle of practice: Agency and emergence in the sociology of Science. *American journal of sociology, 99*(3), 559–589.

Prout, A. (2011). Taking a step away from modernity: Reconsidering the new sociology of Childhood. *Global Studies of childhood, 1*(1), 4–14.

Sandvik, N. (2015). Posthumanistiske perspektiver. Bidrag til 'barnehageforskning'. In A. M. Ottestad & A. B. Reinertsen (Eds.), *Metodefestival og øyeblikksrealisme eksperimenterende kvalitative forskningspassasjer* (pp. 45–62). Fagbokforlaget.

Spyrou, S. (2018). What kind of agency for children? In S. Spyrou (Ed.), *Disclosing childhood, for a critical childhood studies* (pp. 117–156). Palgrave Macmillan.

Srinivasan, P. (2018). Pookey, poory, power: An actoric powerformance. *Contemporary Issues in Early Childhood.* https://doi.org/10.1177/1463949118759979

UDIR Norwegian Directorate for Education and Training. (2017). *Framework Plan for the content and tasks of kindergartens.* Norwegian Directorate for Education and Training.

United Nations. (1989). *United Nations Convention on the Rights on the Child.* https://downloads.unicef.org.uk/wp-content/uploads/2010/05/UNCRC_united_nations_convention_on_the_rights_of_the_child.pdf?_ga=2.259582415.454887985.1587459175-44770236.1585716747

Valentine, K. (2011). Accounting for agency. *Children and Society, 25*(5), 266–278.

CHAPTER 12

Studying Families' and Teachers' Multilingual Practices and Ideologies in Kindergartens: A Nexus Analytic Approach

Anja Maria Pesch

Abstract

This chapter discusses the methodological opportunities of studying multilingual practices in kindergarten through a nexus analytic approach (cf. Scollon & Scollon, 2004). It is based on an ethnographic study with fieldwork in two kindergartens in Norway and Germany. The first part of the chapter elaborates on how the nexus analytic approach made it possible to gain insight into the kindergarten teachers' and parents' views on multilingualism. As a theoretical background, I draw on views on multilingualism and language ideology theory. The second part of the chapter discusses, which insights the applied nexus analytic approach may contribute with to the field of childhood studies, based on the concept of intersectionality (Alanen, 2016) and generational order (Alanen, 2009, 2016). I argue that the nexus analysis in this study contributes with several interesting perspectives. First, it provides insights into the intersectionality of multilingual children's lives by shedding light on the complexity of intersections of linguistic practices. Second, the analysis sheds light on the relevance of various generational categories as part of these intersections. A question deriving from this complexity is which forms of linguistic practice may be in the best interest of multilingual children (cf. James & James, 2008). Here, my study revealed several contrasts between parents' and teachers' views. With reference to article 12 (UNCRC, 1989), which emphasises the importance of listening to children's voices, I argue that this may challenge both researchers, teachers and parents to listen to young multilingual children's voices, especially as these children are little represented in research.

Keywords

multilingualism – UNCRC article 12 – nexus analysis – parents – children's views

© ANJA MARIA PESCH, 2021 | DOI: 10.1163/9789004445666_012
This is an open access chapter distributed under the terms of the CC BY 4.0 License.

1 Introduction

Vignette 1
It is in the middle of the day at the Sunflower kindergarten when I talk to Helena about school and cooperation with parents. Helena is a kindergarten teacher and is responsible for the preschool club in the kindergarten. She tells me that there are parents who sit down with their children and train them to write the alphabet, and that she often tries to convince them that this is not necessary. Still, it does not seem as though they always listen to her. "And it is like this", she says, "school is very important, kindergarten is not". "Oh", I ask, "is it?" "Yes", she says, telling me about one girl, Finja, the older sister of one of the boys in Helena's department, who attended the Sunflower kindergarten before she started school last summer. Helena recounts that Finja always joined in telling and writing stories and that she used to enjoy this activity a lot. Telling and writing stories together with the children was a common linguistic practice in this kindergarten department. Helena tells me that Finja joined in story-telling less and less and says, "and I wondered whether I had done something stupid in some way. And then I noticed at some point that it was the letters". The girl had to write the alphabet at home. She obviously had learnt it in both Russian and German before she started school.[1] And in the end, she did not take part in story-telling anymore, only when her friend joined. Now Finja attends first grade, and Helena refers to the fact that she asked her mother, "How is she doing at school?" "She is bored", the mother tells her, "she keeps asking when they finally are going to do something proper". "Because they all are busy learning to read and write", I say. "Yes", says Helena, "that's what I told her during the whole last kindergarten year" (Field note, Sunflower kindergarten, October 2015)

Vignette 2
[And I] think that she [Finja] learnt to read and write German that quickly, because she already started with Russian lessons one year before she entered school. She still takes them. [...] And she attends lessons once a week. And there she also learnt to write and read Russian quickly. And since she managed that, she also could read in German quite soon. And also write. [She started] when she was close to six. One year before starting school, exactly. I did not want her to start at the same time as starting school, because I thought it might get a bit complicated, both at the same time. That this would maybe demand too much of her, and then maybe something would not work out, and then she would neither get something good out of school nor out of the Russian lessons. And then I

thought, okay, one year earlier. She could, she wanted to, she always asked me, because her friend attended Russian lessons already, and then she said "I want, too" and "I also want to be able to read that". I thought, okay, we will try. We tried, she is happy, we, I am also happy. [...] And I also think that [when] you have this language as your mother tongue, why not be able to write and read it? That is an advantage, I think. (Excerpt from interview with Finja's mother Susanne, February 2016)

The two texts presented above are excerpts from the data collected for my PhD study (Pesch, 2017). Both excerpts are centred on Finja, who was a first grader at the time I collected the data but had attended the Sunflower kindergarten, where I carried out part of my fieldwork. I chose these excerpts to begin this chapter because they point to several contrasts between the kindergarten teacher's view and that of Finja's mother regarding language practices, multilingual language development and formal or non-formal language education. In my dissertation, I discuss these contrasts in relation to multilingualism, including how views on multilingualism create discursive conditions for linguistic practice with multilingual children and influence cooperation between kindergarten teachers and parents. The first aim of this chapter is to elaborate on how the nexus analytic approach developed by Scollon and Scollon (2004) helped me gain insight into the teachers' and parents' language ideologies and views on multilingualism. The second aim is to discuss in which way these insights may contribute to the field of childhood studies, drawing upon the concepts of intersectionality (Alanen, 2016), generation and generational order (Alanen, 2009, 2016; Honig, 2009), transformation (James, 2009) and the best interests of the child (James & James, 2008). The question of the best interests of the child is connected to the UN Convention on the Rights of the Child (in the following: UNCRC) (United Nations, 1989), and has in Norway and the other Nordic countries often been discussed related to juridical issues, as violence and assault, divorce, adoption and taking children into care (Adolphsen et al., 2019). The topic of this chapter does not involve juridical considerations, and hence the question of the best interests of the child is treated slightly different. The discussion is based on article 12 of the UNCRC (United Nations, 1989) and evolves around the importance of listening to young multilingual children's perspectives on multilingualism.

2   Theoretical and Methodological Background

The methodological opportunities and challenges of studying multilingual practices in kindergarten with a nexus analytic approach are starting points for this chapter. For my PhD, I conducted ethnographic fieldwork in two kindergartens, Sunflower in Northern Germany and Globeflower in Northern Norway, both of which were public and located in medium-sized cities. The data are organised into two cases, and the study employed both a case study (see Yin, 2014) and ethnography (see Gulløv & Højlund, 2010; O'Reilly, 2012) as methodological approaches.[2] The data include interviews with the teachers and parents of multilingual children, pictures of the kindergartens' semiotic landscapes, field notes about teachers' linguistic practices and relevant policy documents. For this chapter, I draw upon the data I gathered from Sunflower. Although this chapter is based on the data as a whole, the field notes and interviews are of particular interest. I first introduce the theoretical framework and then present nexus analysis as an analytical approach.

My PhD study draws upon theory from the fields of early childhood education and sociolinguistics. It adopts a socio-epistemological view of kindergarten, proposed by Ødegaard and Krüger (2012), in which kindergarten is understood as a social and cultural arena where people (i.e. children, teachers and parents) with various agendas, aims, views and desires meet. One important aspect is that these 'actors' – as Ødegaard and Krüger (2012, p. 28) refer to them – have different roles in the kindergarten context. The authors emphasise the relevance of talking to these actors to gain insight into their implicit views and understandings as well as observing their practices to understand what they actually do (Ødegaard & Krüger, 2012, p. 28). A related debate in the field of language ideology about whether language ideology can or should be studied through observation of linguistic practices in addition to other methods (Kroskrity, 2004; Woolard, 1998) forms part of the theoretical background for my study. In my study, I gained insight into the language ideologies of parents through discursive reading of interviews about their linguistic practice with multilingual children and into the ideologies of kindergarten teachers through discursive reading of observations and interviews. I found that the different views on multilingualism between teachers and parents were connected to their different language ideologies as well as different choices, aims and agendas (cf. Ødegaard & Krüger, 2012), which framed the conditions in which multilingual children developed their language practices. Here, I focus on the differences between teachers' and parents' views.

Another important theoretical aspect of the socio-epistemological framework is that kindergarten is understood as a social, cultural, historical and political field with different practices that create discursive conditions for learning, formation and development (Ødegaard & Krüger, 2012, p. 20). The present study focuses on the discursive conditions for linguistic practice with multilingual children, a main theoretical part of which are views on multilingualism and norms of linguistic behaviour (Garcia & Li Wei, 2014; Jørgensen, 2008). Garcia and Li Wei (2014) and Jørgensen (2008) refer to different ways of understanding multilingualism and how these connect to different views on multilinguals' linguistic practices. Both authors discuss traditional views of multilingualism as a form of double monolingualism or an additive view of multilingualism and recent views of multilingualism as integrated linguistic repertoires with features from several languages (Garcia & Wei, 2014; Jørgensen, 2008). In addition, both emphasise and argue for a distinction between multilingualism and polylingualism (Jørgensen, 2008, p. 169) or translanguaging (Garcia & Li Wei, 2014, p. 13), which are complex linguistic practices in which individuals draw upon various linguistic features in a communication context and the question of which language these features belong to becomes immaterial.[3] The different views of multilingualism are illustrated below. Figure 12.1 diagram depicts multilingualism[4] as consisting of several autonomous languages, Figure 12.2 refers to Cummins' (2000) idea of interdependence between the individual's languages, while Figure 12.3 depicts the idea of translanguaging.

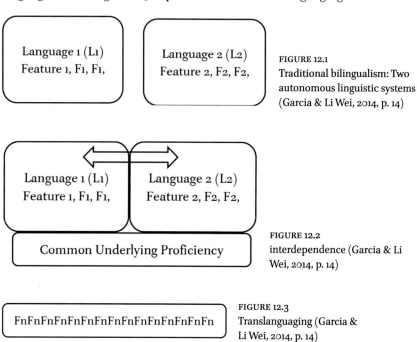

FIGURE 12.1
Traditional bilingualism: Two autonomous linguistic systems (Garcia & Li Wei, 2014, p. 14)

FIGURE 12.2
interdependence (Garcia & Li Wei, 2014, p. 14)

FIGURE 12.3
Translanguaging (Garcia & Li Wei, 2014, p. 14)

Behind these distinctions lies the ideological question of what counts as language (Woolard, 1998, p. 16) and whether languages are relatively solid systems or more fluid and dynamic constructions. In my data, language ideologies are expressed through teachers' and parents' views on multilingualism as well as through the choice to use particular languages and the values attached to them (see Jaffe, 2009) or a focus on language separation on the one hand and translanguaging practices on the other (see Garcia & Li Wei, 2014; Riley, 2011). In this chapter, I use the term *multilingual* to refer to children who grow up speaking more than one language because one or both of their parents' mother tongue is different from the country's majority language and used with the child. The term *mother tongue* is complex and has various definitions (Sollid, 2014; Øzerk, 2016). I choose to use it here because it best covers the dynamic nature and changeability of the participants' multilingualism.

2.1 Nexus Analysis

Nexus analysis is a type of discourse analysis that uses human action as a starting point (Scollon & Scollon, 2004, p. 64). It draws upon theories from different linguistic and anthropological fields as well as critical discourse analysis (Hult, 2017; Lane, 2014; Scollon & Scollon, 2004). Since sociocultural theory is an important theoretical background for nexus analysis, action is always regarded as social and mediated (Lane, 2014, p. 2; Scollon & Scollon, 2004, p. 12). However, action is not connected to a particular group, which distinguishes the concept of a *nexus of practice* from a *community of practice* (Lane, 2014, p. 6). This also becomes evident in the connection to ethnography; Scollon and Scollon (2004) point out that nexus analysis adopts ethnography not only as a research approach but also as a theoretical position:

> A nexus analysis is a form of ethnography that takes social action as the theoretical center of study, not any *a priori* social group, class, tribe, or culture. In this it departs to a considerable extent from traditional ethnography in anthropology or sociology. (Scollon & Scollon, 2004, p. 13, italics in original document)

This distinction – that nexus analysis studies social action and not a group of people – is important, not least as an ethical consideration when presenting the findings, and relates to Ødegaard and Krüger's (2012) view of teachers, children and parents as actors. Discourses may seem personal when they are revealed in interviews or actions, but they are always connected to one's role and aim within the kindergarten context. Teachers and parents are not studied as people, but as actors with linguistic practices in relation to the discursive frames they experience. In this context, it is important to identify participants' motives for action, not objectively but in relation to relevant discourses (Scollon & Scollon, 2004, p. 11).

2.2 Central Terms and Concepts

Nexus analysis depends upon three terms *action*, *practice* and the *nexus of practice* (Scollon & Scollon, 2004, p. 62f.).[5] Both Scollon and Scollon (2004) and Lane (2014) point to time and repetition as important differences between action and practice. Similarly, I understand a practice as an action that has been established over time. Moreover, a practice is a nexus of trajectories of participants, places and cycles of discourses. These trajectories and discourses intersect and enable action, and an action or practice may alter these discourses or trajectories (cf. Scollon & Scollon, 2004, pp. 28, 159). Cycles of discourse are related to three key factors that intersect in social action: participants' *historical bodies*, the *interaction order* and the *discourses in place* (Hult, 2017, p. 94; Lane, 2014, pp. 7–8; Scollon & Scollon, 2004, p. 19–20).

Hult (2017) argues that, due to its integration of principles from different research traditions, nexus analysis makes it possible to focus on three complementary scales: (inter)personal, community and societal scales. The historical body is about a personal scale and involves beliefs that are related to an action and based on one's experiences through education and socialisation as well as the beliefs of earlier generations passed on through an individual's language socialisation (Hult, 2017, p. 94). It also includes the possibility for individuals to influence society. *Interaction order* refers to the typical patterns of interaction between participants that occur during an action or practice at a particular location and time (Scollon & Scollon, 2004), and it takes place mainly at the interpersonal scale (Hult, 2017, p. 95). Important aspects of the interaction order include individuals' social positions, their expectations for each other and the possibility of developing certain kinds of interactions during encounters between individuals (Hult, 2017). Interaction orders often relate to norms and expectations that have developed over time, and to understand why an interaction order works as it does, it is important to map its sociohistorical evolution (Hult, 2017, p. 96). Thus, one could argue that the interaction order also involves the community and societal scales.

Discourses in place are connected to particular places. Even though they become relevant for an action at a particular moment in time, they also cycle on wider community and societal scales (Hult, 2017, p. 97). Some discourses are more foregrounded and thus more relevant for a particular action or practice. One main aim of nexus analysis is to find the foregrounded discourses within the studied practice, and one challenge is that some discourses are so implicit that they may be difficult to find (Lane, 2014, p. 8; Scollon & Scollon, 2004, p. 14). Hult (2017, p. 93) suggests searching for joint values, attitudes, stances and ideologies to which certain actions relate.

Another main aim related to the three different scales is to connect discourses at the (inter)personal and local levels to discourses at different macro levels. This is possible due to a twofold understanding of discourse in nexus analysis. As Scollon and Scollon (2004, p. 2) point out, in the simplest sense, discourse can be understood as 'the use of language in social interaction'. In addition, they make use of Gee's (1999) understanding of discourse as a connection between linguistic and non-linguistic elements, including emotions, values, symbols and artefacts (Scollon & Scollon, 2004, p. 4). This understanding implies that we attach values to material and non-material elements and view some as more valuable than others. In that respect, discourse involves power. While the first understanding of discourse is connected to action at the micro level, the second understanding includes the development of discourses over time and within society, groups or institutions. Still, it is important to note that the distinction between the micro, meso and macro levels might only be applicable to analysis, and in reality, discourses are interconnected and not necessarily found on only one level.

3 Reading the Excerpts from a Nexus Analytic Perspective

The excerpts presented in the introduction to this chapter are two different descriptions of Finja's participation in and enjoyment of non-formal activities at a kindergarten and formal Russian lessons that she attended in the afternoon. Helena and Susanne almost seem to be describing two different children. Looking at these descriptions from a nexus analytic perspective might not give insight into Finja's actual experience, but by viewing the choices made by Helena and Susanne as mediated actions, one can ask questions about the discourses connected to them.

Helena's description of Finja's decreasing participation in story-telling highlights to a discourse in my data from Sunflower regarding the relevance of exposing children to literature, encouraging them to create stories and helping them to understand how to construct a story to support their language development. Another discourse in place circulating through this practice is connected to the child-centred approach at Sunflower and its opposition to the common pedagogical approach of learning through memorisation. For Helena, the joy children feel while telling stories is important, as evidenced by her criticism of Susanne and other parents who train their children to memorise and write the alphabet before they enter school. In the excerpt, these discourses seem to be situated mostly in Helena's historical body, which is connected to her professionalism and experience as a kindergarten teacher. But, as mentioned above, they also are connected to discourses in place at Sunflower. Regarding interaction orders, the excerpt also highlights the expectations that, as an expert, Helena's advice should be heeded. In the last sentence of the excerpt, for example, after Susanne mentions that Finja is bored at school, she points to her recommendations the previous year. Many of Helena's colleagues also believe in this interaction order (i.e. kindergarten teachers are the experts, not parents). Thus, in many respects, it is a general interaction order that exists at Sunflower regarding linguistic practice and preparation for school. It also directly references the kindergarten as a context of interaction (Ødegaard & Krüger, 2012), in which studies on cooperation have identified a field of tension between professional roles and equal partnerships between kindergarten teachers and parents (Alasuutari, 2010; Einarsdottir & Jonsdottir, 2018; Kultti & Samuelsson, 2016).[6]

The excerpt of the interview with Susanne confirms Helena's statement that parents do not always take her advice or the advice of teachers in general. Susanne might not share the expectation that she is less of an expert, partially due to the different discourses affecting her choices regarding Finja's language development. For example, at the end of the interview excerpt, she emphasises the advantage of being able to read and write in one's mother tongue. In addition, she considers it to be too complicated for children to start reading and writing in two different languages simultaneously. Thus, she chooses to let Finja start learning Russian before she enters school, related to a discourse regarding the importance of formal schooling. At the beginning of the excerpt, she supports her choice, saying that her daughter learnt to read and write in German so quickly because the groundwork was laid during her Russian lessons. In line with Garcia and Li Wei (2014), this refers to a view of multilingualism as dual and languages as interdependent (see Cummins, 2000). From a language ideological perspective, she emphasises the importance of separating languages (Riley, 2011), but with the underlying idea that children benefit from certain competences in all their languages, even though they are acquired in one language first. Both Susanne's emphasis on formal schooling and view on multilingualism contrast the kindergarten's practice and discourses.

It is important to note that, during the interview, Susanne voices some concern about her daughter's competence in German when she started school, which seems to be an important aspect of her choice regarding formal schooling. She also states that, in hindsight, her concerns probably were exaggerated, adding an interesting aspect to the expectations regarding roles in the interaction order. To a certain degree, Susanne now confirms Helena's role as an expert. Concerning motives (Scollon & Scollon, 2004), both Helena and Susanne refer to their motive to do what is in Finja's best interest (cf. James & James, 2008). Since this is related to their discourses on multilingual children's language development and education, their choices – and evaluations of these choices – are quite different.

4   Cycles of Discourses at Different Levels

My data contain several references to connections between discourses at the inter- or intrapersonal level and the macro level. One such connection is revealed in the excerpts with regard to the question of formal or non-formal education. The focus on non-formal linguistic practices with a child-centred approach at Sunflower is not only connected to discourses at this kindergarten but also general discourses on children's participation and language development in national policy documents (Schleswig-Holstein Ministerium für Soziales, Gesundheit, Familie und Gleichstellung, 2012). In the interviews with parents, school emerged as an important discursive condition for the choices regarding language and linguistic practices they made on behalf of their children. Concerns regarding the children's language competence in German was a main factor in their choices; to compensate for the kindergarten's non-formal approach, the parents engaged in various formal linguistic practices with their children. This is also evident in the following excerpt from an interview with Manuel, who describes his son, Niko's, linguistic practice:

> Yes, sometimes it is like that, well, that you catch them when you fetch him or so, you know? That you catch them, if they now speak the same language, Turkish or so. Then they babble Turkish. Where I tell them, "Guys, you have to speak German". So it will be a bit easier in school later on. But it is, well, they are young – in here, out there and then they still do what they want. (Interview excerpt with Manuel, Sunflower kindergarten, February 2016)

In this excerpt, Manuel focuses on his son's German language development, referencing school as a reason for the relevance of German. It is also interesting that he chooses the word 'babble' when referring to his son's choice to use Turkish, implying criticism of this linguistic practice. During the interview, Manuel expressed that German should be the primary language at the kindergarten, while Turkish should be spoken at home, in contrast to Sunflower's view of the kindergarten as a multilingual space. To some degree, this view was shared by all the parents I interviewed, although Manuel made the strictest distinction. Unlike Susanne, Manuel chose to enrol Niko in formal German lessons roughly a year before Niko started school. Manuel refers to the same discourse as Susanne – that learning two languages at the same time would be too much – but he regards German as the more important language. In terms of language ideology theory, this points to a view of languages as separate entities (Riley, 2011) and having different values (Jaffe, 2009); German is seen as the main language that is important for participating in society, while Turkish is seen as belonging to the family.

The discourse about the importance of school was also referenced by the third family I interviewed. The father, Thorben, describes how he often sits down with his children in the evening to learn English, including names of colours and numbers, using an iPad. Thorben notes that the children are able to learn new languages quickly and that he wants to give them an advantage when they start learning English in school:

> And I try to lead them a bit closer to English, so they maybe through this, maybe get a little help. I think, in third grade, they start with English already. My son, that he at least knows some words by then. Maybe also the numbers, so up to, what do I know, ten or twenty, and so. (Interview excerpt with Thorben, Sunflower kindergarten, February 2016)

Thorben is focused on his children's English language development, not German, but the discourse to which he refers is similar to that of the two other parents. School is an important discursive condition affecting many of the language choices the parents make for their children, and it is connected to their motive (Scollon & Scollon, 2004) to do what is best for their children.

Another important discursive condition that emerged in the interviews is migration, and it intersects with school in many of the parents' practices. While these discourses primarily relate to the parents' inter- or intrapersonal-level historical bodies (cf. Hult, 2017), they also relate to society-level discourses regarding equality in the education system, as Oberhuemer (2015) points out. Programs such as Sprach-Kitas (Bundesministerium für Familie, Senioren, Frauen und Jugend, 2017), for which kindergartens can apply to get extra funding to support multilingual children's language development, are part of this discourse. By making these connections between micro- and macro-level discourses, I do not mean that they connect in only one way (i.e. from the society level to the micro level or vice versa). Rather, they meet and intersect in the families' choices. Still, the macro-level discourses are important. As Lane (2010) points out in her study on language shift from Kven to Norwegian, parents do what they think is best for their children, but their choices are influenced by societal discourses and attitudes towards minority languages. Although my study was carried out in a quite different context, some of the same patterns of connections between micro- and macro-level discourses emerged. One of the interesting aspects of my study is that what the parents and kindergarten teachers regard as best for the children (James & James, 2008) is fundamentally different.

5 Decisions about Children's Future Made in the Present Based on the Past

Nexus analysis studies action situated in a moment in time and space (Lane, 2010, p. 68) with the underlying idea that action refers to past experiences and future expectations. My data revealed many such trajectories, where both parents and kindergarten teachers referred to past experiences on the one hand and goals for the children's future on the other. In the excerpts, school is a clear reference to the children's future, and choices related to the future are made in the present. However, the relevance of the past became visible through the kindergarten teachers' references to the development of their multilingual practice and through the parents' views on migration as part of their historical bodies. As Hult (2017) states, historical bodies contain the beliefs of earlier generations, which became salient when the parents referred to their own or their parents' experiences of migration. Some parents referred to their own childhoods and experiences with the German school system as factors affecting the choices they made for their children. Some viewed migration as part of their personal history that distinguished them from non-migrant Germans, while others included their own migration in the German society in general. As with school, these discourses on migration connect to different levels and intersect in various ways in the parents' choices for their children. In my opinion, it is the insight in the intersection of discourses affecting choices regarding children's future that contribute to the field of childhood studies, as I will discuss in the last sections of this chapter.

As mentioned in the introduction, two important concepts from the field of childhood research are intersectionality and generation or generational order (Alanen, 2009, 2016). According to Alanen (2016, p. 158), intersectionality in research has been used as an additive approach to individual identity as well as a non-additive approach to differences between individuals. In relation to the view that children's lives are intersectionally structured, she criticises the fact that intersectional thinking "appears to be a [...] thought experiment" in childhood studies (Alanen, 2016, p. 159). Referring to Qvortrup (2008), she argues for *generation* or *(inter)generationality* as an important category for confronting the challenges of intersectionality, as childhood can only be understood as interdependent with a counter-category, such as adulthood or a "differently constructed generational category" Alanen (2016, p. 159). Honig (2009, p. 46) argues that children become children – and adults become adults – through institutionalised practices of differentiation.[7] In this regard, the positions of children and adults in relation to the constructed concept of childhood are important (Honig, 2009). This relates to *generational order* (Alanen, 2009,

p. 161), according to which childhood exists in relation to other social categories and involves the idea of a system of social order. It connects children to social circumstances in which they participate in social life. Childhood extends beyond the differences between generations as age categories; Honig (2009, p. 48) argues that childhood is a social position that is influenced by various factors, such as age, gender, social-cultural environment and ethnicity.

Both Alanen (2016) and Honig (2009) describe childhood as a fluid category that is interrelated to other categories. I also understand both of these descriptions as intersectional views on childhood. My point is not to analyse these intersections for single children, focus on diversity within the category or add different sections to create a full picture of multilingual childhood. Rather, I think that these concepts, similar to nexus analysis, draw attention to the complex intersection of linguistic practices and the choices experienced by the children in my data. As James (2009, p. 42) points out, "children live their lives in and between any numbers of social institutions", including families, educational institutions and society. These institutions, and discourses at different levels (Hult, 2017), contribute to the complexity of children's lives.

Generation and generational order are important not necessarily in relation to age, but in relation to the roles of parents, children and kindergarten teachers in the kindergarten context (Ødegaard & Krüger, 2012). James (2009, pp. 42–43) argues that people (in this case, teachers and parents) occupy specific social positions and may transform the social structure, thus shaping the conditions for children's agency. Bergroth and Palviainen (2017) make a similar point in their discussion of the interplay of educational and language policies in bilingual kindergartens and bilingual children's agency. Their analysis shows how practice structures in the studied kindergartens, the teacher's pedagogical linguistic solutions and official language policies and educational policies shape conditions for bilingual child agency. In nexus analysis, this process of transforming social structures can be connected to the individual's historical body, which has the potential to influence other people's life experiences through mediated action (Hult, 2017). In interrelationship with their parents, children belong to a certain social category, and in interrelationship with their kindergarten teachers, they belong to a different category. Honig's (2009) reference to institutionalised practices of differentiation applies to the institutions of both kindergartens and families, but as they intersect with macro-level discourses, society also plays a role.

The multilingual children in my data have different positions in their family and in their kindergarten. Nexus analysis of their parents' and teachers' language choices reveals the complex intersections of linguistic practices that frame their childhoods. In the interview excerpt presented in the introduction,

Susanne refers to Finja's wish to start attending Russian lessons as part of the reason for her choice regarding formal schooling. Helena references the joy Finja showed in the story-telling activities. In elucidation of article 12 of the UNCRC (1989), which emphasises the right of the child to express its views, one could argue that Finja's views have been included in Susanne's and Helena's choices. However, since my nexus analysis does not include children's voices, Finja's experience remains unclear. Still, the analysis shows how the different positions adopted by parents and teachers transform the social structures that shape the conditions for children's own linguistic practices. One may ask which choices and practices are in the best interest (James & James, 2008) of Finja or multilingual children in general. In the present, it might be best to support children in their multilingual expressions through translanguaging. In the future, these complex multilingual practices may be challenged by the monolingual orientations of a community aiming to preserve minority languages or a majority-language-oriented educational system. As Bergroth and Palviainen's (2017, p. 396) study showed, declared monolingual policies in kindergartens were no hinder for children's active bilingual agency. Article 12 of the UNCRC (United Nations, 1989) may challenge both teachers and parents to listen to multilingual children's voices, to create space for and include their agency. Moreover, this raises a question regarding the sustainability of linguistic practices and indicates the need for more research on young multilingual children's voices and experiences of multilingualism.

Notes

1 Like most of the children at Sunflower, Finja can be considered multilingual as she uses Russian, German and Arabic as part of her daily linguistic practice.
2 The literature mentions both critical views on the combination of these methodologies (see Postholm, 2011) and possible similarities and benefits (e.g. Ødegaard, 2015). For further discussion of this topic in relation to my study, see Pesch (2017).
3 There are several other related terms, such as *translingual practice* (Canagarajah, 2013) and *flexible bilingualism* (Blackledge & Creese, 2010). All these terms have also been critically discussed (MacSwan, 2017), but this is beyond the scope of this chapter.
4 Garcia and Li Wei (2014) use the term bilingualism to also include individuals who use more than two languages.
5 Action and practice are sometimes treated as equivalent in the literature on nexus analysis (e.g. Hitching & Veum, 2011; Lane, 2011).
6 For further discussion on this topic in relation to my study, see Pesch (2018).
7 'Kinder werden zu Kindern, und Erwachsene zu Erwachsenen durch institutionalisierte Praktiken der Unterscheidung (*generationing*)' (Honig, 2009, p. 46, original emphasis).

References

Adolphsen, C., Hrefna, F. Hartoft, H., Leviner, P., Sandberg, K., & Stang, E. G. (2019). Barneretten i de nordiske land: Temaer i tiden. *Barn, 37*(3–4), 15–39. https://doi.org/10.5324/barn.v37i3-4.3389

Alanen, L. (2009). Generational order. In J. Qvortrup, W. A. Corsaro, & M.-S. Honig (Eds.), *The Palgrave handbook of childhood studies*. Palgrave Macmillan. https://ebookcentral.proquest.com/lib/tromsoub-ebooks/detail.action?docID=485290

Alanen, L. (2016). 'Intersectionality' and other challenges to theorizing childhood. *Childhood, 23*(2), 157–161. https://journals.sagepub.com/doi/abs/10.1177/0907568216631055

Alasuutari, M. (2010). Striving at partnership: Parent-practitioner relationships in finnish early educators' talk. *European Early Childhood Education Research Journal, 18*(2), 149–161. doi:10.1080/13502931003784545

Bergroth, M., & Palviainen, Å. (2017). Bilingual children as policy agents: Language policy and education plicy in minority language medium early childhodd education and care. *Multilingua, 36*(4), 375–399. doi:10.1515/multi-2016-0026

Blackledge, A., & Creese, A. (2010). *Multilingualism. A critical perspective*. Continuum International Publishing Group.

Bundesministerium für Familie, Senioren, Frauen und Jugend. (2017). Bundesprogramm Sprach-Kitas. Weil Sprache der Schlüssel zur Welt ist. *Bundesprogramm Sprach-Kitas*. http://sprach-kitas.fruehe-chancen.de/

Canagarajah. (2013). *Translingual practice. Global Englishes and cosmopolitan relations*. Routledge.

Cummins, J. (2000). *Language, power and pedagogy: Bilingual children in the crossfire*. Multilingual Matters.

Einarsdottir, J., & Jonsdottir, A. H. (2018). Parental engagement in icelandic preschools. In E. E. Ødegaard & S. Garvis (Eds.), *Nordic dialogues on children and families* (pp. 143–156). Routledge.

Garcia, O., & Li, W. (2014). *Translanguaging. Language, bilingualism and education*. Palgrave Macmillan.

Gee, J. P. (1999). *An introduction to discourse analysis: Theory and method*. Routledge.

Gulløv, E., & Højlund, S. (2010). *Feltarbejde blandt børn: Metodologi og etik i etnografisk børneforskning*. Gyldendal A/S.

Hitching, T. R., & Veum, A. (2011). Introduksjon. In T. R. Hitching, A. B. Nilsen, & A. Veum (Eds.), *Diskursanalyse i praksis. Metode og analyse* (pp. 11–39). Høyskoleforlaget AS.

Honig, M.-S. (2009). Das Kind der Kindheitsforschung. In M.-S. Honig (Ed.), *Ordnungen der Kindheit. Problemstellungen und Perspektiven der Kindheitsforschung* (pp. 25–51). Juventa.

Hult, F. M. (2017). Nexus analysis as scalar ethnography for educational linguistics. In M. Martin-Jones & D. Martin (Eds.), *Researching multilingualism: Critical and ethnographic perspectives* (pp. 89–104). Routledge.

Jaffe, A. (2009). The Production and reproduction of language ideologies in practice. In N. Coupland & A. Jaworski (Eds.), *The new sociolinguistics reader* (pp. 390–404). Palgrave Macmillan.

James, A. (2009). Agency. In J. Qvortrup, W. A. Corsaro, & M.-S. Honig (Eds.), *The Palgrave handbook of childhood studies* (pp. 34–45). Palgrave Macmillan. https://ebookcentral.proquest.com/lib/tromsoub-ebooks/detail.action?docID=485290

James, A., & James, A. (2008). *Key concepts in childhood studies*. Sage Publications.

Jørgensen, J. N. (2008). Polylingual languaging around and among children and adolescents. *International Journal of Multilingualism, 5*(3), 161–176. http://dx.doi.org/10.1080/14790710802387562

Kroskrity, P. V. (2004). Language ideologies. In A. Duranti (Ed.), *A companion to linguistic anthropology* (pp. 496–517). Blackwell Publishing.

Kultti, A., & Samuelsson, I. P. (2016). Diversity in initial encounters between children, parents an educators in early childhood education. In K. Fischer, I. Kaschefi-Haude, & J. Schneider (Eds.), *Voices on participation: Strenghtening activity-oriented Interactions and growth in the early years and in transitions* (pp. 140–152). GINALS, EU Lifelong Learning Program. http://www.signals-eu.com/

Lane, P. (2010). "We did what we thought was best for our children": A nexus analysis of language shift in a Kven community. *International Journal of the Sociology of Language, 202*, 63–78. https://doi.org/10.1515/ijsl.2010.014

Lane, P. (2011). Neksusanalyse – minoritetsspråkpolitikk og språkskifte i et tospråklig samfunn. In T. R. Hitching, A. B. Nilsen, & A. Veum (Eds.), *Diskursanalyse i praksis. Metode og analyse* (pp. 239–256). Høyskoleforlaget AS.

Lane, P. (2014). Nexus analysis. In J.-O. Östman & J. Verschueren (Eds.), *Handbook of pragmatics* (Vol. 18, pp. 1–18). John Benjamins Publishing Company.

MacSwan, J. (2017). A multilingual persepctive on translanguaging. *American Educational Research Journal, 54*(1), 167–201. doi:10.3102/0002831216683935

Oberhuemer, P. (2015). Parallel discourses with unparalleled effects: Early years workforce development and professionalisation initiatives in Germany. *International Journal of Early Years Education, 23*(3), 303–312.

Ødegaard, E. E. (2015). The importance of looking at someone looking through a pirates telescope: Reflections on the making of knowledge from empirical data. *Tidsskrift for nordisk barnehageforskning, 11*(1), 1–17.

Ødegaard, E. E., & Krüger, T. (2012). Studier av barnehagen som danningsarena – sosialepistemologiske perspektiver. In E. E. Ødegaard (Ed.), *Barnehagen som danningsarena* (pp. 19–47). Fagbokforlaget.

O'Reilly, K. (2012). *Ethnographic methods* (2nd ed.). Routledge.

Øzerk, K. (2016). *Tospråklig oppvekst og læring*. Cappelen Damm Akademisk.

Pesch, A. M. (2017). *Å skape rom for flerspråklighet: En studie av diskursive vilkår for barnehagens språklige praksis med flerspråklige barn* (Ph.D. thesis). UiT Norges arktiske universitet, Tromsø.

Pesch, A. M. (2018). Syn på flerspråklighet som diskursive vilkår for samarbeid med foreldre til flerspråklige barn. *NOA: norsk som andrespråk, 1–2,* 158–188.

Postholm, M. B. (2011). *Kvalitativ metode: En innføring med fokus på fenomenologi, etnografi og kasusstudier* (2nd ed.). Universitetsforlaget.

Qvortrup, J. (2008). *Diversity's temptation – And hazards*. Paper presented at the 2nd international conference representing childhood and youth, University of Sheffield.

Riley, K. C. (2011). Language socialization and language ideologies. In A. Duranti, E. Ochs, & B. B. Schieffelin (Eds.), *The handbook of language socialization* (pp. 493–514). Blackwell Publishing Ltd.

Schleswig-Holstein Ministerium für Soziales, Gesundheit, Familie, und Gleichstellung. (2012). *Erfolgreich starten: Leitlinien zum Bildungsauftrag in Kindertageseinrichtungen.* http://www.schleswig-holstein.de/DE/Fachinhalte/K/kindertageseinrichtungen/downloads/kindertageseinrichtungen_Bildungsauftrag_LeitlinienBildungsauftrag_BildungsauftragLeitlinien.pdf?__blob=publicationFile&v=1

Scollon, R., & Scollon, S. W. (2004). *Nexus analysis: Discourse and the emerging internet.* Routledge.

Sollid, H. (2014). Hierarchical dialect encounters in Norway. *Acta borealia, 31*(2), 111–130. doi:10.1080/08003831.2014.967969

United Nations. (1989). *Convention on the Rights of the Child.* Retrieved March 27, 2020, from https://www.ohchr.org/en/professionalinterest/pages/crc.aspx

Woolard, K. A. (1998). Language ideology as a field of inquiry. In B. B. Schieffelin, K. A. Woolard, & P. V. Kroskrity (Eds.), *Language ideologies. Practice and theory* (pp. 3–47). Oxford University Press.

Yin, R. K. (2014). *Case study research: Design and methods* (5th ed.). Sage Publications.

CHAPTER 13

Studies of Child Perspectives in Methodology and Practice with 'Osallisuus' as a Finnish Approach to Children's *Reciprocal* Cultural Participation

Liisa Karlsson

Abstract

This article discusses the methodology and practices involved in *studies of child perspectives*, which is an orientation of research and action focusing on children's perspectives and social participation as a cultural phenomenon. The objective of this orientation is to examine children's and youth's views and their ways of operating and acting as well as the data they produce. It includes listening to children's varied signals and information through multiple methods and analysing their experiences, views, actions, values, and ways of operating and expressing their thoughts.

Studies of child perspectives can be described as part of a holistic approach, which covers the relationships between humans, non-humans, objects, and different phenomena. Furthermore, it focuses on children's lives and childhood as comprehensive phenomena through interdisciplinary and cross-disciplinary research by applying multi-method approaches, which may include, for example, ethnography, narration, movements, playing, constructions, photos, and drawings.

Conducting research on children and engaging in activities with them can be justified from a number of viewpoints: the realm of rights, the realm of needs and learning, and the realm of listening, encountering, and sharing. The article explores these realms because they represent important aspects of why we need to observe and apply children's perspectives in research. Children's social participation, which is a multi-faceted phenomenon, forms the central concept for each realm. The article discusses essential elements of children's perspectives and the multiple possibilities offered by the elements for research and working with children. The need to listen to children's perspectives has been emphasised since the U.N. Convention on the Rights of the Child (UNCRC, 1989) was signed worldwide.

This article discusses the Finnish concept 'osallisuus' (in Swedish 'delaktighet'). 'Osallisuus' involves not only participation (in Finnish 'osallistuminen') but also acting, involvement, feeling and experiencing, relatedness, belongingness, togetherness, inclusion, and influencing as well as representation, democracy, organising, and governance.

Empirical research will be presented in order to introduce how studies of child perspectives and social participation can more comprehensively reveal different phenomena related to communal and other relationship networks. The empirical data gathered through a focus on child perspectives show that in order to achieve social participation from a child's perspective as a broader concept of a cultural participation, it is crucial to build a reciprocal participatory culture. A reciprocal participatory culture calls for a comprehensive, communal, and systemic understanding of the complexities and relational aspects of time, place, and space, which are in continuous and evolving processes.

Keywords

children's cultural participation – childhood studies – child perspective – UNCRC article 12 – 'osallisuus'

1   Introduction

Children and childhood have become a growth area in research and are regarded as interesting and important topics in more and more areas of life. Thus, there has been an increase in studies focusing specifically on children (i.e., persons under the age of 18). Furthermore, there has also been a call to explore in more detail children's actions and the ways in which they communicate, grow, learn, and create their own and shared cultures within a community and in relation to participation (e.g., Farrell, Kagan, & Tisdall, 2016; Karlsson & Karimäki, 2012; Corsaro, Honig, & Qvortrup, 2009).

When studying a child's perspective and social participation, it does not suffice to simply have children produce the research data. The topic should be discussed not only from an adult's point of view but also from that of the children. Therefore, I argue that it is relevant to focus on the concept of participation, which is a central concept both in research and practice (in Finnish 'osallisuus', in Swedish 'delaktighet') from a broader cultural standpoint. When studying children's participation through the lens of children's perspectives, we need to pay special attention to the ways in which the subject, agency, power, and influence are all intertwined. Next, I will discuss the different approaches of child studies, childhood studies, studies of child perspectives, and a child-centered viewpoint in order to reflect on the premises of the Finnish concept of reciprocal cultural participation.

2   Participatory Data Production with and by Children

Researchers in childhood studies have been engaging in multidisciplinary research in social studies, education, and cultural studies. A key part of these efforts has been the goal shared by different academic disciplines and researchers to understand children in their societies and communities and as agents, as well as to discern how childhood relates to the surrounding society, its structures, and cultures (Alanen, 2009, p. 9; James et al., 1998/1999; Corsaro, Honig, & Qvortrup, 2009; Corsaro, 2018). As a result, childhood studies and child culture studies have increased and become more diverse.

Depending on the approach, research can highlight very different issues. The essential consideration is not the academic discipline as such, be it cultural studies, education, psychology, sociology, or some other social science, but the theoretical background and the paradigm on which the study is based. As childhood is by nature a multi- and cross-disciplinary phenomenon, a combination of scientific viewpoints provides a more comprehensive outlook on the subject. James and James (2008, p. 25) define childhood studies as an interdisciplinary study of persons under the age of 18 with an active and social child at its center.

We should not overlook the fact that children are experiencing their childhood right now, in real time. They also have their particular manners of being present in the world, acting, learning, and growing, all of which differ from their adult counterparts. Therefore, an orientation of research and action focusing on a child's perspective is needed as well. The aim of this orientation is to uncover children's views and ways of operating and acting. When conducting research or working with children, a concept is needed that describes the child as a subject, a participant, and a data producer, while also including the passive and reluctant sides of children. Figure 13.1 shows the relationships between child studies, childhood studies, and studies of child perspectives in relation to each other and to other cultural, material, and biological contexts.

Data and topical knowledge are relevant to, for example, decision making, education, pedagogy, social sciences, and the cultural sector. Different needs for research data – in other words, who needs information and where – contribute to choosing a research paradigm, perspective, and methodology. In studies focusing on children, data and knowledge can be generated by children, parents, or experts. Involving children in the process of producing data allows them to likewise participate in the research as well as in the practical

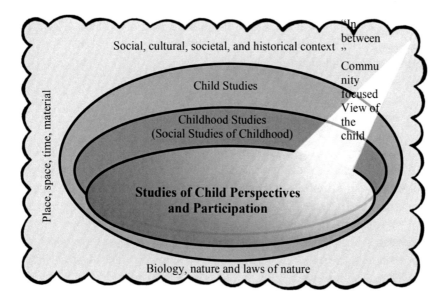

FIGURE 13.1   Child studies, childhood studies, studies of child perspectives, the child-centered view, and social participation in different contexts

phases of the study. Several methods are typically employed when gathering data on children, and they can be divided into five categories (Karlsson, 2012a):

1. Data may be gathered from children in real time by recording, filming, photographing, or observing children and the adults around them, or by utilising applications such as smartphones.
2. Both children and adults can produce data in retrospect by answering questionnaires, participating in interviews, reminiscing, and expressing their thoughts verbally or in writing, or by using symbols, emojis, pictures, or body language.
3. Valuable data can also be obtained from children's works, for example stories, writings, journals, presentations, recordings, constructions and crafts, photos, videos, movements, maps, and drawings. The material can be produced as part of normal daily activities or specifically for research purposes. Adults' works can also depict their own childhoods or the children with whom they interact.
4. Research materials can include documents, such as statistics, procedural texts, laws, regulations, political programs, and historical documents. These materials are created by adults.
5. One type of data consists of public information, including information presented by the media, social media content, and forum discussions, which are mainly produced by adults.

Even in studies on children, adults still produce most of the data. Another potential issue is that studies focus on a single phenomenon and therefore do not provide an overall picture of childhood.

3 The Essential Elements in Studies of Child Perspectives

The aim of the studies of child perspectives is to examine children's and youth's (persons under 18) views, the data they produce, and their social participation (Karlsson, 2010, 2012a, 2013). This leads to listening to children's signals and information in various ways and to analysing children's experiences and views, their actions and values, and their ways of operating and expressing their thoughts. Children should not be romanticised or isolated from other age groups, although the special traits of childhood should be taken into account. Moreover, children should not be viewed as a uniform group; rather, different childhoods and viewpoints should be observed. Furthermore, children's points of view and words are best viewed in relation to other perspectives, which can be those of adults, communities, or animals and which may originate as a shared outcome between different elements, such as space, expectations, matter, biology, or habits of action (Karlsson, 2012a, 2013).

An empirical example provided in one study (Hohti & Karlsson, 2013) clearly shows how the phenomenon in question appears differently when the child perspective is applied. During fieldwork, the researchers focused on a single school day from different perspectives. On that particular day, the class was preparing for their spring festival. The researchers found that the discursive frame of the festival allowed children only a narrow space for their actions and voices. Children were supposed to stand still and they could use their voices only for singing, but even then, they had to use their voices carefully. Those children who behaved well in the rehearsal were given lollipops. The researchers wanted to use the Storycrafting Method, a participatory method to listen to children's perspectives; the children were able to tell a story about anything they wanted to because the aim of the method is to give the child freedom and space to tell their own story (Karlsson, 2013). Surprisingly, the stories that the children told were about the festival rehearsal and the control they had experienced:

> The title of Jani's story:
> Jani, who didn't like Matias because he ate lollipops all the time, which Jani didn't like. Once upon a time, there was Jani, who didn't like lollipops. Or the lollipops that Matias is munching next to me. The end.

This empirical example from the research data shows that the phenomenon being researched, as well as our understanding of social participation, becomes more comprehensive and multi-dimensional when applying a child's perspective; in this example, the researcher took the position of the listener and had the physical space and time to listen to the children's voices. Without the participatory space, the children's voices would not have been heard.

The study of child perspectives focuses on a holistic approach (Karlsson, 2010, 2012a). There is always the question of what happens 'in between' in the relationships between humans, non-humans (Prout, 2005), objects, and various phenomena. Disciplines should not limit the subject being studied nor its analysis; instead, the focus should be on children's lives and childhood as comprehensive phenomena on cultural participation. Thus, this field of research is interdisciplinary and cross-disciplinary by nature (see Mikkeli & Pakkasvirta, 2007). Nothing occurs on its own or in a vacuum, but rather in relation to other issues, as self-expression and its various forms and types of content are linked to the cultures, subcultures, and environments in which people operate as well as to social, societal, historical, material, and biological contexts. Consequently, the studies of child perspectives also investigate children's interactions with adults and others as well as broad contexts in different macro and micro cultures. This means that research on child perspective is community-focused, implying that researchers should not just adopt concepts that highlight children, such as child-focused studies or child-centered studies (Karlsson, 2012a). The studies of child perspectives overlap with other research orientations, such as research on minorities and marginalisation.

Researchers have started to employ methods that encourage subjects to participate more in the study and have developed multi-method approaches that utilise, for example, ethnography, photos, and narration (Honkanen et al., 2018; Kinnunen & Einarsdóttir, 2017), as well as the mosaic approach (Clark & Moss, 2011). Children are included as co-researchers in a variety of modes of action (e.g., Kjær, 2015; Hakomäki, 2013; Lundy, Mcevoy, & Byrne, 2011; Clark & Moss, 2011; Karlsson, 2014, 2005; Tisdall et al., 2009; Christensen & Prout, 2000; Jørgensen & Kampmann, 2000; Alderson, 2000). Here, children are considered active producers of data and knowledge instead of research subjects. Especially in the 21st century, children have been included in the research process as active participants (see also Sommer et al., 2010). They take part in ways that come naturally to them, such as playing (e.g., Cederborg, 2020; Vuorisalo, Rutanen, & Raittila, 2015; Rainio, 2010), talking and telling stories (e.g., Engel, 2006; Karlsson, 2013; Weckström et al., in press), and taking photos (e.g., Honkanen et al., in press). Children can study a variety of phenomena (e.g., Weckström et al., in press; Stenvall, 2009; Raittila, 2008). In some cases, children have been encouraged to form their own research questions, which they then try to answer through research, and their research question has also been included in the scope of the actual scientific study (e.g., Hakomäki, 2013; Hakomäki & Karlsson, in press; Tuovila, 2003). Researchers may also present their findings to the children before the study results are published (e.g., Hohti, 2016). Hence, we could argue that this discipline is currently undergoing a paradigm shift (e.g., Fargas-Malet, 2010; Karlsson, 2012a, 2013).

The child perspective affects the whole research process: forming the research task and questions, producing the data, choosing the methodology, conducting the analysis, drawing conclusions based on the findings, and publishing the results (Karlsson, 2012a). However, researchers can never truly experience what life is like for those who participate in the study or get inside the participants' heads. This naturally applies to all research (Karlsson, 2012a). In short, the studies of child perspectives highlight issues discussed by children or arising from children, while placing the complexity of these phenomena in a broader context.

James and James (2008, p. 19) suggest that child-focused or child-centered research is the core element of childhood studies. Children are seen as subjects and actors rather than as the objects of research (James & James, 2008, p. 17). Children are not merely actors with something to say. They have views that they are capable of presenting in a research-oriented context (Jones & James, 2008, p. 17). The "studies of child perspectives" approach includes the concept of "children's perspectives", which "represent children's experiences, perceptions, and understanding in their life-world" (Sommer et al., 2010; see also Lewis & Lindsay, 2000).

With the studies of child perspectives, information provided by children forms the basis of child-perspective activities. This information is paired with expert knowledge and skills through activities, which are communal and reciprocal. The orientation of actions comprises inquiry, experimentation, and wonder: both the children and the professionals pose questions and try to answer them on their own. Even though children's perspectives are considered, it will not result in excluding or belittling the capabilities and actions of adults. On the contrary, it is essential to observe everyone's perspectives and the community as a whole. When working with a focus on children's perspectives, these overall ideas form the basis for research activities.

It could be argued that there is no need for a separate 'child perspective', and instead we could focus on the perspectives of all actors, agents, and communities. The risk then lies in children's perspectives being overshadowed by stronger and more forcefully presented points of view, which is hardly a novel outcome. Adults' positions of power, practiced writing skills and verbal skills, wealth of experience, and specialist knowledge can easily take over and dominate. For example, there is a trend of engaging in problem-centric discussion, where the focus is placed on children's shortcomings, hardships, and points of development. In reality, children are similar to adults, as well as special and different from them. Studies and activities with a child perspective pay attention to all sorts of signals from children, which means that children's strengths and skills are also observed as opposed to only their weaknesses and troubles. Furthermore, the manner in which children act, express themselves, and deal with issues differs from how adults operate. This calls for special attention. Table 13.1 presents some visible differences between the currently predominant child research approach and the studies of child perspectives.

TABLE 13.1 Differences between the currently predominant child research approach and the studies of child perspectives

Predominant approach	The approach of the studies of child perspectives
Adults define and produce information and knowledge. Research focuses on the views of teachers, experts, and parents on matters affecting children.	Children and youth produce information and knowledge (together with adults). Since the research focuses on children, issues are studied together with children.
Discussions revolve around adult-centric definitions and often negative phenomena and indicators (e.g., incapability, health problems, impairments in interaction, learning disabilities).	In addition to problems, positive, constructive, and joy-inducing elements of children's and youth's lives, perspectives, and experiences are observed.
Adult perspective	Child and community perspective
Phenomena are often examined from one discipline's point of view and using one method.	Answers (to a holistic and systemic, multifaceted whole) are sought utilizing a multidisciplinary and often multi-method approach.

Research on children and engaging in activities with them can be justified from a number of perspectives. The next section expands on some points that can be used as arguments for why we need to observe and apply a child's perspective. Research and activities with children can be seen as different realms: the realm of rights, the realm of needs and learning, and the realm of listening, encountering, and sharing. In these realms, children's social participation is the central concept, which is a multi-faceted phenomenon.

4   The Convention on the Rights of the Child – Realm of Rights

Children's (persons under the age of 18) rights in society are globally defined by the United Nations Convention on the Rights of the Child (UNCRC, 1989), which all UN member countries have ratified except for the U.S. The convention includes all the key principles of the Declaration of the Rights of the Child (1959). It is a legally binding document, and it has greatly affected national laws. Some noteworthy examples include the Finnish constitution (Section 6, 1999/731), inter-branch laws, political agendas, and curricula.

Article 12 of the UNCRC (1989) asserts:

> States Parties shall assure to the child who is capable of forming his or her own views the right to express those views freely in all matters affecting the child, the views of the child being given due weight in accordance with the age and maturity of the child.

It stands to reason that children shall also have a say in matters affecting them in studies of children and activities with them. The need to consider the views of children based on their age, capabilities, and stage of development should not be taken to mean that young children or children with disabilities are unable to make an impact. Instead, the inclusion of age and stage of development into the equation challenges researchers, professionals working with children, and others to look at issues from a child's perspective. We should aim to develop the ways of operating that come naturally to children. There are several ways to include children in studies and listen to their voices. Next, I will discuss how the rights of the child are put into effect and what matters demand particular attention.

When children are considered in line with the UNCRC, we are operating in the realm of rights. Children as a group can be observed in several other realms, such as the romantic, advocacy, needs, learning, institutional, and proactive realms (Francis & Lorenzo, 2002, p. 164). Furthermore, children can be discussed within the realm of listening, encountering, and sharing (Karlsson, 2012a; see also Rainio, 2010). The next sections concentrate on several of those realms.

4.1   Realm of Needs and Learning

In the realm of needs and learning children can be observed from the standpoint of a child's level of self-determination and motivation (see Isola et al., 2017). Ryan and Deci's (2000, 2017) theory of self-determination examines people as actors striving to achieve goals that they have personally set. The theory suggests that people have three basic psychological needs: autonomy, showing competence, and relatedness. The theory has been developed, studied, and expanded since the 1970s. For example, the theory has recently received a fourth dimension: benevolence (Martela & Ryan, 2015). According to self-determination theory, motivation is a result of satisfying basic needs. When autonomy is promoted by listening to subjects and providing them with options, studies have found, for example, the onset of more beneficial exercise behavior (Hynynen & Hankonen, 2015, p. 483). When subjects have been presented with an opportunity to show benevolence, they have felt a sense of purpose, appreciation, and dignity.

Another point of view has been offered by Bandura (1977), who discusses the concept of self-efficacy as entailing a person's trust in their own abilities in a certain situation. People with a strong sense of self-efficacy tend to accept more challenging tasks and achieve goals more efficiently than others (e.g., Kavanagh & Bower, 1985). Research indicates that students with higher self-efficacy display more effort and perseverance, for example when engaged in demanding writing tasks (Schunk, 2003). Self-determination, motivation, and self-efficacy are important phenomena that create space for children to act and present their views. The studies of child perspectives provide this space, and thus, participating in the study often inspires and motivates children and supports their possibilities to improve self-determination and self-efficacy. However, in order to create a more holistic perspective, I will next discuss in detail the child's whole community and its dynamic operational environment.

4.2   Subjectivity, Agency, Community, Social Participation, and Power – Towards the Realm of Listening, Sharing, and Encountering

When children are viewed as part of a community and an operational environment, the following concepts arise: the states of subject (subjectivity) and object, agency and sense of community, social participation and non-participation, and the power involved in providing room for the subject state and participation, or in limiting them. What do these concepts mean in practice, though?

As mentioned earlier, a child is not an independent or isolated actor. When a child is born, he/she grows, learns, and undergoes changes within a certain social, cultural, and material environment and exists in a constant state of interaction. Both children and adults can simultaneously be considered beings or persons acting in the moment and becomings, or subjects-in-process (Lee, 2001; Prout, 2005; Kennedy, 2006; Rainio, 2010). They are both strong, fragile, and active agents and in need of protection, and they are capable as well as learners. The states of subject, agency, participation, or power do not define an individual as an absolute, nor are they measurable and static features. Instead, these concepts should be regarded as dynamic phenomena: they are ever-changing, connected to people and various matters, and contextual. The phenomena and the concepts that represent them are overlapping and connected, network-like relations. They are born in context-specific interactions in communities and spaces. Hence, subjectivity, agency, participation, and power are dynamic, communal, and relational concepts (e.g., Prout, 2005). Power and the states of subject or agency cannot simply be taken for granted; rather, they reflect a constantly changing relationship with others. In some situations, agency is easily accessed and allowed to surface, but in others it is not available, or the person does not want to strive for a position of agency. On the other hand, self-exclusion and opposition are expressions of agency and power.

Any situation can involve various areas of power and agency. For example, it may prove to be less difficult to utilise power when facing a peer than to exercise that power over an adult who is in charge of an activity. Each actor's visible or implicit actions, or intentions, have an impact on others and are simultaneously affected by others' actions. Predominantly, several conscious and unconscious actions occur at the same time. Therefore, actions or events are not linear in relation to each other; rather, they are intertwined like a net and partially entangled. Power is a social resource, as well as a network of sociocultural interpretations and communication (see also Thomson, 2007), but it involves other factors as well, such as the operational environment and material and biological bases (see also Barad, 2007). The world is comprised of entanglements of both 'social' and 'natural' agencies, and nature and culture interact and change over time (Barad, 2007).

In summary, the concepts of subjectivity, agency, community, participation, and power always exist in connection with the observed phenomenon and with time, place, and space. Subjectivity, agency, community, participation, and power are not individual, static features. Instead, these phenomena emerge among human beings, in dialogue, through listening to each other, encountering one another, and sharing together. Consequently, subjectivity, agency, community, participation, and power help to create a realm of listening, encountering, and sharing.

5 'Osallisuus' – A Finnish Approach to Children's Social Participation

In this section, I will examine social participation in more detail. Social participation allows us to discuss essential parts of the child perspective and its chances of being realised in research and in working with children. I shall also discuss what additions the child perspective can bring to defining and realising participation as a broader cultural phenomenon.

There are multiple definitions for the phenomenon and concept of social participation and involvement. In a broad sense, participation can be characterised by three dimensions: having, acting, and belonging (Raivio & Karjalainen, 2013; Allardt, 1976; Isola et al., 2017). The last two could be included in the social participation of children, which entails mechanisms for people to participate in making social decisions.

Children's social participation, and especially the Finnish concept of 'osallisuus' (in Swedish 'delaktighet'), is a multifaceted phenomenon. The concept involves participation, acting, involvement, feeling and experiencing, relatedness, belonginess, togetherness, inclusion, influencing and representation, democracy, organising, and governance (see also Isola et al., 2017; Kangas, 2016; Karlsson, 2012a; Weckström et al., in press). Social participation consists of an entangled union of the states of subject, agency, power, and influence. When a child is treated as a subject or actor with meaningful thoughts and views, the child has an opportunity to enter the position of an active participant within the community. Whoever organises an activity also possesses the power to affect whether space and opportunities are presented for others to achieve the states of subject, agency, and participation. Then again, the child may or may not accept the role of active agent. Additionally, numerous factors influence participation and agency, such as other children and adults, experiences, expectations, an operational culture or community culture, space, objects, biology, and other phenomena, as well as the relationships and tensions between all of these elements.

The key to social participation is giving the child an opportunity to participate and to have an effect as well as allowing the child to feel involved and included. Social participation manifests itself as mutual respect, equality, and trust within a community. Taking part and having influence are gateways to social participation. The concept of social participation has been specified according to different dimensions and levels. Shier (2001, p. 110; see also Hart, 1995) has introduced five levels of participation: (1) children are listened to, (2) children are supported in expressing their views, (3) children's views are taken into account, (4) children are involved in decision-making processes, and (5) children share power and responsibility for decision making.

These levels of social participation resurface in a new light if they are examined from a qualitative perspective and from the perspective of power and decision making. This highlights not only what action is taken, but even more what kinds of issues these actions address, who makes decisions regarding the actions, and on what grounds. In other words, from the qualitative perspective the essence of the first level of social participation inquires as to whose views are listened to and what criteria are used in deciding what is worth listening to. On the second level, we should ask what types of expressions and content are allowed in children's self-expression, what types are not acceptable, and why. The third-level's qualitative questions include, for example, which of the children's ideas are taken into consideration, by whom, and how. The fourth level of qualitative questions asks what activities the children can affect, are they allowed to have an influence on crucial and important actions, and who decides what is considered a crucial and important action. The method of determining what is important to the children also has a significant role in shaping this level. On the fifth level, attention should be given especially to how and by whom decisions are made in situations where children are also responsible for the outcomes, what the decision-making process involves, on whose initiative the decisions are made, how and by whom the decisions are arrived at, and how these decisions are addressed.

The requirements for social participation of children have noteworthy counteractions and downsides. Active and participating children may become a norm, which isolates children from each other (see Prout, 2003, p. 22). Discussions of agency and social participation can place a heavy focus on an individualistic point of view. If children's activity is highlighted as a trait, it may distort or blur the meaning of the boundaries in the community and culture, the historical and biological factors, and political and financial structures. Children should not have limitless opportunities for agency, and action should not be a venture of omnipotent individuality. The rise of individualism (e.g., Koskelainen, 2017) is present in criticisms of child-focused activity (Hytönen, 2008). The social effects of one person's actions on others may become difficult to detect. The current life of any person is a result of the person's, community's, and society's history. Goals and boundaries for any action are based on current structures and cultural norms. When attention and focus are placed on actively pursued actions, they simultaneously marginalise the silent, passive, and invisible (e.g., Gordon et al., 2002; Rainio, 2010). The studies of child perspectives and childhood studies face the challenge of combining micro- and macro-level perspectives with a discursive, evolving, and societally influential research genre.

6 The Key to Children's Social Participation Can Be Found in a Reciprocal Participatory Culture

How does adopting a child's perspective affect our ideas of social participation? Does a child's perspective inspire new understanding or revelations? First, I introduce and define the concept of *reciprocal participatory culture*. With a reciprocal participatory culture, all participants – children and adults of different ages – have an opportunity to be heard and appreciated. Everyone can take initiative and affect the decision-making process, regardless of their age, skills, or backgrounds. Thus, the different ways in which participants take action are respected. A reciprocal participatory culture involves a shared understanding of 'we' rather than 'us and them'. Reciprocal participatory culture calls for a comprehensive, communal, and systemic understanding of the complexities and relational aspects of time, space, and place, but also of relations with the biological bases and material aspects of the phenomena of power. This understanding is shared and invoked in continuous and evolving processes as part of a broader continuum or process and not as a set of individual actions. Reciprocal participatory culture involves the creation of a (transparent) system, certain attitudes, views, spaces, and actions, which are justified and agreed upon together as a community.

From an adult's perspective, in a reciprocal participatory culture both adults (e.g., researchers, teachers, parents) and other children see a child as an interesting person who shows initiative and has her/his own ideas, knowledge, views, and ways of acting, all of which are worthy of examination. Adults give children an opportunity to have an influence on their daily activities. In a reciprocal participatory culture, the adults are also active subjects and participants. Social participation can be regarded as a shared process between children and those who are acting with them. The process affects both the individual and the community. In a reciprocal participatory culture, adults cannot fully plan ahead or know the outcomes of particular actions. The views of children and the expectations and intentions of adults set the boundaries or provide the opportunities for children's actions and a framework for how children see their position and chances for acting in relation to that of others. The focus lies in achieving a clear sense of the activities and shared goals involved. Additionally, interaction, place, space, material, and biological factors affect the larger whole. A reciprocal participatory culture requires mutual understanding and that the participants take steps to build a reciprocal participatory culture through practical actions. This shared process helps create a better understanding of the concept involved.

When we take a closer look at the levels of children's social participation and their qualitative aspects, it becomes apparent that they are based on an adult's perspective. Social participation is in fact defined through adults' actions. When a child's perspective is introduced into the equation, the phenomenon can be observed more comprehensively, through communal and other relationship networks. This approach uncovers new issues and provides new focal points. Our understanding of social participation becomes more thorough, and some parts of it may change notably. This could either become a sixth level of social participation or rather a new, more comprehensive, qualitative, dynamic, and emerging way of dissecting social participation.

Here, I would like to highlight the empirical research example from a prior study (Hohti & Karlsson, 2013) already presented in this paper because it shows that children's social participation is not unitary and complete, but rather emergent and contingent upon the discursive, social, material, and physical resources available. Hohti and Karlsson's (2013) study tracked the voices of the children through three different discursive spaces. They discovered that the observational space, which was constructed by observing the class rehearse for a spring festival, illustrated a struggle between the controlling institutional voices of the teacher and the voices of the children. Children's voices appeared to be mostly defined by the teacher as largely irrelevant, disturbing, and as signs of behavioural problems. Hohti and Karlsson (2013) additionally found that the participatory space was created via a participatory narrative method, Storycrafting (Karlsson, 2013, 2014). With the method, children were given an opportunity after the rehearsal to tell any story they wanted to the researcher (Hohti & Karlsson, 2013). In this space, it became possible to hear the children's voices in (the physical and) the discursive senses, and children's narratives were positioned as knowledge. The stories – the narrative voices of children – provided diverse and surprising perspectives on classroom interactions. The analysis revealed children's performative styles of elaborating on the power relations they had experienced, in which reciprocity, friendship, and humor were crucial. The researchers were now able to see how the children talked about the rehearsal situation and their individual ways of coping with that situation. The participatory method allowed children to construct meanings, which was not the case before.

The reflexive space of listening was entered when the researchers started to question their own ways of selecting and interpreting children's voices (Hohti & Karlsson, 2013). After focusing on the discursive, social, and physical dimensions of the narratives, attention was turned to listening to voices, and more stories that had been left out of the study at an earlier stage were analysed. The reflexive space showed that by listening to the easier-to-understand voices, a gendered and simplified picture of children's worlds was realised. Through reflexive listening, it was possible to embrace children's diversity and to bring to the center the cultural and collaborative dimensions of children's narrative activity.

This empirical example of the holistic and reflexive approach shows that in order to promote social participation, adults must take responsibility for creating spaces for children's voices. Hence, time is needed for reflexive listening through repeated considerations and experimentation on the researchers' part. Furthermore, entering the reflexive spaces of telling and listening can also help intervene in the persistent controlling practices in schools and early childhood education and to build spaces for the complex and diverse voices of children.

When social participation is understood as an emotion arising from the experience of communal inclusion, it cannot be considered a specific action taken at a given moment, after which a new way of acting is adopted. Actions seem contradictory and confusing from a child's perspective if in one moment the child is expected to show initiative and present ideas, while similar active participation becomes a distraction during the next task. In order to achieve social participation from the child's perspective, participation must be viewed as part of a broader continuum or process and not as a set of single actions. This, in turn, is a fundamental shift in a reciprocal participatory culture. Here, reciprocal and social participation is present in subtle actions, word choices, and objects, as well as in lengthier processes, larger environments, and principles guiding people's actions. The attitudes of the adults in charge are a decisive factor (e.g. Olli et al., 2012). Adults' views about children in general and about the children with whom they interact are essential. The views, expectations, and intentions of adults set boundaries for children's actions and provide a framework for how children see their position and chances for acting in relation to that of others.

As discussed earlier, social participation is often observed from an individual's perspective instead of focusing on the point of view of a community. People operate within a community, and there can be no social participation without community-level activity. When we observe social participation from a child's perspective, shared activities and spending time with others become important matters. Virkki's (2015) research indicates that educators emphasise individualistic elements, but children place more value on community or group activities. For children of all ages, friends as well as family members are extremely valuable (e.g., Hayball et al., 2018; Honkanen et al., in press). Children's participatory actions correlate positively with peer relations, play, and positive emotions (Arvola, Lastikka, & Reunamo, 2017). School children who are popular with their peers offer more positive evaluations of their own behavioral and emotional strengths than children who are rejected by their peers (Rytioja et al., 2019). Friendships and a sense of belonging are even connected to learning. According to research, children who enjoy positive relationships with their peepers experience more emotional well-being, have a greater sense of self-worth, and excel at academic tasks compared to those without positive peer relationships (Wentzel, Donlan, & Morrison, 2012, p. 79). Research (Rytioja et al., 2019) shows that children in the 'popular' status group perform better academically and report less emotional distress in their self-evaluations than others.

A child's perspective challenges scholars to delve deeper into the less researched community perspective. This involves shared activity, interaction, and relationships where both human and non-human participation in social life is addressed (Prout, 2005).

7 The Studies of Child Perspectives Open New Avenues

The studies of child perspectives have revealed new ways of looking at several phenomena. When researchers studied residential areas from a child's point of view, children were able to introduce many issues relevant to developing residential areas and services for families (Honkanen et al., 2018). To a child, place and space are linked. The concepts of place and space are defined differently. In humanistic geography, the understanding of place has recently been changing. The place can be seen as both a socially produced and personally experienced space (Hyvärinen, 2014; see also Campbell, 2018). However Duhn (2012) defines place as a recognizable, physically built, or natural place. But for humans, lived places constitute not only a physical environment. A place has different meanings when it is connected with emotions, actions, and memories. Here, the starting point is that space is relationally produced through everyday actions and interactions in a process that is intertwined with physical environments and places and concrete objects, personal interpretations of physical and cultural space, and cultural and collective views (Vuorisalo et al., 2015; Soja, 1996; Bourdieu, 2000; also Zhou et al., 2019). Space is not a neutral context or background for action, but involves collective definitions and ideas (Vuorisalo et al., 2015).

According to a recent study (Honkanen et al., in press), a place becomes meaningful to children when it serves as a location for activities with friends, or when children can feel safe and experience a feeling of togetherness with other people, like parents or siblings. The researchers identified two essential types of places where children experience a sense of well-being: open public places where children meet up with friends (e.g., day-care centers, schools, playgrounds, family parks, shopping malls, youth centers) and bordered private places where children feel safe (e.g., home, the yard, a grandparent's home, 'secret places') (Honkanen et al., in press).

Children can also help determine how different methods, such as the Storycrafting or Storycomposing, work. In one experiment (Hakomäki, 2012, 2013), a young researcher together with a Ph.D. assistant, and music therapist used the Storycomposing method as well as the co-researcher's past experience with music therapy to create a place for children to tell their own stories. Storycrafting allows researchers to hear the thoughts of children and adults of different ages, get to know them, and build a reciprocal participatory culture for the community (Karlsson, 2013; Karlsson et al., 2018). Children also use the Storycrafting method to engage with power structures. Piipponen and Karlsson (2019) found that children participate in an intercultural Storycrafting exchange by narrating stories in a complex cultural web of connections, one which included their classmates, their teacher, and the partner class in another country. Story exchange promoted reciprocal intercultural encounters within and between the two groups of children, where the children find a way to connect as equals. Thus, the Storycrafting method creates a qualitatively deeper and reciprocal means for cultural exchange. The story exchange between the two classes was not only intercultural; important intracultural encounters occurred within the groups as well.

Research in nursing science (Olli et al., 2012, 2014) has shown that a child's perspective is rarely acknowledged in traditional, professional-centered nursing care or habilitation nursing, which emphasises vulnerability, and in the medical model of disability. These nursing functions and the procedures they generate are based on an adult's, and more specifically on a professional's, perspective. According to one study (Olli et al., 2014), the lack of consideration for a child's perspective is seldom recognised by healthcare professionals, because nurses feel that they are working with the child's best interest at heart. Nurses already treat children with kindness and give them opportunities to express themselves, for example by choosing their own toys or what they want to drink. When a habilitation program is developed, no consideration is apparently given to how matters seem from a child's perspective or the underlying thought patterns guiding the procedures. Olli et al. (2012) found that the lack of consideration for a child's perspective is also seldom recognised by other professionals, for instance teachers in early childhood education and school, educators at different levels, or social workers.

Several studies of child perspectives take an ontological post-humanist approach, highlighting how important it is to note the relationships and entanglements between multiple entities. Children and childhood are part of larger relational situations. The human, non-human, material, and place are all intertwined. Findings presented by Rautio, Hohti, Leinonen, and Tammi (2017) tell us how inseparable childhood is from place, and how they form side by side. The complexity of childhood and the concept of multispecies childhood is discussed by Hohti and Tammi (2019). Schooling, pedagogy, social participation, and childhood are redefined when the relational scope is expanded beyond human relationships in the studies of child perspectives (Tammi, 2019, 2020). Children may hold in high value mundane, material, funny, and contradictory objects, such as the pages of a book, seats, football cards, pens, jokes, animals, and children's stories, all of which have an impact on children's existence and learning, even though they have not always been taken into consideration in educational research (Hohti, 2016). For children, such institutions as schools or early childhood education settings are an inseparable aspect of their lives. For example, most Finnish school children own a smartphone, and the phones connect children's daily lives and school by becoming entangled in a web of things, bodies, emotions, time, and space (Hohti, Paakkari, & Stenberg, 2019).

8   Conclusions: Communal, Collaborative and Shared Social Participation in a Reciprocal Participatory Culture

Finally, I will connect the child perspective to a reciprocal participatory culture. In this reciprocal participatory culture, adults see children as interesting persons who show initiative and have ideas, knowledge, views, and specific ways of acting that are considered worthy of examination. In this context, children have an influence on daily activities (see also Turja, 2016; Kangas, 2016; Kangas & Lastikka, 2019; Weckström et al., 2017).

The supervising adult's views of an active child have an impact on the ideas and actions of the whole community. In a reciprocal participatory culture everyone can show initiative and affect decision making, regardless of their age and skills (Karlsson, 2012a, 2013; Riihelä, 2000). Initiatives can mean suggestions, ideas, and questions, but they can also simply be expressions conveyed through body language or actions, such as playing, acting silly, or excluding oneself from a shared activity. In fact, adults need to be particularly alert and sensitive to these kinds of initiatives and expressions. Above all, they should be able to register the subtlest of signals during activities, their planning, and their realisation. It is also a matter of adults' communication skills (Olli et al., 2012):

how adept are they as listeners, and can they communicate without words, for example by playing or utilising humor or through observation and recognition? The person in charge of an activity, who is usually an adult, has power and influence. It is the adult's responsibility to ensure that he/she sees, hears, and understands even the most laconic initiative or signal and that those messages are included in activity planning. It is also important to develop ways of acting that promote children's initiatives.

In a reciprocal participatory culture, the adults are also active subjects and participants. Social participation can be regarded as a shared process between children and those who work with them, and the process affects both the individual and the community (e.g., Hart, 1992; Kiili, 2006; Venninen & Leinonen, 2013), as well as time, space, place, and material. Research suggests that a group of children struggles with social participation if the workers in the group do not experience social participation as well (Karlsson, Weckström, & Lastikka, 2018). Parents' active social participation has also proven to be a crucial factor. According to a number of studies, parents' active social participation is connected to their children's academic success (e.g., Díez, Gatt, & Racionero, 2011; Gatt, Ojala, & Soler, 2011; Epstein, 2009). Also, parents' sense of academic efficacy and aspirations for their children are linked to their children's academic achievement. In turn, children's beliefs in their efficacy to regulate their own learning and academic attainments contributed to scholastic achievement (Bandura et al., 1996).

A reciprocal participatory culture involves taking a critical stance towards 'the other' and towards classifying a person as the other (Hummelstedt-Djedou et al., 2018). A child should not be considered 'the other', a person who needs to swiftly adjust to adult norms. In this way, children and families avoid viewing employees as the other, or as someone who should be opposed or pleased. Furthermore, parents should not be considered, for example, customers who require special treatment. Instead, all actors should be viewed as members of 'our community', where people share the same main goals. Each individual should still be respected and valued as a unique person and exactly as he/she is. However, a single father, a Nigerian mother, a special education teacher, or a disabled child does not represent being 'special'. They should primarily be viewed as individuals with different goals, ideas, dreams, ways of acting, and skills, who are valued members within the same community. Everyone should receive the same treatment as an interesting subject and actor. Alongside human contact, children have been found to hold animals in high value as subjects and co-actors (Hohti & Tammi, 2020; Karlsson, 2012b). Considering the abovementioned findings, a sense of community and individualism are closely connected.

In a reciprocal participatory culture, adults cannot fully plan or know the outcomes of their actions. When making plans, the focus lies instead on achieving a clear sense of the activities and goals involved, and therefore, planning should emphasise how, where, and with what equipment activities should begin and seek procedures where children have the opportunity to reflect, do, and create as much as possible. Additionally, interaction, place, space, material, and biological factors affect the larger whole.

Social participation should not be promoted only 'from above'. Instead, social participation involves the whole community and is often active by nature, but it can also simply be a sense of belonging. Social participation is not a constant or static state of being, and various degrees of participation can be observed in different situations. Still, from a community and child perspective, social participation is a starting point and always present in some form. An active effort should be made to allow children room to participate in activities wherever they may take place.

When we examine social participation from a child's perspective, we discover that in order to achieve participation, one must foster a reciprocal participatory culture in which a comprehensive, communal, and systemic understanding of the complexities and relational aspects of time, place, and space as continuous and evolving processes exists. Then, social participation involves the creation of a (transparent) system, certain attitudes, views, spaces, and actions that are justified and agreed upon together as a group. This, of course, does not suggest that a reciprocal participatory culture should be completed and achieved at once. Once a mutual understanding has been reached, people can start taking steps to building a reciprocal participatory culture. Taking practical action helps participants to better understand the concepts involved, and as a result, the next step can prove to be more profound than its predecessor. This should be considered an adventure; it is a matter of seeking, finding, questioning, failing, wondering, enjoying, delving deeper into the work, and laughing.

The 1989 UNCRC has had a crucial effect on our understanding of children and the studies of child perspectives. Listening to children's perspectives has been emphasised and will continue to be emphasised even more in the future.

Acknowledgements

Heartfelt thanks to the *'Child perspective'* research group: Otto Burman, Hanna Hakomäki, Timo Hirvonen, Riikka Hohti, Kati Honkanen, Satu Vasenius, Anna-Leena Lastikka, Johanna Olli, Antonina Peltola, Oona Piipponen, Noora Räihä,

Tuula Stenius, Tuure Tammi, and Elina Weckström. They provided and discussed novel, emerging, revealing, and thought-provoking points of view. The warmest thanks to Oona Piipponen and Anna-Leena Lastikka for their help.

References

Alanen, L. (2009). Johdatus lapsuudentutkimukseen. In L. Alanen & K. Karila (Eds.), *Lapsuus, lapsuuden instituutiot ja lasten toiminta* (pp. 9–30). Vastapaino.

Alderson, P. (2000). Children as researchers: The effects of participation rights on research methodology. In P. Christensen & A. James (Eds.), *Research with children: Perspectives and practices* (pp. 241–257). Routledge Falmer.

Allardt, E. (1993). Having, loving, being: An alternative to the Swedish model of welfare research. In M. Nussbaum & A. Sen (Eds.), *The quality of life* (pp. 88–95). Oxford University Press.

Arvola, O., Lastikka, A.-L., & Reunamo, J. (2017). Increasing immigrant children's participation in the Finnish early childhood education context. *The European Journal of Social and Behavioural Sciences (EJSBS), 20*(3), 2538–2548. http://dx.doi.org/10.15405/ejsbs.223

Bandura, A. (1977). Self-efficacy: Toward a unifying theory of behavioral change. *Psychological Review, 84*(2), 191–215. doi:10.1037/0033-295x.84.2.191 PMID 847061.

Bandura, A., Barbaranelli, C., Caprara, G. V., & Pastorelli, C. (1996). Multifaceted impact of self-efficacy beliefs on academic functioning. *Child Development, 67*(3), 1206–1222. doi:10.1111/j.1467-8624.1996.tb01791.x

Barad, K. (2007). *Meeting the universe halfway: Quantum physics and the entanglement of matter and meaning.* Duke University Press.

Bourdieu, P. (2000). *Pascalian meditations.* Stanford University Press.

Campbell, C. J. (2018). Space, place and scale: Human geography and spatial history in past and present. *Past and Present, 239*(1), e23–e45. doi:10.1093/pastj/gtw006

Cederborg, A. (2020). Young children's play: A matter of advanced strategies among peers. *Early Child Development and Care, 190*(5), 778–790. doi:10.1080/03004430.2018.1491561

Christensen, P., & Prout, A. (2002). Working with ethical symmetry in social research with children. *Childhood, 9*(4), 477–497.

Clark, A., & Moss, P. (2011). *Listening to young children: The mosaic approach* (2nd ed.). National Children's Bureau.

Corsaro, W. A. (2018). *The sociology of childhood* (5th ed.). Sage Publications, Inc.

Corsaro, W. A., Honig, M., & Qvortrup, J. (2009). *The Palgrave handbook of childhood studies.* Palgrave Macmillan.

Deci, E. L., & Ryan, R. M. (2000). The "what" and "why" of goal pursuits: Human needs and the self-determination of behavior. *Psychological Inquiry, 11*(4), 227–268. Retrieved January 4, 2019, from https://users.ugent.be/~wbeyers/scripties2012/artikels/The-what-and-why-of-goal-pursuits.pdf

Diez, J., Gatt, S., & Racionero, S. (2011). Placing immigrant and minority family and community members at the school's centre: The role of community participation. *European Journal of Education, 46*(2), 184–196.

Engel, S. (2006). Narrative analysis of children's experience. In S. Greene & D. Hogan (Eds.), *Researching children's experience* (pp. 200–2016). Sage Publications. doi:10.4135/9781849209823

Epstein, J. (2009). *School, family and community partnerships. Your handbook for action* (3rd ed.). Corwin Press.

Fargas-Malet, M., McSherry, D., Larkin, E., & Robinson, C. (2010). Research with children: Methodological issues and innovative techniques. *Journal of Early Childhood Research, 8*, 175–192.

Farrell, A., Kagan, S. L., & Tisdall, E. K. M. (2016). *The Sage handbook of early childhood research*. Sage.

Gatt, S., Ojala, M., & Soler, M. (2011). Promoting social inclusion with everyone: Learning communities and INCLUD-ED. *International Studies in Sociology of Education, 21*(1), 33–47.

Gordon, T., Lahelma, E., & Tolonen, T. (2002). Katseelta piilossa. Hiljaisuus ja liikkumattomuus kouluetnografin havainnoissa. In S. Aaltonen & P. Honkatukia (Eds.), *Tulkintoja tytöistä* (pp. 305–325). Suomalaisen Kirjallisuuden Seura.

Hakomäki, H. (2012). Storycomposing in music therapy. A collaborative experiment with a young co-researcher. In G. Trondalen & K. Stensæth (Eds.), *Barn, musikk, helse* (pp. 147–171). NMH-publikasjoner.

Hakomäki, H. (2013). *Storycomposing as a path to a child's inner world. A collaborative music therapy experiment with a child co-researcher* (doctoral dissertation). Jyväskylä Studies in Humanities 204, University of Jyväskylä, Finland.

Hakomäki, H., & Karlsson, L. (in press). Child perspective in practice; A child as a co-researcher in a music psychotherapy research. *Journal of Music Therapy*.

Hart, R. (1992). *Children's participation. From Tokenism to citizenship* (Innocenti Essays No. 4). UNICEF.

Hart, R. A. (1995). The right to play and children's participation. In H. Shier (Eds.), *The article 31 action pack*. Play-Train.

Hayball, F., McCrorie, P., Kirk, A., Gibson, A. M., & Ellaway, A. (2018). Exploring children's perceptions of their local environment in relation to time spent outside. *Children and Society, 32*, 14–26. doi:10.1111/chso.12217

Hohti, R. (2016). *Classroom matters: Research with children as entanglement* (doctoral dissertation). Opettajankoulutuslaitos, julkaisuja; No. 387. http://urn.fi/URN:ISBN:978-951-51-2069-4

Hohti, R., & Karlsson, L. (2013). Lollipop stories: Listening to children's voices in the classroom and narrative ethnographical research. *Childhood*, 1–15. doi:10.1177/0907568213496655

Hohti, R., Paakkari, A., & Stenberg, K. (2019). Leaping and dancing with digitality: Exploring human-smartphone-entanglements in classrooms. In P. Rautio & E. Stenvall (Eds.), *Social, material and political constructs of arctic childhoods* (pp. 85–102). Springer.

Hohti, R., & Tammi, T. (2020). The greenhouse effect: Multispecies childhood and non-innocent relations of care. *Childhood, 26*(2), 169–185. doi:10.1177/0907568219826263

Honkanen, K., Poikolainen, J., & Karlsson, L. (2018). Children and young people as co-researchers. Researching subjective well-being in residential area with visual and verbal methods. *Children's Geographies, 16*(2), 184–195. doi:10.1080/14733285.2017.1344769

Honkanen, K., Poikolainen, J., & Karlsson, L. (in press). Well-being places: Children's and young people's experiences of subjective well-being, social relations, emotions and action. *Children's Geographies*.

Hummelstedt-Djedou, I., Zilliacus, H., & Holm, G. (2018). Diverging discourses on multicultural education in Finnish teacher education programme policies: Implications for teaching. *Multicultural Education Review, 10*(3), 184–202.

Hynynen, S.-T., & Hankonen, N. (2015). Autonomiaa tukien aktiivisemmaksi? Itsemääräämisen teoria lasten ja nuorten liikunnan edistämisessä [Supporting Autonomy to Create a More Active Adolescence? Applying Self-Determination Theory in Increasing Adolescent Physical Activity]. *Kasvatus, 46*(5), 473–487.

Hytönen, J. (2008). *Lapsikeskeisen kasvatuksen ydinkysymyksiä*. WSOY.

Hyvärinen, R. (2014). Paikan käsitykset paikkalähtöisen kasvatuksen tutkimuksessa. In E. Estola, M. Hiltunen, & E. K. Hyry-Beihammer (Eds.), *Paikka ja kasvatus* (pp. 9–30). Lapin yliopistokustannus.

Isola, A.-M., Kaartinen, H., Leemann, L., Lääperi, R., Schneider, T., Valtari, S., & Keto-Tokoi, A. (2017). *Mitä osallisuus on? Osallisuuden viitekehystä rakentamassa* (THL: TYÖPAPERI 33/2017). http://urn.fi/URN:ISBN:978-952-302-917-0

James, A., & James, A. (2008). *Key concepts in childhood studies*. Sage Publications.

James, A., Jenks, C., & Prout, A. (1998/1999). *Theorizing childhood*. Polity Press.

Jørgensen, P. S., & Kampmann, J. (2000). *Børn som informanter*. Børnerådet.

Kangas, J. (2016). *Enhancing children's participation in early childhood education through the participatory pedagogy*. Department of Teacher Education, Faculty of Behavioral Science, University of Helsinki. https://helda.helsinki.fi/bitstream/handle/10138/159547/enhancin.pdf?sequence=1&isAllowed=y

Kangas, J., & Lastikka, A.-L. (2019). Children's initiatives in the Finnish early childhood education context. In S. Garvis, H. Harju-Luukkainen, S. Sheridan, & P. Williams (Eds.), *Nordic families, children and early childhood education* (pp. 15–36). Palgrave Macmillan.

Karlsson, L. (2005). Lapset tiedon ja kulttuurin tuottajina [Children as informants and knowledge actors]. In S. Hänninen, J. Karjalainen, & T. Lahti (Eds.), *Toinen tieto. Kirjoituksia huono-osaisuuden tunnistamisesta* (pp. 173–194). Sosiaali- ja terveysalan tutkimus- ja kehittämiskeskus.

Karlsson, L. (2010). Lapsinäkökulmainen tutkimus ja aineiston tuottaminen [The child perspective study and data collection]. In K. P. Kallio, A. Ritala-Koskinen, & N. Rutanen (Eds.), *Missä lapsuutta tehdään?* (pp. 121–141). Nuorisotutkimusseura. Verkkojulkaisuja 106. http://www.nuorisotutkimusseura.fi/images/julkaisuja/missa_lapsuutta_tehdaan.pdf

Karlsson, L. (2012a). Lapsinäkökulmaisen tutkimuksen ja toiminnan poluilla [The child perspective study and action]. In L. Karlsson & R. Karimäki (Eds.), *Sukelluksia lapsinäkökulmaiseen tutkimukseen ja toimintaan* [*Diving into study and action on the child perspective*] (pp. 17–63). Suomen kasvatustieteellinen seura, Jyväskylän yliopistopaino.

Karlsson, L. (2012b). Lapset toimivat – aikuiset valistavat: lasten kertomuksia syömisestä [Children act – Adults enlighten]. In L. Karlsson & R. Karimäki (Eds.), *Sukelluksia lapsinäkökulmaiseen tutkimukseen ja toimintaan* [*Diving into study and action on the child perspective*] (pp. 235–283). Suomen kasvatustieteellinen seura, Jyväskylän yliopistopaino.

Karlsson, L. (2013). Storycrafting method–to share, participate, tell and listen in practice and research. *The European Journal of Social & Behavioural Sciences, 6*(3), 1109–1117. http://www.futureacademy.org.uk/files/menu_items/other/ejsbs88.pdf

Karlsson, L. (2014). Children's voices in context of art education and circumstances for interaction. In I. Ruokonen & H. Ruismäki (Eds.), *Voices for tomorrow: Sixth international journal of intercultural arts education* (pp. 25–34). University of Helsinki, Department of Teacher Education. http://hdl.handle.net/10138/44696

Karlsson, L., & Karimäki, R. (2012). *Sukelluksia lapsinäkökulmaiseen tutkimukseen ja toimintaan* [*Diving into study and action on the child perspective*]. Suomen kasvatustieteellinen seura, Jyväskylän yliopistopaino.

Karlsson, L., Lähteenmäki, M., & Lastikka, A.-L. (2019). Increasing well-being and giving voice through storycrafting to children who are refugees, immigrants, or asylum seekers. In J.-A. Aerila & K. J. Kerry-Moran (Eds.), *Story in children's lives: Contributions of the narrative mode to early childhood development, literacy, and learning* (pp. 29–53). Springer International. https://doi.org/10.1007/978-3-030-19266-2_3

Karlsson, L., Weckström, E., & Lastikka, A-L. (2018). Osallisuuden toimintakulttuuria rakentamassa sadutusmenetelmällä [Building a Culture of Participation through Storycrafting]. In J. Kangas, J. Vlasov, E. Fónsen, & J. Heikka (Eds.), *Osallisuuden pedagogiikkaa varhaiskasvatuksessa 2 – Suunnittelu, toteuttaminen ja kehittäminen* [*Participatory Pedagogy in Early Childhood Education 2 – Planning, Implementing and Developing Practices*] (pp. 73–99). Suomen Varhaiskasvatusry.

Kavanagh, D. J., & Bower, G. H. (1985). Mood and self-efficacy: Impact of Joy amd sadness on perceived capabilities. *Cognitive Therapy and Research, 9*(5), 507–525.

Kennedy, D. (2006). *The well of being. Childhood, subjectivity and education*. State University of New York Press.

Kiili, J. (2006). Lasten osallistumisen voimavarat. Tutkimus Ipanoiden osallistumisesta. In *Studies in education, psychology and social research*. Jyväskylän yliopisto.

Kinnunen, S., & Einarsdóttir, J. (2017). "Look mother! Mother look!" Young children exploring life with their mother. In M. Narey (Ed.), *Multimodal perspectives of language, literacy, and learning in early childhood. Educating the young child* (Advances in Theory and Research, Implications for Practice, Vol. 12, pp. 109–126). Springer International. https://doi.org/10.1007/978-3-319-44297-6_6

Kjær, B. (2015). Children as co-researchers. *Arv: Nordic yearbook of folklore, 71*, 189–192.

Koskelainen, J. (2017). *Mahtava minä. Itsekkyyden voima ja vastavoimat*. Atena.

Lähteenmäki, M. (2013). *Lapsi turvapaikanhakijana: Etnografisia näkökulmia vastaanottokeskuksen ja koulun arjesta* [*The Child as an Asylum Seeker: Perspectives on Reception Centres and Daily School Life*]. http://urn.fi/URN:ISBN:978-952-10-8205-4

Lee, N. (2001). *Childhood and society. Growing up in an age of uncertainty*. Open University Press.

Lewis, A., & Lindsay, G. (2000). *Researching children's perspectives*. Open University Press.

Lundy, L., Mcevoy, L., & Byrne, B. (2011). Working with young children as co-researchers: An approach informed by the United Nations Convention on the Rights of the Child. *Early Education and Development: Children's Rights and Voices in Research: Cross-National Perspectives, 22*(5), 714–736. doi:10.1080/10409289.2011.596463

Martela, F., & Richard, R. (2015). The benefits of benevolence: Basic psychological needs, beneficence, and the enhancement of well-being. *Journal of Personality, 84*(6), 750–764.

Mikkeli, H., & Pakkasvirta, J. (2007). *Tieteiden välissä? Johdatus monitieteisyyteen, tieteidenvälisyyteen ja poikkitieteisyyteen*. WSOY.

Olli, J., Vehkakoski, T., & Salanterä, S. (2012). Facilitating and hindering factors in the realization of disabled children's agency in institutional contexts – Literature review. *Disability & Society, 27*(6), 793–807. doi:10.1080/09687599.2012.679023

Olli, J., Vehkakoski, T., & Salanterä, S. (2014). The habilitation nursing of children with developmental disabilities – Beyond traditional nursing practices and principles? *International Journal of Qualitative Studies on Health and Well-being, 9*(1). doi:10.3402/qhw.v9.23106

Piipponen, O., & Karlsson, L. (2019). Children encountering each other through storytelling: Promoting intercultural learning in schools. *The Journal of Educational Research*.

Prout, A. (2005). *The future of childhood. Towards the interdisciplinary study of children*. Routledge Falmer.

Qvortrup, J., Corsaro, W. A., & Honig, M.-S. (2009). *The Palgrave handbook of childhood studies*. Palgrave Macmillan.

Rainio, A. P. (2010). *Lionhearts of the playworld: An ethnographic case study of the development of agency in play pedagogy* (doctoral dissertation). University of Helsinki, Institute of Behavioural Sciences Studies in Educational Sciences, 233. http://urn.fi/URN:ISBN:978-952-10-5959-9

Raittila, R. (2008). Retkellä. Lasten ja kaupunkiympäristön kohtaaminen. *Jyväskylä Studies in Education, Psychology and Social Research, 333*.

Raivio, H., & Karjalainen, J. (2013). Osallisuus ei ole keino tai väline, palvelut ovat! Osallisuuden rakentuminen 2010-luvun tavoite- ja toimintaohjelmissa. In T. Era (Ed.), *Osallisuus – oikeutta vai pakkoa?* (pp. 12–34). Jyväskylän ammattikorkeakoulun julkaisuja, No. 156. University of Jyväskylä.

Rautio, P., Hohti, R., Leinonen, R.-M., & Tammi, T. (2017). Shitgulls and shops are nature: Urban child-within-nature reconfigurations. *Environmental Education Research, 23*(10), 1379–1390.

Riihelä, M. (2000). *Leikkivät tutkijat*. Edita.

Rutanen, N. (2007). Two-year-old children as co-constructors of culture. *European Early Childhood Education Research Journal, 15*(1), 59–69. doi:10.1080/13502930601161825

Ryan, R. M., & Deci, E. L. (2017). *Self-determination theory: Basic psychological needs in motivation, development, and wellness*. Guilford Publishing.

Rytioja, M., Lappalainen, K., & Savolainen, H. (2019). Behavioural and emotional strengths of sociometrically popular, rejected, controversial, neglected, and average children. *European Journal of Special Needs Education, 1*(7), 1–15. https://doi-org.ezproxy.uef.fi:2443/10.1080/08856257.2018.1560607

Schunk, D. K. (2003). Self-efficacy for reading and writing: Influence of modeling, goal-setting, and self-evaluation. *Reading and Writing Quarterly, 19*(2), 159–172. doi:10.1080/10573560308219

Shier, H. (2001). Pathways to participation: Openings, opportunities and obligations. A new model for enhancing children's participation in decision-making, in line with article 12.1 The United Nations Convention on the Rights of the Child. *Children & Society, 15*. https://ipkl.gu.se/digitalAssets/1429/1429848_shier2001.pdf

Soja, E. (1996). *Thirdspace. Journey to Los Angeles and other real-and-imagined places*. Blackwell.

Sommer, D., Samuelsson, I. P., & Hundeide, K. (2010). *Child perspectives and children's perspectives in theory and practice*. Springer.

Stenvall, E. (2009). *"Sellast ihan tavallist arkee" Helsinkiläisten 3.-6.-luokkalaisten arki ja ajankäyttö*. Helsingin kaupungin tietokeskus. http://www.hel2.fi/tietokeskus/julkaisut/pdf/uudet_julkaisut_2009.pdf

Tammi, T. (2017). *Poliittinen prosessi ja demokratiakokeilujen tartunnat koulun arjessa* [*The political process and the contagions of democratic experiments in every-day life in school*] (Doctoral dissertation). Helsinki Studies in Education, No. 2. Faculty of Educational Sciences, University of Helsinki.

Tammi, T. (2019). Breathing well at the wastelands? Indoor climate change in schools and the daily lives of arctic children. In P. Rautio & E. Stenvall (Eds.), *Social, material and political constructs of arctic childhoods – An everyday life perspective* (pp. 17–34). Springer International.

Tammi, T. (2020). What if schools were lively more-than-human agencements all along? Troubling environmental education with moldschools. *Environmental Education Research.* doi:10.1080/13504622.2019.1584881

Thomson, F. (2007). Are methodologies for children keeping them in their place? *Children's Geographies, 5*(3), 207–218.

Tisdall, K., Cree, V. E., Davis, J., & Gallagher, M. (2009). *Researching with children and young people: Research design, methods and analysis.* Sage.

Tuovila, A. (2003). *"Mä soitan ihan omasta ilosta!" Pitkittäinen tutkimus 7–13 -vuotiaiden lasten musiikin harjoittamisesta ja musiikkiopisto-opiskelusta* (doctoral dissertation). Sibelius Academy, Helsinki.

Turja, L. (2016). *Model of children's participation in ECEC.* https://www.researchgate.net/publication/316895844_Model_of_children%27s_participation_in_ECEC

United Nations. (1989). *Convention on the Rights of the Child (UNCRC).* Author. https://www.ohchr.org/en/professionalinterest/pages/crc.aspx

Venninen, T., & Leinonen, J. (2013). Developing children's participation through research and reflective practices. *Asia-Pacific Journal of Research in Early Childhood Education, 7*(1), 31–49.

Virkki, P. (2015). *Varhaiskasvatus toimijuuden ja osallisuuden edistäjänä* (Doctoral dissertation). Dissertations in Education, Humanities, and Theology, University of Eastern Finland.

Vuorisalo, M., Rutanen, N., & Raittila, R. (2015). Constructing relational space in early childhood education. *Early Years, 35*(1), 67–79. doi:10.1080/09575146.2014.985289

Weckström, E., Jääskeläinen, V., Ruokonen, I., Karlsson, L., & Ruismäki, H. (2017). Steps together – Children's experiences of participation in club activities with the elderly. *Journal of Intergenerational Relationships, 15*(3), 273–289. doi:10.1080/15350770.2017.1330063

Weckström, E., Karlsson, L., Pöllänen, S., & Lastikka, A.-L. (in press). *Creating a participatory culture: Early childhood education and care educators in the face of change.*

Wentzel, K. R., Donlan, A., & Morrison, D. (2012). Peer relationships and social motivational processes. In G. W. Ladd & A. M. Ryan (Eds.), *Peer relationships and adjustment at school* (pp. 79–107). Information Age Publishing.

Zhou, V. X., & Pilcher, N. (2019). Revisiting the 'third space' in language and intercultural studies. *Language and Intercultural Communication, 19*(1), 1–8.

CHAPTER 14

Global Paradoxes and Provocations in Education: Exploring Sustainable Futures for Children and Youth

Jorunn Spord Borgen and Elin Eriksen Ødegaard

Abstract

Global trends in education are accompanied by both paradoxes and provocations. The paradoxes constitute inherent educational dilemmas, such as the paradox of institutional education, wherein social rules and mandatory tasks are played out as a means of imparting lessons about freedom and independence. Our argument in this chapter is that we should reconsider the 'future' of planned and controlled education and instead become open to the perceptions of two groups that are at the forefront of educational futures – namely, children and young people and various experts on children and childhood. They meet face to face or indirectly on a daily basis in various educational contexts, and their experiences are interdependent and often paradoxical. This chapter explores possible sustainable futures in education as articulated by children, youth and child experts and highlights several qualities that sustainable futures will require, in relation to UNCRC article 28; children's right to education and article 29; that education must develop every child's personality, talents and abilities to the full.

Keywords

education – sustainable future – child experts – children and youth – awareness pedagogy

1   Introduction

As pointed out in the present volume's introduction, 'sustainable futures' is a political and utopian concept that has become prevalent in the global agenda. On a global scale, we have recognised that world cooperation, global and local agreements, and common actions are necessary to solve problems and secure further life for generations of humans, animal species, and plants. As a concept, sustainability encompasses dimensions such as social justice, health, nature and natural science, economics, and government as well as local practices and individual agency and participation. We agree with Peter Kemp's claim that sustainability is an ethical concept addressing the questions of what is considered a good and worthy life for generations to come and how to live according to values that can ensure the longevity of life on Earth (Kemp, 2013).

Futuristic thinking is embedded in all forms of education as children are the hope and future of any society. At the threshold of the twentieth century, discussions about the future were certainly different, but they shared certain similarities to corresponding discussions today. In *The School and Society*, Dewey (1899) argued that modernity brought with it industrialism and the growth of big cities and that society as an organic entity was thus rendered invisible to most people. The purpose of education was to make society visible again and, since culture is the condition for learning, to make culture 'cultural' again (Lundgren, 1986). Ellen Key, in this volume (Chapter 2) followed up on the strategic role that education occupies in society.

Education consistently seems to function as a societal tool for keeping society visible and perceptible. The character formation that is a key objective of education then becomes a matter that is not merely for our own time but for posterity. Global trends in education are accompanied by both paradoxes and provocations. Paradoxes in education are inherent educational dilemmas, such as the paradox of institutional education, wherein social rules and mandatory tasks are played out as a means of imparting lessons about freedom and independence. It does not necessarily follow that freedom and autonomy are compatible with actions that are considered necessary in the name of sustainable futures (Gough & Scott, 2007; Hafner-Burton & Tsutsui, 2005). Sustainable futures should consistently impart knowledge about what is needed, political decisions and actions, sensitivity to local culture and global solidarity, and awareness of relations from both a micro and macro perspective. Since the Brundtland Report (WCED, 1987), sustainability has commonly associated with the appeal to not compromise future generations' ability to meet their needs. Sustainable futures will require advocacy and action for a better balance between social needs, resource consumption, and economic growth. In our study, we touch upon these well-known connections related to the United Nations Convention on Children's Rights (UNCRC) (United Nations, 1989) article 28; children's right to education, and article 29; that education must develop every child's personality, talents and abilities to the full. More specifically, this study aims to contribute to new ideas for education, ideas that take into consideration the message from young people around the world and from an interdisciplinary group of child experts. Entering dialogue and making decisions regarding how best to organise societies and education systems may lead to provocations on both the political and personal levels that will challenge education as a system as well as local practices. A recent example of provocative action on the part of the younger generation is the school strike movement, which began with Greta Thunberg's silent protest every Friday from August 2018 outside the Swedish Parliament and grew rapidly to become one of the biggest environmental protests the world has ever seen.

According to the Norwegian educational philosopher Lars Løvlie (2008), a central pedagogical paradox that is frequently discussed in German and Nordic education traditions and is often associated with the paradox of making rules and regulations for the purpose of educating the autonomous child, is as follows: "discipline the child without making the child a slave; impose rules on the child but remember to allow for his free judgment; praise him but don't foster his vanity; constrain him but let him taste his freedom" (Løvlie, 2008, p. 1). The pedagogical paradox in education is that "autonomy – the freedom of self-determination – both belongs to the child and has to be brought into being by the intervention of others" (p. 5). Thunberg's personal initiative shows radical autonomy and is an example of a provocation directed towards the older generation as well as education as a system and as a set of practices. Even if her initiative was originally individual, it was founded on the principle of solidarity with planet earth.

The need to engage explicitly with values when making decisions about the future direction of education has been overlooked, particularly in times when effective education, big data, and cultures of measurement have been dominant (Biesta, 2010). 'The future' is unpredictable and still very present in educational policy. The future can also be considered an attitude and thereby represents a value judgement. When we consider 'the future we want', do we then mean progress, or do we imply value? Built into educational policy is the optimistic idea that through education the future will be better. In *The Beautiful Risk of Education*, Biesta (2014, p. 2) argues against 'strong' ideas and practices of education and advocates for a 'weak' approach through seven 'themes': creativity, communication, teaching, learning, emancipation, democracy, and virtuosity. He argues against the current dominant ideas in education and the "desire to make education strong, secure, predictable, and risk-free" (Biesta, 2014).

Our argument in this chapter is that we must reconsider the 'future' of planned and controlled education and instead become open to the perceptions of two groups that are in the midst of educational futures – namely, children and young people and various experts on children and childhood. These groups meet face to face or indirectly on a daily basis in various educational contexts, and their experiences are interdependent and often characterised by paradoxes. To be positioned a 'child' or 'young person' and the notion of 'adults' itself places children and young people in a generational temporality as not yet adults, even if their life experience can be as rich and varied as adults' (Kraftl, 2020). This chapter seeks to explore possible sustainable futures in education as articulated by a group of children and youth and a group of child experts selected by the authors. The authors have for many years led a Nordic network of children's culture researchers, participated in dialogues, and witnessed a change in discourse, which shifted from a primary interest in children – in their right to play and to enjoy childhood in the here and now, largely inspired by the UNCRC – towards a prime interest in children's connection with society at large, nature and child-created culture in a complex world. With this background in mind, our research questions are as follows:

a   What concerns and ideas regarding the 'future' we want do children and young people articulate?
b   What are the concerns and ideas about the 'future' we want for children from the perspective of an interdisciplinary group of child experts?
c   How can these 'futures' contribute to the development of sustainable pedagogies for the future?

The chapter will begin with a discussion of how we might manage global paradoxes and provocations in education. The chapter goes on to present statements and perspectives on the kind of future that children, young people, and child experts want and concludes with insights that have the potential to inspire new improvements aimed at achieving sustainable pedagogies for the future.

2   Paradoxes in Education

Education's role in global development and its impact on the well-being of individuals, society, and the future of our planet are unequivocally highlighted in scenarios for education, such as the Education for Sustainable Development (ESD, 2030) launched by UNESCO and The OECD Future of Education and Skills 2030 Project launched by the Organisation for Economic Co-operation and Development (OECD). Across different visions of 'the future we want', these scenarios offer metaphors of time travel towards an unknown future.

These scenarios also define 'learning objectives' (UNESCO, 2017) and 'learning frameworks' (OECD, 2019) that not only address learning and skills but also each student's well-being within a sustainable future. This optimism is also built into practice; we can see the continuation of global policy ideas of controlling education by measurement, for example, in the OECD Programme for International Student Assessment (PISA) project, which has had a substantial impact on children and young people in kindergartens and schools in many countries. However, it has also prompted a substantial amount of research that criticises the ideas embedded in PISA.

Education is increasingly governed by digitisation. At the global, national, and local levels, we have witnessed a rise in big data made possible by digitisation. Database architectures, datasets, codes, algorithms, analytic packages, and data dashboards are all among the emerging technologies that are contributing to the development of the 'quantified teacher' (Buchanan & McPherson, 2019, p. 28). This wealth of data has generated new norms against which students are measured as well as new moral codes and social expectations and has defined students against data-derived categories (p. 33). Ronaldo Beghetto (2019) has highlighted the paradox of combining large-scale assessments (LSA) with creativity, problem solving, and personalised learning in the context of LSA formats. For instance, PISA assessment emphasises sameness, and any instincts towards creativity are hampered by time-limited test conditions. This emphasis on sameness is also found in the school system, wherein groups of students will typically be of the same age, doing the same thing, in the same way, at the same time, in pursuit of the same outcome. Sameness in LSAs is reflected in the fact that they tend to be standardised measures. Test designers aim to control for or remove any interfering factors that may result in inaccurate inferences with respect to observed differences in scores between test takers (Beghetto, 2019, p. 313). Conversely, personalised learning is unique. Judgements about creativity are situated both temporally (in a particular time) and contextually (in a particular place). As such, that which is considered creative in a fourth-grade classroom, Beghetto argues, may not be considered creative in another fourth-grade classroom, in an eighth-grade classroom, or in any classroom in the next year. Creativity is dynamic and dependent upon each individual person. A teacher's awareness of such dynamics appears to be crucial in enabling them to supervise, coach, and develop new approaches to teaching and evaluation. Critical voices claim that various alternatives to measurement exist for ensuring a good education.

The idea of progress through control as a means of evaluating education can be replaced by addressing values related to education, and to UNCRC article 28 and 29 about respect for children's dignity and the development of every child's personality, talents and abilities to the full. In their study of PISA results, Faldet, Pettersson, and Mølstad (2019) compared countries with high performances in PISA to lower-performing countries, in relation to the Human Rights Watch World Report 2017 (Roth, 2017). Based on their review of this report, they ascertained that physical punishment is implemented in all five countries ranked at the top of the PISA list (OECD, 2016). In some of the countries, physical punishment is banned from school but allowed in homes, and several of the countries with high PISA rankings are guilty of human rights violations. Among the countries that stand out with good results in terms of high levels of well-being and quality of life, with, according to PISA, good results in math, that prohibit physical punishment of children and students, and appear to be relatively successful in international comparisons, is Norway (Faldet, Pettersson, & Mølstad, 2019, p. 50), and other Nordic countries (p. 48).

In education, paradoxes are troublesome and of no benefit to educational practices; they are also a nuisance for those with a definite goal in mind (Løvlie, 2008). While the manner and evidence-based practices of the politics of education are 'what works', educational researchers argue that no direct causal relationship exists between teaching and learning (Kvernbekk, 2016). Education in kindergarten, early childhood institutions, primary, and secondary schools is dependent upon practitioners' and teachers' careful consideration of how something can be made to work within their cultural context (Kvernbekk, 2017), and employ educational tools and didactics that allow students' voice (Aarskog, Barker, & Borgen, 2018). Thus, in a study of Norwegian education policy documents, Mølstad and Prøitz (2019) found that teachers are expected to be interpreters and translators of policy and also to play the paradoxical role of delivering expected learning outcomes to children. They are simultaneously expected to provide these children with life opportunities and to support them as unique and autonomous individuals. Teachers appear to be obliged to strike a fine balance between 'strong' and 'weak' ideas and practices of education (cf. Biesta, 2014).

Futures are not fixed. They are imagined and created, but the past will always create premises, some of which can come as a surprise, as the Covid-19 pandemic outburst in 2020 highlighted a new concern regarding the prevention of the spread of communicable diseases. Teachers will face new demands. School attendance in the midst of epidemics or pandemics will demand new considerations, not only for the sake of the children, but also for the teachers themselves and the population in society at large. Sue Robertson reminds us that we must be willing to imagine the creation of institutions and social relationships that maximise outcomes for all individuals rather than for a few (Robertson, 2005). When we look to the past, nostalgia is not necessarily the best guide. The future, as well as the past, is a product of human action and agency and of how we as societies, professions and individual teachers respond to the unexpected. Connell's (2009) historical overview of teaching notes that education has never been static, and that education constitutes a complex assemblage of actions that cannot be reduced to 'tick-box' standards. Education is an embodied activity, a form of emotional labour, and it is located within systems.

According to Elliot Eisner (1984), imagination is required in education. While theory is general, classrooms and students are particular in character. Teachers must be able to perceive any connections that exist between the principle and the case. Unless teachers connect with their students, they will not contribute to their formation as participants in society. What skilled teaching requires, Eisner argues, is the ability to recognise dynamic patterns, to grasp their meanings, and the ingenuity to invent ways to respond to them: "It requires the ability to both lose oneself in the act and at the same time maintain a subsidiary awareness of what one is doing" (p. 25). When teachers draw on educational imagination, they consider options and can invent moves that will advance the situation from one stage to another. Preparedness for the protection of children will require the ability to imagine the unexpected and to systematically work upon the ideas, ways of thinking and procedures for new scenarios. "An imaginative leap is always required" (Eisner, 1984, p. 25), for instance to see the potential and invent moves that will advance situations and understandings, local and global.

As the Covid-19 pandemic that swept the world beginning in from early 2020 is a fresh example of the need to be prepared for the unexpected. Society agrees upon the necessity of innovation, new ideas, and solutions to new and old problems. To understand the relationships between political conditions, both global and local, and the people living within those conditions, focus should be on the children and the professionals they meet. We should also focus on the child experts that children and young people may not necessarily meet in person during their school day, since experts can possibly have power through their impact on knowledge transfer and innovation-action at a macro- and micro-level. Awareness as a dynamic approach is instrumental to understand the fundamental relationality in which children live their lives conditioned by so many aspects also by own agency in the world, as the Swedish young girl, Greta Thunberg, can illustrate. Starting out with a personal engaged action, she has inspired numerous peers and adults all over the world, becoming an icon of children's agency, and has had an impact on global conversations (for example, at her appearance at the UN in autumn 2019).

Here, we take a closer look at how children and youth and child experts, when invited to participate in different processes of collaborative exploration, conceptualise their engagement and operate between societal and institutional frameworks, rules and regulations, and their personal intuitive and creative engagements in education. As described earlier, the OECD Education 2030 project is among the global initiatives of future planning in education. This project operates a website on which interviews with students are posted. First, we explore how these students articulate their concerns and ideas for the 'future' that they want in videos from this OECD 2030 website. Second, we explore child experts' concerns and ideas for the 'future' that they want, as expressed and discussed in an interdisciplinary workshop.

3   The Future Children and Youth Want

Considering the global impact of projects undertaken by UNESCO and OECD that seek to pave the way for a future-oriented education system projects on policy development in education, our interest here was in how students talk about the future they want and how their voices are expressed and heard within this context. To ascertain what children and young people from all hemispheres think about the future of education, we have built on information from video-recorded interviews with students who were selected and given a voice on the OECD Education 2030 project's website. Through "a common language and understanding about broad education goals that is globally informed and locally contextualised", the OECD 2030 project position paper (OECD, 2018) explains how this language is "under construction in co-creation processes" among policy makers, researchers, school leaders, teachers, students, and social partners from around the world (OECD, 2018, p. 2). Such language supports 'weak' ideas and practices in education (cf. Biesta, 2014). However, when discussing which competencies are needed to transform our society and shape our future, the OECD position paper also echoes a desire to make education 'strong', secure, and predictable:

> If students are to play an active part in all dimensions of life, they will need to navigate through uncertainty, across a wide variety of contexts: in time (past, present, future), in social space (family, community, region, nation and world) and in digital space. They will also need to engage with the natural world, to appreciate its fragility, complexity and value. (OECD, 2018, p. 5)

Key transformation processes include the mobilisation of (student) knowledge, skills, attitudes, and values through a process of reflection, anticipation, and action; these processes develop the inter-related competencies that students require to engage with the world. Set out as a 'learning framework', differing explicitly from the PISA assessment framework, the project still reflects the pedagogical paradox by defining the competencies (and constructs and measures for such competencies) that students will need to thrive in the future and for young people to be individually creative, responsible, and aware. Rather than reshape the invisibility of society to references in the material world, as Dewey (1899) asserts education can do, the future of education in the twenty-first century, as described in the OECD 2030 project, seems fluent, nonmaterial, and language dependent. Our starting point for the analysis of these video-recorded interviews is the understanding that the educational paradox is embedded in all educational thinking, and we are particularly interested in how students articulate their understanding of these paradoxes.

On the OECD 2030 website, from spring 2019, students were given the opportunity to give statements about the future they want. The OECD asked students to describe their desired future and "to articulate their hopes, dreams and the actions needed to attain well-being. Listen to what they're saying". These interviews with students are video-recorded and edited by OECD staff. We interpret the videos as developed through a process in which the students voluntarily, having given their consent for the interviews' appearance on the website, have chosen a topic that they wish to talk about, and that they have received a degree of help with scripts and points. We do not know the details of these recording and editing processes. Therefore, we presume from the information regarding the intention to give voice and agency to students that they have had a voice and been heard. Video interviews can convey a sense of ordinariness of mediated communication amongst many young people and can counter the 'pressure of presence' of being heard and seen by unspecific others, with a sense of ease (Weller, 2017). However, a limitation of our use of these interviews is that the videos are aimed at various audiences within a particular context and were not created specifically for research purposes.

During the two-week study period in the summer of 2019, 17 interviews with students aged 10–18 were available on the OECD 2030 web site. Based on available information about their place of living, country, age and school, we found that these students live in all hemispheres and are from various social groups. We selected these 17 students as informants for our study. Later, several more interviews with children and young people were made available on this website. Due to ethical considerations regarding the anonymity of the students, who have no control over the use of these internet resources, we have chosen not to give more detailed information about each informant in our study. We transcribed the 17 interviews, and then conducted a conventional content analysis (Hsieh & Shannon, 2005) of these transcriptions. We then searched for key topics related to education and statements that illustrated how the students articulated their concerns and ideas of the 'future' that they want in terms of education. We organised the statements around topics of concern: education, individuality/agency, capabilities, community, health, quality of life, and environmental issues. Generally, we saw that economic and cultural contexts had considerable influence on the students' concerns, which is also reported in a study of student experiences and quality of life in South Africa, by Savahl, Malcolm, Slembrouk, and September (2015).

3.1 *What Children and Youth Say*

In these interviews, when students talk about education, they often refer to 'we' and talk about 'our' experiences in school and in teaching. In discussing educational futures, some students express concerns about the availability of education for all. "What I want for the future of my community is a bigger school so that kids would want to go to school more" – while an older student reported that "what is currently missing in my education is that I must come away from my home to get that education that I need". Other students, who perhaps take the availability of education for granted, wanted a future in education where mentorship is valued and a curriculum that encourages students to do voluntary work (and for such work to be credited in school), and "where different types of compassions can thrive, and change can happen in the world".

Messages from the students about individuality and agency convey ambivalence. Greater awareness of students' individuality is required. Everyone learns in different ways at different times, and "all education should be about all the possibilities of life and [to] find out what our strengths and interests are". However, students also commented on the challenges of understanding the individuality vs standardisation complex – "are we equal or does the system want us to become all equal?" – and argued that "we need open-ended projects that can help us to bring out the best in ourselves and focus on the areas that interest us". School and teachers' trust in student capabilities seems to be a concern shared by these students, and one student said that "many adults still don't have faith in our ability". Another student said that "teachers need to have knowledge about us children having the virtue of being creative".

In discussing the school and the community, a student stated, "I want to become a member of a community in which students can make a difference". Another student talked about "the others" in the community that they want to help. Social inequalities became evident when a third student said, "I would like the community to be safer", and "the future I want for the community is more awareness of people's health". These students also voiced their awareness of challenges in their communities and for the future. For example, one student wanted social education in order to raise awareness on what a good community is and how to maintain it for future generations. Another student, who had to leave home to get further education, said, "I want to go back to my community and tell the kids what I have been doing and try to inspire them to get education". A well-situated student wanted to know more about the issues with which people in other countries (particularly countries with more poverty and rural areas) struggle and to help them solve their problems.

Housing is a key quality-of-life concern for many: "I want everyone in the world to have their houses to live in where they can feel comfortable, safe and happy". One student said: "Quality life to me means that a person could have access to good health, good education and facilities such as hospitals near-by and schools". Only a few students mentioned their concerns about environmental issues; this statement, however, contained a clear message of concern: "Western consumption harm[s] the environments and [our] communities".

From these interviews, we learned that these students' desire for the future they want are governed by material issues, such as security, housing, health care, environmental care, and access to education for all. They understand the impact these primary needs have on their well-being. They are also concerned about their role in society and wish to be given the trust and space they need to use their capabilities in school as well as in their communities. A few students referred to their difficulties of understanding the individuality vs standardisation complex and wanted more space for individuality in school. It seems that all students lack access to the discourse surrounding the educational paradoxes and dilemmas of which they are aware and which they experience throughout their everyday school lives. However, the students seek awareness among adults, teachers, and society regarding the issues they raise with respect to individual agency and challenges in their communities and for the future. All in all, the students' language echoes weak ideas about education within a context of strong messages, ideas, and educational practices (cf. Biesta, 2014).

4   The Future That Child Experts Want

We were interested in the perspectives of experts because we consider expertise to be of high value for children's futures. The roles of expert competencies and insights into policy design and practices in institutions for our children and young people – such as kindergartens, schools, and health institutions of various kinds – are seldom celebrated, often vaguely integrated, and sometimes contested (Young & Muller, 2014). Even if cross-sector partnerships, alliances, and collaborations have become commonplace in education and important for the promotion of kindergartens and schools as arenas for future societal policy designs, these professionals' experience, nonetheless, is that the complexity of their expertise has little or no voice in policy formation. Particularly at the science–policy interface, heterogeneous and often competing discourses come into play among researchers vs. political decision makers vs. first-line professionals (Lange & Garrelts, 2007). This heterogeneity is characterised as a transdisciplinary paradox (Hollaender, Lobl, & Wilts, 2008), since transdisciplinarity offers perspectives on how problems can be faced and solved (Klein, 2015).

The starting point for this workshop was interdisciplinary expert exchanges concerning which practices and pedagogical research topics are expected to be valid in the future in an urban municipality of Norway. The aim of the workshop was, first, to collect and create research data through a dialogue about 'the future we want' for children from the perspective of children and childhood experts; the second aim was to initiate a common exploration that addresses the paradoxes that experts live by and to create a common space for sharing ideas of what is required to contribute to sustainable futures. This workshop gave opportunities to share thoughts and expertise across disciplines.

We chose to hold a workshop as a research methodology for several reasons. Of chief importance were time efficiency and the motivation to engage in activities with the possibility of sharing, developing, changing, and learning. Acknowledging that experts are often dedicated professionals with work opportunities and restrictions, it appears that they will need to critically consider how they spend their time while still satiating their interest in learning from other experts. Since they also often will be self-determined in the judgement of time-use, we decided to create a situation that would include opportunities for learning as well as networking for future collaborations. A future-oriented workshop could fill these criteria.

According to Merriam-Webster (2016), the term 'workshop' can be traced back to 1556 with the definition of "a small establishment where manufacturing or handicrafts are carried out". Today, the term 'workshop' is used in various contexts, often with respect to an arrangement whereby a group of people learn, acquire new knowledge, perform creative problem-solving, brainstorm, or innovate in relation to a domain-specific issue. The methodology was further inspired by 'futures workshops', which refers to the work of Austrian futurist Robert Jungk, who developed the basic form of the workshop for the purpose of enhancing democratic municipal decision making in the 1950's (Müllert & Jungk, 1987). The main purpose at that time was to activate a basis upon which people could cooperate to create ideas and strategies for the future. Originally, these future-oriented workshops were a tool for collaborative problem solving. In social sciences, workshops are also used for collecting information and creating ideas through dialogues comparable to focus group interviews. In addition to collecting and creating information, a future-oriented workshop can act as a tool for sharing and social learning, which is particularly beneficial if the people taking part in the workshop are also responsible for bringing about change and have the power to assert influence within their fields (Vidal, 2005). In this study, "Workshop – The Future We Want" was a half-workday arrangement whereby a group of childhood experts shared their knowledge and motivations for concern about children's futures; in the workshop, they brainstormed, performed creative problem-identification, and unraveled ideas about possible directions for future research and pedagogical practices.

The participants (12) were invited based on their special expertise in their fields so that they would be complementary to one another with respect to expertise. They were either (a) high-profile scholars (professors) in fields such as psychiatry, medicine, physiotherapy, education, and early childhood pedagogy; (b) teacher educators and PhD students; (c) leaders and administrative personnel representing owners of schools and kindergartens; or (d) experts representing children's best interests, such as non-governmental organisations (NGOs). The overall framework for the workshop was 'sustainable future', and the aim was to draw attention to a range of expert knowledge on children. Before the workshop, the special invitees were informed that a research assistant would take notes for research purposes and they were given a series of questions to prepare for the discussion. These questions were as follows:

> What is needed for us, as experts in various areas of interdisciplinary cooperation, to help create the future we want for our children within and in relation to education? What do we want to achieve on behalf of each child? What can interdisciplinarity bring about for research? What might sustainable pedagogy for the future look like?

The workshop was led by the authors, Elin Eriksen Ødegaard and Jorunn Spord Borgen. A research assistant took manual notes from the shared dialogue and generated four pages of clean data altogether, all of which are included in the material. Post-it notes from the group sessions and the authors' personal notes are also included in the material. The organisation of the workshop was as follows:

1. Introduction of experts and sharing expert statements about the future we want
2. Identification of main topics, which led to the identification of three main topics
3. Group session working more concretely with issues concerning problem-solving related to the three topics
4. Groups shared main ideas
5. Dialogue about main ideas and outcomes and possibilities for future research
6. Short evaluation
7. Analysis of the presentations and dialogues.

According to Ørngreen and Levinsen (2017), the existing research predominantly focuses on how to conduct workshops and less on workshops as research methodology. As this workshop was organised foremost for the purpose of generating data for empirical research and involved preparation, critique, and imaginative thinking about the future we want for children as experts in children and childhood, we analysed the qualitative data accordingly. We organised the prepared statements and dialogues according to the topics of concern:

– Interdisciplinarity: what values, contributions, and pitfalls can interdisciplinarity bring about?
– Critiques and provocations: what kinds of critiques and provocations were highlighted?
– Wishes and ambitions on behalf of children: what are the main ideas for the future?

The presentation of self and agenda resulted in a series of meta-perspectives. In the following, we present the experts' perspectives on the future they want for children organised into four main categories and a fifth point that sums up their views.

4.1 What Experts Say

During the workshop, the main concerns that emerged in the experts' discussion about the future were the pedagogical paradox and dilemmas that they face in their role as experts in addition to discussions about what is 'good' for children and young people. In discussing their role in society, some experts expressed concerns about how they might come close to and keep in touch with the children who are their clients: "All the ideas that we as professional[s] have, of what children need, take up a lot of space in policy design and what we consider 'good' professional practice". We can lose sight of what the child is here and now. Are we losing the language of awareness and closeness in micro-practices and responding merely to the signals and language of politics? For instance, one expert was "concerned about the concern" about children as sedentary beings and objects of health policy. Rather, we can learn from each other – both children and adults – that we are all corporeal beings in the world and that physical experience and language are interdependent and should not be separated. As experts, they are also concerned about the ways in which their professional language differs from the everyday language. More reflection on our own language as professionals will generate greater opportunity for change in micro-practices and everyday moments in kindergartens and schools.

4.1.1 The Paradox of Early Efforts and 'Future' Prospects

The experts were also more concerned about the very young than they were about older children and adolescents, and this was justified by the sense of responsibility for the possible future of every single child. These concerns were related to the pedagogical paradox; Certain boundaries must be set; however, the child must also find his or her own way. The question of what constitutes pedagogy in this framework is a professional one: if you frame the child in a certain way, why and how do you know it will work well? The experts wanted greater awareness of procedural thinking: how to proceed should be more thematised and should include asking questions such as "What if?".

Early efforts can lead to positive results. That positive outcomes is key, but we know little about the long-term outcomes of our professional decisions here and now. This is a dilemma, as one should not do anything for which there is no good evidence. However, it takes a long time for results to make themselves known and there is a lot from which you get no evidence. Should we ignore it simply because we do not know if it has an effect? For example, we can see that some children are living in difficult conditions. Controlled trials cannot be conducted among children experiencing neglect. Regarding children who have developed an identifiable disorder, perhaps related to these circumstances, should we not give them some support? As experts, we have some evidence that if these children are supported, they will visibly improve (at least in the short term), but it is difficult to say whether this will continue for 10 or 20 years. Recommendations may be made according to the level of evidence available, with some levels of evidence higher and some lower, but even if a measure does not have the perfect level of evidence it can be implemented nonetheless, as it is based on a comprehensive professional assessment. On the other hand, society and child experts know little about children's first years of life prior to their attendance at kindergarten. Should we work more systematically to provide parents with instrumental aids, teaching parents how to interpret and communicate with children? This is a key issue for some experts with respect to health and pedagogy.

4.1.2 Knowledge Dialogues and Good Practices

The positive aspects of kindergarten and school are not always made visible; rather, they must be experienced through shared practices. Experts often enter classrooms and stay for a short time before leaving again. Experts and researchers must challenge practices but not destroy that which is good within the educational context. For instance, when children's involvement (cf. UNCRC, art. 12) became integrated into the curriculum, kindergartens suddenly had to professionalise the space and circumstances to accommodate children's participation. One of the researchers observed kindergarten practices and found that some activities were democratic and that a lot of good pedagogy was evident, but the activities were also guided by the employees' understanding of democracy. Can asking children what they want to eat and where they want to go be said to constitute democratisation? In that study, they saw that children became very tired of deciding these things. "Who am I to play with?", on the other hand, was of more immediate importance for the children. The experts recommend more open and inclusive institutions with the aim of developing dialogical practices that achieve common understandings of culture and context for the children. It is not sufficient to merely talk to and understand each other; rather, the practice of doing something meaningful together is required for transformation to happen.

4.1.3 Ideas of the 'Good' Expert

Experts have a common mission and social mandate. This changes over time, and experts and researchers also contribute to these changes. For instance, one of the experts at the workshop was fascinated by how rapidly things can change: "The way we think the world is and the image of the child (within which our mandate lies) can suddenly change". For instance, politicians who earlier paid no attention to children in their municipality changed their conceptualisation of small children in kindergarten and set out demands for changes of routines and practices. The experts involved appreciated these changes because this was more in line with the professional understanding of small children's needs. However, knowledge exchange across the various sectors of society is lacking. For instance, kindergarten education knowledge and pedagogy are not transported to other institutions and sectors in society, such as into the school and health system and vice versa. Parallel insights that do not become synergy between sectors become society's smallest multiples of knowledge about children and young people and are not sustainable for the future. Sustainable pedagogy must be thematised through more dialogue to develop our common language about what this means to us and the possible positive impact for children and young people.

Sometimes, the experts agreed, we must look up to determine whether we are on the right course. Changes in the global agenda include the examples of Greta Thunberg and a new word in Sweden known as 'flight shame' – who could have predicted this? Suddenly, a sympathetic wave has swelled around this that we can either join or resist. What does this mean for our understanding of children and young people, power, and agency? As experts, we have some of the evidence for knowledge but, at the same time, we should remain open and do the investigative work to understand where we are headed and where we want to go? According to the experts, ambiguity and imprecision are present in everything they do. They can be caretakers with good intentions without agreeing on what is best in a particular practice. However, the experts agreed that it is important to consider what kindergartens and schools are already doing. Sustainable pedagogy already exists: "we have to find it and spread it" and make it visible. In sustainable pedagogy, those paradoxes should be discussed more so that it is easier to agree on an ideological level and so that 'the child and I' are partners in this. Ultimately, it is the child's understanding and awareness of what they experience that is the end result and not what experts thought was best for the child. They also posed the question of whether we can create a pedagogy that makes us present in the moment, a pedagogy of awareness that constantly renews us and in which we are constantly asking "Where is the world now?".

5   Conclusion and Provocations

So, how can these 'futures' contribute to the development of sustainable pedagogies for posterity? The pedagogical paradox is that education is dependent upon what is understood as important knowledge at a certain time within each new generation, but that education is also instrumental for the development of independent thinking and acting subjects in a future, unknown world. Biesta (2014) argues for a 'weak' approach to education, emphasising creativity, communication, teaching, learning, emancipation, democracy, and virtuosity. From the interviews and the workshop, we have many examples of these features of what is described as the desired future of education. However, paradoxes are not followed by solutions, and among the dilemmas are the many versions of visibility/invisibility of the world (cf. Dewey, 1899), the fluency and non-materiality of education in the twenty-first century, and the significance of language for dialogues across sectors and societal, institutional, generational, and personal perspectives.

The OECD 2030 interviews with children and young people yield new insights into the concerns that children and young people have regarding their well-being and access to education. They want safety and the opportunity to be themselves and become who they want for the future. At the same time, they want belonging and to see themselves as participants in the good of society. When it comes to the specific learning context, they emphasise the importance of being taken seriously as learners and as individuals, particularly with respect to their knowledge, skills, and creativity, in line with article 12 in UNCRC. From these interviews, it seems children and youth echoes weak ideas of education, thus have little access to language and dialogues about pedagogical paradoxes and dilemmas they are aware of and experience within the context of strong ideas and practices in education (cf. Biesta, 2014).

The workshop brought different knowledge and topics from the perspectives of child experts to the forefront, some of which we could predict and some that we could not have foreseen. This can be explained by the choice of research methodology. As the workshop included many participants and took the form of a dialogue, it made space for prepared utterances (answers to a research request), listening, sharing, and collaborative problem solving; as such, new ideas and understandings easily arose.

We found that the experts are working towards a future for the best of the child (cf. UNCRC, art. 3). Experts are aware of the contradictory messages of strong and weak pedagogy (cf. Biesta, 2014); however, they require more extensive access to the micro context to be able to assess what measures are best both for the present and for children and youth to have the future we want for them. This implies time and space for the children and young people to talk and express themselves. However, as the students seem to have opinions and make choices, they also require access to a language with which to communicate with adults about the paradoxes they experience. Beyond the opportunity to speak and express themselves, children require an audience, their voice and expressions must be listened to and their view must be acted upon, as appropriate (Lundy, 2007, p. 933). Even if UNCRC is high on the educational policy agenda, this gives no guarantee of an interpretation that will function in a complex practice. When practice isolates children's participation from other concerns, the risk of a one-sided understanding with a focus on self-determination and individual choice ensues. This is in line with the critique coming from Nordic researchers of the UNCRC's interpretations of pedagogy. It seems to be biased towards a practice wherein the child's right to voice and influence is interpreted as denoting individual choice (Ødegaard, 2006; Lundy, 2007; Kjørholt, 2008).

How we deal with and talk about the educational paradox seems to be significant. An awareness pedagogy will be directed towards the ethical aspects of rights and obligations in society and will simultaneously safeguard the individual child. An awareness pedagogy will also need to consider paradoxes when judging the best interest of the child. Since the best interest of the child can be difficult to determine, balancing information and imagining scenarios is necessary in order to ensure the best possible situation. Educational imagination requires the ability both to lose oneself in the act and at the same time maintain a subsidiary awareness of what one is doing, according to Eisner (1984); an imaginative leap is always required. Some paradoxes that must be considered are outlined below.

We perceive, based on the material from these students and from our experts, the primacy of the belief in the free, informed individual who seeks knowledge and aims to develop a future in which everyone is an equal participant in society. However, the kind of student agency that is at the forefront of the OECD 2030 project could become an individual responsibility and a burden for children and youth, assuming that these competencies are typically middle-class characteristics and thus are not as inclusive as we want. Do students get help and support within a liberal education logic where standardised measures are laid down as proof of sustainable education for the future? Is there room for dialogues and language development about imagined possible futures and paradoxes?

Educational systems and policymakers voice the need for control and governance, implying that standards and measures should be implemented. The OECD 2030 project aims at developing a future imagined in the here and now, and, since the time span of the project is 15 years, it also implies ideas about how the future might possibly change. However, the kind of future the measures are aiming at, while also arguing for an imagined future over a longer time span, is dependent on the short time frame of the next political term.

The experts, on the other hand, owing to their knowledge of the complexities of social dynamics (particularly regarding how the weak always become outsiders), argue for acting here and now upon what they imagine to be possible futures for the children and youth they meet in their professional work. As these experts argue for a combination of horizontal and vertical transdisciplinarity (Sandström, Friberg, Hyenstrand, Larsson, & Wadskog, 2004), they also argue for a transdisciplinary attitude (Augsburg, 2014) between themselves as experts and researchers in different disciplines and people who know the problem area, for example, by working with it in practice or being affected by it in other ways.

We suggest an awareness pedagogy that will be directed towards the ethical aspects of rights and obligations in society and, at the same time, safeguarding the individual and securing the well-being of children and society, that is in accordance with UNCRC article 28; children's right to education and respect their dignity and rights, and article 29; that education must develop every child's personality, talents and abilities to the full. Such a pedagogy must be further theorised in line with the educational philosophy briefly introduced in this chapter. Sustainable futures will require greater awareness of children's situations, critical reflection, and new transdisciplinary initiatives and actions. Awareness must include reflections and actions towards the world and ourselves, towards actual life experiences. Or, will we – even despite this awareness and willingness to follow what the world is now – forget the educational paradox and dilemmas that are included in all pedagogy? Is acknowledgement of this paradox a premise for a sustainable pedagogy for the future we want?

References

Aarskog, E., Barker, D., & Borgen, J. S. (2018). What were you thinking? A methodological approach for exploring decision-making and learning in physical education. *Sport, Education and Society*. https://doi.org/10.1080/13573322.2018.1491836

Augsburg, T. (2014). Becoming transdisciplinary: The emergence of the transdisciplinary individual. *World Futures, 70*(3–4), 233–247. https://doi.org/10.1080/02604027.2014.934639

Biesta, G. J. J. (2014). *The beautiful risk of education*. Paradigm Publishers.

Biesta, G. J. J. (2010). *Good education in an age of measurement*. Paradigm Publishers.

Beghetto, R. A. (2019). Large-scale assessments, personalized learning, and creativity: Paradoxes and possibilities. *ECNU Review of Education, 2*(3), 311–327. https://doi.org/10.1177/2096531119878963

Buchanan, R., & McPehrson, A. (2019). Teachers and learners in a time of big data. *Journal of Philosophy in Schools, 6*(1), 26–43.

Connell, R. (2009). Good teachers on dangerous ground: Towards a new view of teacher quality and professionalism. *Critical Studies in Education, 50*(3), 213–229. doi:10.1080/17508480902998421

Dewey, J. (1899). *The school and society*. Chicago University Press.

Eisner, E. W. (1984). The art and craft of teaching. In J. Reinhartz (Ed.), *Perspectives on effective teaching and the cooperative classroom* (Analysis and Action Series, pp. 19–31). National Education Association.

Faldet, A. C., Pettersson, D., & Mølstad, C. E. (2019). Jeg, du, meg og deg: Hva kan vi egentlig lære av PISA? [I, you, me and you: What can we really learn from PISA?], *Norsk pedagogisk tidsskrift, 103*, 42–52. https://doi.org/10.18261/issn.1504-2987-2019-01-05

Gough, S., & Scott, W. (2007). *Higher education and sustainable development: Paradox and possibility*. Routledge.

Hafner-Burton, E. M., & Tsutsui, K. (2005). Human rights in a globalizing world: The paradox of empty promises. *American Journal of Sociology, 110*(5), 1373–1411. https://doi.org/10.1086/428442

Hollaender, K., Loibl, M. C., & Wilts, A. (2008). Management. In G. Hirsh Hadorn (Ed.), *Handbook of transdisciplinary research* (pp. 385–397). Springer.

Hsieh, H. F., & Shannon, S. E. (2005). Three approaches to qualitative content analysis. *Qualitative Health Research, 15*(9), 1277–1288.

Ideland, M., & Malmberg, C. (2015). Governing 'eco-certified children' through pastoral power: Critical perspectives on education for sustainable development. *Environmental Education Research, 21*(2), 173–182. https://doi.org/10.1080/13504622.2013.879696

Kemp, P. (2013). *Verdensborgeren – Pædagogisk og politisk ideal for the 21. århundrede [World citizen – Educational and political ideal for the 21st century]*. Hans Reitzels Forlag.

Kjørholt, A. T. (2008). Retten til lek og fritid (The right to play and leisure). In N. H. Høstmælingen, E. S. Kjørholt, & K. Sandberg (Eds.), *Barnekonvensjonen. Barns rettigheter i Norge [The children's convention. Children's rights in Norway]* (pp. 219–231). Universitetsforlaget.

Klein, J. T. (2015). Reprint of 'discourses of transdisciplinarity: Looking back to the future'. *Futures, 65*, 10–16.

Kvernbekk, T. (2016). Comparing two models of evidence. *OSSA Conference Archive, 72*. https://scholar.uwindsor.ca/ossaarchive/OSSA11/papersandcommentaries/72

Kvernbekk, T. (2017). Evidence-based educational practice. In *Oxford research encyclopedia, education* (oxfordre.com/education). Oxford University Press. doi:10.1093/acrefore/9780190264093.013.187

Kraftl, P. (2020). After childhood: Re-thinking environment. *Materiality and Media in Children's Lives*. Routledge.

Lange, H., & Garrelts, H. (2007). Risk management at the science–policy interface: Two contrasting cases in the field of flood protection in Germany. *Journal of Environmental Policy & Planning, 9*(3–4), 263–279. https://doi.org/10.1080/15239080701622758

Løvlie, L. (2008, March). *The pedagogical paradox and its relevance for education*. Paper presented at PESGB, Oxford Conference. https://www.researchgate.net/profile/Lars_Lovlie2/publication/242678544_The_Pedagogical_Paradox_and_its_Relevance_for_Education/links/56a6183d08ae2c689d39d060.pdf

Lundgren, U. P. (1986). John Dewey in Sweden: Notes on progressivism in Swedish education 1900–1945. In I. Goodson (Ed.), *International perspectives in curriculum history*. Croom Helm.

Lundy, L. (2007). 'Voice' is not enough: Conceptualising article 12 of the United Nations Convention on the Rights of the Child. *British Educational Research Journal, 33*(6), 927–942.

Merriam-Webster Dictionary and Thesaurus. (2016). *Workshop*. Retrieved July 7, 2019, from http://www.merriamwebster.com/dictionary/workshop

Mølstad, C. E., & Prøitz, T. S. (2019). Teacher-chameleons: The glue in the alignment of teacher practices and learning in policy. *Journal of Curriculum Studies, 51*(3), 403–419.

Müllert, N., & Jungk, R. (1987). *Future workshops: How to create desirable futures*. Institute for Social Inventions.

Ødegaard, E. (2006). Kaptein Andreas og hans mannskap – drøfting av en datakonstruksjon om en gutts stemme og hans innflytelse på barnehagens innhold [Captain Andreas and his crew – A discussion on the construction of data regarding one boy's voice and his influence on the content of the kindergarten]. *BARN, 1*, 67–89.

OECD. (2016). *PISA 2015 results: Excellence and equity in education* (Vol. I). PISA, OECD Publishing.

OECD. (2018). *OECD future of education and skills 2030*. Position paper. Author. http://www.oecd.org/education/2030-project/

OECD. (2019). *Video interviews with students*. http://www.oecd.org/education/2030-project/teaching-and-learning/learning/well-being/

Ørngreen, R., & Levinsen, K. (2017). Workshops as a research methodology. *The Electronic Journal of eLearning, 15*(1), 70–81.

Robertson, S. L. (2005). Re-imaging and rescripting the future of education: Global discourses and the challenge to education systems. *Comparative Education, 41*(2), 151–170.

Roth, K. (2017). *World report 2017*. https://www.hrw.org/world-report/2017

Sandström, U., Friberg, M., Hyenstrand, P., Larsson, K., & Wadskog, D. (2004). *Tvärvetenskap – en analys [Interdisciplinarity – An analysis]*. Vetenskapsrådet.

Savahl, S., Malcolm, C., Slembrouk, S., Adams, S., Willenberg, I. A., & September, R. (2015). Discourses on well-being. *Child Indicators Research, 8*(4), 747–766. doi:10.1007/s12187-014-9272-4

United Nations. (1989). *United Nations Convention on the Right of the Child*. Retrieved April 21, 2020, from https://downloads.unicef.org.uk/wp-content/uploads/2010/05/UNCRC_united_nations_convention_on_the_rights_of_the_child.pdf?_ga=2.259582415.454887985.1587459175-44770236.1585716747

United Nations Educational, Scientific and Cultural Organization (UNESCO). (2017). *Education for sustainable development goals: Learning objectives*. United Nations Educational, Scientific and Cultural Organization.

Vidal, R. (2005). *The future workshop*. Chapter 6. http://www.imm.dtu.dk/~rvvv/CPPS/6Chapter6Thefutureworkshop.pdf

Weller, S. (2017). Using internet video calls in qualitative (longitudinal) interviews: Some implications for rapport. *International Journal of Social Research Methodology, 20*(6), 613–625. doi:10.1080/13645579.2016.1269505

World Commission on Environment and Development (WCED). (1987). *Our common future*. United Nations/Oxford University Press.

Young, M., & Muller, J. (Eds.). (2014). *Knowledge, expertise and the professions*. Routledge.

Index

activities and practices in kindergartens and schools   9, 122, 125, 236
aesthetic and playful   50, 61, 64, 198, 207
agency   x, 2, 5, 8, 9, 14, 19–21, 39, 41, 44, 47, 77, 107, 163, 181, 200, 204, 206, 207, 214–220, 223–226, 241, 242, 247, 255–258, 275, 280, 282–284, 290, 292
awareness pedagogy, vii, xi, 291, 292

being and becoming   2, 7, 54, 56, 76, 77, 192, 215, 226

century of the child   7, 13–19, 23, 25, 28, 29
child experts   ix, 9, 276, 277, 280, 281, 284, 288, 291
childhood fears and pleasures   ix, 23–25
children and the social constructions of risk   179
children and youth   183, 274
children with severe, multiple disabilities   54, 55, 57, 58, 60–62, 64, 66–68
children's culture   21, 22, 26, 28, 198–200, 203–206, 209, 277
China   3, 8, 89, 105, 123–128, 131–135
conditions for learning, formation and development   232

digital media use in everyday life   8, 162–165

early childhood education   20, 24, 216, 232, 261, 263, 264
education   vii, ix, x, 1–6, 8, 9, 14–16, 20, 24, 38, 39, 45, 50, 60, 63, 76, 107, 108, 121, 123, 125, 128–135, 156, 164, 179–181, 185, 190, 193, 216, 223, 224, 232, 239, 291–293

food practices   8
frustration education   121, 123, 125, 128–135
future-oriented and sustainable   30
transdisciplinary research designs   30

Germany   16, 92, 98, 105, 204, 232

inequality   1, 128, 283
infant   x, 2, 6, 7, 23, 37–51, 87, 110, 205

methodology   9, 21, 79, 81, 85–105, 110, 170, 171, 182, 202, 246, 248, 252, 285, 287, 291
modes of communication   7, 23, 27, 38, 40, 41, 54–56, 59–69, 79, 111, 256, 276, 290
multilingual practices   9, 229, 231–234, 237, 239, 240, 242
multimodality   8, 39, 41, 44, 45, 48, 109–111

nexus analytic approach   9, 229, 231
Nordic   vii, ix, x, 3, 5–8, 10, 14–16, 18, 19, 23–25, 79, 163, 173, 175, 181, 192, 207, 231, 276, 277, 279, 291

public health policy   8, 178, 180, 182–184, 189, 191–193

resistance   8, 9, 197–200, 203, 205–209, 225

spaces for transitions in intergenerational childhoods   7, 23, 74
studies of child perspectives and participation   9, 246–253, 255, 258, 262, 264, 266
sustainable future   viii–x, 9, 18, 274, 275, 277, 278, 285, 286, 289, 293

the future children and youth want   281
transformation of childhood in a globalised era   23, 26

UN Convention on the Rights of the Child (UNCRC)   vii, x, xi, 1–5, 7–9, 14, 17–19, 24, 28, 29, 78, 123, 134, 179, 183, 191, 192, 198, 210, 231, 242, 254, 266, 275, 277, 278, 291, 293

vulnerable children   vii, 5, 17, 29, 192

Printed in the United States
By Bookmasters